BONN and
JERUSALEM

also by Inge Deutschkron

For Theirs Was the Hell
(Denn ihrer war die Hölle)

BONN and JERUSALEM

JERUSALEM

The Strange Coalition

by Inge Deutschkron

CHILTON BOOK COMPANY
Philadelphia · New York · London

Copyright © 1970 by Inge Deutschkron

First Edition
All rights reserved

Published in Philadelphia by Chilton Book Company
and simultaneously in Ontario, Canada,
by Thomas Nelson & Sons, Ltd.

ISBN 0-8019-5265-4
Library of Congress Catalog Card Number 79-121109
Designed by Harry Eaby
Manufactured in the United States of America
by Vail-Ballou Press, Inc.

CONTENTS

21375

PREFACE

In the entire field of politics there can hardly be a theme more difficult to present and analyze than that of the relations between Germans and Jews. The emotions and feelings that characterize their every phase must inevitably influence anyone who attempts to trace the course of their development. Strict objectivity is almost impossible. Yet, such is its burning topicality that the theme must concern all leaders of the political and cultural life of the two peoples—indeed, all thinking Germans and Jews.

The relations between Israel and Germany are an inseparable part of the whole subject matter. It is to Inge Deutschkron's credit that, with her book, she has made a contribution to the understanding of the events that led to the taking up of diplomatic relations between the two countries. In many of them she was personally involved. Having escaped, with the aid of German friends, the Nazi murder machine she was an eyewitness to the collapse of Hitler's Reich in Berlin. As correspondent of an Israeli newspaper in West Germany she has followed every phase of the development of the relations between Germany and Israel. It is her particular merit that—although at no time uninvolved—she never allows herself to be misled by her own feelings into passing judgment where straight reporting is needed. A book has thus been written which throws interesting light on events about which details, in many cases, have never been published.

Inge Deutschkron emphasizes both the psychological and political factors that stood in the way of making contact: the burden of the past and the facts of the present. The background of the Luxemburg compensation agreement is examined and the political pressure described by which the Arabs sought to wreck the approaches being made. The effects of the Eichmann trial on the relations be-

tween Germans and Israelis are described. Of particular interest is the description of the meeting of those two great statesmen who more than all others contributed to bringing about diplomatic relations: Adenauer and Ben-Gurion. One chapter is devoted to relations with East Germany. It makes clear how vast the gap is between the attitude of the two German states to Israel. The events that led to the start of diplomatic relations between West Germany and Israel form the absorbing final stage of this interesting book.

It is left to the reader to make his own judgment on the matters described. Knowledge of the facts is both a vital and a valuable aid to a better understanding between the two countries. The official relations now in existence can only be the starting point for continuation of the dialogue on a new basis.

> Asher Ben-Nathan,
> First State of Israel Ambassador
> To West Germany, 1965–1969

ACKNOWLEDGMENTS

This has been a difficult book to write. Most of the agreements were secret; so were a good number of the meetings. Consequently, there is little or no documentation available. Information could be obtained to a great extent only from people who had had a hand in the relations, secret or otherwise. Some of them are now dead, such as former Chancellor Adenauer and his Minister of Foreign Affairs, Heinrich von Brentano.

It is only human that people forget, confuse events or, to this day, feel bound by secrecy like Dr. Kurt Birrenbach who felt he could not yet talk about his experiences in Israel. Therefore, I cannot exclude that future research will add new aspects and question my statements. I have tried, to the best of my ability, to present a fair picture. But, unfortunately, my task was hampered by the unreadiness of some German politicians to receive me or to give information which, it seems to me, should have been their duty. History has a right to the truth.

To those who even failed to reply to my request I express only my regrets.

The more cordially I thank those in Germany who were kind enough to receive me and assist me with their wealth of information: Banker Hermann-Josef Abs, former Minister Ernst Benda, former Ambassador Dr. Herbert Blankenhorn, Professor Franz Böhm, former Chancellor Professor Ludwig Erhard, Dr. Abraham Frowein, Dr. Otto Küster, Baron von Preuschen, Parliamentarian Fritz Sänger and former Minister Dr. Ludger Westrick.

I am deeply indebted, also, to the former Israeli Prime Minister David Ben-Gurion, Minister Shimon Peres, Dr. Nahum Goldmann, President of the World Jewish Congress, Ambassador Asher Ben-Nathan, Ambassador Zeev Shek, Dr. Chaim Yahil and the many officials in Israel.

Mrs. Luise Bauch of the German Press and Information Office and officials of the Foreign Office deserve thanks for assisting me in my task.

I am most grateful, too, to the SPD archives, the American Jewish Labor Committee, the archives of the All-German Affairs Ministry, the *Germania Judaica* (Cologne), the archives of the Catholic Church in Germany, the *Bundestag* library and the *Maariv*, editors and staff, for the help they have given me to obtain a rounded picture of this intricate subject.

I.D.

BONN and
JERUSALEM

1
A German Trauma

A man shuffled along the street. He wore the striped pajamas which once had been the concentration camp garb. They dangled around him as though on a coat hanger in the wind. Only the gaunt outline of a body was visible. The face was haggard; the eyes without light, as if they lay sightless in their sockets. He appeared not to see the world around him. Nor did the people in the street take note of him. They hastened by the ruins, the rubble, the debris, the skeleton of what once had been their capital, Berlin. They did not see him.

Nor did they see the man in what once had been the proud uniform of a German soldier, hobbling on dirty rags tied around his feet in place of shoes. He held out his mess tin, begging for food, the unshaven face shy yet urgent, as if desperate for a crumb. The people did not take note of him, either; at the most, they showed indignation, brushing him aside with a hasty movement of their arms. They even failed to note the spring which, as if to spite the events of 1945, had come and sewn green patches amid the ruins that marred the face of the city of Berlin. The people no longer noticed anything that did not concern them directly; they no longer showed feeling.

When the war had turned against the Germans, when it had come directly to their doorstep, when the bombs had fallen and no longer was there any escaping the horrible reality of war in their own country, they had learned to think of themselves, only; to clutch what was left to them; to hide what was their own. Fear for their lives, anxiety for their loved ones at the front or elsewhere, the search for food and shelter had made the individual selfish, immensely self-centered, totally egoistic. The neighbor no longer existed. A man in his pain could not expect any compassion. When the war finally had been lost, they saw the foreign soldier, to be sure—but as nothing else than a dupe to be bribed for food, for cigarettes or dollars. He was not the conqueror, the enemy that they had been told for many years to hate; on the contrary, he was considered a source of income; he seemed to offer a chance for survival.

The Germans, then, were guided solely by this animal instinct that excluded all passions or interests in other things but their very own fate. This lasted well into the second and even third year after the war; with some who had to set up a new home or to start from scratch—having lost everything in the war—it lasted longer.

It was then that the full extent of the crimes that the Nazis had committed against the Jews and the opponents of National Socialism became known. None in Germany could escape the photographs of the inmates of concentration camps, the living skeletons so horribly dehumanized until the Allies had liberated them. As soon as newspapers became available again (all under Allied censorship), the truth about the organized murder of the Jews was revealed. In some areas, the occupation authorities ordered visits to the French film, *Night and Fog,* depicting, in detail, the machinery of murder which the Nazis had built up. Unless the admission ticket could be produced there was no ration card and, during those years of food shortage, that assured a full attendance. In Weimar, the American military commander made the population pay visits to the nearby concentration camp of Buchenwald. Yet, all this seemed to have little or absolutely no impact on the people.

They seemed to look away, to see nothing. The outcry at the horrors, which was the natural reaction of the whole world, failed to be heard in Germany. Instead, in tests of a cross section of the population, the majority claimed to have suffered, too—through bombing; when driven out of their homes by Poles or Russians; or, at the end of the war, when they had so little food. The Germans gave the impression of being eaten up by self-pity, of thinking only of their own sufferings, but they refused to search or ask themselves for the cause of their personal misery. In their plight—the country greatly destroyed and split up, and most men missing or feared to be dead—this, perhaps, could be called a normal human reaction. It would be wrong, however, not to mention that, in some cases, a guilty conscience sealed their lips.

Undoubtedly, there were those who were shaken to the bone by the revelation that six million Jews, millions of Russians and an endless number of people of many nationalities had been brutally and systematically murdered by Germans. But they were mostly those who had already known, or, at least, had heard in general terms of crimes being committed. For, it was possible to know, even during the war, that something dreadful was being done to the so-called "enemies of the state." Any ordinary citizen could have seen, if only he had wanted to, the deprivations of the Jewish population; their degradation; their suffering, mental and physical; their expulsion, which was bad enough from any humanitarian point of view, but which, unfortunately, proved to be nothing compared to what happened to them later in Auschwitz, Maidanek and Treblinka. Again, how many *wanted* to see it—this injustice against a minority—or *could*, without coming into conflict with their own conscience?

Admittedly, there were those few in Germany who had helped Jews in their plight, even to the extent of risking their own lives for them. Far too little, or almost nothing, is known to this day about those who, in this way, often had expressed their hatred of the Nazis. Certainly the German nation did not acclaim them as their heroes. But those few were in the forefront right after the war, demanding atonement for the extermination of Jews in Germany and for the cruel fate that other nations had had to suffer at the hands of Germans.

The general public, however, displayed indifference during and after the war, especially to the revelation of the crimes committed against the Jews. There can be no doubt that even after the war quite a few harbored their own kind of anti-Semitism; partly, because of indoctrination by the Nazis which had fallen on fertile ground, and again because the human being likes to have a scapegoat to blame for his own shortcomings. Moreover, anti-Semitism was an old prejudice, the origin being religious or just indefinable, and based on arguments, however illogical; dormant, perhaps, until the Nazis' rise to power. Here was a situation, then, which may have been no different in some other European countries; the Jews disliked as a minority who clung to customs and habits alien to the majority of citizens. Yet, it was in *Germany* that millions were systematically murdered.

The Nazi slogan, "The Jews are our misfortune!" (of course, no longer hurled at the world after the war) somehow continued to exist—perhaps, subconsciously; perhaps, in a new version; perhaps, spoken in the full consciousness of guilt. The occupying powers left no doubt as to the truth of crimes committed against humanity; also, that it was they, not the Germans themselves, who had liberated Germany from a criminal regime. Insofar as the Allies were concerned, the entire German nation was guilty, and they demanded payment for it. The theory of "collective guilt" which they emphasized continually (and which was not only incorrect, but also short-sighted in its application) produced nothing but stubbornness among the German people. The de-Nazification procedure, to which everyone was subjected, was in many ways a foolish arrangement—foolish because the foreign powers showed that they had failed to understand the intricacy of the German or, perhaps, of any dictatorial system. More often than not, they passed judgments that punished the "little" man and let the "big" ones escape; or gave them sentences that were in no way commensurate to the crimes.

This procedure only strengthened the unreadiness of the people to accept any guilt, or to atone for any of the crimes. In quite a few it also aroused new anti-Semitic feeling or reawakened the old one that once again the Jews had brought upon them all this misery. The fact that young people joined in anti-Semitic incidents again in the first years after the war was an indication of this new bigotry.

In June, 1947, the American military government found that 22 percent of the population in its zone declared allegiance to the National Socialist racial theory and 19 percent to National Socialism.[1] One can safely assume that the percentages actually were higher and tallied with the attitudes of people in other zones of Germany. German reticence and so recent a collapse of the Hitler Reich, and all the charges that had been raised against it, surely increased the reservation of people to reply frankly to questions testing their political opinions.

In times when fear, hunger, need and distress are uppermost in the minds of the people, religion's influence is greatest. This was also the case in Germany after 1945, when people flocked to religious services in an unprecedented number. Yet, the churches did not use the opportunity to make clear to the Germans that their present misery was nothing but the consequence of their own doing; that the Ger-

[1] *New York Herald Tribune*, reprinted in *Der Weg*, Berlin, June, 1947.

man people had sullied their name with unspeakable crimes. Nothing of that. The clergy remained completely silent on the Nazi responsibility for catapulting practically the whole world into a horrible war, and on the systematic annihilation of millions of Jews. In the case of the clergy, this also might be attributed, to a great extent, to the guilty consciousness that, apart from individual cases, they had done nothing to prevent mass murder.

Although it is presumed that the churches should act as the public conscience and give guidance to the weak they, too, had remained, almost until the last stages of the war, virtually silent. It would be useless to revive the old dispute over this attitude. However, when the crime of euthanasia was practiced in the years of 1941-1942; when hundreds of thousands of old, infirm and mentally deranged Germans were gassed by German doctors complying with Hitler's orders, the Church spoke up and it was its opposition that brought this action to a close. Well-known in this connection are the sermons of the Bishop of Münster, Cardinal Graf Galen (the "Lion of Muenster"), in 1941. Galen (who, no doubt, was in danger for his brave outspokenness), however, had nothing to say against the persecution of Jews or non-Germans which already was in full operation. Not until 1943, when hundreds of thousands of Jews had been murdered did some clergymen mention from the pulpits of their churches (and then without going into detail) the suffering of guiltless people. But the protests were far too late and too isolated to influence the killers or even stop the machinery of murder running at full speed. Nevertheless, it must be stressed that the churches produced a few heroic figures.

Soon after Hitler's rise to power in 1933, a group of Protestants founded the *Bekennende Kirche* (Confessional Church) to demonstrate their resistance against the Nazi policy of introducing a "state" church. With this policy, the Nazis intended to deprive the Protestant Church of its ideological basis—Martin Luther's theses of a reformed church. The *Bekennende Kirche* soon found supporters all over the country. For its belief and its efforts to save at least baptized Jews, or Jews converted to Christianity, quite a number suffered in concentration camps. Most prominent among them were Pastor Niemoeller, and Propst Heinrich Grueber, a Protestant minister, who, immediately after 1945, spoke up and denounced the churches for having failed in their responsibility during the war. The German people, Pastor Niemoeller said in February, 1946, had left it to one man to determine good and evil. And this had been possible only because the churches had allowed these crimes to happen and had not challenged the people's conscience.[2]

It may be disputed whether or not the intervention of the churches beyond the group of the *Bekennende Kirche* would have changed the evil intentions regarding the Jews as it did in the case of euthanasia. But it is surely right to say that, at least, it would have made it very difficult, if not impossible, for some practicing Christians to execute the Nazis' criminal orders.

When the war was over, the churches again failed to give guidance to their followers. True, in the German bishops' first pastoral letter[3] after the war, dated August 23, 1945 (read on September 9, at the grave of Saint Bonifacius at Fulda), the crimes committed by the Germans against mankind are mentioned in general terms:

. . . horrible crimes were committed before the war against Germans, and during the war by Germans in the occupied countries. We deplore this deeply. Many Germans, also from our ranks, were infatuated by the false teachings of National Socialism; they remained indifferent to the crimes; many encouraged the crimes by their attitude; many became criminals themselves.

The pastoral letter then goes on to excuse those who had remained silent, or who even had joined the Nazi party, saying that this could not be called "tolerating" the awful crimes of the Nazi regime. And this was precisely what the people were eager to hear. It was their absolution. Especially words like: ". . . Some people joined (the Nazi party) in ignorance of the activities and the aims of the party; some compelled, others, in good faith, to prevent bad deeds . . ." The Catholic Church adapted itself once again to popular feeling. No word was uttered about the murder of the Jewish people.

Nor is there any mention of the Jewish suffering in the *Stuttgarter Schuldbekenntnis* (Confession of Guilt) produced by the Protestants in October, 1945[4]: "With great sorrow we state: through us unspeakable suffering has been brought upon many peoples of the world. . . ." This declaration, incidentally, found more

---

[2] Speech in Ludwigsburg before German internees in an American camp, reported in *Stuttgarter Zeitung*, February 27, 1946.

[3] Archives of the Catholic Church, Bonn.

[4] *Das Verhältnis der Christen zu den Juden in Deutschland, Der ungekündigte Bund*, p. 248, Kreuz-Verlag, Stuttgart, 1962.

opponents than supporters in Germany.[5] Some Germans even considered it treason as it clearly blamed Germany for being solely responsible for starting the war. It is probably correct to assume that
the churches actually were in the same conflict as their followers
concerning the Jews. In its *Wort zur Judenfrage* (Word on the
Jewish Question) issued on April 8, 1948, the Protestant clergy ad-
mits for the first time: ". . . The official church, in general, approved of the policy with regard to the Jewish people, openly or
clandestinely, and allowed the measures of the Nazi regime to be
taken within and without the Church. . . ." It said in its preface:
". . . In view of the past, one could have expected that the Protestant Church would have had something to say immediately after the
collapse of the Nazi Reich . . ."

But no reply is given as to why this was not the case. Heinz
Schmidt, a well-known German theologian—who, earlier in 1947,
had expressed his surprise at the fact that eighteen months after the
war the Church had failed to speak up on the crimes against the
Jews—came to the conclusion that perhaps time and distance were
needed, as well as a spiritual integrity," to account for the horrors
which still keep us spellbound." [6]

What he did not mention was that the churches had as yet to
purge their own teachings of anti-Jewish tendencies. Such phrases as
"The Jews murdered Christ" lived on as a charge, having been
passed on from one generation to the next. But the Protestant
Church, in its *Wort zur Judenfrage*, April 8, 1948, tried to check a
new type of anti-Semitism, saying that the danger existed, that:
"Now when we have to pay for our guilt concerning the Jews" . . .
"we resort to a new type of anti-Semitism. . . ."

Only a few months later, September, 1948, in Mainz, the Catholic
Church also made the appeal "to every Christian to do his share, and
that the Christian population refrain from the anti-Semitism that is
already newly developing. As fathers of families, as mothers, as
teachers, as spiritual advisors we should live and teach the right
Christian attitude of love towards the Jews."

The Church then implored the Jews to fight together with all
those of good will against every trend of demoralization. In the
same resolution, the Catholics spoke of the need to make up for the

---

[5] Erwin Gross, *Die Schuld der Kirche, Die Wandlung,* p. 38, Heft, February 2, 1947.

[6] Heinz Schmidt, *Die Judenfrage und die christlichen Kirche, in Deutschland,*
p. 9, Kohlhammer Verlag, Stuttgart, 1947.

injustice done to the Jews "within the framework of what is possible." [7]

What, then, had made the churches suddenly wake up to their responsibility? It must be assumed that it was the recognition of several anti-Semitic incidents, such as the daubing and desecration of Jewish graves and the slander of Jewish citizens that occurred in the first years after the war, and the realization that anti-Jewish feeling was still very much alive among the people. The churches must have been aware of the consequences for Germany at the time; anti-Semitism would again discredit the nation in the world and mar its future. And it was an anti-Semitism that was not confined to the guilty, older generation.

To begin with, it was an anti-Semitism practically without Jews. About fifteen thousand Jews of German origin were counted in Germany right after the war, in comparison with 500,000 who had lived there before Hitler came to power.[8] Most of these fifteen thousand were married to Christians and were raising baptized children. There were a few who had survived concentration camps or had lived in hiding. But their number was minute. The majority did not want to stay on in Germany. The few privileges they had been granted right after the war (for instance, being given the use of an apartment which once had belonged to a Nazi, or being appointed trustee of Nazi property) had disappeared as soon as the Nazis had been de-Nazified by special de-Nazification courts.[9] In fact, the Jews had to recognize a kind of re-Nazification in the sense that often the same officials returned to the same posts in Germany's restored administration or justice department which they formerly had occupied in the Third Reich. Irrespective of the fact that they had served a criminal regime, now they were to help introduce a democratic system. Those who in the early stages of military government had been appointed officials were soon replaced by de-Nazified officials demanding their "rightful posts." On September 13, 1947, the organ of the Jewish community in the British Zone described the situation as, "two years of the most bitter disappointment." [10]

The Jews soon were made to feel those anti-Semitic tendencies.

---

[7] 72 Conference: *Deutscher Katholikentag*, Archives of the Catholic Church in Germany.

[8] Harry Maor, *Über den Wiederaufbau der jüdischen Gemeinden in Deutschland nach, 1945*, p. I, Mainz University, 1961.

[9] *Neue Zeitung*, February 24, 1949.

[10] *Jüdisches Gemeindeblatt für die Britische Zone* II-11.

German Jewry, at a delegates' conference of Jewish communities, meeting in Berlin from October 19 to 23, 1947, gave vent to their bitterness and disappointment, declaring: ". . . Delegates expressed their grief and their disgust at the growing wave of anti-Semitic incidents in Germany and demanded that a legal framework for the persecution of collective offenses against the Jewish communities be introduced. . . ." [11]

Later on, anti-Semitic tendencies increased to some extent regarding the "Displaced Persons" camps. In fact, it appears as if these DPs were a welcome target for the Germans with antagonistic feelings towards the Jews. Hundreds and thousands of Jews, survivors of concentration camps, escaping from Communism and anti-Semitism, fled from Poland, Czechoslovakia, Hungary, Rumania, and Lithuania to the nearest Western country—Germany.[12] They came with the firm intention of emigrating to Palestine. But, as the British, still in charge of Palestine, were not ready to provide facilities for immigration beyond the quotas fixed for normal times, these poor people were herded together in camps in Germany. Quite a number of them were in Bavaria, others near Berlin, and in the provinces of Lower Saxony, Schleswig-Holstein or Hesse. Once again behind barbed wire, these unfortunate people—having miraculously escaped from annihilation, but having witnessed the most horrible crimes committed by the Germans—hated to be in Germany and hated the Germans. But, ironically, they had nowhere else to go.

According to official sources, President Truman had given instructions in 1945 to General Eisenhower to see to it that the inhuman conditions under which many Jews had to exist in the camps of the American Zone of Germany were changed.

General Eisenhower, then High Commander of the United States

[11] Quoted in the German Press, October 24, 1947.

[12] American Joint Distribution Committee Study published in the *Sueddeutsche Zeitung*, November 17, 1948: There were 94,000 Jews in Germany in 1946 of whom about 74,000 (85 percent from Poland and 15 percent from other countries) were not of German origin. Until June, 1946, about five thousand Jews had entered the American Zone each month. From July to September (the consequence of a *pogrom* in Kielce), seventy thousand Jews fled to Germany during the three months of July, August and September. At the beginning of 1947, a great number of Rumanian Jews crossed into Germany. In March, 1947, 126,000 Jews were cared for as DPs in the American Zone, twelve thousand in the British, 2,300 in the French (of whom 108,000 were from Poland, the rest from Czechoslovakia, Rumania, Hungary and Lithuania). Very few settled in Germany, the majority gradually leaving for Israel in illegal and, later on, legal immigration.

Zone, confiscated an estate on which some of the Jews were to learn to work on the land as a preparation for their emigration to Palestine. When David Ben-Gurion, shortly after the end of the war, visited one of the DP camps, Eisenhower told him that the Jews had refused to work there. Ben-Gurion was "shocked and ashamed." But, Eisenhower explained to him that he fully understood their reactions, which were solely emotional. It was impossible for the Jews to work on Nazi land.[13]

The American representative of the Refugee Committee, Earl Harrison, said, "We seem to treat these Jews like the Nazis before us; only we do not annihilate them. They are overcrowded; often, unhygienic camps behind barbed wire are similar to some notorious concentration camps. They are cut off from every kind of contact with the outside world and, without work, await the day on which the world will be reminded of them again." [14]

True, these camps were showered with food and clothing from all parts of the world; many of the gifts were beyond the needs of the inmates. It was not surprising that they used the opportunity to sell the surplus at black market prices to the starving Germans who, on their part, detested them for it. They did not take the refugees' previous suffering into account. They just saw that these people toyed with delicacies in front of their eyes and would not share them, unless at exorbitant prices. In Munich, as well as in Berlin, certain streets became notorious as trading grounds for black marketeering and often were raided by the police. Only the German citizens were punished, the DPs being beyond German jurisdiction—at least until 1947. The hatred of the Germans turned against these people in particular; against people who were not earning their livelihood through honest work; against those who exploited their plight—a fate which so many of them refused to accept as being deserved.

But, at the same time that the churches tried to check the new rise of anti-Semitism—partly because they were afraid of added guilt, and partly because they realized the disastrous effect anti-Jewish tendencies in Germany would have on people abroad—they continued to show that they, along with the German people, would not go the whole way. They still were not ready to acknowledge the enormity of the German guilt. For example, in 1948, in letters to the American Military Governor, General Lucius D. Clay, the German

13 Ben-Gurion, in a conversation with the writer, August 7, 1968.
14 Archives of *Neue Zeitung*.

clergy objected to the manner in which the trials against the Nazi criminals at Nuremberg were conducted.[15]

The victors were charged with trying the accused according to laws that had not been codified anywhere in the world. This created the suspicion that the Allies were less concerned about justice than about exercising their power over the defeated. Church leaders of both Christian denominations did not take into consideration that the crimes of which those in the dock had been accused were indeed so monstrous and so unique in the history of mankind that no mention of the need to adhere to the established law, or of any mercy on the part of the judges, should have been raised.

The clergy complained, among other things, that the trial of officers by a civilian court was as contradictory to international law as the fact that the officers had been deprived of their military status before the trial. This called to mind the inhuman treatment of the German officers who had attempted to overthrow Hitler on July 20, 1944. It is not surprising that the Jewish weekly, *Juedische Wochenzeitung*, in January, 1949, remarked with bitterness that there had been no protest on the part of the clergy when the mass murders had been committed:

. . . They worry about justice of the Allies which made an end to the Nazi regime and also saved the Church from destruction. They express their doubts as to whether or not the trials against the criminals have been prepared thoroughly enough and believe it necessary now to come to the rescue of the condemned . . . criminals against humanity. . . .

There had indeed, been no difference in the reaction of the German people to the very first Nuremberg trial that put the remaining top Nazi leaders in the dock. The *Stuttgarter Zeitung* of February 2, 1946, analyzed the reaction and came to the conclusion that the general public still had no opinion of its own (did not want to have any) as to the Nuremberg trials and to the crimes revealed there. The Germans were either too preoccupied with their own problems or claimed not to believe in anything any more, having been una-

[15] Josef Cardinal Frings (Cologne) protested on November 8, 1948, to General Clay, in the name of the Bishops' Conference at Fulda, against the war crime trials. Protestant leaders, at almost the same time, expressed their misgivings, also. Chairman of the Protestant Church Council, Dr. Theophil Wurm, had written on October 14, to the American Secretary of State, Foster Dulles, protesting the resumption of executions of condemned war criminals: ". . . For over one or two years condemned men are held in death cells without clarity about their fate. . . ."

ware of any "misleading" during those twelve years. Others paid no attention to the trials, saying that surely what was done in Nuremberg would be all right, just as they had expressed their trust in the Führer before. There were small groups of people expressing odd views, saying that they felt it a shame or even a national disaster that German military men "who had done nothing but their duty" had to be tried by an international court. Others rejected Nuremberg as a mere show and suggested that the Nazi criminals be sent to build up Siberia. But, as always, there was the small minority that grasped the sense of the trials and spoke of the need to expose, before the whole world, the political system of the Third Reich in all its details; the system that had brought so much misery to all mankind. And it was this minority, also, that articulated its misgivings at the acquittal of the three accused—Franz von Papen (Hitler's versatile diplomat, in many ways responsible for his ascent to power); Hjalmar Schacht (for a time Hitler's Minister of Economic Affairs and president of the German Bank); Hans Fritzsche (one of Hitler's most loyal propagandists).

"There is, apart from Adolf Hitler, none more guilty than this Mr. von Papen; he is actually a symbol of what is called the German guilt. . . . This acquittal signifies in the eyes of many also a political acquittal for the regime which brought about those horrors," declared Dr. Kurt Schumacher, Chairman of the Social Democratic Party (SPD) and himself a concentration camp inmate for many years.[16] Hesse Legislative Assembly requested that the three acquitted now be tried by a German court for high treason. They described von Papen as having been "the chief culprit" for the past twelve years. Bavaria's Prime Minister Hoegner (SPD) called von Papen's acquittal "a truly astonishing affair." It was no different in Baden-Wuerttemberg where the Legislative Assembly demanded that the three be tried before a German court. On behalf of his three colleagues in southern Germany, Premier Maier of Baden-Wuerttemberg explained that von Papen had undoubtedly committed high treason (for unseating the Prussian government of July 20, 1932). More than 200,000 workers and employers downed tools in Berlin for ten minutes to register their protest against the acquittals.

General Clay saw the German criticism of the Nuremberg verdict as an "encouraging" sign.[17] What he did not see was that this criticism came mainly from politicians and Germans who had been orga-

[16] *Stuttgarter Zeitung*, October 5, 1946.
[17] *Stuttgarter Zeitung*, October 9, 1946.

nized workers or politicians, active or passive opponents of Hitler; in other words, those belonging to that small minority of Germans who were staunch Democrats before Hitler's rise to power and after his downfall. And here, for the first time, appears the discrepancy of published and genuine "public opinion" [18] in Germany, a disparity which continued to exist for years. Leading politicians, installed or encouraged by the Allies to take an active part in political life because of their integrity during the Third Reich, and they themselves ready to come forward to help set up a democratic Germany, were sincere when they condemned the Nazi Reich and all it had represented. Their statements and declarations were tolerated by the Germans—although opinions might have differed—often because the people felt it was better for them to accept the new trend, or because they were so used to being led. This was reflected, also, in the attitude towards Jewry.

There were some German politicians and statesmen who never failed to mention the terrible Jewish fate, disdainful of it being popular or not. Prominent among them was Professor Theodor Heuss.[19] It was he, in 1949, who created the expression of "collective shame." He rejected the term "collective guilt" with which foreign countries stigmatized the entire German nation with the crimes of the Hitler era. Heuss said: "The word 'collective guilt' is a primitive simplification, is a twist of the kind that the Nazis used to apply to the Jews, the fact that to be a Jew already contained in itself the guilt phenomenon. But something like a collective shame has grown from this period and remained. The worst that Hitler has done to us . . . . . . after all, has been that he forced us into that shame to have in common with him and his fellows the name 'Germans'." [20] There can be little doubt that Professor Heuss, a leading Liberal, was sincere when he spoke in this spirit. Some of his critics might say that his own guilty conscience had led him to react in this way. For, in 1933, Heuss, as a member of Parliament, had voted in favor of Hitler's Enabling Laws, which became the legal basis for his crimes. But, be that as it may, others whose conscience should have been burdened much more said much less or nothing at all.

[18] Quotation from the first Israeli diplomatic emissary to Germany, Ambassador Asher Ben-Nathan.

[19] President of the Federal Republic of Germany from 1949 to 1959.

[20] At a ceremony of the Society for Christian-Jewish Cooperation in Wiesbaden, December 7, 1949. Printed in the *Stuttgarter Zeitung*, December 8, 1949.

Another leading Liberal, Dr. Reinhold Maier, when introducing himself as Prime Minister of Baden-Wuerttemberg, in October, 1945, recalled the fate of the Jewish citizens of his state: ". . . Surely, countless Germans who were not concerned felt sympathetic and suffered terribly, yet the majority of the population remained unaffected and unmoved. . . ." [21] There were similar statements from some leading Christian Democrats; Professor Franz Boehm,[22] for instance, who was to become one of the architects of the Restitution Agreement drawn up between Germans and Jews at a later stage, or from Dr. Eugen Gerstenmaier,[23] connected with the abortive anti-Hitler *Putsch* of July 20, 1944. But there are no statements or declarations on the Jewish fate by the Christian Democratic Union (CDU) which rapidly became the leading political force in Germany in the early postwar years.

Several reasons may account for this. The party, unlike the Social Democrats, was not based on tradition. It was newly created and, for the first time, it combined the various wings of Christian politicians. It united its supporters as much for opportunistic reasons as for genuinely democratic or idealistic aspirations. It took some time for the party to be properly established in the whole of the country, due to the differing regulations of the occupation powers for their individual zones. From the start it also lacked the rigidity of organization that is typical of the Social Democrats. It became a voters' party rather than a membership party so that attitudes and opinions were not the result of views formulated from within the party but were rather the independent thinking of leading individuals. (This, incidentally, may also apply to the small Liberal Party which, although having a tradition, lacked mass membership.) Over and above this, the Christian Democrat leader, Dr. Konrad Adenauer— one of the cleverest party politicians in Germany—no doubt realized that the people whom he wanted to attract as voters were far more interested in subjects other than those connecting them with the unpleasant past. And, undoubtedly, problems existed that required urgent solving at that time; the refugees, the homeless, the chaos, the dismantling. Dr. Adenauer surely sensed that he would not find any response for himself and his party, should he turn to the people

---

[21] *Stuttgarter Zeitung*, October 6, 1945.

[22] Minister of Culture in Hesse province, 1945-1946: Member of the Bonn Parliament, 1953-1965.

[23] President of the *Bundestag* from 1954 to 1969.

with the demand to atone for their crimes first and foremost—crimes for which many people, rightly or wrongly, did not feel responsible. Today, Christian Democratic politicians maintain that, to have solved all these burning problems, the leadership would have had to be dependent on the cooperation of the people. Lastly, Dr. Adenauer had been a staunch Catholic all his life. The Catholic Church eradicated the charges against the Jews from its liturgy, but not until 1967. This is not meant as a charge against Dr. Adenauer. Nevertheless, it cannot be excluded that, if only subconsciously, the Catholic attitude towards the Jews may have influenced him to be lax in his pronouncements on the Jewish question (as the Church in general proved to be in the first postwar years), notwithstanding his general morality all during his life. But, apart from this assumption, it is a fact that, in the first postwar years, the Christian Democratic Union failed to declare itself the haven for the Jewish survivors or to condemn in unambiguous terms the crimes committed against the Jews during the Hitler era.

The relationship between Jews and Social Democrats was different from the very start. It was to them that the Jews could turn at any time with their grievances, knowing that they would be understood. There are several reasons for this. First of all, bias never existed in the Socialist movement from its very inception. According to its teachings, in a Socialist society every man and every woman would have equal opportunities and rights, and religious grounds for anti-Semitism would disappear with the gradual reduction in religious beliefs. There were quite a number of Jews in the leadership of the Socialist movement in Germany whose adherence to the Socialist principles was such that they virtually forgot their Judaism until the Nazis dug it out again. In fact, the contact between Jews and Socialists in Germany never ceased, despite the Nazis' threat to punish all those who would fraternize with Jews. Social Democrats and Communists were the first to suffer from Nazi persecution in 1933. They were arrested, put into concentration camps, others fled abroad, and some remained to work in the resistance movement, however small it may have been. The connection with Jews was, for former Social Democrats within Germany, often the only form of expressing their hatred against the Nazis. And, in many cases, Social Democrats helped Jews to survive the Nazi regime.

The Jews themselves never entirely severed contact with the Socialists. A most striking example in this regard is the fact that the

American Jewish Labor Committee [24] tried to save leaders of the German Labor movement at a time when it was very difficult, indeed, for the outside world to differentiate between the Germans. The Committee's argument with the State Department was that, after the defeat of Hitler, Europe would need these leaders to reconstruct a democratic regime there. Sponsored by the president of the American Federation of Labor (AFL) William Green, a rescue operation was started in the south of France where a number of Socialists had found temporary shelter. The American Socialist, Dr. Bohn, was sent to Marseilles to assist the refugees in their dealings with the American Embassy which had received instructions from the State Department to issue six hundred visitors' visas to German Socialists and German writers on the run from the Nazis. Those chosen had been declared reliable by German Socialists already in the United States; for example, Max Brauer, the first postwar Mayor of Hamburg, and Dr. Richard Katz, a judge of the postwar German Supreme Court. Their Socialist liaison officer in France was Fritz Heine, a postwar leader of the German Social Democratic Party. The rescue operation, for which the American Jewish Labor Committee took over all the technical and financial burdens, lasted from August, 1940, to January, 1941. Although it was not easy to get transit visas through Spain and Portugal—some had to travel via Africa—a good many German Socialists were saved in this way. When they reached the States, the Jewish Labor Committee provided them with money to start a new life and had apartments ready for them.[25]

It might sound odd, considering the events during the war, that it was the Jewish *Bund* [26] in Paris that helped German Socialists to return to Germany from France with the purpose of rebuilding the Socialist movement there. After heated discussions within its ranks, the *Bund* managed to wring from the French occupying power permits for prominent German Socialists to enter Germany. This, in 1945, was by no means easy. In fact, they became the first to be allowed to enter Germany from abroad, long before those who had been refugees in England were permitted to return. The *Bund* granted these Socialists a loan which was not only to cover their

---

[24] Founded in 1934 for the purpose of supporting the fight against Hitler and helping the resistance movement in Germany by arranging a boycott against German exports and other activities.

[25] Information obtained from the American Jewish Labor Committee.

[26] International Jewish organization adhering to Socialistic principles.

traveling expenses but also to get them off to a good start in Germany.[27]

It is clear that it was easy for the German Socialists to meet the Jews and to be confronted with their problems. In fact, the Socialists became the only ones in Germany who had no reason to shy away from the Jews, to apologize to them or to fear that their hand of friendship would be turned down. And this did not only concern the Jewish question. The Socialists—with their record of noncooperation with Hitler—who had been detained in concentration camps and forced into exile also, showed in all their postwar statements no indication of the shame, guilt complex or servility that became the second nature of some people in Germany.[28] The Socialists knew no inhibitions in their attitude towards either the occupying authorities or towards the Jews.

Kurt Schumacher, the postwar leader of the Social Democratic Party, often was accused of a nationalistic and unbending attitude when it would have befitted a German to be modest and servile. One may or may not have doubts as to the manner by which Schumacher tried to make the Allies understand that a new Germany, a democratic Germany as they wanted it, could not be built on subjugation. But this manner certainly was the consequence of the development of the man himself and his party. Schumacher and his party never failed to remind the German people of the crimes they had committed against the Jews. The German Social Democrats, regardless of the unpopularity of the demand, requested the severest punishment for the criminals and called for a declaration by the new German leaders that anti-Semitism constituted a serious crime. Schumacher would not have been a politician, had he, too, not realized that the Germans disliked the subject. But for him the moral aspect seemed to stand far above all other considerations. It is quite understandable that he was the first German politician to be interviewed by the publisher of the weekly of German Jewry at the beginning of 1947, and that he was the first to demand that the Jews be compensated for their material losses [29]—a demand other parties would not have dreamed of making at that time. This request was taken over

---

[27] Information obtained from G. Markscheffel, Bonn.

[28] Ben-Gurion, in conversation with the writer, August 7, 1968, recalled the "slave-like servility" of the Germans which he had found unbearable during his visit to Germany in 1945.

[29] Repeated in speech before the delegates of the AFL in San Francisco, October, 1947.

by the Social Democratic Party Congress of June-July, 1947, in Nuremberg and reintroduced by the Congress of September, 1948, in Düsseldorf.

But the Social Democrats were not the German people. (Officials of the occupation forces at that time say that they used to divide the Germans into "Social Democrats" and "other" Germans.) Nor were the politicians, Professor Theodor Heuss and Professor Franz Boehm, representative of the people. Neither could certain German intellectuals be considered the voice of the public. For example, the rector of the University of Heidelberg, the first German university to be reopened, declared that the Nazis, by their organized mass murder had desecrated medicine.[30] Journalists, working for the many publications established after the war, wrote—spirit released from suppression—expressing their horror at the crimes. We hear of rallies all over Germany in 1949, where speakers promised to punish those who had committed the crimes. But, was reality exposed in the outcome of a test that *Radio Munich* reported at the beginning of 1949?

A teacher had put the following questions to 124 young individuals, their ages averaging about twenty-five: "A cordial and friendly relationship develops between you and another young person. By chance you learn that he is Jewish. Would you break off the friendship?" Replies were plain and to the point: "Break off at once"; some adding a few exclamation marks. The second question: "Would you take a Jewish pupil into your class?" was answered, "Yes, to see how he developed." Third question: "Do you know of any group of people whom you dislike more than the Jews?" The majority replied: "No." [31]

On July 27, 1949, the French news agency *Agence France Presse* (AFP) reported an analysis by an institute for Jewish affairs, saying:

The position of the Jews in Germany is completely hopeless. The yellow star of the Nazis has been removed on orders of the Allies. But the German Jews feel that there is another kind of anti-Semitism at work now; not so visible, but no less deadly than the one which landed millions in the crematoria. . . . . In industry and trade, Jews have great difficulties; German wholesale dealers give priority to non-Jewish customers

[30] Professor K. H. Bauer, *Stuttgarter Stimme*, August 31, 1945.
[31] *Frankfurter Neue Presse*, February 15, 1949.

and this means certain death for a businessman in times of shortage, still existing in Germany.

And the Jewish Lawyers' Conference in Wiesbaden in July, 1949, arrived at the conclusion that: ". . . The German people have not changed in their attitude towards Jewry. . . ." In an August, 1949, opinion poll inquiring into the people's general attitude towards Jewry, 41 percent indicated a tolerant attitude. Anti-Semitic replies came from 23 percent and 15 percent gave no definite answer. Fifteen percent offered no opinion at all, while 6 percent expressed philo-Semitic views.[32]

Dr. Nahum Goldmann, the president of the World Jewish Congress, declared at their Paris meeting, on August 30, 1949, that German nationalism was as strong as it used to be under Hitler; anti-Semitism had increased constantly while de-Nazification had failed; for the Jews and the world, Germany indicated danger.[33]

But, at least the Basic Law, the constitution of the Federal Republic of Germany (adopted on May 8, 1949, by the Parliamentary Council, the predecessor of the elected Parliament), granted the Jews, or all minorities for that matter, equality before the law: ". . . No one may be prejudiced or favored because of his sex, his parentage, his race, his language, his homeland and origin, his faith or his religious or political opinions."

Some conditions under which Jews lived in the Russian-occupied zone of Germany after the war—later forcibly cut off and turned into a Communist state—differed little from those in the three zones under Western Allies' rule. In *Der Weg* (issued May 5, 1947, in undivided Berlin in the early postwar years, also serving the Eastern Zone since the Jewish community and all other groups were split up only as a consequence of the establishment of the two German states in 1949), mention is made of desecrations of cemeteries just as much as in the Western areas of Germany: "Half of the Jewish cemetery of Zittau was destroyed . . . the damage done was worse than that caused during the Third Reich. . . ."

In the first years, the Russian-controlled East German authorities, already predominantly Communist, were helpful to the Jewish citizens or those who still declared themselves to be Jewish. Some people

[32] Elisabeth and Peter Noelle-Neumann, *The Germans, public opinion polls, 1947-1966*, p. 186, Verlag für Demoskopie, Allensbach, 1967.
[33] *Neue Zeitung*, Munich, August 31, 1949.

of Jewish stock believed that, thanks to Communist rule, their origin no longer played a part. Government authorities gave the Jewish communities facilities according to their needs regarding their cultural and religious institutions and helped them to restore cemeteries or synagogues destroyed or neglected during the Nazi era. Jews who had returned to the Eastern Zone from concentration camps, or who had survived Nazi persecution by other means, were given the status of "Victim of Fascism" as were all other sufferers from Nazi persecution. This entitled them to a number of privileges, such as priority in the distribution of flats and more generous food rations. Those who had suffered physical injuries were given a pension. On no occasion, however, was there any mention of the Communist regime's readiness to compensate the Jews for their material losses.

The Communists—and there we find a difference between the Western Zones of Germany and the Eastern Zone—from the start never failed to distinctly charge the Nazis with the responsibility for the war and the past sufferings of certain sections of the population. As they themselves had become victims of the Nazi persecution, this may not be surprising. They assured the world that the introduction of Socialism in their zone would make it impossible for Fascism and Nazism ever to raise their ugly heads again, and that there would never be a problem of anti-Semitism as long as Socialism was firmly in the saddle.

The Social Democratic Party existed as a separate party only until the spring of 1946, when it was, more or less forcibly, merged with the Communists. Until then it had shared the views of the West German SPD on the need to compensate the Jews and to reinstate them to full citizenship.

The churches and the political parties were just as silent on the issue of the Jews as their colleagues in the west with whom they still were joined organizationally. The more the Communist regime established itself in the Eastern Zone, supported by the Russian occupation authorities and army, the less freedom of speech was granted to the population. Anti-Semitism was not in line with the pronouncements of the Communist authorities, therefore, it is practically impossible for an observer to judge the East Germans' attitude towards the Jewish people, or on any issues that would reveal whether or not the East German population still had an ideological affinity for Nazi teachings.

In Heidelberg, on July 30, 1949, the American Zone's High Commissioner, John McCloy, said, "The manner in which the Germans treat their Jews is the test for German democracy." [34]

It would be easy to conclude from all that has been said so far that no definite judgment could be made about the East Germans regarding their attitude towards the Jews, but it soon became evident from the political development in East Germany that its rulers did not intend to build up a democracy. As to West Germany, one would have to say that the people had failed, up to then, to prove themselves democrats. Their treatment of the Jewish people showed that they had learned little or nothing from the past.

Yet, a little later they democratically voted their first post-Hitler Parliament into power, causing German Jewry to state, sarcastically: "They have put the cart before the horse. The Hitler voters of yesterday have been permitted to be voters for Parliament today." An analysis of the outcome shows that the Social Democrats, the only democratic party which at first had not allowed former Nazis to become members, and which had proved its integrity throughout the Hitler regime, could muster only 29.2 percent of all votes cast. The Christian Democrats and the Christian Social Union, its Bavarian counterpart, became the strongest political force with 31 percent. Its following consisted, no doubt, of sincere democrats, but also of opportunists or former Nazi members. It was no different with the Free Democrats polling 11.9 percent, although at the time we still find in them the Liberals of the old school, destined to die out a few years later. Apart from scattered votes polled in favor of other small democratic parties, one can say that roughly 9 percent of all votes went to right-wing parties, half of them outspokenly Nazis.

This may not appear to have been a dangerous trend. Yet, at that time, the reasons for voting for democratic parties were far less easy to define than they are today. They included opportunistic angles or careerist hopes, as well as misunderstood aims and personal attachments to certain leaders. Adenauer attracted many partisans, following the chaos during which he himself had not been misled. He was the "father figure" which the German nation needed then. Dr. Schumacher, the victim of Nazism, was too much the image of German guilt. Thus, Adenauer became the chosen German leader.

At least fifty-three of the elected parliamentarians, in 1949, had been members of the National Socialist German Workers' Party (NSDAP) which means that one-eighth of all parliamentary seats

[34] *Neue Zeitung*, Munich, July 31, 1949.

were occupied by members who had once pledged their allegiance to Adolf Hitler. Three of them had also been members of the fearful Storm Troopers (SS) and one of the Brownshirts (SA). With the exception of ten, all were members of the new government parties (Christian Democratic Union, Free Democrats and the German Party).[35]

As Chancellor, in his address to the first post-Hitler Parliament on September 20, 1949, Dr. Adenauer did not mention any German liability towards the Jewish people. He merely said: "We consider it disgraceful and actually unbelievable that, after all that happened during the National Socialist era, there should still exist people in Germany who persecute or despise Jews solely because they are Jews. . . ."

It also cannot be overlooked that, by the time the first postwar German government and its Parliament were constituted, the state of Israel already existed. And, although the founding of the state of Israel was in some way connected with the fate that Jews in Europe suffered at the hands of the Germans, not a single reference was made by the new German government to this fact, an omission which must again be considered the result of psychological as well as political motivations.

On September 21, the leader of the Social Democratic Party, Dr. Kurt Schumacher, in his reply to the government declaration, expressed his astonishment at the few words on the subject of the Jews, and said:

. . . . What was said yesterday about the Jews and the horrible tragedy of the Jews in the Third Reich is too colorless . . . . it is the duty of each German patriot to emphasize the fate of German and European Jewry and to give the necessary help . . . Hitler's barbarism has degraded the German people through the annihilation of six million Jewish people; we shall have to bear the consequences of this degradation for unforeseeable time. . . .[36]

But Dr. Schumacher and his party were only the opposition, with little or no power to face the government and other parties then represented in Parliament. They were, with all their good will, not strong enough to act as the basis for relations between postwar Germany and the Jews, although they were a glimpse of hope for the

[35] Archives of *Neue Zeitung*, Munich.
[36] Minutes of the *Bundestag*, vol. I, pp. 27-36.

future development of Germany—for those who wanted to see any. But, the majority of the Germans, however difficult it may be to judge many of them in view of their silence, failed to inspire this confidence.

2
Israel Trapped by Realpolitik

Jews were not wearing the concentration camp garb when they reached the shores of Israel. But the suffering of the years past was deeply engraved in their faces and the physical state of each of the survivors left no doubt as to the inferno from which they had miraculously escaped. The stories they had to tell about their years in German concentration camps and the fate of the others who had not survived seemed incomprehensible—yet they were true to the smallest detail, as official facts and figures soon bore out. There was not a single family in Israel of European origin that had not suffered the loss of a close relative, a friend or a neighbor. The outcry of a whole nation that followed the reports of the murders and the mental torture endured hearing of the methods of annihilation knows no comparison. It is practically impossible to describe in adequate words.

The whole world shared the grief at the cruel extinction of a people, systematically organized by other humans. Many a responsible statesman of the world must have felt the guilt of not having done everything possible to save European Jewry when there still had been time to do so. Many a Jew who had escaped in time, almost broke down under the burden that, perhaps, he could have done something more to save his next of kin from a horrible fate and a torturous end.

Next to grief, a wave of hatred mounted in Israel against those who had committed such crimes and against those who had permitted them to happen. It was as if a good German never had existed; it was as if Jews never had spent a happy period in Germany; it was as if Goethe and Schiller never had lived to add to the world's finest literature. All that once might have been dear to some Jews in Germany; all that once had been contributed to the world's knowledge and wisdom by a German seemed a dream, an unreality, and was buried, it appeared then, once and for all.

No distinction was made between the Germans. It was not and could not be seen then and there that Germans, also—though a minority—had suffered at the hands of the Nazis; that Germans, too, though their number minute, had stuck out their necks to save Jews. What was clear—if, at the end of the Nazi era anything at all *was* clear to those who had lost their loved ones—was that six million Jews had been killed off in the most horrible, perfidious and gruesome manner by Germans, by many Germans; watched without protest by Germans, by most Germans. The "collective guilt" of the entire German nation seemed well proven and unshakable. This meant, then, for an Israeli, no contact with Germans, no reconciliation, no acceptance of advances on the part of Germans, ever.

When the state of Israel was founded in 1948, the Jews were so much concerned with their own problems (the taking in of thousands of immigrants and the war that the Arab states had carried into the newly founded state of Israel), that they cared little about the development in postwar Germany. This might be called an advantage from the German point of view, as the Israelis thus missed the first recurrences of anti-Semitism in Germany so soon after the destruction of the Hitler Reich. This might have strengthened their hatred for the Germans and made it even less extinguishable. As matters stood, the attitude of every Israeli towards Germans then seemed fixed and seemed beyond any revision or revoking. The fact that the Germans, preoccupied with their own postwar troubles, failed to take notice of the founding of the state of Israel, or that many, for psychological reasons, pretended not to take any notice of the new Jewish state, made this attitude even easier. At the most, some Germans noted with satisfaction, at last, the unwanted "DPs" gradually had disappeared from Germany.

The only anti-German action initiated by Jews during this period came in 1949, from the World Jewish Congress which protested to the American Foreign Office on behalf of its millions of members against delegating power to the Germans. In the statement of May 18, 1950, the World Jewish Congress, explaining its objection, maintained that too many Nazis or their former sympathizers were employed in German government services.[1] Of course, this was an unrealistic step to take on the part of the Jews as, the Western Allies, already aware of the impact of the Russian offensive against the free world, believed that West Germany would be needed as a bulwark against the Communist onslaught. They seemed to have thought that, under their occupation, turning the Germans into their enemies might have driven them into the arms of the Communists. The Allies definitely needed the Germans as friends now. The handing over of power in 1949, and the permission granted the Germans to make use of democratic institutions only four years after the collapse of a totalitarian regime seemed logical consequences from the Allies' point of view. The crimes that had been committed by the Germans were virtually reduced to incidents and, though they were not forgotten, no longer were decisive. The commutation of many sentences which, in Nuremberg, had been imposed by the Allies with all harshness on war criminals only a few years earlier is the best proof of this contention. The Jewish people and the state of Israel could not follow this trend of thought.

The new German government rejected the charges of the World Congress, but it still failed to say anything about the guilt it was burdened with, or an intention, at least, to make reparation for the material losses of the Jews. Needless to say, the Jews and the Israelis had expected some kind of admission of guilt on the part of the Germans. This admission did not materialize. Professor Heuss, later on, argued that such admission of guilt—a collective guilt—would have meant identifying the whole nation with the crimes; this would have been not only incorrect but similar to Hitler's collective statements with reference to the Jews. This argument, however valid it may have been for Professor Heuss and some others, was unacceptable, (at least to some extent), to the Israelis who were aware of the fact that, after the 1945 disclosure of the most devastating genocide, nothing had been said officially by those in whose name the crimes had been committed. Admittedly, such a statement might not have had an immediate impact on the survivors or might not have changed their attitude towards the Germans instantly. But the omission of it seemed to prove even more the immorality of the German people.

The first German Chancellor, Dr. Konrad Adenauer, spoke up on the Jewish question on November 25, 1949, to Editor Karl Marx, of

[1] Joachim Kreysler and Klaus Jungfer, *Deutsche Israel-Politik*, p. 19, Wolf von Tucher Verlag G.m.b.H., Diessen-Ammersee, April 1965.

the Jewish weekly, *Allgemeine Wochenzeitung der Juden in Deutschland*, two months after he had been elected head of the newly founded Federal Republic of Germany. The realistic Adenauer must have sensed that he could gain worldwide confidence for himself and his country if he did so. As he put it many years later: "I tried to achieve reconciliation with the Jews because of the injustice that has been done to them and because of the fact that world Jewry is a power." [2] But, surprisingly, the first postwar Chancellor of a democratic Germany did not deal with the relationship between Germans and Israelis, between the two newly founded states, or even Germans and Jews. He simply dealt with materialistic issues. He offered the state of Israel: ". . . a gift of goods to the value of $2,380,000 for the purpose of the building up of Israel, and this is to be a first direct sign that the injustice inflicted upon the Jews the whole world over by Germans must be made up for."

Adenauer had no other word for Israel except admiration for what had been achieved there, yet he said so, not within the framework of the interview, but in the private conversation preceding it. Then he went on to offer the Jewish people in Germany the setting up of an office within the Interior Ministry with the sole task of safeguarding the rights of the Jews in political, cultural and economic life in Germany; an office which, incidentally, never was created, as the $2,380,000 never was given. Admitting that not enough had been done since 1945 for the Jewish people, Adenauer assured the Jews then that the German government would do all in its power to protect them against anti-Semitism and expressed deep regret that such tendencies still existed in Germany.

In this first address to the Jewish people when he made his offer of a $2,380,000 gift, Dr. Adenauer entirely ignored the fact that very definite requests on the part of Israel for adequate compensation for the material losses incurred by the Jews due to their persecution already existed. On September 20, 1945, Chaim Weizmann, spokesman for the Jewish Agency for Palestine, had asserted in a note [3] to the Four Powers—the United States, Great Britain, the Soviet Union and France—that the Jews demanded compensation from the Germans. Weizmann reminded the Allies that:

. . . In executing their declaration of war, Germany and her associates murdered some six million Jews, destroyed all communal institutions

[2] The eve of Adenauer's ninetieth birthday, January 4, 1966, on West German television.

[3] Felix E. Shinnar, *Bericht eines Beauftragten*, p. 20, Rainer Wunderlich Verlag, Tübingen, 1967.

where their authority extended, stole all their treasures on which they could lay their hands . . . the mass murders, the human suffering, the annihilation of spiritual, intellectual and creative forces are probably without parallel in the history of mankind.

Weizmann also mentioned the problem of restitution concerning the buildings, plant equipment, money securities and valuables of various kinds taken from Jewish institutions and individuals, as well as Jewish cultural treasures, religious articles and communal properties which he estimated at $8,000,000,000. Recalling the system of reparations payments after World War I, he demanded "that the Jewish people also be allotted a proper percentage of reparations to be entrusted to the Jewish agency for Palestine" for the relief and rehabilitation of Jewish victims of racial and religious persecution.

In view of the actual losses, a $2,380,000 gift to Israel appeared almost a mockery. The reaction in Israel was unanimous. Comments ranged from, "We shall neither now nor in future accept any gifts from Germany, for we do not sell our honor" to "Germany bears the responsibility for the difficult situation in which the young state of Israel is placed today since hundreds of thousands became homeless because of Germany. Germany is guilty of the death of six million people and it has to acknowledge this guilt." The Israeli government refused to comment, declaring that it had not been directly addressed.

The World Jewish Congress called $2,380,000 totally insufficient and expressed its regret that, above all, the statement had been issued only by an individual (although the Chancellor himself), but that it failed to have the backing of the new German Parliament or any other government institution. And, of course, the World Jewish Congress pointed out that it lacked the admission of guilt as much as the binding obligation to pay compensation for the material losses.[4]

Emotions, most certainly justified emotions, guided the political attitude of the state of Israel. It was determined not to enter into any political, economic or other relationship with Germany. It could not be otherwise, considering that the state of Israel had become the haven for many who had been able to escape the great annihilation. Up to 1952, more than 500,000 Jews from Germany and the Nazi-occupied territories during the war had come to settle in Israel; a high percentage of Israel's population. Antagonistic feeling

[4] Joachim Kreysler and Klaus Jungfer, *Deutsche Israel Politik*, p. 14, Wolf von Tucher Verlag G.m.b.H., Diessen-Ammersee, April, 1965.

against Germany prompted a demand in the *Knesset* that the Israeli Consulate in Munich be closed.[5] Until the founding of the Federal Republic, it had been accredited, at first, only to the American occupation army; later, also to the British and French, without contact with the German authorities. The tasks of the consul were restricted to matters relating to DP camps and to the United Nations Relief and Works Agency (UNRWA). After 1949, the accreditation was to apply also to the German authorities.

On January 9, 1951, when the Western Powers requested all non-Communist members of the United Nations to end the state of war with Germany, forty-seven declared their readiness to do so. Israel was not among them.[6] From the formal point of view, no state of Israel had existed when war had raged in Europe; therefore, there was no obligation on the part of the Jewish state to end war with Germany. But, under different circumstances, it might have been a matter of diplomacy between nations to express the readiness to establish friendly ties after the majority of the free world had made such a move. In August, 1951, Ben-Gurion referred to this, saying that official postwar Germany had so far failed to declare that it differed from Hitler's attitude towards the Jews. There was no concrete proof of a change of mind in Germany, and no readiness to compensate the Jews.[7]

But, by that time there were contacts between Germans and Jewish representatives seeking a basis for a *rapprochement* and a reconciliation. Ben-Gurion must have known this, although Israel had left the negotiations to the World Jewish Organization as if not concerned. On the other hand, Israel did not allow itself to be taken by surprise when the subject of restitution was broached. In the beginning of 1950—that is, in the early stages of Jewish-German negotiations—the Israeli Finance Ministry had requested that the legal advisor and director of the Jewish Relief Unit for the British Zone of Germany, Hendrik van Dam, work out a memorandum as to the legality and prospects of restitution of heirless property to the state of Israel.[8] There had been contacts since the early fifties.

[5] *Ibid.*

[6] According to *The New York Times*, January 10, 1951, the three Western Powers were informed by the Israeli government that it could not agree to an ending of war with Germany.

[7] Erich Lüth, *Viel Steine lagen am Weg*, p. 271, Marion von Schröder Verlag, Hamburg, 1966.

[8] Rolf Vogel, *Deutschlands Weg nach Israel*, p. 22, Seewald Verlag, Stuttgart, 1967.

According to German government sources, a German-Jewish businessman is said to have made the first direct approach to Dr. Herbert Blankenhorn, Adenauer's most trusted assistant, who intimated that now the German government was not disinclined to consider the Jewish issue. Dr. Blankenhorn's current recollection was that the topic of making amends had been an object of frequent discussion between him and Dr. Adenauer from the very outset of Adenauer's chancellorship. But, too much still blocked the road in the problems of rebuilding Germany from the shambles the war had left behind. Consequently, anything concerning the Jews could take shape only in the later phases of the development. And even in 1950, Dr. Blankenhorn said, it could not have been done simply by issuing a declaration admitting the German guilt and perhaps also expressing readiness to compensate the Jewish people for their material losses. Dr. Blankenhorn referred to the need to "prepare the psychological basis among the German people for such a declaration." The German people had to be in agreement with the government's efforts to achieve reconciliation with the Jews, as it would have been disastrous for Germany's standing in the world, had objections been voiced. That reconciliation was not an easy matter for some German circles to accept is apparent from the reluctance of German institutions to mention this issue at all after the war.[9] The fact that Adenauer made his first offer to the Jews and Israel two months after he had been elected Chancellor also may serve as a pointer to the apprehensions of the government concerning this delicate issue. Some Germans admit quite freely today that they felt rather annoyed at the Israeli request for a share in the reparations payments in some of the notes presented by the Israelis to the Allied powers. They state that they considered the issue purely from the legalistic point of view; Israel had not existed at the time of the war and was therefore not entitled to reparations. The moral aspect played virtually no part in their considerations.

With the consent of Dr. Adenauer, Dr. Blankenhorn eventually entered into negotiations with Dr. Noah Barou, a leading personality at the European desk of the World Jewish Congress in London. The aim was to find out on what conditions Jews and Germans could meet. Barou told Blankenhorn that Israel and the Jews would negotiate with Bonn, "only after Adenauer had solemnly acknowledged before the German Parliament his nation's responsibility for

[9] Conversation with the writer, London, March 8, 1968.

the acts of the Nazi regime against the Jews." [10] Another condition, of course, was a public declaration that West Germany would make amends for the material losses suffered by Jewry and that representatives of Israel and world Jewry should be officially invited to discuss the matter. These terms were accepted by Dr. Adenauer.

Barou and Blankenhorn battled for many months over the wording of the declaration which Chancellor Adenauer was to deliver in Parliament. "We met at least a dozen times until we reached a compromise," Dr. Blankenhorn recollected.

Obstacles to reaching an easy agreement were raised on both sides. The Germans felt that they could not allow the entire nation to be blamed for the execrable crimes as this did not comply with the truth, nor were they ready to promise to undertake compensation payments without limitations. On the other hand, it was not easy for the Jews to relinquish their uncompromising attitude. For them, the losses were unforgettable—the people who had been murdered in the name of Germany, mainly by Germans, and the vast amount of property that had been stolen. Dr. Blankenhorn expressed the belief that it was due only to "the understanding attitude of Dr. Barou" that the declaration was at last completed. Barou realized the German difficulties, Blankenhorn said. The declaration had to be acceptable, for moral and political reasons, not only to the Chancellor and his party, but also to all political parties represented in Parliament and all those who bore the responsibility for the new democratic state. Dr. Blankenhorn did not conceal the fact that there were quite a number of reactionaries within the ranks of those representing democratic parties for whom a reconciliation with the Jewish people was not imperative, let alone desirable. And, above all, it had to be acceptable to the German people. Step by step, they had to get accustomed to their responsibilities towards the Jewish survivors.[11]

The Israeli government continued to give the impression that it took no note of the negotiations between Jews and Germans. The antagonistic feelings in Israel against Germany would not have allowed any other attitude at that time. It also continued to address its requests for compensation to the Four Powers, even after the founding of the West German state. Israel's note of January 16, 1951, in which it complained about the meager and unsatisfactory restitution

---

[10] Nicholas Balabkins, "The Birth of Restitution," p. 10, The Wiener Library Bulletin, London, Autumn, 1967.

[11] Conversation with the writer, March 8, 1968.

and indemnification legislation that had been in existence in West Germany, demanded the adoption of a general claims law for the Federal Republic and started off a series of exchanges between Israel and the Western Powers. The Soviet Union never replied, and does not even acknowledge Israel notes to this day. In their replies, reaching Israel in March, 1951, the three Western Powers agreed that the handling of individual restitution claims in their occupation areas was far from satisfactory. The British added that this was "occasioned by the reluctance of His Majesty's Government, with the United States and French governments, to abandon attempts to reach an agreement in the Control Council on a unified program throughout Germany for internal restitution of identifiable property." Which meant that the Western Powers were still hoping to obtain Russian support for restitution payments to be introduced in their zone of occupation.[12]

Israel's note of March 12, 1951, with the very specific demand for compensation of $1,500,000,000 to Israel as payment for the resettling of 500,000 Jews caused some more headaches for the Allies. Felix von Eckardt, German government spokesman and Adenauer's confidant for many years, in his book wrote about this note: "The Allies did not quite know what to do with it at first." They recognized the moral justification for the demand, yet they did not know on what legal grounds to base it. The request had nothing to do with individual compensation, the legality of which could not be disputed. It was different with the request of the state of Israel. During the Hitler Reich no state of Israel had existed which meant that Israel and Germany had not been at war with each other and the term of "reparations" was, therefore, not applicable. The reply of the Allies was cautious and evasive. On July 5, 1951, the United States expressed regret "that it cannot impose on the government of the German Federal Republic payment of reparations to Israel." [13] In other words, Israel could not continue to ignore the German state if it wanted it to pay restitution. Only direct negotiations would be the right approach to the problem. Several prominent Jewish persons (mostly of former German origin, and with ties to the new German leaders stemming from the pre-Hitler era), tried

[12] Kurt R. Grossmann, "Germany's Moral Debt," *Public Affairs Press,* Washington, D.C., page 9.

[13] Felix von Eckardt, *Ein unordentliches Leben,* p. 199, Econ Verlag, Düsseldorf, 1967.

their hands as mediators, making it clear to the Israeli government that the Germans were quite willing to discuss a compensation treaty with them.

Robert M. Kempner, United States Chief of Counsel and Chief Prosecutor in the Nuremberg trials is said to have told Israeli government officials, when on a lecture tour in Israel, "Such matters cannot be dealt with by means of telepathy." [14] The German government, however, refused to comment on the Israeli note. The sole spokesman for the Finance Ministry declared that the Federal Republic was ready to consider all individual claims handed in by German Jewry; which, of course, was not what the state of Israel was driving at.[15]

The good will reported to exist on the German side was believed with reluctance in Israel. Watching developments in Germany, it did not escape notice that, on February 22, 1951, in the *Bundestag*, when the Social Democrats proposed to the Allies that Germany recognize Israel as the legal successor to all heirless property and indemnification claims, the House could not be stimulated. Carlo Schmid, spokesman of the Social Democratic Party (SPD), declared that Germany had by no means done enough to absolve "our moral and legal guilt." He said, "No matter how much Germany atones in this regard, it never will be enough to permit us to forget." Yet, despite this appeal, the legislation did not come about. The matter was referred to the Legislation Committee and there it was pigeonholed for several months and finally forgotten.[16]

Israel's economic situation deteriorated from 1950 on, so much so (due to the influx of the thousands of survivors who had to be housed, clothed and fitted into society again, also because of the Arab-Israel War) that it had to tap all sources of promising income. Compensation seemed to be such a source, and a big one, too. Israel finally had to realize that it could not request compensation from the German state by ignoring its existence. The notes of the Western Powers had made this quite evident; common sense did the rest. Obviously, it was not easy for the government in Israel to accept this as a fact, being fully aware of the public feeling.

[14] Kurt R. Grossmann, *Die Ehrenschuld*, p. 21, Ullstein Verlag, Frankfurt/ Berlin, 1967.

[15] Joachim Kreysler and Klaus Jungfer, *Deutsche Israel Politik*, p. 23, Wolf von Tucher G.m.b.H., Diessen-Ammersee, 1965.

[16] Minutes of the *Bundestag*, 120th Session, vol. 6, p. 4589, February 22, 1951.

But, while the Israeli government made it appear to the outside world—for good reasons, particularly with regard to its own countrymen—as if it left all responsibility for negotiations to the Jews outside, it made preparations to meet the Germans.

The first meeting took place only one month after the Israeli government had handed in its note of March, 1951 (which was to become the basis for the compensation agreement signed between Germany and Israel in September, 1952). When Dr. Adenauer visited Paris in April, 1951, he received the Israeli Ambassador to Paris, Maurice Fischer, and the Director General of the Israeli Finance Ministry, David Horowitz. The meeting—which had been arranged with the help of a Jewish member of the German Parliament, Jakob Altmaier (SPD) and the Israeli Consul in Munich—was top-secret. It served the purpose of weighing the chances of future negotiations between the two states. Dr. Adenauer received the two gentlemen in the private suite of his hotel. Horowitz is said to have put before Dr. Adenauer, in a most impassioned manner, what his government thought to be a legal claim of the state of Israel to compensation from the Germans based on his government's note of March 12, and which had been drafted by Horowitz himself and Dr. Pinchas Cohen.

He described to Dr. Adenauer, in detail, the suffering of the Jewish people while the Chancellor is reported to have listened patiently to what some German observers called painful and embarrassing words. The fact, however, that Dr. Adenauer and his government had so far failed to make an official statement as to the shocking crimes committed against the Jews by Germans reenforced the Israelis in the moral right to approach Adenauer as they did.

Adenauer, it is said, never forgot Horowitz' passionate address and conceded that, in view of the past, one had to have understanding for these Jewish sentiments. Yet, he merely promised the two Israelis that, preceding possible negotiations, he would examine Israel's case and the request for a German declaration accepting the moral, political and material responsibility for the events during the Third Reich. No more came of this meeting.[17]

The Israelis took the negotiations between the Jews and the Germans seriously, despite the fact that they had the impression of having been slighted. On July 1, 1951, a special department was set up in Jerusalem's Foreign Office to deal with the claims of the state

[17] Kurt R. Grossmann, *Die Ehrenschuld*, p. 29, Ullstein Verlag, Frankfurt/Berlin, 1967.

of Israel against Germany. Dr. Felix Shinnar, who later became the head of the Israeli Mission in Germany, was in charge of it.[18]

But all this went on in the strictest secrecy. The German people knew nothing about the negotiations. Understandably, then, disgust was rising among some German circles, having experienced Nazi persecution themselves, at the continued silence of the German government with respect to the Jewish people. The repeated charges against Germany on the part of Jewish statesmen and politicians at least prompted some Germans to come forward and suggest that something had to be done to ask forgiveness for what had happened in the past. On August 31, 1951, Erich Lüth, Director of the Hamburg State Press Office, published an article with the plea, "We beg Israel for peace." [19] Joined by other journalists, a "Peace with Israel" movement sprang up spontaneously all over the country. The appeal said: "We Germans must not shirk the Jewish problem! . . . We must say, 'We beg Israel for peace'. As a call to Israel from all pulpits, from all desks, from all government benches, this request ought to go out to reach the smallest and most isolated community in Germany; in the name of humanity, of justice to which we want to return, and in the name of a happier future."

Nahum Goldmann, the leader of the World Jewish Congress, was the first to congratulate Lüth on his initiative:

> . . . You surely realize that the failure of some kind of official or spontaneous statement—be it from official sources, be it from public opinion in Germany—concerning the crimes which the Nazi regime committed against the Jewish people cannot be understood by the Jewish public. . . .

Lüth's initiative may have helped to persuade reluctant Jewish and Israeli groups to look at Germany with more leniency.[20]

Yet, the Israelis' objections to meet with the Germans continued. One incident took place at a meeting of the Inter-Parliamentary Union in Istanbul (August 31 to September 6, 1951) when the leader of the Israeli delegation, Yitzchak Ben-Zvi [21] objected to the presence of German parliamentarians at the meeting, calling it "an

---

[18] Felix E. Shinnar, *Bericht eines Beauftragten,* p. 20, Rainer Wunderlich Verlag, Tübingen, 1967.

[19] *Deutsche Presse Agentur,* August 31, 1951.

[20] Erich Luth, *Viel Steine lagen am Weg,* p. 274, Marion von Schröder Verlag, Hamburg, 1966.

[21] President of the State of Israel from 1952-62.

offense to every honest and decent human being to be forced to deliberate with Germans as if they had done no harm to mankind. . . ." Professor Carlo Schmid, vice president of the German Lower House recalled, "It was a horrible speech . . . I have hardly ever heard anybody speak with such passion. . . ." [22]

After the president of the meeting had ruled that this problem was not for the Union to solve, efforts were made to reconcile the Israeli and the German delegations. A Swiss parliamentarian acting as a mediator succeeded. Carlo Schmid, Heinrich von Brentano (later Germany's Foreign Minister) and Robert Tillmanns (Minister without Portfolio until 1953) met with Ben-Zvi, the very same delegate who had opposed the presence of Germans at the international gathering, together with David Hacohen, leading member of the Israel Labor Party (MAPAI) and Jacob Klebanoff, a leading Israeli Liberal. The conversation, held in French, was halting at first, Professor Schmid remembered. It dealt with the issue of restitution, the Germans urging the Israelis to be ready to accept money. They were aware that this would not minimize the German guilt, but it would help them to gloss over their past. Only after Klebanoff revealed that he had studied in Munich some time in 1910 under a relative of von Brentano and the conversation continued in German did the tension lessen. The talks ended with the assurance of the Israeli partners that an offer from the Germans for negotiations on compensation would find serious consideration in the Israeli Parliament.[23]

Now it was certain that the German government would at last address itself officially and openly to the Jewish people; the efforts of Jewish and German officials to draft a declaration had reached the final stage. Two reasons may have speeded up the deliberations and helped to reduce the German reluctance to issue the statement, one being interlinked with the other. The Americans, German politicians relate now, did not conceal the fact that they would appreciate something that would help to improve German relationship with the Jews. And, since Dr. Adenauer was eager to pay his first visit to the United States—clever strategist that he was—he realized, no doubt, that such a statement would strengthen his reception there.

On September 27, 1951, more than six years after the war and two

[22] Rolf Vogel, *Deutschlands Weg nach Israel*, p. 19, Seewald Verlag, Stuttgart, 1967.

[23] Rolf Vogel, *Deutschlands Weg nach Israel*, p. 20, Seewald Verlag, Stuttgart, 1967.

years after the founding of the Federal Republic of Germany, Dr. Adenauer, on behalf of the government, at last submitted the statement to the *Bundestag* that was to commit the Germans to a relationship of accordance and an understanding of Israel and the Jewish people.[24] Rarely has a statement shown so manifestly the scars of tough battling. It did not start off with the admission of guilt towards the Jews. On the contrary, the statement's first paragraphs made clear that, in view of the past, the German government had done all to assure equality of opportunity for its Jewish citizens and to protect them against renewed persecution. However, it went on to admit that all these measures could become effective only if "the ethical attitude from which they spring becomes the common property of, and is shared by the entire people." This was an allusion to the anti-Semitic incidents that had occurred during the first postwar years which had done much to support the world's adverse opinion of Germany.

The government then pledged itself to do all in its power to indoctrinate the entire German people "with the spirit of human and religious tolerance." To make sure that this educational task would not be interrupted, the Federal government announced that it would combat "those circles which continued to engage in anti-Semitic incitement with rigorous and unforgiving prosecution and punishment." Only in the third part did the statement deal with the past suffering of the Jews at the hands of Germans; the German government aware, as always, of the interests of its people. No mention is made of the fact that, by their membership alone, millions of followers of the NSDAP or other Nazi formations became, to a great extent, accomplices in the crimes. Instead, it said:

The great majority of the German people have abhorred these crimes perpetrated against the Jews and have taken no part in them . . . there were many among the German people during the time of National Socialism who, at great risks to themselves and for religious motives, compelled by conscience and from the sense of shame at the defilement of the German name, came to the aid of their Jewish fellow-citizens.

If, indeed, this had been true to the extent the government stated, many more Jews would have been saved than actually was the case.

Nevertheless, Dr. Adenauer admitted that unspeakable crimes had been committed in the name of the German people, "which called

---

[24] *Deutschland und das Judentum, Erklärung der Bundesregierung uber das deutsch judische Verhaltnis,* Deutscher Bundes-Verlag, Bonn, 1951.

for moral and material restitution." In the last part of the statement
he then dealt with this obligation on the part of the Germans, yet
he warned that limits had been set due to dire needs of many Germans, war victims and refugees. However, the Chancellor promised
his government's readiness "to work out in conjunction with representatives of Jewry and the state of Israel that has given shelter and
refuge to so many homeless Jewish refugees, a solution of the problem of material restitution and compensation, and thus also ease the
path towards a healing of the spiritual wounds."

The government declaration was followed by statements of speakers from some of the political parties represented in Parliament. The
seventy-six-year-old Paul Loebe, former Speaker of the German
Reichstag, representing the Social Democrats, spoke of Germany's
moral obligation to strive for a reconciliation with the state of Israel
and the Jews all over the world, and to do this by taking the first
step in this direction. Loebe expressed criticism of the government
when he said: "We only wished that they [the steps] had been
taken earlier and with greater emphasis." He thus reiterated the criticism that his party has uttered for six years against the government.
Unlike Dr. Adenauer, Loebe, in view of "the horrible extent of the
crimes," demanded sacrifices from the Germans to prove by deeds
that this effort to make up for the crimes was the measure for the
restoration of justice in Germany. Although some parties, including
the Communists and right-wingers, failed to speak up on the issue,
they were ready, perhaps for reasons of expediency, to support the
statement. When the president of the *Bundestag*, Dr. Hermann Eh-
lers, suggested, "As a sign that we are united in our sympathy for
the victims, and in our willingness to accept and make amends for
the consequences of past happenings, members should rise from
their seats," the entire House, including the government and the visitors, rose to observe one minute's silence.

The World Jewish Congress commented that it had noted with
special interest that the declaration of the Federal government referred to all questions which the World Jewish Congress considered
imperative. Even though the crimes committed by the Nazi regime
could never be eradicated from the memory of the Jews, the World
Jewish Congress had taken note of the German authorities' intention
to take definite steps on the road to making amends for the past.[25]

The Israeli government reacted to the statement with caution and

[25] Kurt R. Grossmann, *Die Ehrenschuld,* p. 26, Ullstein Verlag, Frankfurt/
Berlin, 1967.

scepticism. Once again, it declared,[26] in plain language, the extent of the Jewish losses and the collective guilt of the Germans in this respect. Yet, it admitted that the statement appeared to be at least an attempt of the German government to face this grave issue and to initiate some measure of moral and material reparations. As if to pacify its own people, it drew their attention to the passage in the statement whereby the German government appealed to the German people to divest themselves of the cursed heritage of anti-Semitism and racial discrimination; it expressed the intention of working out legislation and introducing educational means to eradicate, once and for all, those dangerous trends and tendencies among the Germans. It seemed to the Israeli government that the German government was ready to admit the crimes committed in the name of the German people, and to feel the obligation to compensate the Jewish people, morally and materially, both on an individual and on a collective basis. But, it called it imperative that the Germans make a major contribution towards the absorption and rehabilitation of the survivors of Nazi persecution, the bulk of whom had found refuge in Israel.

The conciliatory tone of the Israeli government statement, ending with the promise to further examine the Chancellor's statement and to make known its own attitude in due course, makes it clear today that the Israeli government had realized by then that it could not do without German restitution payments and that it could not obtain them without dealing directly with the German government. It was evident that this could not possibly be broken to the country bluntly. Dr. Adenauer's mention that negotiations would be needed to work out a restitution scheme with the Jewish people sparked off heated debates and anti-German demonstrations in Israel; extremists rejected such ideas outright. The objectors thought that the acceptance of money from the Germans implied moral approval of the new West German state, which surely was not deserved, considering, above all, that former Nazis served in high government positions, and that anti-Semitic and Neo-Nazi tendencies had survived the Hitler Reich.[27]

It surely is not incorrect to say that the Israeli people were then practically united in the refusal to accept the hand stretched out to

---

[26] Declaration to the German government via the Israeli Consulate in Munich, September 29, 1951.

[27] Kurt R. Grossmann, "Germany's Moral Debt," p. 16, Public Affairs Press, Washington, D.C., 1954.

them from Germany. At that time, political motives of certain Israeli parties to undermine the government's position in opposition to
a restitution agreement with the Germans did not play a part as it
would do at a later stage. The Israeli government, however, felt that
it had no other choice.

3
The First Treaty Between Jews and Germans

On March 20, 1952, at 9 a.m., sharp, a group of Germans in dark suits enter the conference hall of the Hotel Kasteel d'Oud in Wassenaer. Nobody speaks. An uneasy silence is in the air. They take their positions behind the table away from the door. They are not to have "physical contact" with the group of men who enter, as arranged, five minutes later. The Israelis and the representatives of the Jewish Claims Conference bow mutely to the Germans. Nobody shakes hands. The leaders of the two groups introduce the delegates. Again, one bows to the other. Then, standing up, they read out their opening statements in English. This having been done, the next meeting is suggested by the Israelis, and is agreed upon. The Germans leave the room first, again with deep bows.

This was the opening ceremony of the conference to lead to German compensation payments to Israel and the Jewish Claims Conference, or the first treaty that was to be signed by Jews and Germans after the end of the war.

"To describe what went on in us then, seven years after Hitler and the end of the war, is almost as difficult as to grasp and to realize the tragedy which was the reason for the meeting. . . ." Dr. Shinnar said in his account [1] of the Wassenaer Conference. Professor Böhm, the leader of the German group, said afterwards, "You

[1] Felix E. Shinnar, *Bericht eines Beauftragten*, p. 37, Rainer Wunderlich Verlag, Tübingen, 1967.

can imagine what we felt at this moment of our first encounter with the representatives of Israel." [2]

It was eleven years after the idea that the Germans should compensate the Jews had come to light following the destruction of the Nazi Reich. Dr. Nahum Goldmann, president of the World Jewish Congress, had raised this subject in a speech in Baltimore in 1941, at a time when the Nazis were at the peak of their military successes and had only just begun the organized murder of the Jews.[3]

As the war went on, some Jewish refugees in the United States went to work on the formulation of future Jewish demands against Germany. In the autumn of 1943, Dr. George Landauer, a leading Zionist of German origin, wrote a memorandum in which he stressed that, after the victory, the Jews as a nation should be allowed to make claims against Germany. He was aware of the fact that it would be extremely difficult for such a collective claim to be recognized by the victorious powers; reparations, according to international law, could be requested only by states. Nevertheless, he had argued that Jews and Germans had special accounts to settle.[4]

Dr. Siegfried Moses, the future comptroller of the state of Israel, had supported Dr. Landauer's insistence that the Jews, although a nation without a state, had a claim against Germany; not on legal but on moral grounds. Specifically, Dr. Moses felt that an agency representing the Jews must establish a claim for the heirless property of Jewish religious and nonreligious institutions, and demand compensation for the sufferings inflicted on the Jews as a nation.

The German term, *Wiedergutmachung* (to make amends), which was to become the *terminus technicus* for the payments later made by the Germans, was introduced into the discussion by "a German refugee" [5] in America (possibly by George Landauer when, in 1943, he had made his first suggestions for Jewish claims against Germany). In a way, the word implied more than the Jews probably wanted it to express; it inferred that repentance was possible through material values. In fact, the word later was called a very

[2] Rolf Vogel, *Deutschlands Weg nach Israel,* p. 46, Seewald Verlag, Stuttgart, 1967.

[3] Kurt R. Grossmann, "Germany's Moral Debt," p. 5, *Public Affairs Press,* Washington, D.C., 1954.

[4] Nicholas Balabkins, "The Birth of Restitution," p. 9, *The Wiener Library Bulletin,* London, Autumn, 1967.

[5] Dr. Otto Küster, in conversation with the writer, Stuttgart, September, 1967.

bad one, as nothing could make up for the crimes, most certainly, not money. But the term was there and had a legal basis in Germany. It remains in the juvenile penal code, having been introduced by the Nazis in 1943 to give young people the opportunity to pay for damage they had done with good deeds rather than by serving a jail sentence. The Stuttgart lawyer and restitution expert, Dr. Otto Küster, explained that this term caught on in Germany after 1945 because it "made sense" to the people, and it was also taken up by the legislature.

Dr. Goldmann recalled that, soon after the war, Jewish organizations in America discussed the question of compensation and restitution time and again.[6] He went to Germany for the first time in 1946 to see the former concentration camps. This was the opportunity to meet with the heads of the occupation forces with whom the question of compensation had been brought up for the first time. Of course, the subject was not alien to the four occupation powers. On January 5, 1943, a conference of eighteen allied governments—including the United Kingdom, the United States and the Soviet Union—had issued the first Allied pronouncement on the principle of restitution and indemnification. But the problem was much bigger and more complex than was realized at the time, due to the considerable amount of property belonging to Nazi victims who had no heirs. In those first postwar years when Germany was split up, each of the four zones had its own laws and regulations. The American occupation authorities, in 1946 and 1947, introduced laws that stipulated compensation and restitution for those who had been persecuted by the Nazis (and their heirs) from a special fund to be formed by contributions from formerly active Nazis, as well as by other means. The council of the South German *Länder* (States), on March 5, 1946, ordered that all those who had actively supported the National Socialist regime, or who were otherwise guilty, be compelled to pay compensation. The property of those considered the chief culprits was to be confiscated, entirely or partly. The Jewish Restitution Organization was appointed the legal successor to heirless and unclaimed Jewish property by the United States military governor. Its counterpart in the British Zone was the Jewish Trust Corporation, and a similar organization handled the problem in the French Zone. Thus, compensation and indemnification for the

[6] Conversation with the writer, October 16, 1968.

victims of Nazism were not alien to the Germans on an international
level.[7]

A moral blow was dealt when on March 10, 1951, the Bavarian
government arrested the State Commissioner for Restitution, Philip
Auerbach, on his return from Bonn. So far, Bavaria (in the American Zone) had been a pioneer among the German Länder with respect to restitution for Nazi victims. Auerbach was held in high esteem at first, as he had promised and managed the emigration of
thousands of DPs who, having escaped from the Communist countries, had reached Bavaria shortly after the end of the war. He had
hardly completed this task when he was accused of swindling the
state of enormous sums—charges that never were proven but which
were exploited by right-wing factions against restitution and, indirectly, also against the Jews. However, it appeared in the end that
Auerbach had not always been quite correct in the application of his
powers and of the money with which he had been entrusted. The
trial against Auerbach dragged on for a year. He was then sentenced
to two and a half years imprisonment and committed suicide in his
cell.

But this unfortunate incident did not alter the determination of
the Jewish parties to demand restitution and compensation from
Germany. From 1945, they continued to address appeals to the victorious authorities. Though sympathizing with the Jewish claims,
they made it clear that this was an issue that had to be settled between the Jews and the Germans themselves. In the note of July 5,
1951, in reply to Israel's note of March 12—which later became the
basis for the talks between Jews and Germans on this subject—the
three Western Powers said that they "could not impose on the government of the Federal Republic an obligation to pay reparations to
Israel." This threw Israel into a quandary. It, in fact, meant that Israel itself would have to initiate negotiations with Germany, an undertaking which, for psychological reasons, seemed out of the question. Dr. Hendrik van Dam, a Jewish leader in Germany, at a
meeting of liberated Jewish concentration camp inmates, had said in
July, 1948, "Israel can ill afford to give up claims against Germany
because of emotionalism." [8] In 1950, Dr. van Dam again reminded
the Jews and Israelis that, "the corresponding factor of the German

---

[7] Kurt R. Grossmann, "Germany's Moral Debt," p. 17, *Public Affairs Press*,
Washington, D.C., 1954.

[8] Nicholas Balabkins, "The Birth of Restitution," p. 10, *The Wiener Library
Bulletin*, London, Autumn, 1967.

people's moral obligation is the moral claim of the Jewish people."
He urged Jews not to burden their claim against Germany with
moral and historical imponderables and to accept what was long
overdue. Still, no matter how much Israel might have wanted it, it
dared not seek direct contact with Bonn. The World Jewish Congress could do so in its stead. But secret contacts had, indeed, been
initiated between Germany and Jewish officials and had lasted for
many months during which time they drafted the declaration to be
delivered by the German Chancellor in Parliament. This had been
one of the preconditions of the Jews for entering into negotiations
with the Germans on restitution.

On September 27, 1951, Dr. Adenauer read the declaration to the
Bundestag, in which he stressed "the obligation to make moral and
material amends to the Jews." A number of preparatory talks, but
no formal conferences, ensued right then. Dr. Nahum Goldmann
now assumed the Jewish leadership. Dr. Adenauer, who realized that
he would have to negotiate not only with Israel but also with Jewry
from all over the world, requested that the Jews form an organization which would act on behalf of the many Jewish groups
concerned.[9]

Under Dr. Goldmann's chairmanship, representatives of Jewish
organizations met in Paris in October to consider the German offer
of negotiating restitution and indemnification. A second meeting attended by Israeli representatives on the instigation of Israel's Foreign
Minister, Moshe Sharett, led to the formation of the conference on
Jewish material claims against Germany. This "Claims Conference,"
as it was called, was attended by twenty-two Jewish organizations.
On October 25, at its founding in New York, the Claims Conference passed a resolution in which it agreed to play second fiddle,
saying that it supported all claims advanced by the government of
the state of Israel with respect to rehabilitation in Israel of victims of
Nazi persecution. It requested satisfaction in all other Jewish claims
against Germany, including individual ones. It called for:

immediate steps to improve existing restitution and compensation legislation; to enact it where it did not exist.[10]

The Israeli government, in a new note on November 20, 1951, once
again reminded the Western Powers:

[9] Dr. Goldmann, in conversation with the writer, Bonn, October 16, 1968.
[10] Kurt R. Grossmann, "Germany's Moral Debt," p. 17, *Public Affairs Press,*
Washington, D.C., 1954.

to impress upon the government of the Federal Republic of Germany the urgent and compelling necessity to give effective satisfaction to its claim.

In their replies to this note, the Western Powers reiterated their previous contention that they could not intervene in the matter. The United States government suggested "direct negotiations." [11] And, in fact, there seemed to be no more obstacles standing in the way of direct negotiations.

Dr. Goldmann, who had refused to meet Adenauer before he had issued a declaration that would clarify the German obligation towards the Jews, now was ready for a talk with the German leader. But Goldmann insisted on it being a secret meeting as he was aware of the opposition among the Jews to such negotiations. Before meeting Adenauer, Goldmann requested and received authorization from Ben-Gurion to speak on behalf of Israel.[12] The meeting took place on December 6, 1951, in London. Dr. Adenauer recalled in his *memoirs* [13] that Goldmann had been accompanied by the Israeli ambassador to London, whose real name had not been given to protect him against attacks by the Jewish organizations which had refused contacts with the Germans. Dr. Goldmann said that Dr. Blankenhorn had been present to assist the Chancellor, and that he had been accompanied by Dr. Barou. In its note of March 12, 1951, Israel had requested a compensation of $1,000,000,000 from the Federal Republic and $500,000,000 from the East German state, the German Democratic Republic, which was the amount that Israel claimed it cost them to integrate 500,000 refugees from Hitler's persecution. Goldmann therefore told Adenauer that before he could recommend to Israel direct negotiations with Germany Adenauer had to agree, in writing, to the request for $1,000,000,000 as a basis for negotiations. Blankenhorn immediately objected, saying that the Chancellor could not do so as it was against all rules of Parliament and the Constitution. "I had spoken for over twenty minutes," Goldmann said. "I analyzed the Jewish situation for him and asked him to appreciate what it meant for me, as a representative of the Jewish people and Israel, to meet with the head of the German government, after all the sufferings the Nazis had inflicted upon the Jewish people. . . . I said to the Federal Chancellor, 'either this problem is

[11] *Ibid.*

[12] Dr. Goldmann, in conversation with the writer, Bonn, October 16, 1968.

[13] Konrad Adenauer, *Erinnerungen, 1953-55*, p. 137, Deutsche Verlagsanstalt, Stuttgart, 1965

treated as a moral issue, and a truly great gesture is made by you on behalf of the new Germany, or it is better not to engage in such talks at all, because they can end only in failure and are bound to poison German-Jewish relations still further. . . . I hope to be able to leave you today with the assurance that you accept the claim of the state of Israel for $1,000,000,000 as a basis for our negotiations. . . .' "

Adenauer listened attentively, then replied: "You don't know me yet. I dislike big words and pathos. But when you spoke I felt the wings of history brushing my shoulders." Goldmann continued to express his view. "I cannot recommend negotiation to Ben-Gurion and the *Knesset* unless $1,000,000,000 are guaranteed by you as a basis for negotiations. Dr. Blankenhorn says there are difficulties. I judge that now you will disregard these difficulties. Write a letter to this effect." Adenauer laughed and said: "You know me better than Blankenhorn. Go and dictate the letter to my secretary. I shall sign it." And he did after he had made minor alterations.[14]

In the letter, addressed to Goldmann, Adenauer referred to his government's declaration of September 27, in which acknowledgment had been made of readiness to enter into negotiations with representatives of the Jewish people and Israel regarding restitution and indemnification for loss and damage caused by the Nazi regime, stating: "I wish to inform you that the Federal government considers the moment to have arrived for such negotiations to begin. . . ." He repeated that his government viewed the problem of restitution and indemnification primarily as a moral obligation and considered the German people in honor bound to do everything possible to repair the injustice inflicted upon the Jewish people: "In this connection, the Federal government would welcome an opportunity to make a contribution to the building of the state of Israel by supplying goods and services. The Federal government is prepared to accept the claims made by the state of Israel in its note of March 12, 1951, as a basis for these negotiations." [15] This letter was important not only for moral reasons and the fact that it accepted the Israeli demands at least as a basis of negotiations but it also mentioned for the first time the possibility of restitution being made in the form of goods.

[14] Dr. Nahum Goldmann, in conversation with the writer, Bonn, October 16, 1968.
[15] Rolf Vogel, *Deutschlands Weg nach Israel*, p. 39, Seewald Verlag, Stuttgart, 1967.

Public opinion in Israel was dead set against any direct negotiations with Bonn. The issue was hotly debated in the press, and the spokesmen of the extreme "left" and the extreme "right" were its most outspoken opponents. *Kol Ha'am*, a Communist paper, the right-wing *Heruth* and *Al Hamishmar*, the mouthpiece of the *Mapam*, were adamant in their opposition to direct contacts. None of them took into consideration Israel's economic needs which had, no doubt, prompted the government to be ready for such negotiations with Germany. It surely would be unjust to assume that the Israeli government arrived at the decision to negotiate with Germany for money easily and without reservations.

The extremists adopted every means and method to stop their government from proceeding with these talks. Menahem Begin, leader of the *Heruth*, organized a fierce campaign against the government and Ben-Gurion, whom he called "that maniac who is now Prime Minister." According to Begin, certain things were worse than death; direct talks with the Germans for one. The "what do we get for Grandpa and Grandma?" argument induced many people to agree with Begin. The Israeli Communists, in addition to purely emotional objections, denounced restitution as a "trick by the Western Powers designed to facilitate the grooming of West Germany as the spearhead of new hordes to attack Russia." [16] The term "blood money" became popular; it was used in a pamphlet against talks with Germany.

Ben-Gurion and Foreign Minister Moshe Sharett were of the opinion that a *Knesset* decision was needed to have a mandate for negotiations with Germany on as broad a basis as possible. The debate was set for January 7. Israel's extremists tried to prevent the debate from taking place. More than ten thousand demonstrators converged on the *Knesset* building in Jerusalem, stoned its walls, smashed windows and threw tear-gas bombs. The battle with the police raged for two hours. It was one of those occasions destined to happen more often in the state of the Jews. Many a policeman might have shared the feelings of the demonstrators; ninety-two of them were injured, and hundreds of demonstrators had to be taken to hospitals.

While windows were shattered, ambulance sirens wailed and screams and shouts were heard, Ben-Gurion explained to the *Knesset* why he sought its permission to begin formal talks with Western

[16] Nicholas Balabkins, "The Birth of Restitution," p. 11, *The Wiener Library Bulletin*, Autumn, 1967.

Germany. He told the members that, if they were to refuse this permission, Israel could not collect the millions of dollars worth of unclaimed Jewish property. Using Biblical language, he tried to make parliamentarians understand that the murderers should not get away with stealing their victims' property, also: "And thou shalt speak unto him saying: thus saith the Lord: 'Hast thou killed and also taken possession?' " [17] The debate was stormy. It lasted two days, during which the *Knesset* was surrounded most of the time by barbed wire and patrols of steel-helmeted police. The meetings had to be interrupted on several occasions as, within the *Knesset*, the opponents fought with all bitterness. A representative of the orthodox *Misrachi* party said one should not honor Germany by accepting money from that country; that one should not sit down at the same table with wild beasts.[18]

Foreign Minister Sharett, winding up the debate on January 9, assured Parliament that the negotiations with Germany did not mean recognition of that country; Israel considered the entire German people responsible for the Nazi crimes and could not discern, at present, any signs of genuine repentance in Germany. At the end of the debate, the *Knesset* supported the request made by Ben-Gurion for direct negotiations with Germany by sixty-one votes to fifty, with five abstentions and only four absentees.[19]

The left- and right-wing parties—*Mapam*, the Communists, and *Heruth*—voted against it. They were joined by the General Zionists, a party generally of moderate views.

In Bonn, the decision of the *Knesset* to empower the Israeli government to commence official negotiations with Germany was welcomed. This was reaffirmed on January 15 by the *Knesset's* Foreign Affairs and Defense Committee. Dr. Adenauer was officially informed of it on February 17 by Dr. Goldmann when they met for the second time in London, and he was equally pleased that his suggestions had not been rejected. He expressed the hope that the negotiations would start as soon as possible.

Shortly after his return from London, Dr. Adenauer wrote to inform Finance Minister Fritz Schäffer of his talks with Dr. Goldmann and his consent that negotiations, starting in March, were to be based on the Israeli request for $1,000,000,000. He asked Dr.

[17] Kings I: Chapter 21, verse 19.
[18] Keesing's Contemporary Archives.
[19] Felix E. Shinnar, *Bericht eines Beauftragten,* p. 31, Rainer Wunderlich Verlag, Tübingen, 1967.

Schäffer to prepare the negotiations, so far as his Ministry was concerned. The Foreign Office would be in charge of the conference. Dr. Adenauer wrote—apparently anticipating Schäffer's opposition—". . . It is my desire that the negotiations . . . be prepared and carried out in a spirit befitting the moral and political weight and the uniqueness of our moral obligations." Adenauer asked Schäffer to pay no attention to considerations which would be presentable in any other case.[20]

But it soon became clear that more in the way of preparations had to be done before the negotiations could actually proceed. Adenauer's decision (as expressed in his letter of December 6, 1951, to Nahum Goldmann) accepting the Israeli request for $1,000,000,000 as a basis of negotiations met with strong opposition in Germany. Representatives of trade and commerce, bankers and industrialists reproached the Chancellor for having accepted a burden that the country's economy could not shoulder.

There was also fierce opposition among his ministers. They felt sure that the subject would be most unpopular, especially in view of the many other financial problems besetting the country—refugees from the Polish-occupied territories, unemployment, housing shortage, dismantling, and so forth—problems which were closer to the heart of the German citizens. The most vigorous opponent was Finance Minister Fritz Schäffer. He was simply furious and, regardless of the moral aspect, he rejected the Jewish claims for financial and legal reasons.

First of all, he doubted the legality of Israel's demands as the state had not been in existence when the crimes had been committed. Over and above this, Israel was in such a plight that it would accept $300,000,000, he is reported to have said to a reproachful Adenauer. Germany was already so overburdened by occupation costs and other consequences of the war that he did not see how such an additional claim could be borne by the state without upsetting its financial balance.

Another outspoken opponent was Dr. Hermann Josef Abs, Director of the German Bank, who is reported to have said that "under no circumstances" could Germany agree to pay such vast amounts. Abs represented Germany at the London Debt Conference which was to settle Germany's prewar debts. He was particularly angry as he had talked to Dr. Adenauer on the third of December in London,

[20] Rolf Vogel, *Deutschlands Weg nach Israel*, p. 40, Seewald Verlag, Stuttgart, 1967.

only three days before Adenauer met Goldmann and signed the letter in which the $1,000,000,000 request of the Israelis was accepted as a basis for the negotiations.

He then implored Adenauer to remember that Germany could not enter into new obligations without obtaining permission from her creditors. But, as we know, Adenauer ignored this. Abs was at first not even told of the new development; he learned of it by accident. The Israeli representative at the London Debt Conference, the ambassadorial councilor Keren, informed the conferees on the second day of deliberation of Israel's demands for a restitution agreement with the Federal Republic and of Chancellor Adenauer's acceptance of Israel's request. The information was given, as Keren put it,[21] to emphasize that no agreement with Germany on its financial obligations would be complete without the justified demands of the Jews being taken into account. Abs, who called Keren "very difficult in his contacts with Germans," [22] immediately demanded new instructions. Summoned to Bonn on March 8, he was, at last, officially told of the forthcoming talks with the Jews on the basis of the $1,000,000,000 request. He wanted to resign at once. His task seemed insurmountable, he explained; on the one hand, he had to try to reduce the total indebtedness of his country while, on the other, Adenauer proposed to enter into substantial new commitments. Dr. Adenauer persuaded him to stay on. On Abs' insistence, the Israeli government was then informed that it was hoped their talks could be coordinated with those of the London Debt Conference. This indicated that the Germans intended to apply the bargaining technique used at the London Conference to the German-Jewish negotiations.

An article published in *The New York Times*, February 11, on the basis of talks with leading official Germans stated that the Jewish demands were far too high and that Israel should be ready to reduce them. It said there that most of the Germans wanted to fulfill the Jewish requests, but that only a few were of the opinion that the German government was in a financial position to do so.

Hints in Bonn that a satisfactory settlement might be arrived at if Israel would agree to accept German goods in place of hard currency were at first ignored by the Jews. Discussions with reference to this were held several times between Dr. Goldmann and Dr.

---

[21] Rolf Vogel, *Deutschlands Weg nach Israel*, p. 47, Seewald Verlag, Stuttgart, 1967.
[22] Conversation with the writer, September 7, 1968.

Barou on the Jewish side and Dr. Blankenhorn and Professor Hall-stein on the German side before actual negotiations started. Lots of difficulties cropped up, and, as Dr. Blankenhorn reviewed the situation, it was greatly due to Dr. Goldmann that they were eventually overcome.[23]

"It was all very secret," to quote Dr. Goldmann. He met the Germans on German soil—in Bad Neuenahr, about fifteen miles from Bonn, in the Hotel Dreesen in Bad Godesberg. The Israeli government had assured the *Knesset* that no Israeli would be allowed to enter the territory of the Federal Republic, and no German would consent to go to Israel to discuss the matter. That was why the negotiations were later held on "neutral ground." The little town of Wassenaer near Den Haag was chosen (according to Dr. Adenauer's *Memoirs*) because Israel favored a small place which was easier to guard, fearing attacks by Jewish extremists on its own or the German delegation.

Goldmann's life would have been at stake, had it been known that he had met the Germans in Germany. Whenever he flew to Israel he was protected by security officials. The excitement over the intention to negotiate with the Germans and possibly accept their money had by no means diminished in Israel. Posters with a black rim, as if they were death announcements, listing all the names of those parliamentarians who had voted in favor of the negotiations with Germany were posted on the walls in Jerusalem. The parliamentarians were charged with betraying the murdered by being ready to negotiate with the murderers. The Ministry of the Interior threatened to ban the *Heruth* newspaper, which was undoubtedly the organizer of the riots, if it continued to incite the people against the negotiations. Yet, one has to understand that the feeling was well founded. Hardly seven years had gone by since the gas chambers in Auschwitz had stopped working. Dr. Shinnar recorded in his memoirs how deeply he and his colleagues were moved by the outcry:

All of us who experienced those three days (in the *Knesset*) were for years deeply impressed by the incidents which could be remembered only as a great outcry against its tragic background.[24]

[23] Conversation with the writer, London, March 8, 1968.
[24] Felix E. Shinnar, *Bericht eines Beauftragten*, p. 32, Rainer Wunderlich Verlag, Tübingen, 1967.

An explosive addressed to Dr. Konrad Adenauer and packed in a volume of the *Little Brockhaus,* a well-known German encyclopedia, was obviously the work of Jewish extremists. On March 27, the parcel had been handed to two schoolboys in Munich for posting to Bonn. The two boys—twelve and thirteen years of age—thought there was something suspicious about it and contacted the police. When the explosive expert, Karl Reichert, examined the parcel in an air-raid shelter it went off. Reichert died four hours later of his injuries. A few days later, several French newspapers received carbon copies of a typewritten letter in faulty French (posted in Geneva) in which an organization of Jewish partisans admitted its responsibility for the crime:

. . . We are at war with the nation of murderers, a war until the end of time. . . . The Germans should know that there is no excuse for their crimes, and that there never will be. There is not enough money in the world to make us forget their crimes. No act of reparation or restoration can ever cleanse them of their sins. The Jewish people will never permit the return of Germany to the family of nations. . . .[25]

Chancellor Adenauer received telegrams from Churchill, Eden, De Gasperi, the three High Commissioners representing the United States, Britain and France, and some Jewish leaders congratulating him on his miraculous escape.

In Germany, the climate of public opinion was tested by a German research institute on behalf of the American High Commissioner of Germany.[26] The result of the poll on the question of whether the Jews should receive help for their suffering under the Third Reich was published on December 5, 1951. Of those polled (1,201 cases), 68 percent replied in the affirmative, 21 percent were of the opinion that Jews should receive no help, 17 percent believed Jews had the least rights, 11 percent gave no answer.

In another question, people were asked to list those who, according to their preferences, should receive help. Jews ranked last. War widows, orphans and people who had suffered bomb damages led the list. Jews had neither the greatest nor the least right to help, 49 percent said. Dr. Adenauer ignored all this. He disregarded public opinion as well as political allies who felt that Germany could not

[25] Paul Weymar, *Konrad Adenauer,* p. 429, André Deutsch, London, 1957.
[26] Kurt R. Grossmann, "Germany's Moral Debt," pp. 18-19, *Public Affairs Press,* Washington, D.C., 1954.

accept such financial obligations at a time when it was saddled with burdens arising from the lost war. It did not occur to these people that a sacrifice would be appropriate in this case since they had failed from the start to repent for what had been done to the Jews in their name.

Dr. Adenauer chose Professor Franz Böhm to head the delegation for the negotiations with the Jews. "From talks with him I knew that he shared my views on these questions," Adenauer wrote in his *Memoirs*. Böhm, the first postwar dean of the Johann Wolfgang von Goethe University in Frankfurt, had, on several occasions, publicly admitted the German culpability. In January, Professor Hallstein, on behalf of the Chancellor, asked Böhm to take on the task. He consented at once.

Kindly Böhm had no Nazi past. He had been a student of law but he had no knowledge of financial dealings. His deputy, Dr. Otto Küster, a lawyer in Stuttgart and a leading authority on restitution as well as indemnification legislation—although no financial expert, either—was also a prominent anti-Nazi. The Nazis had expelled him from his post as a judge in 1933 for his reluctance to comply with their wishes. Dr. Abraham Frowein, a Foreign Office official, assisted Böhm and Küster. He was later put in charge of a special department in Bonn's Foreign Office dealing with restitution matters.

There were a few experts from the Ministries of Finance and Economic Affairs belonging to the delegation. One of the high-ranking officials, Bernard Wolff, was at the same time a delegate to the London Debt Conference, with respect to the German desire to coordinate both conferences. Two young diplomats, still very much in the background, and mere aides, rate mentioning for the roles they would play in the future relationship with Israel; Dr. Rolf Pauls, personal assistant to State Secretary Professor Walter Hallstein of the Foreign Office, and Dr. Alexander Toeroek, who was then at the German Embassy in Den Haag. Pauls was to become Germany's first ambassador to Israel and Toeroek his very controversial deputy.

The delegation from Israel was headed by Giora Josephtal, an authority on the absorption of refugees. Josephtal was Treasurer of the Jewish Agency and head of its absorption department. His delegation as an immigration expert was only natural as Israel based its claims on the integration of refugees.

Josephtal had been born in Heidelberg and had studied at the town's university. During the Hitler regime he had gone to Palestine to live in a kibbutz. Dr. Felix E. Shinnar, in charge of a special department dealing with the claims against Germany in the Jerusalem Foreign Office since July, 1951, shared the leadership of the delegation with Josephtal. Gershon Avner of the Israel Foreign Office was designated the delegation's spokesman. Eli Nathan, Deputy Chief of the Foreign Office's Legal Department, and Besner, Chief of the Foreign Currency Department of the Finance Ministry (killed in a plane crash on his way to Wassenaer) made up the Israeli delegation. Executive Vice-Chairman Moses Leavitt of the American Jewish Joint Distribution Committee, Dr. Nahum Goldmann, president of the World Jewish Congress and Chairman Jacob Blaustein of the American Jewish Committee should be mentioned as leaders of the Claims Conference delegation.

Dr. Josephtal described the atmosphere in a letter to his wife: [27]

. . . The whole thing is quite weird. We are staying at a castle with large grounds, fifteen minutes by car from The Hague. . . . The castle has been converted into a hotel with about fifty rooms and we, the Jewish delegation, are occupying twenty-five of them. There are also some old countesses and a few honeymooners. . . . Every day at 10 a.m. we meet the other side. The first encounter was a dramatic one. . . .

At this first dramatic encounter, Gershon Avner of the Israeli delegation read a declaration which referred to the Israeli note of 1951, the Adenauer declaration of September 27, 1951, and, finally, the letter Adenauer had written to Nahum Goldmann on December 6, 1951. Again, with reference to these documents, the Israelis demanded the payment of $1,000,000,000 as a reimbursement of the costs of resettling 500,000 Jewish people who had come to Israel between 1933 and 1951, Dr. Avner once again described the German crimes in detail. He said that three of every four European Jews had been murdered. No amount of material aid could atone for the crimes; yet, the stolen goods could be returned and the survivors could be paid a compensation. Unlike other countries, Israel had no developed economy and, therefore, had to make special efforts to cope with the influx of diseased, impoverished and broken people. Their claim was based both on the estimated losses of the Jewish people and on the costs of rehabilitating the survivors in Israel— about $1,500,000,000 for 500,000 people. Of this sum, Israel requested

[27] Senta Josephtal, *The Responsible Attitude*, p. 146, Schocken Books, Inc., New York, 1966.

$1,000,000,000 from the Federal Republic and $500,000,000 were to be paid by the East German state.[28]

The opening statement of the Germans was "to the point and negative." [29] Professor Böhm referred to Adenauer's statement of September 27 and declared that Germany's obligation to make amends for their wrongs meant more than material restitution and indemnification. He then listed the predicaments—such as the London Debt Conference which made it difficult, if not impossible, to grant Israel preferential treatment without antagonizing Germany's other creditors, and the foreign currency restrictions due to the occupation status. Unfortunately, the Jewish claims would have to be considered in the light of Germany's other financial obligations. In short, according to Josephtal's memoirs, the Germans said, "We are unable to pay." Josephtal, who presided at all meetings, made a sharp reply to the German statement which he felt indicated that agreement would be difficult to reach. He threatened breaking off negotiations. Yet, there was general interest in keeping the ball rolling, so the discussions continued.

First of all, the Germans doubted that all 500,000 for whom Israel demanded restitution were indeed refugees from Nazi oppression. The figures that the Israelis proposed numbered 115,000 from Germany and Austria and some 158,000 from Poland and the Baltic states; [30] the remainder from Hungary, France and other countries. The question was raised because a number of survivors of concentration camps had returned to their native countries in the East in 1945 and, after only one or two years, had emigrated to Israel.

The Israelis argued that the Jews virtually had been forced to leave because of the hate and resentment which they had encountered upon their return from concentration camps. They had found their former homes occupied by people who were most unwilling to move, and they had also found it difficult to get employment. This made them decide to leave their country once more. The Israelis said that, if the Nazis had not persecuted the Jews and started World War II, the Jews still would be in the countries of their origin.[31]

The second question that the Germans—themselves experts on ref-

28 *The Times*, March 21, 1952.
29 Senta Josephtal, *The Responsible Attitude*, p. 147, Schocken Books, Inc., New York, 1966.
30 Paul Weymar, *Konrad Adenauer*, p. 443, André Deutsch, London, 1957.
31 Professor Franz Böhm, *Junges Europa*, Frankfurt, June 6, 1953.

ugee problems—examined with thoroughness was whether each immigrant did, indeed, cost the Jewish state three thousand dollars. According to Dr. Shinnar, "We had assessed the minimum required by each Jewish refugee to start a new existence. Thus the sum of $1,500,000,000 as total costs was arrived at." [32]

In the course of these first discussions the German delegate, Dr. Küster, despite the frosty atmosphere, wrote a note to Dr. Shinnar saying, "Your English has a Swabian accent." "True," Shinnar wrote back, "I was born and brought up in Stuttgart." Soon the two found out that they had attended the same school. A few days later, the former schoolmates wrote a postcard to one of their teachers whom both had held in high esteem.[33] The ice was broken. The members of the delegations began to speak in German, which was practically everybody's mother tongue. The leaders of the delegations, who at the beginning had bowed to each other mutely without shaking hands, now met over lunch in order "to get to know each other better in this informal atmosphere and to discuss a number of questions more freely than was possible within the framework of the talks at the negotiations." [34] Giora Josephtal wrote to his wife: ". . . It is all unreal. The Germans are unreal, too, for they represent the best aspects of the Weimar Republic and not the Germans of the past twenty years. And I do not know how much influence they have in Bonn. . . ." [35]

On March 24, Dr. Shinnar presented the particulars of the Israeli demands. The payment of $1,000,000,000 was to be made, one-third in hard currency (United States as well as European currencies) within three to four years, and two-thirds in goods to the value of $100,000,000 to be payable in each annual installment. Moreover, 15 to 20 percent would be consumer goods which Germany did not export, but the production of which would be of importance to German employment. Eighty-five percent should consist partly of high-quality consumer goods, such as industrial equipment, which Germany did export.[36] One day later, the Jewish Claims Confer-

---

[32] Paul Weymar, *Konrad Adenauer*, p. 443, André Deutsch, London, 1957.

[33] Nicholas Balabkins, "The Birth of Restitution," p. 12, *The Wiener Library Bulletin*, London, Autumn, 1967.

[34] Felix E. Shinnar, *Bericht eines Beauftragten*, p. 37, Rainer Wunderlich Verlag, Tübingen, 1967.

[35] Senta Josephtal, *The Responsible Attitude*, p. 148, Schocken Books, Inc., New York, 1966.

[36] Konrad Adenauer, *Erinnerungen, 1953-55*, p. 140, Deutsche Verlagsanstalt, Stuttgart, 1965.

ence submitted its demands for $500,000,000 for the relief and reha-
bilitation of Nazi victims not living in Israel, and for an improvement of restitution legislation.

Böhm and Küster were about to return to Bonn to present the
demands of the Israelis to their government. "It was early—7 a.m.,
on March 31—when Professor Böhm rang me to ask whether I had
any mail that had not been opened," Frowein reminisced.[37] The
Dutch police had informed Böhm that under no circumstances
should any parcel be opened. Suddenly, the two secretaries had
come upon one addressed to the German delegation. When the
Dutch police arrived on the scene, careful examination had revealed
"a highly explosive" parcel which surely had come from the same
source as the one addressed to Adenauer a few days earlier and
which had cost the life of a police expert.

On April 1, the two German delegates reported to Dr. Adenauer
in Bonn and gave an account of the Wassenaer Conference in the
presence of some officials concerned—Finance Minister Fritz
Schäffer, State Secretary Hallstein and the banker, Hermann Josef
Abs. Both Schäffer and Abs were known as opponents of the payments to Israel. Abs immediately threatened to resign from the delegation to the London Debt Conference if the plan (which he called
harmful to German currency) should be accepted. Dr. Adenauer
said to Abs: "I should like to know from you in what form we can
pay." Abs and Schäffer suggested that one could perhaps satisfy the
Israeli demands by donating a hospital to them. It was apparent that
Dr. Adenauer disliked this travesty. When Dr. Küster protested,
saying, "This is no true repentance!" Adenauer nodded and said, "I
agree with you entirely." Böhm then suggested that the amount of
$750,000,000 should be taken into consideration. "I told Adenauer
the amount of money to be granted to the Jewish people should
have the character of a genuine effort and had to be recognizable as
such. If this should not be the case, it would only add to another deterioration of feelings."[38]

Abs was not easily convinced of the need for such payments. He
continually expressed the fear of the reaction of the London Debt
Conference. On seeing Adenauer very much inclined to accept
Böhm's proposal, he insisted that the creditors, at least, be told of
the German intention. Dr. Küster stated[39] that Abs vigorously op-

[37] Conversation with the writer, February 9, 1968.
[38] Dr. Küster, in conversation with the writer, September, 1967.
[39] Professor Böhm, in conversation with the writer, February 17, 1969.

posed the plan in the morning but—seeing that Adenauer showed an inclination to agree with Böhm and Küster—that same afternoon eloquently pleaded with John McCloy to estimate the proposal to compensate the Jews. The American High Commissioner represented one of Germany's biggest creditor countries. "This is a strong statement," McCloy said. But he and the other creditors were convinced that Israel would have to be paid eventually, notwithstanding the financial state of affairs of Germany then and the little hope that it would improve.

Against the advice of Abs (protesting that the sum would then be a foregone conclusion), Böhm and Küster published what they planned to inform the Israelis and the Claims Conference on April 7.[40] After thorough examination, the German delegation had come to the conclusion that Israel did incur costs for the resettling of 500,000 Jewish refugees. This, according to German experts, amounted to $1,071,000,000. The Israelis had claimed $1,500,000,000. The German share of two-thirds of these costs, as suggested by the Israelis, would then come to $714,000,000. The delegation announced its recommendation to the government to accept this as a result of their findings. However, in view of the country's financial and economic situation, the delegates were unable to say at that stage what amount, at what time and in what form payments could be made. A concrete proposal would be made on June 19, or one month after the London Debt Conference had reconvened, as a concession to the opponents such as Abs and Schäffer.

The Israelis emphatically opposed this. Josephtal, in another letter to his wife, on April 8, wrote: ". . . I have threatened to break off. The answer was: 'That is too bad. But the other creditors will not agree to your getting everything and their getting nothing.' " [41]

Gershon Avner protested strongly against both the reduction of the figures and the fact that the Germans linked commercial debts with the demands from the Israelis and the Jewish claims. On April 8, the Israelis declared that the German proposal was "entirely unsatisfactory." They demanded a clear statement of the German position on the following basic issues: the amount for which the German government would accept liability; the period over which the discharge of the German obligation would spread; the principles of implementation of the German obligation including the period re-

[40] Professor Böhm, in conversation with the writer, February 17, 1969.
[41] Senta Josephtal, *The Responsible Attitude*, p. 150, Schocken Books, Inc., New York, 1966.

quired for the delivery of the goods (as well as the type) and the extent to which the Israel claim would be settled in the delivery of goods and in hard currency.[42]

The Israelis were deeply disappointed and angry. Dr. Josephtal wrote, again to his wife: " . . . Sacrifices, special efforts and the like are only talked about and every day there is another schmaltzy speech without *takhles*." [43]

The German negotiators consulted Bonn and returned with Adenauer's promise that concrete proposals would be made, but without specifying when. On April 9, the Germans made it clear that they wanted the conference to be suspended. They declared they would be able to reply to Israel's points only after the resumption of the London Debt Conference. Both the Israelis and the Claims Conference delegation made it plain that nothing less than a concrete offer from the German government could make them resume negotiations at Wassenaer. No doubt the negotiations had reached a crisis. It could be of little consolation to the Jews that the curious situation had evolved where even the leaders of the other side—Böhm and Küster—shared their viewpoint.

Of course, neither the Germans nor the Israelis really wanted the negotiations to end in failure. Dr. Adenauer, in fact, argued that the outcome of the two conferences depended on mutual responsibility. In his *Memoirs*, he expressed the view that, if the conference with the Jews had failed, there would have been danger that the London Conference also would have failed, as Jewish bankers exerted considerable influence on the London Debt Conference. On the other hand, a failure of the London Conference would not have led to a successful ending of the conference in Wassenaer. He wrote that the London Conference's success was imperative for Germany to be considered worthy of credit.[44] Only then would Germany's economy develop in such a manner as to enable it to make payments to Israel and the Jewish organizations.

Dr. Adenauer pointed out the enormous burdens that the aftermath of the war had put on Germany. "But, political considerations have to take preference over financial and economic ones."

In a talk with Dr. Goldmann on April 20, he was told that public

[42] Konrad Adenauer, *Erinnerungen, 1953-55*, p. 144, Deutsche Verlagsanstalt, Stuttgart, 1965.
[43] Precise proposals.
[44] Konrad Adenauer, *Erinnerungen, 1953-55*, p. 140, Deutsche Verlagsanstalt, Stuttgart, 1965.

opinion in Israel was very unfavorable and that mistrust of Germany had intensified again.

. . . We could only continue assurance that the German government and the people were serious in their intention to recognize the moral guilt towards the Jewish people and in the intention to make amends for crimes committed. . . . In order to be able to commit ourselves we had to await the outcome of the London Debt Conference. Just because it concerned a moral guilt, we wanted to assume obligations only at such a moment in which we knew for sure that we could also promptly execute them.[45]

The Israelis and the Claims conferees, Dr. Adenauer recalled, strongly protested that the negotiations of Wassenaer were made dependent on the London Debt Conference. They demanded priority for their claims. Although the conference had been interrupted on the German initiative, negotiations continued between German and Jewish representatives. But the differences of opinion persisted and the climate of the relationship just begun deteriorated steadily. Professor Böhm felt the need to put the Jewish case once more to Chancellor Adenauer although he was preoccupied with preparations for the German treaty which was to put Germany's relations with the outside world on a firm basis and the tentative treaty for the European Defense Community. Adenauer wrote, on April 23:

. . . The claims, both of the state of Israel and the organizations, are considerable, comparing them with the capacity of the Federal Republic. But, when compared with the extent of the harm done, they are without any doubt rather moderate. . . .

Once again, Böhm urged Adenauer to give priority to the Jewish claims, considering the moral aspect, and to think of the future, calling efforts to overcome the past a very important aspect of German politics. He pointed out that not only Jewry but the entire world was watching the outcome of the negotiations and that the determination with which the decision would be made also would have an impact on the political and moral education of Germany.[46] In response to the reaction of the Israeli public, it was only logical that the parliamentary opposition in the *Knesset* move that negotiations be broken off at once. In the ensuing debate, Foreign Minister Moshe Sharett said very emphatically that Israel refused to wait its

[45] Konrad Adenauer, *op. cit.*
[46] Rolf Vogel, *Deutschlands Weg nach Israel,* p. 51, Seewald Verlag, Stuttgart, 1967.

turn in London in the queue of Germany's commercial creditors; that there was no comparison between what Germany owed its creditors and its obligation for restitution of Jewish property which had either been deliberately destroyed or stolen. Yet, Sharett also spoke in favor of continuing the negotiations with Germany, provided Germany made "a concrete, satisfactory and binding offer about the amount and the time within which it would pay restitution." [47] The motion requesting the discontinuance of negotiations was voted down, forty-nine against thirty-two votes. With fifty against thirty-four votes, the *Knesset* accepted the suggestion of its Foreign Affairs Commission as it had been formulated by Sharett.

Political circles in Bonn disliked the haggling over the issue in question. Kurt Schumacher, the leader of the official opposition, wrote a letter to the government in which he expressed the view that restitution should not be linked up with commercial debts:

Bundestag (Lower House) and *Bundesrat* (Upper House) in complete unison of view, expressed before the whole world their wish to strive for peace with Israel through restitution. That is why I am greatly concerned that the negotiations with Israel came to a standstill. . . .

Connecting negotiations in London with those in Wassenaer would not only constitute a breach of a decision taken in the *Bundestag* but also tie up two issues which had no connection with each other.[48]

On May 10, the *Bundestag's* Foreign Affairs Commission, under the chairmanship of the Social Democratic politician, Professor Carlo Schmid, expressed agreement with Schumacher's viewpoint which also coincided with that of Professor Böhm.[49] The committee passed a resolution to continue the negotiations on the premise that the obligation for restitution which the *Bundestag* and the government had recognized could be fulfilled only if given the right of priority. This view, which did not bind the government, was undoubtedly shared by the majority of German politicians.

Abs continued to have his misgivings. He insisted that any financial obligation towards Israel depended upon the outcome of the London Conference. He argued that Germany must give equal con-

[47] *Associated Press*, May 7, 1952.
[48] Archives of the Social Democratic Party letter dated May 10, 1952.
[49] Felix E. Shinnar, *Bericht eines Beauftragten*, p. 39, Rainer Wunderlich Verlag, Tübingen, 1967.

sideration to all of its financial obligations, whether they had moral, legal or any other basis. At a press conference in Bonn in May, 1952, he said: "It has to be paid out of the same purse, and you can pay only according to Germany's ability."

Abs hoped to postpone the negotiations indefinitely. With the concurrence of Finance Minister Fritz Schäffer, he offered Israel $23,800,000 per year for twelve years as a substitute for a final settlement.[50] Dr. Josephtal described this stage again in a letter to his wife, from London on May 8: " . . . This will be the beginning of a war of nerves and nobody knows who is going to win it. The Germans have a great *khutspah*, and among themselves they say we are so broke that we will *khapp* (grab at) and accept everything." [51] Professor Böhm was furious. "I went to see Adenauer," he said. "The offer is below our dignity and in contrast to our own declarations." [52] Adenauer—who, in his *Memoirs*, contended that he did not know of Abs' offer—requested Böhm to accompany the banker to London to meet the Jewish leaders. But Böhm declined. Instead, he and Küster decided to resign. Küster wrote a letter of resignation on the nineteenth in which he said that the government had not shown a "sincere will to make a settlement." "I did so in the mood of strong resignation," Küster recalled.[53] He did not believe in the arguments of Abs and Schäffer. He rather thought that they, particularly Schäffer, had no feeling for the Jews and for what had happened. He felt, also, that the German people were not in the least interested in the efforts to compensate the Jews. They just could not have cared less. His feelings were borne out by an opinion poll taken in August, 1952. Only 11 percent of those questioned agreed that Germany should pay $714,000,000, to Israel, while 11 percent called it "unnecessary." Another 24 percent expressed conditional agreement; they thought the amount was too high. Twenty-one percent had no opinion on the issue.[54]

Küster immediately announced his resignation to the press. Böhm waited until Monday. Dr. Adenauer called him to Bonn and, as Böhm looked back on the meeting, in the presence of Dr. Blanken-

[50] Kurt R. Grossmann, "Germany's Moral Debt," p. 23, *Public Affairs Press,* Washington, D.C., 1954.

[51] Senta Josephtal, *The Responsible Attitude,* p. 158, Schocken Books, Inc., New York, 1966.

[52] Conversation with the writer, February 17, 1969.

[53] Conversation with the writer, September, 1967.

[54] *The Germans, public opinion polls, 1947-1966,* p. 188, Verlag für Demoskopie, Allensbach und Bonn, 1967.

horn, "We had a very lively conversation lasting over an hour. When Blankenhorn had to leave the room, Adenauer put his arm on mine and said, 'What are we to do now?'" Böhm, whose resignation (unlike that of Küster) had not been accepted, told Adenauer what he thought should be done, namely to reopen negotiations at once, irrespective of what was going on at the London Debt Conference. "I shall see what I can do tonight in the Cabinet meeting," Adenauer said.

In the middle of the night, Professor Böhm in his home in Frankfurt received a phone call from Dr. Blankenhorn, saying: "He was grand. He carried everybody with him. Besides, we just learned that Abs has failed to convince the Jewish partners that his $23,800,000 offer was worth considering.[55] Abs had met with Dr. Shinnar and Keren, on May 19, in London. There he had made this $23,800,000 offer, adding that he had no definite mandate to do so. When his suggestion met with refusal, Abs spoke of the possibility of increasing this offer in case the German property "frozen" in the United States should be released—an assumption that, at the time, Dr. Shinnar commented, seemed very hypothetical, indeed.[56]

Goldmann recalled that Abs saw him at that time. He offered him advance payments and suggested postponement of any decision for six months, until after the London Debt Conference. "I cannot put emotions on ice for six months," Goldmann remembered replying.[57] Dr. Goldmann wrote a letter to the Chancellor that same day expressing his keen disappointment over the turn of events delaying the concrete offer which Germany had promised at Wassenaer.[58] The "suggestion" made by Abs could be taken only as an insult by Jewry; Abs had shown no readiness to make any sacrifices in order to solve the problems. Moreover, the increasing power of the German economy disproved Abs' arguments. Goldmann pleaded with Adenauer to lead the negotiations back "to the high moral level from which you used to consider them. Do not allow methods which are used at purely commercial negotiations to degrade and endanger these negotiations."

A copy of this letter was sent to High Commissioner McCloy. "I

[55] Conversation with the writer, February 17, 1969.
[56] Felix E. Shinnar, *Bericht eines Beauftragten*, p. 41, Rainer Wunderlich Verlag, Tübingen, 1967.
[57] Conversation with the writer, October 16, 1968.
[58] Rolf Vogel, *Deutschlands Weg nach Israel*, p. 52, Seewald Verlag, Stuttgart, 1967.

was then ready to break off the negotiations," Dr. Goldmann said.[59] About this time Ben-Gurion asked for a report of the situation. When he had heard Goldmann's story, Ben-Gurion said to him, "Don't try to be too clever. Take what you can get." Whereupon Goldmann replied: "I shall not sign. You may. I represent rich Jews and you a bankrupt state."

Adenauer now seemed to realize that he had to do something to prevent a collapse of the negotiations. It is known today that Goldmann's letter played a big part in Adenauer's considerations. In a way, this crisis helped to bring about the eventual success of the Wassenaer Conference. Adenauer asked Böhm and Abs to see him at once. He suggested that the negotiations might be reopened on the basis of the $714,000,000 offer for Israel's absorption of the refugees. The money should be paid over a period of twelve years. For the time being, Israel would receive payment in goods only—the type and amount of yearly installments would be flexible. A mixed commission was to determine, year by year, the particulars of the deliveries, and should Germany receive a dollar loan, such funds would be made available to Israel.[60]

Abs was reluctant to accept this. He thought the Israelis would later demand more, and increased deliveries. Adenauer asked Böhm, "What do you say to this?" Böhm replied, "I cannot imagine any Israeli government that would refuse such an offer." [61] Adenauer then said to Böhm, "All right, you offered your resignation. Are you prepared to meet Goldmann in Paris and put this to him as your private suggestion?" Böhm had neither a passport nor a visa to enter France and formalities were still very strict concerning German citizens. Francois-Poncet, French Ambassador to Bonn, was asked to help. But then, Böhm still had no French currency as it was a holiday and all banks were closed. Hausenstein, German Ambassador to France, lent him some money. Adenauer wanted everything done very quickly. He realized that a crisis in the negotiations with the Jews would not be very auspicious for the future standing of his country. Goldmann said that McCloy phoned him in Paris and advised him to stay at home the next morning—he would have a visitor. But McCloy did not tell him who it would be. It seems that

[59] Conversation with the writer, October 16, 1968.
[60] Kurt R. Grossmann, "Germany's Moral Debt," *Public Affairs Press*, Washington, D.C., 1954.
[61] Conversation with the writer, February 17, 1969.

McCloy was always informed of the developments in these negotiations, and although he never interfered, he made it plain that the Germans should do their utmost to reach an agreement. On the morning of the twenty-third, Böhm rang Goldmann and asked to see him. Upon arrival, Böhm offered his "private" suggestion as a basis for the resumption of the negotiations. "That is an offer," Goldmann said, and accepted it almost at once.[62]

The members of the Israeli delegation were not disinclined to accept but they were critical of some points that Böhm had put forward, especially since there were no foreign currency payments envisaged in the "Böhm" plan. In his lengthy report to Adenauer, dated May 24,[63] on the conversations he had had, Böhm disclosed that the leader of the Israeli delegation (Josephtal) "Came to meet me at the railway station when I was about to depart." [64] Josephtal had informed him that Israel had vainly tried to obtain a foreign currency loan from the British, something that had also come to the attention of Dr. Abs. Therefore, the Israeli delegation would consider a reduction of the sum if they could get some foreign currency.

On May 28, Dr. Adenauer—in Paris to sign the abortive treaty on the European Defense Community—also met Goldmann. He assured him that a definite offer now would be forthcoming.[65] Before the press, Adenauer said that he had gained the impression that an agreement with the Jewish delegation would now be reached. He also announced, on this occasion, that Böhm had withdrawn his resignation, which indicated that the negotiations would take a new turn.

Authorized by Ben-Gurion, Dr. Josephtal announced in Tel Aviv that this new offer made it possible to resume negotiations with the Germans. When he met Böhm again, he told him that people in Tel Aviv streets had reproached him, saying that the German professor had grasped what was going on—referring to Böhm's resignation— "You did not."

On June 9, at the urgent invitation of Dr. Adenauer, Goldmann

---

[62] Conversation with the writer, Bonn, October 16, 1968.

[63] Rolf Vogel, *Deutschlands Weg nach Israel*, p. 59, Seewald Verlag, Freiburg, 1967.

[64] Professor Böhm, in conversation with the writer, February 17, 1969.

[65] Kurt R. Grossmann, "Germany's Moral Debt," *Public Affairs Press*, Washington, D.C., 1954.

flew to Bonn. He was accompanied by Dr. Shinnar and Dr. Barou. The Germans were represented by Walter Hallstein, Secretary of State; Dr. Herbert Blankenhorn, Assistant Secretary; Hermann Abs; Professor Böhm and Dr. Abraham Frowein.

In a relatively brief conference the next day, the two delegations, advised by the experts of both sides, agreed on $821,100,000 to be paid to the Israel government in goods over a twelve-year period. Two installments of $94,200,000 would be payable in 1953 and 1954, while the ten subsequent payments would amount to $59,-500,000 each.[66] This sum included the $107,100,000 which the Claims Conference warranted. Dr. Goldmann had reduced the claim of the Jewish organizations from $500,000,000 to $107,100,000 and suggested that it should all be given to Israel. The Claims Conference would make its own arrangement with Israel to obtain its share in cash. After all, Jewry in America would not have any use for goods nor for restricted currency. This, Goldmann argued, was certainly to the advantage of the Germans. Adenauer replied: "Mr. Goldmann, I can well see that this is to my advantage. And I can also imagine what you will put into the contract with Israel." [67]

The noncovered part of $119,000,000 to $142,800,000 would be discharged from the proceeds of a foreign loan which Germany would try to obtain, or from other sources which the Federal Republic would try to make accessible. If, contrary to expectations, such a possibility failed to fully materialize, it was planned to increase the ten yearly payments by $11,900,000 per year. However, considering the yearly burden, the Federal Republic reserved the right to negotiate with the state of Israel again after about three years, with the possibility of discharging these additional yearly payments in two extended payments. Should the Federal Republic's efforts to raise higher amounts than the $119,000,000 to $142,800,000 be successful, such amounts would be used for the settlement of the respective final yearly payments. The composition of goods to be delivered to Israel by the Federal Republic would be subject to special negotiations and agreement. Finally, such goods should not be limited to German products, only. Inasmuch as the interstate trade agreements and the international payment agreements permitted, wholly or partly raw products should be bought from a third coun-

---

[66] Konrad Adenauer, *Erinnerungen, 1953-55*, p. 152, Deutsche Verlagsanstalt, Stuttgart, 1965.

[67] Goldmann, in conversation with the writer, October 16, 1968.

try. This clause was of particular interest to Israel, eager to buy oil, among other things, in third countries.[68] The goods to be delivered under the agreement should principally serve the development of Israel. Possible sale of the delivered goods should be settled by mutual agreement.

Chancellor Adenauer submitted this tentative agreement to his Cabinet on June 17. After thorough examination it was approved, although there was still opposition from Minister of Finance Schäffer. Abs at last gave his consent to what he once had called "measures harmful to the currency." From that day on, Abs did all to support the agreement. His recent comment: "I would not have signed the agreement, had I not been convinced that we could fulfill the treaty." [69] A few weeks later, Dr. Adenauer, on vacation in the Swiss resort, Buergenstock, asked Dr. Hallstein how the Wassenaer talks were progressing. Hallstein explained that Abs at last agreed. Adenauer, grinning broadly, said: "What? How come: (Agreed) To the measures which are to do harm to our currency?" Hallstein laughingly replied: "If you had delegated Abs to Wassenaer, we would have had to pay $952,000,000."

On June 28, the negotiations were resumed in Wassenaer on the basis of the suggested agreement which had been worked out in its details by a committee of legal experts. Dr. Küster had been replaced by Dr. von Truetzschler, an official of the Foreign Office. The Germans explained that he was an outstanding expert, but it was noted, with misgivings by the Jewish public, that he was a former Nazi. The negotiations in Wassenaer lasted until August 28, as there were still quite a number of details to be clarified. The atmosphere was extremely relaxed and informal. "We are very satisfied, and I cannot really give you a rational explanation of how things have progressed to this point," Giora Josephtal wrote to his wife.[70]

Just one of the details to be settled was what would happen to the agreement in case of a reunification of Germany. The status of the Israel Mission to be established in Germany for the purpose of pur-

[68] Senta Josephtal, *The Responsible Attitude*, p. 162, Schocken Books, Inc., New York, 1966.

[69] Hermann Josef Abs, in conversation with the writer, Bonn, September 7, 1968.

[70] Senta Josephtal, *The Responsible Attitude*, pp. 161-167, Schocken Books, Inc., New York, 1966.

chasing the goods in accordance with the agreement was yet to be determined. A list of goods had to be compiled. The Israelis still tried to reduce the number of payment years. Most of this was cleared up by committees. Dr. Josephtal noted:

. . . This morning I met with five people from the other side and all of a sudden the representative of the Economic Ministry told me that we would have to use German ships. More screaming, more discussions and after four hours I managed to get the fly out of the ointment. And so it goes every day. . . .[71]

But the Germans agreed that the deliveries were to be made by Israeli ships since the German flag was still banned in Israeli ports. But, in case of necessity, only a German ship should be the alternative, sailing under the flag of a third country. Then there was the question of the return of German property in Israel. It concerned the members of the German Templers, ardent Nazis, who had lived in Palestine until their deportation by the British. It was not easy for the Israeli delegation to agree that the state of Israel should make payments to them.[72]

It had been decided to sign the agreement on September 10. Two days prior to the signing Adenauer was to present the treaty to his Cabinet. Adenauer was nervous, Professor Böhm said,[73] because he was not sure how his Finance Minister would react. Schäffer had once before tried to induce his ministerial colleagues to vote against the Israel treaty by threatening to eliminate all their pet projects from the budget plans. But the Israel treaty was saved because it was decided to vote separately on it. Adenauer made sure that Schäffer was still in Mexico at the International Currency Conference when he scheduled the Cabinet meeting to vote on the Israel treaty. Adenauer opened the meeting saying how much he regretted that Schäffer (represented by State Secretary Hartmann), was absent. Then suddenly the door opened and Schäffer entered. But Adenauer could not be nonplussed so easily and cordially welcomed Schäffer.

The two delegations agreed that the signing should take place in Luxembourg. The Israelis were of the opinion that the signing would cause less stir in a small town. The danger of attacks from

[71] *Ibid.*

[72] Felix E. Shinnar, *Bericht eines Beauftragten*, p. 51, Rainer Wunderlich Verlag, Tübingen, 1967.

[73] Professor Böhm, in conversation with the writer, February 17, 1969.

the extremists was still there. Dr. Adenauer decided to sign the treaty himself because of the importance "I attached to it." [74] The other signatories were to be Foreign Minister Moshe Sharett and the president of the World Jewish Congress, Dr. Nahum Goldmann. The place of affirmation was kept secret until the very last minute. On the day prior to the signing it was announced that it would take place in a primary school at 10 a.m. At a last meeting, Adenauer, Sharett and Goldmann decided to change the place of venue, and the time, because both sides felt that this was an act of great significance and should not be turned into a public spectacle. The historic ceremony was to take place at 8 a.m. in the Hotel de Ville of Luxembourg. Sharett, a very correct man, compelled his delegation to leave early. Consequently, they arrived much before the appointed time and an embarrassed caretaker searched for the keys of a room in which the delegation could wait. At last, they were led into the *salle de mariages*. Shortly before 8 a.m. they entered the conference hall where Dr. Adenauer, Professor Hallstein, Dr. Blankenhorn, Professor Böhm, Felix von Eckardt, then Chief of the Bonn Press Office, von Herwarth, Chief of Protocol, Dr. Frowein and Jacob Altmaier, the (Jewish) Social Democratic parliamentarian (who had been used as a "messenger boy" between the two countries' representatives in the beginning), waited for them. Adenauer walked up to Sharett, saying, "I have awaited this day with expectation and joy." Sharett replied in German, "For us, also, this is a special day of great significance." [75] Then the agreement with Israel was signed by Sharett and Adenauer. It contained, apart from the general text of the treaty annexes, nine letters exchanged between Adenauer and Sharett, Böhm, Josephtal and Shinnar. Dr. Goldmann and Chancellor Adenauer affixed their signatures to two protocols, one committing Germany to pay $107,100,000 to the Claims Conference, and one obliging Germany to adopt a legislative program for individual restitution and indemnification.

Professor Hallstein handed a silver pen to Dr. Goldmann for the signing. Goldmann tried once, twice, three times; no ink flowed. Goldmann returned the pen to Hallstein saying: "Mr. State Secretary, the first item that you delivered to us is no good." [76] But, on

---

[74] Konrad Adenauer, *Erinnerungen, 1953-55*, p. 155, Deutsche Verlagsanstalt, Stuttgart, 1965.

[75] Felix E. Shinnar *Bericht eines Beauftragten*, p. 54, Rainer Wunderlich Verlag, Tübingen, 1967.

[76] Dr. Goldmann, in conversation with the writer, October 16, 1968.

the whole, the signing was a solemn act. Afterwards, the leaders of the delegations met for a long chat in one of the reception rooms. When Sharett was asked later, in Israel, in which language he had talked to Adenauer, he replied, "In the language of Goethe and Schiller." [77]

In a Paris press conference, Sharett stated that he was "very satisfied with the agreement." He considered it "of great moral and economic significance which would assume a place in the annals of international relations." The signing, however, did not imply the establishment of diplomatic relations or of trade with Germany.[78]

In Israel, the agreement was again accompanied by outbursts of violent opposition. The extremists organized street battles and demonstrations to express their disgust at the signing of the treaty. The daily, *Maariv*, wrote on September 10, " . . . It is true that it is a historic act. But doubts exist whether history will remember this day to have been for the good of the Germans, or for the good of us. . . ." This agreement was without precedent. *Maariv* stated:

This, too, is true. In the history of peoples there has never been a case when moral debts were recognized and paid for in hard cash. But in the history of nations it has not happened that a whole nation would help in wiping out another. . . . They tore the gold teeth from our sisters' mouths and they return it now, not in gold but in something which is equal to gold. They do not let us buy freely but force us to take it in the form of goods produced by their bloodstained hands. . . .

On October 5, a man was arrested in the Foreign Office in Jerusalem because he was found to have an explosive in his bag. It was due to go off six minutes after he was discovered, very close to the room where Foreign Minister Sharett conferred about the German Restitution Treaty with Israel's Ambassador to the United Nations, Abba Eban.

But, in Germany also, the chapter was far from being concluded. The Arabs managed to influence all those factions which already had great misgivings concerning the treaty with Israel. They held up ratification for six months. It needed a good deal of lobbying on the part of the Jewish representatives and attempts on the part of the Germans to convince the Arabs before the treaty finally reached the House for ratification. Though it had passed the Cabinet on

[77] Sharett, in conversation with the writer, many years before his death.
[78] *Stuttgarter Zeitung*, October 5, 1952.

February 13, a delay afforded new negotiations between the two governments due to the "flag issue."

According to the agreement, goods bound for Israel, but not shipped under the Israel flag, had to be carried in shipping space provided by the German government but not in ships flying the German flag. Strong objections to this clause from shipping circles were reflected in the treaty deliberations of the Foreign Relation Committee of the Upper House. Members announced that they would oppose the ratification unless this clause was changed. Dr. Shinnar was forced to return home to discuss the issue. The Israeli government, in order to prevent endangering the treaty, decided to abolish the clause once the ratification had been achieved.

Dr. Adenauer put the treaty before Parliament virtually in the last minute. It was necessary to get it through all the stages of ratification before March 20, as the budgetary year 1952-1953—for which the first deliveries had been stipulated in the treaty—would end on March 31. On March 4, 1953, Adenauer proposed the first reading of "Paper No. 4141." He pointed out that the Federal Republic was

now confirming through practical deeds the solemnly promised closure of a chapter which to every German must be the saddest in our entire history. The name of our fatherland must regain the respect which corresponds with the historic achievements of the German people in the cultural and economic fields.

The government had concluded this agreement, Adenauer declared: "not in fulfillment of a legally valid claim . . . but in fulfillment of a moral obligation of the German people as represented by the Federal Republic." [79] The treaty was then referred to the Foreign Affairs Committee where it passed on March 12. In this way, the scenery was set for the second and third reading of the bill on March 18. Speakers from Dr. Adenauer's Christian Democratic Party and from the opposition, the SPD, expressed their wholehearted support of the agreement with Israel and the Jews. The Free Democrats (Liberal) were not unanimous on this issue. The fear of alienating the Arab world was uppermost in the minds of some of their politicians. Jewish observers considered it most tactless that Dr. Walter Hasemann spoke on behalf of the Free Democrats. He had been a member of the NSDAP since 1932. The Social Democrats and a few Christian Democrats left the House in protest when he started his speech. The right-wing German Party (DP)

[79] Minutes of the *Bundestag*, vol. 15, p. 12092, March 3, 1953.

also expressed misgivings with reference to the treaty. They felt that there also should have been efforts to compensate the refugees from the Polish-occupied territories for the "injustice" done to them.

Adolf von Thadden,[80] a right-wing extremist, whose party was banned in the course of the legislative period, rejected the Israel treaty. He tried to minimize the crimes committed against the Jews by saying that hardly one million had been murdered. It was wrong to negotiate with Israel, a country from which Arab people had been compelled to escape. With equal vehemence, the Communists refused to vote for the treaty, saying that it had not been drawn up to make amends for the crimes; it was only for the benefit of Israel's industrialists. There were a few parliamentarians who rose to say that they would cast their votes against it either because Israel had no legal right to the claim or because they preferred that German expellees be given compensation priority.

The voting took place late in the evening. Only 360 parliamentarians out of 402 voted on the ratification, twenty being absent, unaccountably. They were, ironically, called "the heroes of March 18," as they had to pay a fine for being absent without excuse.[81] The ratification was carried by 239 votes against 35, with 86 abstentions. The only party that voted *en bloc* for the ratification turned out to be the Social Democrats. The official opposition, Dr. Adenauer's coalition, was split on it. Of the 214 parliamentarians belonging to three coalition parties—Christian Democrats, Free Democrats, and the German Party (DP)—only 106 voted in favor of the treaty. There were even thirty-nine abstentions and five "nos" from Adenauer's own CDU. Among those abstaining were Finance Minister Fritz Schäffer, Franz-Josef Strauss, one of the leading politicians in Bavaria, and a number of parliamentarians representing economic interests.[82]

Once passed in the Lower House, the Upper House dealt with it without much ado and responded unanimously. Professor Theodor Heuss, the president, signed the treaty on the same day, March 20.

In Israel, there was no need for ratification of the treaty by the

---

[80] Chairman of the *Nationaldemokratische Partei Deutschlands* (National Democratic Party) since 1968.

[81] Professor Franz Böhm, in conversation with the writer, Rockenberg, February 17, 1969.

[82] Joachim Kreysler and Klaus Jungfer, *Deutsche Israel Politik*, p. 35, Wolf von Tucher Verlag G.m.b.H., Diessen-Ammersee, 1965.

Knesset. Ben-Gurion put it before the parliamentary Foreign Affairs and Defense Committee on the nineteenth. Seven members voted for it, five against it and there was one abstention. The Israeli Cabinet added its consent to the treaty on March 22. A week later, Dr. Hans Riesser, Consul General of the Federal Republic, and Arthur Lourie, Consul General of Israel in New York, exchanged the documents of "the Law for the ratification of the Agreement concluded on September 10, 1952, between the Federal Republic of Germany and the state of Israel" in the office of the director of the Legal Department of the United Nations in New York. The documents were registered in the Secretariat General of the United Nations. With this act, the law was valid.

Ben-Gurion commented: "This is a great day. But the Germans will never pay." He was sure that it would end the way the Versailles Treaty had after the First World War. And he added: "Whether they pay or not is not so decisive. That they took the decision is of significance. For it is a political decision. It is the recognition of the state of Israel." [83]

But Ben-Gurion was wrong in his estimation. The Germans carried out the terms of the treaty with precision and accuracy. On July 30, 1953, the Israeli freighter, *Haifa*, took the first German consignment, consisting of iron, aboard in Bremen.

[83] Dr. Haim Yachil, in conversation with the writer, Jerusalem, July 27, 1968.

4

German-Arab Tug of War

"Egypt offers Germany the key to the Near East," Prince Abbas Hahim, a cousin of King Farouk of Egypt, said in the theatrical manner of an Oriental monarch while on a trip through Germany in December, 1951.[1] He actually meant that the Germans should be of help to Egypt in developing its industries and cultivating its deserts. Earlier on, in July of that year, Abd el Rahman Azzam, General Secretary of the Arab League, had made his overtures to Germany when he remarked to a correspondent of the semiofficial German news agency, *Deutsche Presse-Agentur*, in Cario, that the Arabs would never look on the Germans as enemies; purely political expediency had forced them, in 1939, to declare war on Germany. The implication was that, as dependent factions, this decision had not necessarily been their own. He said this on May 13, 1951, when Egypt was the first Arab state to declare the end of war with Germany, adding that other Arab states would soon do likewise.[2] This, he thought, should now be followed by a speedy *rapprochement* of Arabs and Germans. Close trade contacts, an intensive exchange of scientists, experts and students should restore the old, friendly relationship between the two nations. No doubt he had in mind, too, that the Germans should help the Arab world to elevate its state of technical and economic underdevelopment.

[1] Reuters, December 7, 1951.
[2] Chancellor Adenauer announced this in the *Bundestag* on July 10, 1951, and added that the German government would send $23,800 to help Arab refugees.

Naturally, the Germans were very pleased at these advances on the part of the Arabs, especially since defeat had left them paupers, and with little esteem among nations. They were eagerly searching for friends in the world and for markets that would help them to improve their practically shattered economy. Although the Germans did not much question why the Arabs had turned to them after they had achieved their independence from colonial powers, and had gladly joined the chorus praising the "traditional Arab-German friendship," the Arabs had been prompted by various reasons. There was, of course, the often praised German technical ability—an invaluable asset in the calculations of the Arabs. But this was only a minor issue; emotional aspects led them to consider the Germans their best friends and allies.

Until the turn of the century, the Germans had not competed with other European nations for political and economic influence in the Near East. But, in 1898, Kaiser Wilhelm II decided to form an alliance with the Turkish Sultan. He was persuaded to do so, in the belief that he could help preserve the *status quo* of the Balkans which seemed endangered by the activities of big and small powers. He also considered this area a potential market for his country's rising industrial output. Germany's prestige actually grew in the Near East through an agreement with the Sultan that a German company construct a railway line from the Bosporus to Baghdad. This railway, started in 1903 and nearly completed in 1914, became the only traffic connection in the Middle East at the time and was, above all, of great strategic value. The completion of each section, therefore, increased both Germany's influence and popularity in the area and fanned the hostility against the other big powers trying to prevent the construction of the line. The Russians saw their access to the Bosporus at stake; the English feared for their land route to India. The railway finally became a bone of contention between the European nations and was one of the reasons for the outbreak of World War I. The people of the Near East who had benefited from the railway continued to consider Kaiser Wilhelm II and his German people their only friends and protectors.[3]

The "traditional German-Arab friendship" persisted even after Germany had lost World War I. German scholars, doctors and teachers went to live and work in Arab lands, attracted by the ro-

[3] Alfons Raab, *Die Politik Deutschlands im Nahen Orient von 1877–1908*, p. 133, Wien, 1936.

manticism of the Orient and the treasures indigenous to that region, which continued to preserve the ties between Arabs and Germans. World War II again found the Arab peoples emotionally on the side of the Germans while, due to their status as dependent countries, they were forced to be at war with Germany. But they made no bones about their sympathies for Hitler and his party.

The reasons, this time, were of a negative character. First, it was hatred for England and France, countries which had failed to honor their promise given during World War I (when they wanted Arab cooperation) to grant the Arab states their independence. The fact that Hitler waged war on England and France turned them into his blind admirers. Then, the Arabs saw in Hitler an ally because of his anti-Jewish policy. Hostility to Zionism and to the Jewish settlers in Palestine made the Arabs lose all sense of proportion in the course of time, so that they did not even find fault with Hitler's slaughter of six million Jews. To this day, Arab nationalists identify Germany with Nazism. It may not be surprising, therefore, that Nazi criminals, wanted in Germany for capital crimes committed against the Jews during the last World War, found refuge in Arab countries and were not even extradited on the request of German legal authorities. For many Arabs, the "traditional Arab-German friendship" is still based mainly on these aspects.

But the honeymoon between Germans and Arabs at the time of the restoration of ties did not last. The Luxembourg Treaty between Israel and the German Federal Republic very soon turned the first advances into a strained relationship. In the course of the negotiations, lasting from March till September, 1952, Arab protests against the treaty were still fairly isolated.

The Prime Minister of Jordan wrote Chancellor Adenauer, warning him that he risked impairing the "century-old good relations between Germany and the Arab East" in establishing close contacts with Israel. The Syrian government handed a memorandum to the Chancellor which read that, should the Federal Republic of Germany decide on restitution payments to Israel, this would not remain without consequences: "Germany would lose the respect and the friendship which exists for it among Arab countries." [4] Furthermore, it made a point of the economic boycott and blockade against Israel, with the threat that, if Germany should pay restitution to Is-

[4] *Die Zeit*, September 18, 1952.

rael in this situation, the Arab countries would find themselves compelled to stop all imports from Germany. As the Federal Republic was not really a sovereign state, the governments of Syria and Lebanon turned to the British government only five days after the negotiations had started in The Hague, claiming a share of the amount to be negotiated as compensation for the Arab refugees. The Arab argument was that, if the Germans accepted the blame for Jews having settled in Palestine, they were also to be charged with the existence of Arab refugees having fled their homeland due to the Arab-Israel war. The Arab High Committee for Palestine wrote in a similar vein in June to the Federal government and to the United Nations. Abd el Rahman Azzam, on August 8, 1952, announced that the Arab states had taken steps to assure restitution payments to Arab refugees subsequent to agreement between the Jews and the Germans on compensation, although he did not disclose any details.[5]

Another argument with which the Arabs tried to dissuade the Germans from granting Israel and the Jews restitution payments was that the money given to Israel would increase Israel's war potentiality. Such payments would, therefore, constitute a breach of neutrality on the part of the Germans in the Near East conflict. They were well aware that the Germans wanted to avoid, at all costs, being made a party to the conflict; not only because they were eager to maintain friendly relations on both sides but, also, having been responsible for World War II, their past did not allow them to become involved in international conflicts.

At first, these protests were not taken too seriously in Germany. Dr. Adenauer was more concerned with reaching an agreement with the Jewish representatives. For, once he had made up his mind about compensating the Jews for their material losses, he intended to go through with it. He knew that it would be disastrous for postwar Germany—from both the moral and the political viewpoint—if negotiations with the Jews were to fail. When even the Mufti of Jerusalem, Haj Amin el Husseini (whose close relationship with Hitler had not been forgotten in Germany) joined those threatening the Germans in case of payments to the Jews, an uneasy feeling towards the Arabs spread in Germany.[6]

Nevertheless, efforts were made from Bonn to pacify them. The

[5] *Deutsche Presse-Agentur*, August 8, 1952.
[6] Heinz Wewer, *Die deutsch-israelischen Beziehungen-Ende oder Neubeginn*, vol. 18, p. 455, Frankfurter Hefte, 18, Jahrgang, July, 1963.

German government spokesman, Secretary of State von Eckardt, time and again, stressed that Germany was eager to preserve the traditionally good relations with the Arab world, and denied that the restitution agreement between Bonn and Jerusalem was, in any way, harmful to the Arab states. In its official bulletin, *Diplomatische Korrespondenz,* of September 12, 1952, two days after the signing, the German government appealed to the Arabs to understand the German position. It said: "No doubt the conflict between the moral obligation that our recent past forced on us and the wishes of our Arab friends, who belong to one of the oldest and the most enduring societies in the world, is felt deeply in the whole of Germany. This feeling should be a guarantee that the conflict can be solved. However, a precondition is that the Arab world be prepared for an objective appreciation of the German reasons for it."

But there was no good will on the part of the Arabs to understand the German point of view. On the contrary. Their anti-Israel attitude was such that no argument seemed sufficient to change their minds. It appeared from the start that the Arabs felt if they could not prevent German-Jewish reconciliation they might at least gain something by their pressure, if only to have the Germans at their mercy. After the signing of the treaty, the Arabs stepped up their campaign to hinder its ratification and its enforcement. Compared to their newly increased efforts, their opposition before the treaty was signed was relatively lax, possibly because they did not expect the Jews and the Germans to come to terms. Or, recalling the old friendship, they might have been under the impression that a hint from their quarter would change the Germans' mind. This sudden fury took the German government by surprise. But, from the start of the Arab campaign, Chancellor Adenauer left no doubt that he would not back out of the Luxembourg Treaty even though some of his Cabinet members lost heart in the course of time. The Arab arguments against the Luxembourg Treaty now boiled down to the following: Israel had no right to compensation since, at the time of the persecutions, the Jewish state had not existed; Israel's demands for absorption of 500,000 Jews were unjustified and too high in view of the fact that the United Nations had estimated the costs of integrating one million Arab refugees at $249,900,000; Israel had so far failed to pay any compensation to Arab refugees; since the Arab states were still at war with Israel, all actions strengthening Israel's economy had to be regarded as a breach of neutrality; such considerable support for Israel would undo the balance of power in the Near East and enable Israel to initiate new acts of aggression against the Arab countries.

To drive home their arguments the Arabs applied tougher methods. They harped on the economic disadvantages to Germany if the projected treaty with Israel were to come into force, knowing well that this would impress the Germans most. A letter, signed by the Arab High Committee for Palestine, addressed to the *Bundestag* and several economic institutions in Germany interested in trade with the Arab states, said: ". . . We might feel compelled to call on all Muslim peoples from Indonesia to Tunisia and from Iraq to Saudi Arabia to issue no more import licenses for goods which are imported via German firms having had a share in the deliveries to Israel." [7] At the same time, the Arabs announced that so-called "black lists" would be issued, noting the names of those firms engaged in business with Israel.

In truth, an economic boycott against the Federal Republic was bound to hurt the Arabs. Eighty-five percent of Egyptian exports to Germany consisted of cotton. Discontinuing them meant virtually an invitation to Brazil to take Egypt's place. Germany was then purchasing 75 percent of its oil in Iraq and in Saudi Arabia. But, other non-Arab, oil-producing countries existed. Germany's imports from Arab countries in 1951 made up only 2.7 percent of the entire bill, while German exports to the Arab world consisted of a mere 1.4 percent of the total sum.[8] Nevertheless, the Germans disliked the idea of an Arab boycott. They were trying hard to recover world markets after the lost war and they were well aware of the prospects which Arab markets might one day present to them.

It was inevitable that Arab propaganda should make some inroads in Germany. German industrial circles, especially, showed apprehension and parliamentarians wrote to the Chancellor asking him to reconsider the restitution agreement, and perhaps entrust its execution to the United Nations, an argument that had been used by the Arabs for some time. They demanded payment aid for the Arabs, too, in view of their refugee problem.

A major politician, Franz-Josef Strauss,[9] one of the leaders of the Christian Social Union, the Bavarian wing of Adenauer's Christian Democratic Union, warned, in the January 5, 1953, issue of *Chemie*

[7] Mittel-und Nahostverein, Hamburg, September 10, 1952.
[8] *Neue Zürcher Zeitung*, October, 1952.
[9] Finance Minister, later Defense Minister.

that the ratification of the Israel agreement might cost Germany a potential Arab market loss of up to $1,190,000,000 over the next ten years.[10]

Four political parties—the German Party, the Free Democrats, the Center Party and the Bavarian Party—implored the government, in a letter dated September 11, 1952, not to ratify the Luxembourg Treaty in view of the Arab reaction.[11] Although two of these parties—FDP and DP—were members of the coalition government, which hardly a year before had petitioned the *Bundestag* to negotiate with the Jews about restitution payments, the government did not take this intervention very seriously since only about thirty parliamentarians had signed the letter.

The German press, also, had second thoughts on the matter; yet, only one year before, they, as well as the politicians, had unanimously supported the government's plan to pay compensation to the Jews. "It would be unwise," the *Koelnische Rundschau* wrote, "to shrug one's shoulders (at the Arab protests)." The paper stressed the economic importance of the Arab states for Germany and pointed out that the Arabs had "warmly recommended the return of Germany to the family of nations, whereas Israel had rejected this proposal." Other German papers suggested either postponement of the ratification until agreement could be reached with the Arab states or entrusting the United Nations with the execution of it.

In December, 1952, the German Ambassador to Egypt, Dr. Guenther Pawelke, tried to convince the Deputy Chief of the Israel Mission in Cologne, Dr. Yachil, that a compromise settlement was also in Israel's interest. Quite evidently under the influence of Arab reaction, Pawelke suggested that restitution payments be transacted through the United Nations. Dr. Yachil rejected this suggestion outright. The Israeli diplomat had the impression that Dr. Pawelke acted without government orders. This was responsible for the Israel Mission's decision not to mention the conversation which had taken place in the middle of the night in a Cologne hotel.[12]

Virtually a one-man campaign was waged against the government's intention to conclude the treaty with Israel by an export businessman, Joachim Georg Adolf Hertslet. In letters and memo-

---

[10] Kurt R. Grossmann, "Germany's Moral Debt," *Public Affairs Press*, Washington, D.C., 1954.

[11] Joachim Kreysler and Klaus Jungfer, *Deutsche Israel Politik*, p. 46, Wolf von Tucher Verlag G.m.b.H., Diessen-Ammersee, 1965.

[12] Doctor Yachil, in conversation with the writer, July 27, 1968.

randa to Ministers and state officials, he called the Israel treaty a "political stupidity." Hertslet had, until then, acted as advisor to Ministers and Secretaries of State and had helped to strengthen Germany's foreign trade relations. His sphere of influence included the Near East. When Dr. Adenauer's government started its negotiations with Israel, Hertslet charged the Bonn diplomats with complete ignorance of the Near East situation and, with all the means at his disposal, helped the Arabs to sabotage the projected treaty.

In a Cabinet meeting, Dr. Adenauer, furious at this obstreperous intervention, impatiently called Hertslet a traitor. From then on, Hertslet found himself locked out from German Ministries. To prove Hertslet a traitor, it is said that (at Adenauer's instigation) Bonn's Secret Service sent the former leader of the banned Neo-Nazi *Sozialistische Reichspartei*, Fritz Dorls, to Egypt with the task of tracing documents and papers which would prove that the man had conspired against his country. The choice of the "delegate" was apparently made to inspire confidence in Egypt. Hertslet, now with a considerable deficit in his business accounts, tried to fight back against the German Chancellor, even with legal means, but he had to wait for exoneration until after Dr. Adenauer's death in 1967.[13]

To make it perfectly clear that the Arabs "meant business," the Saudi Arabians cancelled a $2,000,000 order for the installation of telecommunications by the firm of Siemens, only to reverse this decision shortly after a high-level Foreign Office official had paid a call on the Arab League's authorities in Cairo. Dr. Alex Boeker's method of achievement was not disclosed. But this, and similar examples—like the Lebanon and Saudi Arabia talks on canceling the establishment of diplomatic relations with Germany, or the Syrian government's cessation of negotiations with German firms on the extension of the Port of Latakia, later renewed—gave the German government the feeling that much could be settled in conversation.

So, they reacted favorably when the Arabs decided to send a delegation to Bonn "to convince the Federal government and the German people" that the restitution treaty with Israel should not be ratified under any circumstances. Since there were no German Missions in most Arab states, it seemed a good opportunity to the Germans for explanations, and to come to terms. Germany was quite ready, then, to give aid to the Arabs for development schemes, although at that time, it was far from sure that its own economy would ever flourish the way it actually has.

[13] *Der Spiegel*, June, 1967.

The delegation reached Bonn on Octobr 20, 1952, headed by Ahmed El Daouk, Lebanese Ambassador to Paris and former Prime Minister of Lebanon. Iraq, Syria and Egypt were represented. The message was: "We have come to Germany as friends. We expect to meet with understanding for our cause . . . and that Arab interests will remain untouched; also, that in the future we can hope for cooperation between Germany and the Arab states." [14]

This sounded to the Germans as if the Arabs were ready to accept a compromise backed up by financial means. The four delegates were treated as guests of the Chancellor. Professor Erhard, Minister of Economic Affairs, also received them. They had talks with the Secretary of State, Professor Walter Hallstein, in the Foreign Office, and met with parliamentarians and industrial leaders. All their arguments, written and verbal, and by now familiar, were rejected.[15] Dr. Adenauer made it quite plain to them: "I have put my signature to the Treaty. And I shall stick to my word." [16] He and the other German leaders explained that German restitution payments to Israel were a voluntary, moral atonement for the injustice done to the Jews. Provisions had been made to prevent arms and ammunition being delivered under the treaty. Israel was not free in the choice of the goods; bound by contract, Israel could purchase only such goods as were to serve the integration of the refugees.[17]

Professor Hallstein ruled out the Arab suggestion of entrusting the United Nations with the execution of the treaty ("as the German taxpayer wants to know where his money goes") and suggested that, perhaps, an international committee could be considered. This was rejected by the Arabs on the spot. Referring to the Arab refugees, the Federal German government stated there was "neither the right nor the possibility" of taking a stand, except to wish that

[14] *Deutsche Presse-Agentur,* October 20, 1952.

[15] The delegation submitted a note to the German government containing its views on October 30, 1952: the Arab states were still at war with Israel; the German payments to Israel would upset the balance in the Near East; the state of Israel was no legal successor to the Jews persecuted by the Nazi Reich; the United Nations should be charged with the execution of the Luxembourg Treaty.
Deutsche Presse-Agentur, October 30, 1952.
The New York Times, November 11, 1952.

[16] Kurt R. Grossmann, *Die Ehrenschuld,* p. 45, Ullstein Verlag, Frankfurt/Berlin, 1967.

[17] This declaration was repeated by Dr. Adenauer in the *Bundestag* during the First Reading of the Luxembourg Treaty, March 4, 1953.

this human problem would be solved at the earliest possible moment. The Germans also rejected the accusation that, by giving money to Israel, they had interfered in a conflict and committed a breach of neutrality. Following the armistice agreement of 1949 on Rhodes, a state of war no longer existed between Arabs and Israelis. This had also been confirmed by the United Nations Security Council. Nevertheless, time and again, the Germans assured the Arabs that they would propitiously consider all economic wishes on their part.

The conciliatory tone of the Arabs vanished once they met with such determination. In press conferences and with all kinds of propaganda methods they now tried to sway German public opinion in their favor. They did not hesitate to openly attack members of the German government. After the conclusion of their official visit they continued their lobbying among politicians and industrialists. For obvious reasons, they concentrated mainly on former Nazis and their sympathizers—for example, Dr. Hjalmar Schacht, former Minister of Economic Affairs in Hitler's government and his president of the German Bank. Activities were such that Professor Hallstein refused to meet the delegation a third time, although the Arab gentlemen were already waiting in his office. Finally, it was made clear to them that their assiduity did not warrant a continuation of their stay.

After the return of the delegation, the Arabs increased their threats from Cairo; a new one almost daily. On November 7, 1952, the Prime Minister of Egypt, General Naguib, after a meeting of the Arab League's Political Committee received the newly appointed German Ambassador, Dr. Guenther Pawelke, to inform him that the Luxembourg Treaty threatened Arab interests in both the military and the economic fields.[18] The Arab Press disclosed that, in case of the ratification of the Luxembourg Treaty, the Arab League would call for an economic boycott against the Federal Republic of Germany.

On November 9, the German Ambassador handed a note to the Egyptian Premier in which the German government offered a formal guarantee against deliveries of arms to Israel and trade treaties with individual Arab states for the purpose of developing them.[19] But the Egyptians waived this guarantee as totally insufficient and practically ignored the offer of trade treaties. Meanwhile, Arab

[18] *United Press International.*
[19] Heinz Wewer, *Die deutsch-israelischen Beziehungen-Ende oder Neubeginn* vol. 18, p. 457, *Frankfurter Hefte*, July, 1963.

newspapers, under the influence of the Mufti of Jerusalem, recalled the former mutual struggle against "Zionist-Imperialist aggression" and referred to Adenauer as a "tool of world Jewry." [20] On November 11, the German Cabinet discussed the Arab rejection of their offers and informed the German ambassador in Egypt that they would not change their mind on restitution to Jewry and could not accept any request as to postponement of the ratification of the treaty until agreement had been reached with the Arabs.[21]

On November 12, the Political Committee of the Arab League drafted a note to the German government in which it called the Luxembourg Treaty "a serious threat to the existence of the Arab states" and threatened to sever economic ties following ratification. Reiterating the well-known Arab view points, the Arab states reserved the right to take additional steps to protect their interests.[22]

In an interview on the same day, Dr. Adenauer declared: "It would be shameful, indeed, if we became wavering in our decision only because of being threatened with economic disadvantages. There are higher values than good business deals. . . ." [23]

The German government, also, issued a statement which dealt in detail with the Arab accusations. It assured the Arabs that the deliveries to Israel—as stipulated in the Luxembourg Treaty—did not mean "a breach of neutrality" as, according to international law, the deliveries to a country at war did not constitute such a violation. Although Israel was still at war with the Arab states, the belligerent actions had long ceased. Moreover, the deliveries would not contain any war material. They were also no subsidy for the Israeli government as they were meant exclusively as partial compensation for the injustice done to the Jewish refugees of the Nazi regime. The statement hinted at the possibility of German contributions to the economic development of the Arab states and appealed to the Arabs to respect the reasons which had guided the Germans in concluding the treaty with Israel.[24]

The German government finally announced that a good-will mission to Cairo would make an attempt to improve the situation.

It can be assumed that the Germans were hoping to appease and

[20] *Ibid.*

[21] *Deutsche Presse-Agentur.*

[22] *United Press International,* November 12, 1952.

[23] Joachim Kreysler and Klaus Jungfer, *Deutsche Israel Politik,* p. 39, Wolf von Tucher Verlag G.m.b.H., Diessen-Ammersee, 1965.

[24] *Bulletin des Presse-und Informationsamt der Bundesregierung,* November 12, 1952.

persuade individual Arab leaders by the old method of *divide et im- pera*. The idea was perfectly sound as Arab unity has always been a myth although the dream to achieve it persists to this day. Political and, sometimes, economic interdependencies, as well as fear of one another, made them often act in unison without conviction. But, no doubt, the Germans also wanted to make it known through this delegation—despite all that had happened—that they still wanted to retain the friendship of the Arab peoples and to prove this by helping them in their endeavor to build up their countries.

There were political reasons, too. In the course of the haggling, the Arabs seemed to have discovered that they could make use of the struggle between West and East Germany as part of the cold war. At the beginning, they went about it in an amateurish manner, but they learned this game of playing one side against the other to perfection in later years. In their Economic Service, the Arab League suddenly hinted at the possibility of turning for aid and trade to where one could surely obtain all those products that West Germany delivered—to East Germany. The Arabs knew very well that nothing could hurt the Bonn government more than close contact with the East German Communist regime which, after international recognition, was a second independent German state. However, they must have known, too, that East German goods and trade with the Communist state did not offer, by any means, the profits to be derived, even at that time, from West Germany. East Germany took advantage of the situation and their delegation in Egypt of- fered that nation machinery to the value of $14,000,000; they de- manded, in exchange, cotton, flax, hides and leather.

Dr. Westrick, State Secretary of Economic Affairs, charged with the leadership of the Bonn delegation, had more to offer the Arab League; a $71,400,000 credit with low interest to be divided among the Arab states.

With a number of industrialists, bankers and a Foreign Office of- ficial, Westrick traveled to Cairo in February, 1953. In fact, the del- egation was to have left earlier. Dr. Adenauer had recalled Westrick to Bonn from business talks in Brussels shortly after the Cabinet's decision to send a delegation to Cairo. Knowing that speed was of the essence, Westrick had driven as fast as he could. But it was win- ter and the roads were treacherous. In the hilly Eifel region, he had met with an accident and had been injured. Instead of getting on to Cairo, Westrick had been forced to stay in bed. Adenauer had sent flowers and daily inquiries about his state of health. Westrick, recalling this, smilingly added, "Surely not because he was so concerned about my health, but because he wanted me to go to Cairo." At last, he was well enough to see Adenauer in the Bonn Chancellory, but with a big bandage around his head. Adenauer's first question was: "When will you be able to depart?" [25]

Dr. Westrick remembered that the atmosphere of the first encounter with the Arab league representatives was rather "hostile." Speaking in German, Dr. Westrick once again presented the German reasons for concluding the Luxembourg Treaty and emphasized that this was not meant to inflict harm on the Arab peoples. When requested to speak English, Westrick complied only when the Arabs switched from Arabic to English, too. The German politician, a man with a firm mind and manners, made it clear that the German delegation had come to Cairo as friends and not as debtors. A hint of the German property still confiscated in Arab countries without offer of compensation was ignored by the Arabs, who left no doubt that they were the ones to do the demanding. The $71,-400,000 credit offer was waived at once. The Arabs sneered at it and declared that they saw absolutely no reason for not being granted the same amount that Germany intended to give to Israel. Dr. Westrick declared in unmistakeable terms that he would not, under any circumstances, go beyond the offer—and this would stand only until his departure. In the course of the ten days in Cairo, Dr. Westrick held numerous talks with individual Arab leaders, but to no avail. However, Westrick, too, was adamant. Surely Dr. Adenauer chose him for this mission, knowing him to be unwavering, even in the face of the sweetest blandishments or the toughest pressures.

Incidentally, a member of the Westrick delegation reported a casual meeting with a certain "Colonel Nasser," who expressed his "understanding of the eagerness of the Federal Republic to come to an agreement with Israel."

Westrick returned from Cairo and advised Dr. Adenauer to ratify the Luxembourg Treaty without delay, feeling sure from his talks with Arab leaders that, in the end, the Arabs would do nothing more to impair their relationship with Bonn. This suggests that Arab unity must have appeared very superficial to Dr. Westrick. Furthermore, the $71,400,000 credit never was paid, as the Germans firmly maintained that the offer was no longer valid once it had been rejected. The only assurance that Dr. Westrick held out to the Arabs (and which Bonn was to hold to) was West German assistance for

[25] Conversation with the writer, June 25, 1968.

the building up of Arab industries and agriculture. Dr. Adenauer confirmed this, saying that Bonn was ready not only to examine Egyptian proposals, but also to send delegations into the capitals of other Arab states in order to discuss the economic needs of each country, and a possibility of strengthening the connection with German economy—a point of the First Reading of the Luxembourg Treaty. Dr. Adenauer warned, however: "I hardly need to add that such negotiations will lead to favorable results only if they are carried out in a friendly spirit and if they are not burdened from the start with threats."

Just one month after the return of the Westrick delegation from Cairo, and almost immediately after the ratification of the Luxembourg Treaty, a German study commission went to Egypt [26] to examine, together with Egyptian experts, the technical and economic preconditions for the construction of the Aswan Dam. Economic talks were held soon after with other Arab states. Although there had been a meeting of the Arab League in Cairo after the Luxembourg Treaty had been ratified, the Arab states could not reach agreement on an economic boycott against the Federal Republic of Germany.

The Bonn government had reason to be proud of the outcome—to be proud that it had withstood all pressure, as now there was proof that the Arab threats had been empty words. Perhaps one should add that the government—predominantly Dr. Adenauer—deserved praise for an attitude of courage and conviction. Of course, there is no doubt that the political importance of the Luxembourg Treaty influenced the American attitude toward the postwar German state, and that played its part in the German determination when face-to-face with the Arabs.

Trade between Germany and Egypt increased rapidly after this as if there never had been a clash or a divergence of opinion. In 1953, Germany took second place on the list of Egyptian importer countries, right behind the United States, putting Great Britain in third place. This was quite remarkable in view of Egypt's former dependency on Great Britain. At the end of 1953, West Germany ranked fourth on the Egyptian export list. Germany announced that its export to all Arab countries had risen by 40.5 percent in the past year; its imports by 9.2 percent.[27] This development shows how eager

[26] Bonn Foreign Office, March 20, 1953.
[27] *Bundesamt für gewerbliche Wirtschaft:* In 1961, the Federal Republic's ex-

both sides were to normalize their relationship. But, despite this healthy development, the Arabs never forgot to "remind" the Germans of what seemed a useful handicap, for the sake of their own political or economic advantage. Once it was the Iraq request from the Arab League for a boycott against German firms and goods, as the Arab world could not look on passively when Israel's economy, through the goods from the Federal Republic, became the strongest of the Middle East. The appeal fizzled out, finding no response among the Arab nations. Then, in 1954, after talks with East German government representatives,[28] it was Syria, protesting against West German restitution deliveries to Israel in Berlin at the time of the Foreign Ministers' conference there. And, at a Cairo meeting in July, 1954, the Arab countries decided to let the Germans know that their deliveries to Israel had turned the Arab boycott against Israel into a blunt instrument; that measures should be adopted by the Federal government to alter this, at once, by the exclusion of certain goods from the deliveries to Israel, for example. Again, the effect was nil.

It appeared, at first, as if Germany had hardened to this hot and cold shower-treatment on the part of the Arabs. However, it would be wrong to say that the Germans did not listen to the threats from Cairo at all. Now they culminated in the repeated announcement that the Arabs would extend diplomatic feelers to the GDR should Bonn proceed with Israeli diplomatic relations. The Arab alarm originated in Israel's sudden readiness to consider a German request for expanding diplomatic connections. Rumors of a forthcoming exchange of ambassadors between Israel and Germany having increased (apparently based on the German offer to set up a Mission in Israel similar to the Israeli one in Cologne), President Nasser, in an interview in April, 1956,[29] threatened immediate recognition of the GDR.

The government spokesman declared that neither Germany nor Israel intended to establish diplomatic relations at that time.[30] But, the Germans hoped that, with their economic aid to the Arab countries (which the GDR could not match), they had created a kind of dependency so that the Arabs could not afford to recognize East Ger-

ports to Egypt showed increase of 163 percent: to Syria, 190 percent; to Iraq, 490 percent; to Jordan, 514 percent. (1953 comparison).

[28] *Die Welt*, Essen, February 16, 1954.
[29] *Deutsche Presse-Agentur*, April 4, 1956.
[30] *Der Tagesspiegel*, April 12, 1956.

many. Above all, according to the Hallstein Doctrine,[31] Bonn was to sever all ties to countries propounding diplomatic relations with East Germany—a threat aimed not solely at Near Eastern countries but also at the entire noncommitted world and which was, in fact, carried out in the cases of Cuba and Yugoslavia in later years. This also entailed the danger of a discontinuation of economic aid.

The Arab states appeared to be unconcerned about this threat. On their part, they knew only too well that Bonn, for both economic and political reasons, was not in the least interested in severing connections with them. Obviously, the Germans did not want to give up the Arab markets, however poor they may have been at that time. They did offer prospects, and any other industrial state would be only too glad to step into the breach. To allow the political ties to be grabbed by the GDR, and to permit it to represent postwar Germany in the Arab states, would increase the number of countries ready to back up the Russian theory of the existence of two German states; eventually leading to an international recognition of this fact. Above all, President Nasser was one of the leaders of the noncommitted world, at that time, trying to act as a third united force in world politics. It seemed unwise in the extreme to turn him into an enemy and virtually invite other noncommitted countries to make diplomatic overtures to the GDR.

It is not surprising that the Arabs let no opportunity slip to emphasize the dangers to Bonn's economy and politics in case it decided to normalize its relationship with Israel. Also, under pressure from the Russians—who did all they could to increase their influence in the Near East—some of the Arab states did their best to encourage collaboration with East Germany, just falling short of recognizing it diplomatically.

Syria, for example, agreed in 1956 to the setting up of a Consulate of the GDR in Damascus. The Federal Republic, realizing that it was being "cheated," immediately asked whether or not this was meant to be a diplomatic recognition of the East German Communist state. The Syrian government promptly retorted that, if Bonn intended to sever the ties with them, it would have serious consequences for their trade with the entire Arab world. Bonn almost eagerly accepted the explanation that the opening of a Consulate which later was transformed into a Consulate General—a practice,

---

[31] Named after Foreign Office Secretary of State Professor Walter Hallstein who, in 1955, suggested severance of ties to countries establishing relations with East Germany.

incidentally, copied by other noncommitted countries—was not in any way to be compared with the extension of diplomatic relations.

Both sides then, Arabs and West Germans, assumed a strong stance. The Arabs, generally interested in Russian support, were still not keen on becoming too dependent. They preferred to continue their favorite game of playing one against the other, hoping to reap benefits from both West and East, which they undoubtedly did. Citing the German example, Bonn and Pankow did their level best to vie for the favors of the Arab nations—and for those of the other noncommitted nations, for that matter—as much as Pankow could afford to do with its economic means. From time to time they took a step to prove their friendship with the East, but they never went so far as to extend diplomatic relations to the Communists of Germany.

Misinterpreting the Arab mentality, German diplomats showed alarm whenever the Arabs were playing their game with them. As a result, the Near East ambassadors of the Federal Republic repeatedly warned Bonn of any closer move towards Israel, as this might induce the Arabs to cut off their ties to Bonn.

At the Istanbul conference of German and Near East ambassadors in May, 1956, under the chairmanship of State Secretary Professor Walter Hallstein, this was plainly expressed with the conclusion that absolutely nothing should be done that might impede German-Arab relations any more.[32] This mainly concerned German-Israel relations. The Arabs had achieved their purpose—the Germans refrained from recognizing Israel. At the same time, the Arabs reserved for themselves the issue of German-Israel relations which were bound to increase in some way—even without official ties—as an object of pressure to be used at their whim. The Germans, who had withstood the campaign against them in the case of the Luxembourg Treaty, now fell prey to political gamblers. The Western Powers, themselves on bad terms with the Arabs, were anxious that at least West Germany, as a Western ally, maintain friendly relations. After the Suez incident in November, 1956, the relationship between the West and the Arabs deteriorated even more, with the result that the Germans considered themselves the guardians of Western interests in Arab lands, and felt it a duty not to impair relations with the Arab world under any circumstances. But, by keeping the Arabs from extending diplomatic recognition to Israel, the Germans made

[32] Felix E. Shinnar, *Bericht eines Beauftragten*, p. 114, Rainer Wunderlich Verlag, Tübingen, 1967.

the fatal mistake of showing weakness and inviting political black-mail.

The Arabs saw another opportunity to exert pressure on Bonn to stop restitution deliveries at the time of the Suez conflict. In order to ward off the constant military assaults on its settlements, Israel had taken the initiative—failing a United Nations intervention—to clean up the bases from which these attacks had been carried out. The Ministers of Syria and Lebanon protested to Foreign Minister von Brentano against the continuation of German deliveries to Israel. No doubt there were factions in Germany that felt there was need to comply with the Arab request. In the Security Council, sanctions against Israel, Great Britain and France (having protested with arms against Nasser's nationalization of the Suez Canal) had caused some Germans to feel that the continuation of deliveries might be considered by the world as siding with Israel.

Fear that the Near East flare-up, in addition to the Hungarian uprising against Russian interference, would lead to a world war was great in Germany then. Under no circumstances did the Germans want to be a party to it, nor did they want to run the risk of being accused of having done anything to promote it. The German government discussed the matter at length, then under the strong influence of Adenauer, came to the conclusion that the deliveries were meant for the peaceful building up of Israel and would not increase war potentiality. Dr. Shinnar, Chief of the Israel Mission in Cologne, took note in his book [33] of the determination with which Dr. Adenauer declared that the Federal Republic would continue the deliveries. On behalf of his government, Shinnar had gone to see the German Chancellor with a letter from Prime Minister David Ben-Gurion, explaining the Israeli situation. Adenauer made it perfectly clear that the Germans would not and could not interfere in the conflict. The Arab states, however, vainly continued their appeals to the Federal government in press conferences and statements issued by the Arab League from their office which had been set up in Bonn with the permission of the German government in July, 1956, "for the observation of the economic boycott."

Still, after the end of the Suez warfare, the Arab states, as before, periodically discussed or pleaded for sanctions against Germany because of restitution deliveries to Israel. But again, trade between the Federal Republic and the Arab states flourished and aid was given

[33] Felix E. Shinnar, *Bericht eines Beauftragten,* p. 76, Rainer Wunderlich Verlag, Tübingen, 1967.

with generosity. The West German government, wherever possible, offered liberal aid on favorable terms. It sent experts to the Arab countries for the purpose of introducing progressive, technical methods to the Arabs. Here and there, unauthorized persons—parliamentarians, as well as industrialists—felt the need to assure the Arabs that their government definitely would not subscribe to diplomatic relations with Israel. This never was disputed by Bonn for what was thought to be good reason. About 1958, the Germans felt satisfied, on the whole, with their policy in the Near East. They had no diplomatic connections with Israel but were sure that this did not do any harm to them or to Israel. The fact that reparations were made to Israel and individual Jews (particularly in the later stages) made up for the missing political ties, and had already gained them much political trust in the Western world, predominantly in the United States.

Regarding the Arab world, the Germans were of the opinion that their contacts could not be better. They believed that their policy of aid and allegiance to the Arab countries in international bodies paid them dividends. Their Western partners, being emotionally and politically attached to Israel, did not always share their attitude towards the Arab states. But, as all of them were united in the opinion that the Communist influence exerted over the Near East had to be checked, they did not object to the line pursued to guarantee it. There were politicians in Bonn who felt sure that a good Western relationship with the Arab nations was imperative for peace in the Middle East which, eventually, could turn from an unstable armistice there to a stable situation. As few Western powers were in a position, following the Suez fighting, to maintain good relations with the Arab states, the Germans felt that not only were they doing a service to the Western world, but that they were also playing a part in world politics, at last.

But it appears that whenever the Bonn government felt safe and secure and considered its policy ripe enough to bear fruit the Arabs reminded them of what they must have interpreted as political "reality." At the end of 1958, they invited Otto Grotewohl, the East German Prime Minister, to Cairo. The Egyptians must have thought that again it was about time to pay their dues to the Eastern bloc; also, to eagerly accept their aid. Despite protests from Bonn, Grotewohl was received in Cairo on January 4, 1959, like a chief of government with whom Egypt was on diplomatic terms. Nasser bestowed medals and honors on his guest from Communist Germany.

In the course of their talks the two men agreed to set up an East German Consulate General in Cairo. Bonn was furious and demanded assurances that these consular relations were still far from being diplomatic ones. Bonn's anger was particularly understandable, for shortly before Grotewohl's visit to Cairo there had been negotiations about West German participation in the second phase of the Aswan Dam construction and a generous West German credit to the United Arab Republic. It was one of those occasions when the Arabs made it quite evident that *they* directed German-Arab relations and, therefore, they felt in no way bound to ignore the East German state, particularly since Moscow expected such a move on their part from time to time.

Shortly after Grotewohl left Cairo, Nasser received Bonn's Ambassador Dr. Weber, and assured him that he did not intend to recognize the GDR and that the establishment of a General Consulate would not imply such official ties. But the East German Consulate had come to stay in Cairo and, whether Bonn liked it or not, it enjoyed more than semidiplomatic status.[34] In September, Dr. Weber once more held talks on the matter with the Egyptian Foreign Minister, Dr. Fawzi, and was assured again that there was no change in the policy concerning Bonn and Pankow. But Pankow had advanced one more step. There was no denying this fact.

Once again West German trade and aid improved. In January, 1960, Professor Ludwig Erhard, Minister of Economic Affairs in Bonn, paid a call on Nasser. The Egyptians appealed to the Germans for increased import from the United Arab Republic and better conditions for the repayments of loans on development projects. Professor Erhard promised to look into the matter and, as always, Bonn felt compelled to comply as much as possible in a contest with Eastern "generosity."

The climax of German aid to the United Arab Republic seemed to be reached when, in July, 1961, Germany and the UAR signed the Boghdadi Agreement. The UAR Minister of Planning, Abduleatif el-Boghdadi, and Professor Ludwig Erhard on the German side reached agreement that Bonn make available Arab credits to the value of $119,000,000. This money was earmarked for the construc-

---

[34] On February 17, 1965, in the *Bundestag*, the Foreign Minister, Dr. Schroeder, disclosed that Spain had acted as mediator for the Federal Republic at the time of the Grotewohl visit to the UAR, when the Bonn government feared that the establishment of a GDR Consulate General would mean more than just consular relations.

tion of the Euphratis Dam by German firms to supply water for
700,000 hectares of land in the Syrian region of the UAR. The interest rate of 3 3/4 percent was one of the lowest Bonn had ever
granted. Furthermore, Bonn announced credits to the value of
$35,700,000 for projects of infrastructure for both Syria and Egypt.
German private firms supplying capital goods to the UAR were to
receive government guarantees up to $59,500,000 for transactions on
a long-term basis and an additional $35,700,000 in government guar-
antees for deals on a normal credit basis. With the aim of relieving
the trade and payment deficit, West Germany made every effort to
increase the import of goods from the UAR—especially cotton—and
promised to stimulate tourism to Egypt. When the UAR collapsed
shortly afterwards, and Syria regained its independence, the new
Syrian government questioned Bonn, on various occasions, as to
whether or not it would honor the Boghdadi Agreement. The Euphratis Dam, for which the money had been intended, was in their
region. For many years, West Germany evaded answering on technical grounds, but the problem was solved by the rupture of Ger-
man-Syrian relations in 1965. The Germans then made it quite clear
that the aid had been offered with political intentions. Bonn was
fully aware that it was not Syria but Egypt that did the political
steering of the Arab world at home and in the noncommitted nations.

And so it continued through the years. The catchword of the traditional German-Arab friendship was quoted, whenever it seemed
opportune and by either of the two sides. But, actually, it had
turned into a political tug of war and one day the rope was bound
to slip out of the hands of one of the contestants.

5

Israelis and Germans
at Political Hide-and-Seek

". . . The Federal government, in principle, agrees to set up an office in Israel. . . . The time of the setting up of this office and its tasks would have to be determined in negotiations with you at a later date. . . ." This is an excerpt from a letter that the Foreign Minister, Dr. Heinrich von Brentano, wrote to Dr. Felix Shinnar, head of the Israel Mission in Cologne, dated March 14, 1956.[1] On reviewing this letter, the question is, what were the German Foreign Minister's intentions? For, it contains no commitment, whatsoever. That the Federal government agreed, "in principle," to the setting up of an office which, *mutatis mutandis*, would correspond to the Israel Mission in Cologne, is nothing but the expression of an opinion or an intention without any formal undertaking. The postponing of the establishment of this office to an undetermined date leaves little doubt that the West German government did not really intend to establish such an institution in Israel—an office, incidentally, which would not have brought about anything like formal diplomatic relations between the two countries. It merely would have been a place to issue visas, to improve the handling of trade between the two countries, to give the Germans a center for their propaganda in Israel. That the Federal government did not even intend to do this (as the letter betrays) proves that, at that time, they were loth to take a single step which would indicate closer relations with Israel. The

[1] Archives of the Foreign Office, Bonn.

question will remain unanswered as to why this letter was written at all. It may well have concerned Dr. Felix Shinnar, who had given the impression in Israel that the Germans were ready for the creation of something like this in Israel. It was, of course, no fault of his that the letter revealed so clearly that the Germans did not really want to honor the promises contained in it. Nevertheless, it was a cause of deep disappointment in Israel. The prospect of a German Mission in Israel had been interpreted as a first step in the direction of diplomatic relations. The blunt refusal on the German part, bared the change of attitude that had taken place in both countries in the course of the years with regard to diplomatic connections.

Naturally, there was no immediate readiness in Israel—of the government or of the public—for diplomatic connections with Germany. In the first years of the existence of both states, the very thought of it would have sounded absurd to any Jew remembering what had happened only a few years before. It may be recalled that the conclusion of the Luxembourg Treaty caused no end of discussion and furious objections on the part of the Israeli people. The majority of those who accepted it ultimately did so because they were made to see in it justified demands for a compensation of material losses.

The West Germans would have liked the establishment of diplomatic relations with Israel immediately after the signing of the contract. They had made this clear to their Isreali interlocutors. At that time, West German diplomatic alliance with Israel could have been of political advantage; obstacles, as seen by the Bonn government in later stages, did not exist then. "Void of instinct," *Der Spiegel*, March 23, 1960, called this German offer, which of course, had been rejected.

On March 4, 1953, Chancellor Adenauer had said: "We have justified hopes that the conclusion of this treaty eventually will lead to an entirely new relationship between the German and the Jewish people; also to a normalization of relations between the Federal Republic and the state of Israel. We shall exercise patience after all that has happened, and rely on the effect of our readiness for compensation and, eventually, on the healing power of time."

Israel could not possibly undertake such a forward step. Apart from the Luxembourg Treaty, many more proofs of German sincerity of feeling for the Jewish people were needed—including a change of mind and true repentance—to convince the Israeli people that West Germany was a state to be trusted. But, some farsighted politicians in Israel had already realized that Israel would have to come to terms with West Germany. It was a country in the heart of Europe, soon to play its part again in world politics, if due only to the East-West conflict.

A memorandum written by Israeli officials to the Israeli Premier and his Foreign Minister as early as March, 1953, a few days before the ratification of the Luxembourg Treaty, had suggested the establishment of diplomatic relations with Germany. The reasons given: the increasing importance of the Federal Republic, both from the political and from the economic point of view; the danger that the Arabs could "conquer" Western Germany and become a sphere of influence if Israel remained unrepresented there.

Both Premier Ben-Gurion and Foreign Minister Sharett shared this political assessment, particularly in view of the existence and the development of various European bodies, such as the European Economic Community, the Coal and Steel Community and the European Atomic Energy Commission. But, both politicians realized that they dared not voice this opinion at the moment. It would have raised a storm of protest and nobody would have listened to the valid arguments in favor of such an early relationship. Nevertheless, Ben-Gurion tested the reaction on one of his committees, the *Mapai*. Having presented all the arguments, he found a majority of one in favor—far too slender a basis for such an important step, Ben-Gurion decided. The ground had to be prepared carefully, and this would take some time. The execution of the Luxembourg Treaty, just signed, would surely play a decisive part in the Isreali people's confidence in postwar Germany.

In the coming years, West Germany consolidated its position as a state to be reckoned with. It became an important partner in European treaties and took its first steps as a sovereign state in the sphere of world politics. Just this strengthened the Federal Republic and the position of Konrad Adenauer. Economically, West Germany was heading for a boom and self-confidence grew.

Union with the Arab world, as with other countries, was strengthened, although it was difficult to say then how firm it was. Israel's position was far less fortunate. General international recognition of its frontiers, in an armistice agreement drawn up after the first Israel-Arab fighting, was remote. Its economic situation was most precarious. Due to the Arab boycott, Israel could not trade with its natural hinterland. The preparations for a European market roused justified fears that third countries no longer could sell in Europe. There were the heavy defense burdens and the cost of immigration for hundreds of thousands (predominantly Asian and African Jews) entering Israel at that time. Once again (in 1954), astute politicians reminded the government of the need to consider the establishment of relations with Germany. "Time is running out," a memorandum read. But a strengthened, self-confident Germany might no longer need alliance with the Jewish state as it had in the first few years after the war. The Arab influence might make West Germany inattentive to Israel. As a matter of fact, contacts between Israel and the Federal Republic, at the time, consisted almost exclusively of the execution of the Luxembourg Treaty. Yet, there were vacillators in Israel.

In 1954, the Germans still would have been ready to establish a diplomatic interchange with Israel. When interviewed by *Die Welt* on September 14, 1954, Dr. Adenauer explained that he considered the effects of the Luxembourg Treaty extremely important in paving the way for relations with Israel: "It goes without saying that I would welcome it sincerely, if the Israeli Treaty should prove to be the first step towards the normalization of relations between the Federal Republic and the state of Israel." At the same time, he pointed out that the Federal Republic (thanks to his government's persistent policy of reconciliation) had overcome the world's hatred which was the inheritance of the German people, as a result of the Nazi regime. He also paid his dues to the German people, saying that, by voting overwhelmingly for democratic parties in the first two postwar elections, they had shown that no longer was there any room for radicalism in Germany. Rising self-assurance could be discerned in his words, quite clearly.

Professor Walter Hallstein, State Secretary of the Foreign Office, interviewed by *Das Parlament*, November 8, 1954, made it manifest that it was not Germany's fault that diplomatic relations had not taken effect. From the Israeli point of view, time was not yet ripe for the extension of diplomatic relations. He said, "We are interested in establishing a clear relationship of trust with Israel." He was confident, he added, that the exact fulfillment of the Luxembourg Treaty would eventually achieve such a state of mind.

Moshe Sharett, Israel's Premier and Foreign Minister, did his share to prepare the ground for future relations with Germany when, in the *Knesset* on November 16, 1954, he said that Israel could not overlook the development of postwar Germany if it wanted to engage in a realistic approach, and, if it did not intend to lock itself out from a world with which its heart, feelings and memories were linked. He stressed that the restitution agreement was being fulfilled with greatest precision: "I have no doubts that the man [Adenauer] who today is at the helm of the Federal Republic sincerely endeavors to make his country a democratic factor for the strengthening of peace in the world and the stability of Europe."

Another proof that the approach of the leading Israelis became less rigid as time passed is that, hardly two years after the signing of the Luxembourg Treaty, about half of the deliveries of goods to Israel arrived on German ships although during negotiations the Israeli government had objected to German ships calling at Israeli ports. When German Hanseatic towns protested this clause, and the ratification of the Luxembourg Treaty was endangered, the Israeli government agreed to annul the clause after ratification. Yet, so soon after this controversy, the fact that German ships—in increasing numbers—could put in at Israeli ports without being molested was unexpected.[2]

The year 1955 was the actual turning point in the declared policy of both Israel and West Germany in relationship to each other. Israel distinctly expressed its readiness to welcome diplomatic relations with the Federal Republic. West Germany just as distinctly rejected diplomatic relations with Israel. The Israeli government had come to the realization that it no longer could ignore Germany, a partner of NATO and the European institutions. Clearly, Israel had suffered under the isolation into which it had been forced in the Near East and urgently needed to strengthen connections with Europe. But, ties to Asia and Africa were also needed; to countries like India, which, although it had recognized Israel *de jure*, had not done so *de facto*. Diplomatic recognition of Israel by Germany, with its relevance to the Arab world, might be another inducement or, perhaps, a model, for uncommitted countries to come to terms with the Jews. It might also force the Arabs to realize that Israel was a factor to be taken seriously by other countries. The fulfillment of the Luxembourg Treaty—due to which German machinery, ships and railways reached Israel and undoubtedly helped the country's economy to progress—was a decided asset in the government's plan to break the news of a change of policy towards Germany to the Israeli people.

[2] Third protocol to the Luxembourg Treaty, August 5, 1954.
  Joachim Kreysler and Klaus Jungfer, *Deutsche Israel Politik*, p. 56, Wolf von Tucher Verlag G.m.b.H., Diessen-Ammersee, 1965.

Two Germans reported it. Professor Boehm had gone to Israel about this time under an assumed name, at the suggestion of the Israel government. In his report, Boehm recalled a conversation in which Prime Minister Moshe Sharett believed it likely that such a proposal would be passed by the parliamentary foreign political committee. He thought, however, that the request for relations should be presented to Israel by the Germans.[3] Dr. Abraham Frowein, member of the Foreign Office's special department for the execution of the Luxembourg Treaty [4] had similar conversations with Israeli officials during a trip to Israel in 1955. It seemed as if a political dialogue between Israel and the Federal Republic was "in the air."

But, precisely at this time, the Germans must have drastically reconsidered their relations with Israel. The fear that the Arabs with all their affiliations would feel challenged by the extension of diplomatic relations to Israel must have gained the day. It is known that German ambassadors accredited in Arab countries added to these fears. And it seemed clear to Bonn that Israel, in need of Europe, would not again be torn away from Germany. At this time, too, the Americans, who so often had been the spokesmen for Israel, did not press the Germans. They, too, felt that it was imperative for the West—any of the Western-orientated countries—to preserve what was left of a good relationship with the Arab world.

Germany's change of mind was put on a political platform—the Hallstein Doctrine. It was formulated on the return of Chancellor Adenauer from Moscow in September, 1955. The German government had decided to establish diplomatic relations with the Soviet Union; an exceptional step to secure the return of the German prisoners of war. For the first time, the Bonn government consented to diplomatic recognition of a country which had official linkage with the GDR. Nevertheless, there was great anxiety that this step should not be misinterpreted as an encouragement to other countries to recognize the GDR. The Hallstein Doctrine was defined by Dr. Adenauer in a *Bundestag* speech the same month: [5] "The Federal government will, in future, regard the establishment of diplomatic relations with the GDR, through third countries with which it has official ties, as an unfriendly act calculated to aggravate the division of Germany." Such an act, he said, would lead the Federal government to

[3] Professor Franz and Martha Boehm, *Eine Reise nach Israel, Schriftenreihe der Israel,* Mission No. 3, 1955.
[4] Dr. Frowein in conversation with the writer, Überlingen, February 9, 1968.
[5] Minutes of the *Bundestag,* vol. 26, p. 5643, September 22, 1955.

examine its own relationship with those third countries. The Doctrine, rigidly applied in two cases (Yugoslavia, in 1957 and Cuba, in 1963), was also aimed in the direction of the Arab world.

The Bonn government felt that it now had found a weapon to hinder noncommitted countries from recognizing the GDR.[6] It was thought that it might upset the political balance already established if Germany were to extend diplomatic relations to Israel while demanding that the Arabs refrain from doing so in the case of the GDR.

In July, 1955, Dr. Shinnar reported to Jerusalem that there was a German plan to set up a German Mission in Israel. In the middle of 1955, Dr. Shinnar noted in his book [7] that von Truetzchler, Chief of the Foreign Office's Political Department, had asked him to sound out the possible reaction in Israel on the founding of such an institution; it would help to improve the issuing of visas for the Federal Republic which, until then, had been handled by the British Consulate in Haifa.

Although this was by no means what the Israelis aspired to, many politicians considered it a first practical step towards official connections. When it was evident, on the basis of Dr. Shinnar's reports, that diplomatic relations were not to be realized at the time, the Israeli government agreed to accept this German Mission.

Dr. Shinnar was instructed by the Foreign Office in Jerusalem to negotiate in January, 1956. According to Dr. Shinnar's reports, there was sincere intention in Bonn to establish this base in Israel. Great was the surprise, then, to receive a letter on March 14, in which Foreign Minister, Dr. von Brentano, made it known (between the lines) that Bonn no longer desired any association with Israel that could appear to the Arabs as a concession towards the Jewish state.

A conference of German ambassadors accredited in Near East countries, took place in Istanbul in May, 1956, under the chairmanship of the State Secretary, Professor Walter Hallstein. It confirmed this course, and emphatically recommended doing nothing that could give the Arabs an incentive to recognize the GDR, including any such move towards Israel. The Germans chose to forget the Luxembourg Treaty experience, when the Arabs had threatened

---

[6] *Die Zeit*, June 6, 1969, called Professor Wilhelm Grewe, Chief of the Foreign Office's Political Department, the "spiritual father" of the Doctrine, and said that Professor Hallstein had helped to "give birth" to it.

[7] Felix E. Shinnar, *Bericht eines Beauftragten*, p. 113, Rainer Wunderlich Verlag, Tübingen, 1967.

West Germany with vehemence, and in the end had done nothing at all.

Professor Hallstein tried hard to make Israel understand this attitude. He explained Bonn's predicament to Dr. Shinnar and said that West Germany could not afford to do anything that might endanger the reunification of the country. A diplomatic recognition of the East German Communist state by the Arabs, activated by German relations with Israel, might bring about a strengthening of the division of Germany. Hallstein assured Shinnar that, as soon as circumstances allowed, the Federal government would be only too pleased to offer full diplomatic relations to Israel and not just this provisional solution suggested in the Brentano letter.

It probably never will be known whether the Germans did not make their change of mind quite understandable to Dr. Shinnar, or whether he had misinterpreted the situation when he had reported to Jerusalem of the German intention to establish a German Mission in Israel. In a way, the letter signed by the Foreign Minister could be interpreted as adding insult to injury.

But it seems that Professor Hallstein, the man who had lent his name to the doctrine, was to be a stumbling block to future Israel-German relations: an objector to any pro-Israel action. He is said to have inspired the letter signed by Dr. von Brentano. It was drafted by consul Voigt, Chief of the Foreign Office's Near East Department from 1953 to 1962. Voigt's inclinations were undoubtedly attuned to the Arabs. He spoke Arabic fluently, having been Consul of the Ribbentrop Foreign Office from 1936 to 1938 in Jerusalem—a factor which made life and work in Bonn even more difficult for Israeli diplomats. It can be understood why they had nothing to do with this man, remembering only too well the activities of the German diplomatic representation in Jerusalem during the Nazi period. Dr. Shinnar was plainly handicapped, as not all the details of policy could be learned just from occasional meetings with the figureheads of German policy.

Dr. Shinnar was in a difficult position, anyhow. He had been appointed Chief of the Israel Mission in Cologne because of his qualifications as an economist. From the very founding of the state, Shinnar had been entrusted with the handling of some of Israel's precarious economic institutions. As a law student of Heidelberg, Tuebingen, Frankfurt and an editor of the oldest Hebrew newspaper in Israel, *Ha'aretz*, Shinnar had finally specialized in economics. In 1948, he had been appointed Controller of Fuel; in 1949, Economic Counselor in London. When he returned in 1951, he was charged with the founding of Israel's Fuel Corporation and, at the same time, he inaugurated a department in the Jerusalem Foreign Office for the assertion of claims of the Jewish people against Germany. Only a year later, he took part in the negotiations with Germany on the question of restitution. His appointment as Chief of the Israel Mission in Cologne for the purpose of purchasing goods in Germany under the agreement at Luxembourg was only logical. He remained in this post until diplomatic relations took effect in 1965.

In the beginning, the Israel Mission was no more than an institution with economic tasks, although very soon after its founding (May, 1953), the Foreign Office appointed a Deputy Chief, Dr. Chaim Yachil, whose main tasks were of a political nature. From the very beginning, the Israel Mission was considered by the German public *the* representative of the state of Israel, about which many people in Germany were very curious. To distribute information, to lecture on Israel, to sustain contacts with German politicians (for which the basis was laid in the course of the negotiations for the Luxembourg Treaty) was one task; the observation of the political development in Germany, another. Ben-Gurion had come to the conclusion that Germany was one of the neuralgic points in world politics.

A truly political function for the Mission, as representative of Jerusalem's Foreign Office, developed in 1955 after Israel had decided that diplomatic relations were essential, although this was not the purpose for which the mission had been set up. Dr. Shinnar, the economist, now was forced more and more to be a diplomat in the full political sense of the word, rather than the economist, duty-bound to purchase goods most profitably. He soon acquired a vast knowledge of Germany and Germans—he had excellent contacts with Dr. Adenauer and his State Secretary and confidant, Dr. Hans Globke. No one in Israel could match him in those years. This is why he remained in this post which, in its changed character, was not his *métier*. There was a good deal of criticism of Shinnar, especially after the failure of 1956, that probably affected his political backing in Israel. Yet, because of his special knowledge, he seemed irreplaceable.

Dr. Shinnar had also become the personification of the 750 million-dollar bill that the Luxembourg Treaty had granted Israel. For Finance Minister Levi Eshkol, therefore, Shinnar was enormously valuable—indeed, indispensable—as he helped Eshkol out of financial difficulties. One more reason, perhaps, why nobody dared touch Dr. Shinnar was the obvious fact that, after the 1956 debacle, no political ties with Germany seemed to be in sight. This seems to have made Jerusalem leaders again see the Cologne Israel Mission as nothing more than an economic institution of the state.

There was genuine disappointment in Israeli government circles over the Brentano letter, which was considered by many a moral and political blow to Israel. After all, the Germans should have realized that it had not been easy for Israeli leaders to arrive at this decision; closer alliance with Germany ran the risk of causing friction and sparking emotions once again among their own people. Even a first, halting step towards closer relations (the setting up of a German Mission) would have been difficult for the Jewish people to stomach. But more than that, it had to be taken as a political victory for the Arabs, whose policy of blackmail could, once again, register a success. This letter, then, became a milestone in the struggle as its repercussions determined the course of the contacts for some years; in fact, until the establishment of diplomatic relations in 1965.

Israeli leaders, deeply hurt and dejected, separated into three groups regarding their attitude toward Germany. Foreign Minister Moshe Sharett virtually "turned away" from Germany. It was for him, a man of great integrity and honesty, a breach of trust. Golda Meir, Labor Minister, had been against any steps leading to a *rapprochement* from the very beginning for purely emotional reasons. In later years, she could not endure even a brief stop in Germany. Because of her refusal to step on German soil, when traveling by air, she would not leave the plane even when it was refueling at German airports with fire engines drawn up around it. She took over the Foreign Ministry after Sharett's resignation in June, 1956, but treated the subject of Germany as if it did not exist. It may sound ironical that it should have been under her jurisdiction that diplomatic relations with Germany came about in 1965.

Another small group, which included Moshe Dayan—first, General and later, Minister of Agriculture—thought that this should not be taken lying down and that it should be made public. It was, apart from everything else, a political victory for the Arabs, which deserved resistance. Everything should be done to achieve these relations, despite all odds against them. The longer Israel remained without official connections with West Germany, the more difficult it would be to attain them. For, if the Germans thought that Israel would resign itself they would not find it essential to withstand the

Arab pressure. Even a possible "compensation" for the lack of diplomatic relations in the shape of aid of all kinds could not convince this group of the necessity of silence on this issue. They were of the opinion that secret deals—which did develop in later years—were bound to be discovered one day, and then Israel would have neither relations nor aid. But this group remained a minority. It has often been argued that all the hidden manipulations between Bonn and Jerusalem, in the economic as well as in the military field, would not have come about had it not been for the lack of diplomatic relations.

The majority accepted the situation as it was, and no longer bothered about diplomatic alliance with the Federal Republic. Being practical men, first of all concerned about the well-being of Israel, they resolved to reach a greater "practical" cooperation with West Germany.

Thus, there was another chance for Dr. Shinnar, the economist, to prove his worth. It is known that he was stimulated in his efforts to achieve results by Finance Minister Levi Eshkol whose orientation was far less political than determined to make ends meet. Later on, Shimon Peres, Director General in the Defense Ministry, entered the picture to conclude the arms deal with Germany, a deal by which the Germans made their first political commitment towards Israel. There was, at that time, no specific conception of a policy towards Germany. Peres pursued his line; Shinnar and Eshkol, theirs. Ben-Gurion, back at the head of government, continued to express his hope for diplomatic relations with the Federal Republic of Germany, fully aware, no doubt, of the "other" relations that would develop later on.

The Israeli people knew nothing of the incident. The question of the establishment of diplomatic connections with Germany had to be dealt with secretly in order to avoid the whipping up of emotions against Germany. This was still very easy in Israel, and often was "inspired" by opposition parties hoping to deal a blow to the government in this way. Yet, during the Suez crisis the atmosphere changed drastically: there was nothing but praise for Germany and its attitude towards Israel.

On October 29, 1956, Israel tried to stop the Arab infiltration into its territory, and threatening its very existence, by marching into the Sinai Peninsula. The United Nations threatened to use its sanctions against Israel, and America cut off its aid practically the day on which Israel marched. The Arabs immediately urged Bonn to stop its deliveries under the Luxembourg Treaty. There were some

German politicians who believed it better to interrupt deliveries—at least for a short period—to avoid being accused of aiding an "aggressor country."

Brentano voiced the opinion that if the United Nations decided on sanctions the Federal Republic should ignore it. It did not belong to the United Nations and, therefore, was not bound by its decisions. Moreover, German deliveries to Israel were carrying out "a moral obligation." This did not fail to make an impact on Israel, especially since the United States had discontinued aid at once. In June, 1957, from Israel, A. J. Fischer reported in *Deutsche Rundschau* that Brentano's remarks, particularly the one on the "moral obligation," had touched the hearts of people in Israel.

This, and the exact execution of the restitution agreement, brought about Israel's first decisive swing of public opinion in favor of postwar Germany. It would have been an auspicious moment to establish diplomatic relations with the Federal Republic of Germany. Another attempt was made by Israel, or, more precisely, for the first time, it was Israel that openly suggested and requested diplomatic relations with Germany. So far, the idea had been that, even though the Israelis desired the diplomatic interchange, the request had to come from West Germany.

Adenauer and Foreign Minister Heinrich von Brentano traveled to America in spring, 1957. Israeli Ambassador Abba Eban, in Washington, asked the State Department to use its influence by speaking up on Israel's behalf, in favor of diplomatic relations between the two states. Foreign Secretary Foster Dulles called it "a good idea" and conveyed this message to Brentano. But Brentano had nothing to say.[8] Ben-Gurion was not put off. In a press conference in Tel Aviv on June 28, 1957,[9] he expressed the hope that "normal relations" shortly would be established between the two countries. He praised the precision with which the Luxembourg Treaty had been carried out and declared: "Pessimists said this would cease after the first year. . . ."

In July, 1957, Ben-Gurion told a German interviewer of the *Suedwestfunk*, "Up to now we have had only economic and financial relations. I would like to see full diplomatic relations established between the two states."

That same month, when Mrs. Raziel-Naor of the right wing *Her*

[8] *Der Spiegel*, March 23, 1960.
[9] *Die Welt*, June 29, 1957.

uth party demanded a *Knesset* debate on Israel's relations with Germany, Ben-Gurion stated that diplomatic relations with the Federal Republic were a necessity; European union was about to be established. This would constitute an important economic and political factor and West Germany was to be an important partner in this union. Economic and financial connections with the Federal Republic were of great significance to the future of Israel: "Our relations with Germany are, in my humble opinion, and from every point of view including the political one, likely to turn out a blessing for the country." So far, the government had made no decision on the establishment of a diplomatic alliance. This question was not topical for the time being. But Ben-Gurion thought it quite possible, and expressed the view that Israelis and Jews all over the world had to be prepared for it. *Davar*, the daily of the *Histadruth*, the Israeli trade union movement, agreed with the Premier. The *Ha'aretz* wrote that it was about time for the public to stop identifying present-day Germany with the Germany of Hitler. The question of diplomatic relations might not be topical, but Israel had to get used to it. The atmosphere between the two countries, the *Jerusalem Post* asserted, had changed entirely. In the first place, the scrupulous execution of the Luxembourg Treaty had something to do with it. German trade unionists and leaders of the SPD had been able to visit Israel without any incidents.

Gradually, the climate of cooperation between the two peoples had been made possible. The German press welcomed this change in the atmosphere. "The Federal Republic should be greatly pleased about this development, which was by no means natural," the *Stuttgarter Zeitung* wrote, July 17, 1957, and suggested that the Federal Republic should make advances to Israel; the regard for people like Nasser should not prevent Bonn from accepting the hand which Ben-Gurion offered, despite the rift of the past. The *Sueddeutsche Zeitung*, July 19, also remarked that Bonn should not hesitate to honor the Israeli advances.

But Bonn did not react. State Secretary Felix von Eckardt, government spokesman, merely said that negotiations would start on this subject "in the not too distant future." The result was a threat from the Prime Minister of Syria that he would immediately recognize the GDR, should diplomatic ties be established with Israel.[10] The West German Mission chief in Damascus and other German

---

[10] *Der Spiegel*, March 23, 1960.

diplomats in the Arab capitals were notified hastily that the question of diplomatic relations with Israel was not being considered "at the present moment."

Before the *Bundestag* on October 29, 1957, Dr. Adenauer declared that Bonn would "avoid any step that could increase tension" in the Near East. What this meant was explained, vaguely, by the Foreign Minister, speaking before the foreign press in Bonn on November 4. Brentano expressed his opposition to diplomatic relations at that time. In his opinion, it was no good to come to a decision "in which no one had the benefit, but which would do harm to many." He said that tension existing in the Near East could not be denied and that the Federal Republic would not increase this tension through diplomatic steps: rather, that Germany endeavored to contribute to a *lessening* of tension. He did not clarify in what way diplomatic relations between the Federal Republic and Israel could affect the Near East conflict. The argument appeared to be a very poor excuse for something that should have been done without much fuss.

Ben-Gurion did not give up so easily. Good relationship with the Federal Republic was, for him, just one more means to help Israel out of its isolation—politically, economically and militarily. As the Sinai campaign had shown, it had turned out to be bad policy to rely solely on the United States for support. Ben-Gurion's bid to have his country accepted in NATO failed before it was formally proposed. Israel needed strong friends in Europe; France's friendship alone was insufficient. That amity had come about when the Socialists, who felt an allegiance to the Jewish state also based on Democratic Socialism, were in power in France. Another regime might change this, or at least feel less bound by it. Also, France and Germany had shed their century-old enmity for a treaty of friendship. Israel could not be linked in cordial friendship with one country and be merely courteous to the other.

The military aspect played an important part in Ben-Gurion's thinking. The United States, after the Sinai campaign, refused to deliver arms to Israel. The only country that could possibly help out in this field was the Federal Republic. It must have been then that Ben-Gurion fully accepted the views of his friends who had long given up bothering about diplomatic ties and who concentrated on the possibilities of a "practical" cooperation with Germany.

The first contacts between Director General of the Israeli Defense Ministry Shimon Peres and Defense Minister of the Federal Republic Franz-Josef Strauss had just been made when it was let slip in Israel that a "high-ranking personality" was to go to see Adenauer for the alleged purpose of reaching a military treaty with Germany. It was soon an open secret that the "high-ranking personality" was General Moshe Dayan, yet his mission never came about.

On December 15, Bar-Yehuda, Israel's Minister of the Interior, and member of the left-wing *Achduth Ha'avoda*, spoke up in a Cabinet meeting and warned the government of his strong protest in case the mission of the "high-ranking personality" to Bonn would lead to a military treaty with the Federal Republic. He made himself the spokesman of the two left-wing Socialist [11] parties, *Achduth Ha'avoda* and *Mapam*, both in Ben-Gurion's coalition. Both disliked the government's general foreign policy which, in their opinion, was too closely involved with the West. A policy of neutrality in foreign affairs would have suited them better, if not—in the case of *Mapam*, in particular—a greater orientation towards the Communist bloc. From its point of view, West Germany was too much a "stooge" of the United States, and all closer alliances with it would be to the detriment of Israel. But more so, of course, the hope was to benefit from the emotional opposition to a treaty with Germany. According to reports, a compromise was reached on a majority of one vote only, which meant that Ben-Gurion would not aspire to a military treaty with Germany, but was empowered to explore the possibilities of arms purchases in the Federal Republic.

All this never would have come to the knowledge of the general public, had not the *Achduth Ha'avoda* disclosed Ben-Gurion's plans in its newspaper. Ben-Gurion, thereupon, demanded the resignation of the party's Ministers on the basis that Cabinet discussions and decisions were confidential, and their disclosure harmful to the state. But the party's political committee rejected the suggestion. The right-wing *Heruth* party, which was against Germany for totally different reasons than the two left-wing parties, made the request that the government outline its policy towards Germany in the *Knesset*.

On December 24, 1959, Ben-Gurion took the floor to make it clear that Israel had no other possible supplier of arms than the Federal Republic.[12] He said the Soviets had delivered arms to Israel's

---

[11] Joachim Kreysler and Klaus Jungfer, *Deutsche Israel Politik*, p. 62, Wolf von Tucher Verlag G.m.b.H., Diessen-Ammersee, 1965.

[12] Early in December, Dr. Giora Josephtal, General Secretary of *Mapai*, on behalf of Ben-Gurion, had discussed with Adenauer Germany's disposition towards Israel's security, which seemingly prompted the Israeli Premier to make this statement.

enemies while the United States had refused to support Israel with war material in 1956. He reminded the listeners that he had suggested sending a "high-ranking personality" to Bonn to negotiate the purchase of military equipment there. He said Israel had succeeded in obtaining equipment to match the Arab states in two dimensions, land and air; but the danger, "not only to our security, but also to immigration before it ever reached our shores had recently arisen in a third dimension" (obviously referring to Egypt's recent purchase of submarines). The purpose of a proposed mission to West Germany had been to obtain equipment which was not available elsewhere. He told a press conference, the following day that the mission had not been cancelled. As a matter of fact, Israel's Defense Ministry Director-General, Shimon Peres, left for Bonn on December 25, to initiate a deal which was to become of tremendous importance and was to have far-reaching consequences. The motion by the *Heruth* that Ben-Gurion account for his policy towards Germany was lost by fourteen to forty-six votes. The two left-wing parties abstained.

The Israeli Cabinet, on December 24, had adopted two resolutions proposed by Ben-Gurion. The first one explained that the gravity of the security situation in which Israel had been placed made it essential to increase the defense capacity by acquisition of equipment from any quarter or source. In other words, even Germany could not be excluded if it had arms to sell. The second one censured the behavior of the Ministers of the *Achduth Ha'avoda,* saying that the government considered the publicity given to its confidential decision harmful to the state and a grave violation of the principles of collective responsibility.

The indiscretion of the two left-wing parties, therefore, could not go unpunished, especially as it was felt that the disclosure had been made for purely political party motives. Having failed to persuade the Ministers to resign, on December 30, Ben-Gurion announced that he had not succeeded in his efforts to assure collective responsibility of government and coalition parties which was essential to prevent injury to the international position of Israel and for her requirements of security. Therefore, he intended to resign. He did so on December 31. President Ben-Zvi asked him, as the leader of the strongest party, to form a new government. Ben-Gurion reconstituted his Cabinet on January 6, with the same membership, binding the Ministers to strictest secrecy.

The government in Bonn reacted sharply to the disclosures in Jerusalem, always mindful of its relationship to the Arab states. In an official statement of December 27, 1957, it expressed surprise as to what exactly had caused the Israeli government to believe that it could purchase arms in Germany. It said that it would not supply Israel with arms or other military equipment nor would it allow private German firms to execute such orders for Israel. The German Near East policy would remain unchanged. In view of the Arab-Israel conflict, Bonn would not take any step that would be considered instrumental in increasing tension, in either case.

A new government crisis, also due to German relations, followed hardly eighteen months later.[13] As early as 1957, Dr. Shinnar had orders from Jerusalem to acquaint the German Defense Minister with Israel's Uzi, a submachine gun which could well compete with anything of this kind that was produced on the world market.[14] Israel wanted to sell Uzis to Germany. After all, to exist and to pay for its enormous financial burdens caused primarily by defense and immigration, Israel had to explore the world for marketing prospects. Since it was less costly to produce in large quantities than small, it was essential to sell Uzis abroad. It also would be of great importance to Israel's economy, on the whole, if a technically advanced country like Germany would be ready to buy Israel's goods.

After thorough examination of the quality and the price, the German Defense Ministry decided on the purchase of Israel's guns. Strauss explained these purchases of Israeli arms when interviewed on June 2, 1963, by the Israeli paper, *Ha'aretz:* "I was told that these purchases would help the Israeli economy and, indirectly, Israel's security. At the beginning, I was against it. There were also quite a few Germans opposing it. But just in this matter, the Israelis were smarter and the purchases were effected." Strauss, however, did not want to create the impression that he had bought the Uzis simply to help Israel. In an interview on January 19, 1967,[15] or years after the deal had been accomplished, he disclosed that, over a considerable period, his Ministry had examined all types on the market, among them Swedish, French, German-Finnish, English, Italian and German models. The Uzi turned out to be the best from every viewpoint. And, Strauss added, the Uzi had proved itself in the Sinai

---

[13] Joachim Kreysler and Klaus Jungfer, *Deutsche Israel Politik*, p. 64, Wolf von Tucher Verlag G.m.b.H., Diessen-Ammersee, 1965.

[14] Felix E. Shinnar, *Bericht eines Beauftragten*, p. 139, Wunderlich Verlag, Tübingen, 1967.

[15] Rolf Vogel, *Deutschlands Weg nach Israel*, p. 141, Seewald Verlag, Stuttgart, 1967.

fighting. He said: "Until now we have no reason to regret this decision, nor to go back on it. The Uzi has also proved its worth as a standard machine gun in the *Bundeswehr....*"

In June, 1959, *Der Spiegel,* reported that on March 27, a Haifa armaments factory had signed a contract for the supply of 250,000 grenade throwers for the West German army and that other such agreements on arms deliveries to Germany were about to be concluded. Strong protests were published in the majority of the Israeli newspapers, including the organ of the government-represented, left-wing *Achduth Ha'avoda.*

At subsequent Cabinet meetings, June 28 and 29, Ben-Gurion rejected the demands by the two left-wing partners for a cancellation of the contract. He referred them to a Cabinet meeting of December 14, 1958, in which formal approval for the sale of arms to foreign countries had been given. No objection had been raised then by the Ministers of the two left-wing parties. It appears that these Ministers had failed to understand then that this decision also entailed the sale of Israeli arms to Germany. The two Ministers, both of the *Achduth Ha'avoda*—Israel Bar-Yehuda (Interior) and Moshe Carmel (Communication)—had become aware of arms sales to Germany on March 29 at a government meeting when Ben-Gurion had announced that such a deal had been signed. On request of the *Mapam* Minister of Health, Israel Barzilai, Ben-Gurion had promised discussion of the subject at a later date. They finally objected to the contract with Germany in letters to Ben-Gurion on April 29 and on May 4. They also demanded that no such transaction should be carried out before it had been discussed by the Cabinet.

Ben-Gurion replied that they were entitled to propose the cancellation of the contract, but pointed out that they had not raised the matter at any of the preceding Cabinet meetings. The two Ministers more or less admitted that they had not been aware of the full meaning of the decision made on December 14, 1958, which had dealt with the sale of Israeli arms to foreign countries.

The Communists suffered a crushing defeat when they found no support for their "no confidence motion" in the *Knesset* on June 30. It was rejected by fifty-seven to five votes and thirty-seven abstentions. Ben-Gurion then proposed a motion opposing the cancellation of the arms contract. In the ensuing debate, the two left-wing Socialist parties once again expressed their leanings toward the East, voicing fear that this new contact might cause a deterioration of relations with the Communist bloc.

The right-wing party argued that the arms deliveries to Germany impaired the national honor. It was still too early to forgive and to forget. It was apparent that some of these arguments were the result of genuine feeling, although the greater part can be ascribed to political polemics. The arguments of the majority party, Ben-Gurion's *Mapai,* that such sales were an economic necessity for the country and that the Federal Republic had developed into Israel's third strongest trading partner, did not make the slightest impact on those who wanted to oppose the new contacts. In a reply to a debate, Ben-Gurion said,

. . . I do not say that there are no Nazis and anti-Semites in Adenauer's Germany or that there would not be in the Germany of the Social Democrats if they should come to power tomorrow . . . but, when I say that the Germany of today . . . . is not the Germany of Hitler, I am referring not only to the new regime . . . but also to the geopolitical transformation that has taken place in Western Europe and in the world . . . It does not limit itself to Israel whether Germany is with our enemies or with us. Germany as a force hostile to Israel . . . also endangers the friendship of the other countries of Western Europe and might even have an undesirable influence on the United States and other countries of America. . . .

The *Knesset* approved his motion, and with it the sales of Israeli-produced arms to West Germany. The voting on July 1, showed fifty-seven votes in favor, forty-five against and six abstentions. The motion had been opposed by *Mapam, Achduth Ha'avoda, Heruth,* the Communists and the National Religious party. Those voting against the motion included the four Ministers of the two left-wing parties. In an explanation of their attitude; the two parties published, a letter to President Ben-Zvi on July 7, in which they called the contract with West Germany inconsistent with the resolution condemning Germany's rearmament which had been adopted by the *Knesset* in November, 1954.[16] On July 5, the resignation of the four Ministers had been demanded at a Cabinet meeting at which Ben-Gurion himself had tendered his resignation. He declared that the *Knesset* debate had done harm to Israel's standing in the world and that he could not remain in a government with four Ministers who

---

[16] Prime Minister Moshe Sharett, before the House: "The *Knesset* expresses its deep concern over the rearmament of West and East Germany. It appeals to the nations of the world to recall and not to forget what an armed Germany had done to the world and to prevent a repetition of these events." November 16, 1954.

had abandoned the obligation of collective Cabinet responsibility. On July 15, Israel's President, Ben-Zvi, once again asked Ben-Gurion to form a government. He failed in the formation of a minority government which he attempted in order to avoid renewed inclusion of the two left-wing Socialist parties. He then agreed to the coalition, as it existed, remaining in office as a "caretaker" government until the general elections, due to take place in four months.

The fact that two government crises could come about based on Israel's contacts with West Germany is indicative that the subject was back to the state where it could be made the playball of political parties. The auspicious moment after the Sinai campaign, when nobody could dispute Germany's leaning towards Israel, and when diplomatic relations could have been established without opposition having much of a chance, had been squandered by the Germans for reasons of their own. The advances on the part of Israeli statesmen, which remained either unanswered or were rejected, hurt the people of Israel. It was, therefore, quite easy once again to rouse feelings against postwar Germany.

The Germans had watched this tussle from afar with phlegmatic interest; their attitude had not changed. While they delivered the goods to Israel punctually, in accordance with the Luxembourg Treaty, they kowtowed to the Arab world, offering aid and understanding. On August 20, 1958, Foreign Minister von Brentano spoke on the radio of Germany's understanding of the Arabs' endeavor for unity and freedom. He pledged generous economic aid without political strings attached, on the basis of partnership.

More curious, however, were the views expressed by Dr. Adenauer, when interviewed by a reporter of *Maariv* on October 5, 1959, which resembled those of his Foreign Minister in 1957. He told the interviewer that the establishment of diplomatic relations would not be in the interest of Israel at that time. Such a move might bring about a mood of desperation in the Arab world which could induce them to close their ranks and embark on a new action against Israel. He then strongly rejected the idea that Bonn had avoided establishing diplomatic relations with Israel out of fear that the Arabs would then recognize the GDR. He said he did not take such threats into consideration. The Arabs, he conceded, had to get used to the idea that Israel existed and was there to stay. It was necessary to aid the Arabs to reach this conclusion. Yet, he felt that diplomatic ties would only aggravate the situation and fan the fires of hatred against Israel.

It was, indeed, a strange argument. An argument which, if any-thing, should have been more appropriate for Israel to have voiced. But, perhaps, the Chancellor felt a twinge of guilt for not having es-tablished diplomatic relations with a country that was, after all, rec-ognized by the majority of countries in the world, and was a full-fledged member of the United Nations. He then revealed that Ben-Gurion had sent him a special envoy, Maurice Fischer, in 1958. The Israeli statesman had suggested that the Middle Eastern coun-tries, including Israel, be permitted to join the European Market: such a move would serve to convince the Arabs of the need to rec-ognize Israel's existence and would turn out to be beneficial to them, too. Fischer, on behalf of Ben-Gurion, asked Adenauer to support this idea. Adenauer agreed at once, explaining that he shared Ben-Gurion's views. With this, Adenauer tried to create the impression that Bonn always had been ready to support Israel wherever possi-ble, but preferred that relations remain informal for the time being.

Adenauer satisfied himself that he had found an argument that suited his purposes. He could easily have consulted an Israeli politi-cian on his worries and he would have found them groundless. Somehow, this interview appeared as odd as the letter that von Bren-tano had written in 1956 when he offered something he had not been ready to give. Israel-German relations, indeed, were at a stand-still—in a blind alley.

6
Ben-Gurion and Adenauer Meet

"He is older." With this remark Israel's Prime Minister David Ben-Gurion cut short a discussion on a question of protocol—of the two statesmen, David Ben-Gurion or Dr. Konrad Adenauer—Which one was to act as host to the other?

On Monday morning, March 14, 1960, at 10 a.m. sharp, the seventy-three year-old Israeli statesman was about to walk down two floors to the presidential suite of New York's Hotel Waldorf-Astoria occupied by the eighty-four year-old German Chancellor, when he was told that masses of journalists and photographers were crowding the hotel. The only way to avoid them was to go down the fire escape. Without fuss, the elderly man and his team chose this exit to reach Adenauer's suite unobserved. Originally it had been intended to keep the meeting strictly secret. But the two national flags fluttering from the flagstaffs of the hotel had betrayed the two visitors and it was quickly deduced that the two men would meet.

It was to be a "casual" meeting; the first one between a German and an Israeli statesman since signing of the Luxembourg Treaty. Public opinion in Israel still was not in sympathy with a formal encounter. It was evident, therefore, that Ben-Gurion could not travel to Germany. And nonexistent diplomatic ties made it impossible for the two statesmen to meet in their respective countries. The suggestion that Ben-Gurion might meet Adenauer in his Italian holiday resort, Cadenabbia, was disregarded, as this would have called for a special

trip on the part of the Israeli Premier. Chancellor Adenauer's visit to
Washington in March, 1960, at last "coincided" with Ben-Gurion's
American journey to see President Eisenhower and to accept an
honorary degree from Brandeis University.

Ben-Gurion was eager to meet Adenauer. He was curious about
the man. "I felt that he was an honest man," Ben-Gurion said, as he
reviewed the situation. "He really wanted to make up for the past."
Adenauer's opponents, the Social Democrats, had strengthened this
belief by telling Ben-Gurion that, although Adenauer was "a fox" in
political matters, in the case of his attitude towards the Jews, he was
sincere. "Maybe he also thought of political advantages for Germany when he decided to meet an Israeli statesman," Ben-Gurion
admitted, but he was quite sure that these were secondary considerations in this particular case.[1]

Ben-Gurion must have known by instinct that both he and Adenauer had a lot in common, despite the fact that he was one of the
leaders of a Labor movement which had laid the foundations for
quite a few Socialist institutions in Israel, while Adenauer was a
staunch Conservative, having held to traditional values all his life.
Both men were strong believers—each one in his cause. Ben-Gurion,
a conscientious Jew, felt it his duty to create a state of the Jews and
assure its existence. Adenauer, a practicing Catholic, saw it as his
task to bring about Germany's readmittance into the family of free
nations after the disgrace of the Third Reich. Just as Ben-Gurion
had accepted a solution for the state in 1947 (a compromise which
was far from his original aspirations), Adenauer realized that there
was little prospect for a reunification of Germany and he made do
with West Germany. He even strengthened the division of the
country when he saw that he could achieve his ends: a free and
democratic state as a member of the free world in West Germany.

The record of both men as founders of their states is remarkable.
Their unusual strength of conviction which inspired their own peoples made them the special hate target of their respective enemies.
Nasser, due to Ben-Gurion's remarkable leadership, had pitted
against him a strong and alert Israel. It was no different for Ulbricht, the East German Communist boss. With such a strong personality as Adenauer as head of state, Ulbricht and Communism had
no chance of influence in West Germany. Both men had no close
friends, nor did they seem to have the desire for any. Plenty of ad-

[1] Conversation with the writer, August 7, 1968.

mirers seemed to satisfy them. A stubborn streak was typical of both. Adenauer did all he could to oppose Professor Ludwig Erhard as a successor, even if this happened to be detrimental to his party. Ben-Gurion treated Moshe Sharett, his successor for a time, and later Levi Eshkol, with no less contempt.

The meeting of the two venerable statesmen was carefully prepared. Dr. Shinnar, Chief of the Israel Mission in Cologne, met Adenauer several times and traveled to Israel to discuss the meeting with political leaders there. In the spring of 1959, one year before the meeting, Ben-Gurion had discussed his views with the German banker, Hermann Josef Abs, during the latter's stay in Israel. For, apart from his desire to make the acquaintance of the German statesman, Ben-Gurion wanted Adenauer to assure him of financial aid for the state of Israel. He was set on some kind of loan: although it was to be given on a proper commercial basis, it was to be earmarked for certain purposes.

"If I am not mistaken about the man," Ben-Gurion speculated, "the idea to use the money for projects to build up the desert will appeal to Adenauer." He then could give the *Bundestag* a good reason for consenting to such a loan. The young people of Germany would come to see what had been achieved with German money and it would give them the proud feeling that they themselves had contributed to the development of the Negev, which made up 55 percent of the state of Israel.[2] Lengthy deliberations led to the suggestion that Dr. Adenauer be asked for a loan of $250,000,000 for ten years. It was further resolved not to raise the outstanding question of diplomatic relations between Israel and Germany. The Israelis were realistic enough to understand that, at that moment, there was no hope of such a realization: most Germans in government were fearful of risking their flimsy relationship with the Arabs. To have touched on the delicate subject of diplomatic relations might have created an atmosphere of tension and reduced the chances of a satisfactory conference result. And, as Ben-Gurion put it: "Money was more important to us then than diplomatic relations."

There were other reasons why the prospects for the granting of Israel's request could be called excellent. Adenauer, in a way, needed this meeting with the Israeli leader. Only two months earlier, the daubing of swastikas on a Cologne synagogue had shaken the little faith that the free world had developed in postwar Germany. The

[2] Conversation with the writer, August 7, 1968.

German leader needed the good will of the American people and of
the American press to assure continued support—both political and
military—for his country. The handshake with the Israeli statesman
could make all the difference in Adenauer's reception in New York
and, last but not least, in his political talks with President Eisenhower. For it implied that the Jewish people were ready to make
their peace with the Germans. Moreover, here was an Israeli statesman who had hardly ever been equalled. He had just won the greatest election victory of his career.[3] His prestige was considerable in
America. Adenauer had yet to meet President Eisenhower while
Ben-Gurion had already seen him. The encounter with Ben-Gurion
and the manner in which it went off was of the greatest political importance.

Considering Adenauer's situation, $250,000,000 was a ridiculously
low sum. This was the sudden thought of one of Ben-Gurion's political advisors; what a waste of an opportunity! And Yitzhak Navon
decided to acquaint his Premier with his considerations. He had to
wait all night, and only shortly before the meeting was to start
could he hope to have a word with Ben-Gurion. When he entered
the suite, twenty minutes before ten o'clock, Ben-Gurion was still in
the bathroom. He came out at about ten minutes later, still strug-
gling with his tie, which he was not used to wearing too often in Israel. His political advisor rushed up to him and, in a few words
hastily spoken in view of the pressure of time, implored Ben-Gurion
to ask for a billion dollars from the German leader. He gave him all
the reasons. "You are crazy," Ben-Gurion replied, recalling that the
sum of $250,000,000 had been arrived at by the experts after careful
deliberations. Navon reduced the figure to $750,000,000. Ben-Gurion
did not seem to listen. $500,000,000 then. It was like bargaining for a
horse. When Ben-Gurion, a few minutes before ten o'clock, reached
for the door he turned to Navon and said: "All right, I shall ask for
$500,000,000."

Adenauer rose from a couch when Ben-Gurion entered. Smiling
broadly, he greeted his guest with a handshake. Except for the two
interpreters, the two statesmen were soon left alone. A historic
meeting was about to start; a meeting about which there are several
contradictory interpretations. Therefore, it is necessary to emphasize that the following description of the conversation is based on
authentic sources.

[3] November 3, 1959.

Adenauer insisted on speaking German as he felt he could express nuances best in his mother tongue. Ben-Gurion admitted that he did understand other languages—among them German—if he wanted to. Turning to his interpreter, he said in Hebrew: "You do not need to translate what he says. We would rather use the time to think over the reply."

At first, the meeting was formal and stiff. Dr. Adenauer tried to overcome the awkwardness of those first few minutes by saying that he followed the reconstruction of Israel "with greatest personal interest," and he went on to express his deep admiration for the courage, power and perseverance of Israel.

Ben-Gurion returned the compliment, answering, "I want to say how much I value what you did to establish a democratic regime in Germany and what you did to resume the relations with other nations; also, what you did for the Jews." He then praised the reparations agreement which, in 1952, had been the first treaty concluded between their two countries. "That the leader of a great country had the courage to accept the moral responsibility for what happened in his country—that is the real significance of the reparations agreement."

Then Ben-Gurion came to the point. He charged that Hitler had not only annihilated European Jewry but that he had also almost destroyed the Jewish state. European Jewry, Ben-Gurion explained: "those of our people who had vision, knowledge, ability, idealism and readiness for sacrifice and the material means . . . they were destroyed. . . ." They had never considered themselves part of the country they lived in, he said; as he himself, although born in Russia, had never considered himself merely a Russian. European Jewry had been the backbone of the Zionist movement. This concerned their cultural contribution as much as their readiness to be pioneers of Zionism.

At this stage, Dr. Adenauer interjected, "The fate of the Jews is somewhat similar to ours. We are also missing the personalities that were lost with that layer." This was to remain the one and only moment of tension in the conversation between the two men. It can be explained only by Adenauer's assurance and his known tendency for somewhat naive simplifications of complicated cases.

Ben-Gurion retorted brusquely that one could not very well compare the two things, "You cannot compare the tragedy that happened to us with anything else. . . ." He quickly returned to his subject, obviously not wanting to jeopardize the meeting: "If we now had four to five million Jews in Israel, no problem for our security would exist. We would not be rich, but our work and our lives would be safe."

For this had become terribly difficult. Israel would need two to three generations to really integrate Jews from Asia and Africa and to train them to be pioneers similar to the European Jews.

Dr. Adenauer then inquired about the birth rate in Israel and was told that among Oriental Jews the usual number was eight children and among European Jews, two, arriving at an average of four. "That is not enough," the German statesman commented.

"I could not agree with you more," Ben-Gurion answered. He then repeated his charge against Hitler saying that the murder of six million Jews would continue to endanger the existence of the state for some time to come. At the turn of the nineteenth century there had been ten million Jews. Now, after World War II, there were merely twelve million—they would not be in such dire circumstances had the six million not been annihilated. Perhaps at the end of the century there would again be eighteen million; yet, from the historical point of view, Hitler had almost murdered the Jewish state: "our hope and heritage for three thousand years." But Israel would not succumb to such a fate. "We shall overcome it," Ben-Gurion said, then set out to enumerate the difficulties that obstructed the building up of the state.

The Jews had not lived as a nation for two thousand years, Ben-Gurion explained, emphasizing that Jews from all corners of the world with different backgrounds and living standards had gathered in Israel. The ideal of a state, however, had persisted. ". . . I think an ideal is more important than knowledge and experience," he said, hinting at the fact that they had undertaken to develop the state without much experience in such a task. And, although the second problem was that Israel was surrounded by enemies, "I have no quarrel with the Arabs. . . . They are against us. We are not against them. Our aim is to live in peace and help others to the extent we can." Thirdly, there was the problem that the greater part of Israel was desert. It was very difficult to work it. But, Ben-Gurion expressed the firm conviction that the Jews would manage to build up the state, ". . . because it is our spiritual heritage. Our prophets said so long ago, and I believe that the multitude that went to the gas chambers went with the hope that there would be a redemption in Israel." He appealed to the religiosity in Adenauer when he said, "No other people can say as much as we that we are the people of the Bible. The Bible made our people. It formed us." That was precisely the strength of the Jews; this was what gave them the faith to know that they would reach their aim.

Then he did not hesitate any longer to explain what he was after. He said to Adenauer, "What I am going to propose to you, you may reject. I cannot demand it from you . . ." He admitted that there was neither formal nor informal obligation on the part of the Germans to accept what he would suggest, making it clear that the Jews had no more legitimate claims on the Germans (for which he was later criticized in his country.) "But this is what I propose you ought to do," Ben-Gurion urged. There was no such thing as reparations for the lives of six million Jews. But something could be done to lessen the terrible damage done. "We want you to participate in developing our country." He explained that Israel had to build up industries, to expand its shipping and agricultural enterprises, to create places of work for one million people: "You can invest in these enterprises or, for a long term, lend us $50,000,000 each year. . . ." That would make it easier to carry out what was necessary for Israel. And he repeated that either the German government should participate in such development projects or it should lend Israel $40,000,000 to $50,000,000 every year for ten years.

Adenauer did not hesitate to assure Ben-Gurion that Germany would help Israel: "We will help you for moral reasons and for reasons of practical politics," he said. Israel was a fortress of the West. It had to be developed—this was in the interest of the whole world: "I can already tell you that we will help you. We shall not leave you alone." Adenauer did not enter into a discussion about the figure that Ben-Gurion had suggested as a German loan. But he did not reject it.

Ben-Gurion returned to the subject in a later stage of the conversation when he suggested that he would send two or three economists to Germany to discuss investments in existing enterprises and the setting up of new industries. "I understand you agree to my proposal in principle," Ben-Gurion said, "I am not an economist. . . ."

Adenauer replied, "I agree completely."

For a third time, Ben-Gurion inquired whether he could say when he returned home that the ground had been prepared. Again Dr. Adenauer answered, "Yes, it is all right."

There seemed to be no flaw in the agreement, considering that the German leader also sanctioned the arms deliveries to Israel. This had come about on Defense Minister Strauss's initiative. Adenauer assured Ben-Gurion that Strauss had his fullest support in aiding Israel with armaments, adding, "He is all right. He thinks as I do."

Ben-Gurion mentioned that Israel needed submarines as the English type his country possessed were not suitable for Israel's purpose; they were built for too long a range and too large a crew. Then, Israel was also in need of missiles. He hinted at cooperation in this field between France and Germany, saying, "The help we received from France both during the war of independence and later cannot be valued highly enough."

When Ben-Gurion urged Adenauer to express his accord with Strauss's actions, Adenauer once more left no doubt about his agreement in this field. Ben-Gurion pressed, ". . . Also, on defense matters? Can I say that Strauss has your support?"

Adenauer replied, "Yes, that is right."

He told Ben-Gurion that he had been approached by a representative of the Weizmann Institute regarding support for its scientific work and added that this, too, would receive hopeful consideration.

Ben-Gurion then mentioned that he had been attacked in his country for meeting Adenauer and for making a distinction between postwar Germany and that of Hitler, adding, "I think it is not Jewish ethics to levy collective responsibility upon a whole nation and to carry this on and on." His conscience was clear, he said; he was doing his duty as a Jew and a human being.

Adenauer thanked him for his attitude. Then the two men showed how they respected each other, probing each other's opinion on world affairs and the statesmen they had to deal with. When photographers were admitted to the room one and a half hours after the talk had begun, the two leaders were still conversing in fragments of German, English and French, trying to convey ideas to each other without the help of interpreters.[4]

In a room nearby, the aides of the two statesmen drafted the communiqué which was to be issued after the historic meeting. The Israeli representatives, intent on the purpose of the meeting, suggested that one clause should clarify the West German design for aid to Israel. It was to contain the phrase, "cooperation with and support for Israel." Foreign Minister Heinrich von Brentano is said to have objected to such a clause, reminding the Israelis that although there was no longer any legal obligation on the part of the Germans towards Israel such a clause would make demands on Germany. He

---

[4] *The New York Times*, March 16, 1960.

suggested "understanding for Israel" instead of "support." Yaakov Herzog, Minister of the Israeli Embassy in Washington, entered the room at that point. He made his Prime Minister understand that the Germans were being difficult. Ben-Gurion reacted at once, saying in Hebrew, "If it concerns the question of money, be tough," and gave him to understand that Adenauer had already given his word to aid Israel. Herzog then explained the dispute to Adenauer who inquired which of his aides objected to the draft. On hearing the name of his Foreign Minister, Adenauer made it evident with a movement of his hands that he did not consider those objections important and agreed to the draft.[5] The vital sentence then read: "I [Adenauer] am sure that the German people, as well as my government, are convinced that our mutual cooperation with and support for Israel will continue to bear fruit in the future." Adenauer added that he had been deeply moved by the meeting with Ben-Gurion whose statesmanship and steadfastness as the chief architect of modern Israel and its remarkable development he had admired for a long time.

In his statement, Ben-Gurion reiterated his belief that the "Germany of today is not the Germany of yesterday." The meeting with the Chancellor had proved to him that the statement which he had made in the *Knesset* the previous summer had been correct. He wished the Chancellor every success in his efforts to guide Germany along the path of democracy and international cooperation.

It could not be expected that the meeting in New York could pass without dispute in Israel. In the *Knesset*, the Communists attempted to unseat Ben-Gurion because of his meeting with Adenauer. Their opposition to the meeting hardly was based on honest arguments. They simply toed the line laid down by the Communist leaders in opposition to Adenauer and Ben-Gurion, the two "cold warriors" who preserved the axis of revanchism. In view of the emotions that could so easily be roused against West Germany, the Communists hoped to find greater support for their motion of "no confidence" in the government (tabled on March 16) than they actually mustered. As a matter of fact, they had to be content with their own votes of three against fifty-five in opposition to their motion, while twenty-four parliamentarians abstained. The position of the Premier, however, was more vulnerable on this issue than the vote indicated.

The left-wing Socialist parties in the coalition, *Achduth Ha'avoda*

[5] *Maariv*, Tel Aviv, June 10, 1966.

and *Mapam,* in a joint statement before the vote was taken, declared that they had opposed the meeting from the start. However, they did not register their opposition by voting for the motion. The reason was that this time they did not want to cause a crisis in the government in which they were represented. Also, they did not want to appear to be siding with the Communists, whose motives were so evident. Thus, all coalition partners rallied behind the government, with the exception of a member of the National Religious Party whose family had been wiped out and whose feelings against Germany were too strong to consider the issue objectively.

The right-wing *Heruth* Party called the meeting a "historic disgrace," yet abstained, only because of its reluctance to be associated with the Communists. So did the General Zionists. While other parties in the coalition did not make statements in the House, their newspapers scolded the Premier for his declaration in New York that the "Germany of today is not the Germany of yesterday."

Al Hamishmar, the organ of the left-wing Socialist *Mapam,* wrote on March 17, 1960: "What happened did not happen decades ago. It is part of our present time. And the swastika demonstrations which occurred recently show again how senseless every attempt is to forget now, or to make us forget."

The *Ha'aretz,* an influential daily, also, on March 17, expressed its concern about the meeting because Adenauer symbolized the most extreme anti-Soviet attitude within the Western camp: "Is it not to be feared that the Soviets will consider the meeting between Ben-Gurion and Adenauer an anti-Soviet demonstration?" After all, Israel could not afford to allow its connections with Russia to deteriorate even more.

But while the country still worried about the meeting as such, Ben-Gurion had other reasons for concern. He and his friends had been quite sure after the meeting that the loan of $500,000,000 was already "in their pockets." Ben-Gurion had actually told his aides when he came out of Adenauer's suite that the German Chancellor had agreed to the suggested sum. Whereupon a heated discussion arose among the Israeli delegation on whether one should publish what they assumed to be an established fact to pin the Germans down. But it was decided that it would be unfair to do so, as such publication should have been agreed upon with the Germans. As a test, one of Ben-Gurion's aides let the news out in London. Adenauer's spokesman denied it outright from Tokyo, where Adenauer had gone after his visit to the States. Those who had felt apprehension from the beginning that a verbal agreement was an insufficient guarantee were right.

It was now difficult to know what would become of "the agreement"; whether, in fact, one existed at all. Analyzing the German Chancellor's reaction to Ben-Gurion's request, the Israelis had every reason to believe in it. It is, of course, impossible to say whether Adenauer was so much overcome by the occasion that he might have agreed to practically anything. Or, indeed, whether he was sure—as the Israelis assumed—that his word was good enough to convince his government of the necessity of such a loan, though this was not binding. He may well have overlooked that, with his agreement, he had ignored the *Bundestag,* which normally votes on every contribution to a foreign country that goes over $35,700,000 per annum, and so legalizes it. (The original sum of $250,000,000 for ten years, as it had been worked out by the experts of both sides, had surely been arrived at to avoid such complication of procedure.) It is also possible that his aides, especially his Foreign Minister, reproached him afterwards for his generosity and for not taking into account the Arab reaction, and that he was persuaded to keep the agreement strictly secret. It hardly can be assumed that Adenauer agreed to Ben-Gurion's request to make sure of a good reception and a good press in America for himself. Ben-Gurion, recently asked why he had not insisted on a written agreement, replied, "I had such faith in him (Adenauer)." [6]

When Ben-Gurion and his aides asked, in their correspondence with Adenauer and the German authorities, for a written agreement on the $500,000,000 loan, the Germans did not comply. Dr. Felix Shinnar recalled in his book [7] that Adenauer and Ben-Gurion exchanged a number of letters on this question. From this correspondence it became clear that Adenauer was still ready to give money, though under the strictest secrecy. As the two elder statesmen had talked to each other without aides or experts they had not touched any of the practical points of the agreement. There had been, for example, no mention of when the payments were to start.

Dr. Adenauer believed that this had to be on the date of the expiration of the Luxembourg Treaty, March 31, 1966. The Israelis wanted the loan to start at the earliest possible date. Adenauer asked Dr. Abs, to whom he gave a more detailed report of the meeting, to

[6] Conversation with the writer, Haifa, August 7, 1968.
[7] Felix E. Shinnar, *Bericht eines Beauftragten,* p. 99, Rainer Wunderlich Verlag, Tübingen, 1967.

examine the possibilities of fulfilling his promise. The recollection of Minister of Economic Affairs, Professor Ludwig Erhard, is that he had met "at least twice" with his counterpart, Finance Minister Levi Eshkol, "on neutral ground" (Brussels) to discuss with him how best the agreement of a loan to the amount of $500,000,000 could be made to work. He convinced Eshkol that a new, formal treaty similar to the Luxembourg one with fixed annual installments could not be "attractive" to either side. Such treaties only created more possibilities for blackmail, Erhard said, pointing out that the Arabs were bound to demand with all means at their disposal similar sums of money and so would make it more difficult for the Germans to help Israel to any greater extent. According to German sources, one of the Arab ambassadors to Bonn informed the German government that they knew of the agreement, yet were ready to refrain from protesting if it remained strictly secret.[8] The result of the meeting in New York was then turned into what Erhard called "a gentleman's agreement" discussed in various letters between the heads of governments; an agreement, incidentally, which Professor Erhard honored as a matter of course when he became Chancellor in October, 1963.

In this first meeting with Eshkol, Erhard made his proposal that each "installment" should be earmarked for a certain project. The Israelis should suggest what seemed to them worthy of financial support. The Germans would then consider and make their decision. The annual payments should not exceed $35,700,000. Ben-Gurion, in a letter to Adenauer on September 27, 1960, advanced his pet idea— that this money be given exclusively for the development of the Negev, just as from the start he had wanted the Germans to have a share in the cultivation of the desert.

Erhard recalled [9] that the projects suggested by the Israelis were immediately accepted without any closer investigation. "It all worked to perfection," he said. However, each one of the annual loans afforded a special agreement. Each of the Ministries concerned (Foreign Office, Ministry of Economic Affairs, Ministry of Finance, Ministry of Economic Cooperation) was to give its sanction each time until the money was actually paid in by the German Bank for Reconstruction to the Industrial Development Bank of Israel, so the procedure was long-winded. In general, 70 percent of the money

[8] Rolf Vogel, *Deutschlands Weg nach Israel*, p. 136, Seewald Verlag, Stuttgart, 1967.

[9] Conversation with the writer, July 11, 1968.

became earmarked for projects of infrastructure, 30 percent for Israel's industrial development. The terms of repayment and all other conditions differed according to the project. On the average, Israel had to pay 3.6 percent interest per annum, and the time for repayment was to be twelve years in cases of industrial projects and twenty years for those of infrastructure; excellent conditions considering German foreign aid agreements of that time.

The negotiations and the procedure turned out to be so complicated that it took twenty-one months after the historic meeting had taken place in the Waldorf-Astoria before Germany made its first payment. Yet, Ben-Gurion had not lost faith, even as time passed. He was quite sure he had made no mistake in assessing the man he had arranged to meet. Exactly one year after his meeting with Adenauer he was asked by a reporter from Israel's biggest newspaper, *Maariv,* to recall his feelings when he went to see Adenauer. Ben-Gurion replied, "I felt that I went to a meeting which might turn out to be a blessing for Israel. To this day, I have no reason to assume that I made a mistake."

7

The Eichmann Abduction

"Who is Adolf Eichmann?"

This was the question on millions of Germans' lips on the evening of May 23, 1960, after the arrest of Adolf Eichmann had been announced on the evening newscast. It followed the announcement of Prime Minister David Ben-Gurion before the *Knesset* in Jerusalem that Adolf Eichmann had been caught and was in jail in Israel.[1] Who, then, was Adolf Eichmann? With a sound instinct, a considerable number of Germans sensed that it was wiser, perhaps, not to formulate the question. At first, an uneasy silence prevailed.

How many Germans, indeed, could have known the name, the special functions of Adolf Eichmann? Even among his victims— those who had been seized by anonymous SS men and brutally driven into the gas chambers—only a small number would have known the answer.[2] Those who had survived the holocaust and those who had watched from abroad, unable to prevent the mass

---

[1] Ben-Gurion: "I want to inform the *Knesset* that one of the greatest Nazi criminals, Adolf Eichmann, who, together with other Nazi leaders, cooperated in the "Final Solution" of the Jewish question—that means in the annihilation of six million European Jews—has been discovered by Israel's Secret Service. He is already under arrest in Israel and will soon be put on trial in Israel."

[2] Simon Wiesenthal, famous in Europe for his efforts to trace Nazi criminals, and himself a former concentration camp inmate, in *Yet the Murderers Are Living:* ". . . He asked whether I had heard of Adolf Eichmann. I replied that Hungarian Jews in concentration camp Mauthausen had spoken of him. To me, the name meant nothing."

slaughter, would find that Adolf Eichmann had been one of the chief executioners of the "Final Solution" of the Jewish question.[3]

The ordinary German, even if he had wanted to (and which might have been a suicidal undertaking), would not have succeeded in delving into the secret police activities of the Nazi regime. Least of all would he have traced the names of those in charge of organized murder. The fact that, immediately after the war, when Jewish circles took up the hunt for those responsible for the murder of millions of their kin, it took a great deal of cunning and many months to obtain a single photograph of Adolf Eichmann—proof that these "desk murderers" (as they are called in Germany today) successfully managed to remain in the dark, only too aware of the dirty business in which they had been involved.

Adolf Eichmann . . . his name and his function had been mentioned several times in Germany, in connection with the murder of the Jews in the Nuremberg trials of 1946.[4] But this had occurred at a time when the German people were interested in almost anything but becoming involved in a trial, much less in this one. Their country in ruins, their own fate and that of their families often uncertain, they worried mainly about being fed, clad and housed and could not have cared less that somehow they, too, were on trial in Nuremberg. If they had anything to say about the past, it was an expression of hatred the majority claimed, for those who had misled them. Adolf Eichmann's name and the charges raised against him, therefore, passed practically unnoticed by the general public in Germany.

In later years, when German orderliness had superseded the immediate postwar chaos and efficient bureaucratic machinery had been reestablished, a section of the German people began to call for punishment of those who had committed these noxious crimes under Nazi rule. Publications abroad—and subsequently in Germany—depicting the horrors did not permit the Germans to "bypass" this period as many would have preferred. In West Germany, the press, the priests and justice (called by a French writer, "the specialists for the German conscience") took up this cry and repeated it with

[3] Eichmann's connection with the "Final Solution" had been known abroad since 1942. It is said to have reached American circles, via neutral countries, in 1942.

[4] Justice Robert H. Jackson, American Chief Prosecutor at the Nuremberg trials, July 26, 1946: "Adolf Eichmann, this shady figure who was connected with the annihilation program, estimated that the anti-Jewish actions caused the killing of six million Jews . . ." Quoted in Robert W. Kempner, *Eichmann und Komplizen*, p. 20, Europa Verlag, Stuttgart, Zürich, Wien, 1961.

varying success. The Germans believed they had "paid," even over-paid, for the Nazis' crimes with their own fate. Others felt that, not having been personally involved in the murders, the issue did not concern them much. They still rejected the thought that they, too, could be called upon to bear a share of guilt because they either had been a member of a Nazi formation or had remained silent.

A direct confrontation with the Jewish people, who might have functioned as constant accusers, did not take place in Germany. The few Jews who had returned to that country by then also did not want to be reminded of the past—in their case, because of their suffering. Otherwise, they might have been unable to live in Germany. Moreover, they lived apart from German society, which was as much their own doing as it was that of the Germans, who were instinctively afraid of their right to challenge them. The contact between the state of Israel and West Germany was still too much confined to certain German groups, or to those who had belonged to the "other Germany" and who, therefore, could make little impact on the German mind.

One exception was when the *Diary of a Young Girl* by Anne Frank was published and brought home the suffering of individuals. Something of compassion was awakened in Germany. But concern was for Anne Frank, the child, as the personification of innocence, and not the genocide of which Anne Frank's fate was but a mere symbol. Fortunately for the Germans, the picture of the crimes faded fast, perhaps because up to the Eichmann trial they had not known their entire ghastliness. They might have had the opportunity to learn from the occasional trials of Nazi criminals—but they did not listen, in their obvious effort to resist the truth. The figures of the victims were too abstract to agitate them, and, wherever Germans admitted wrongdoing, most of them brushed it off impatiently, saying this surely would be dealt with, but at the same time, disavowing personal responsibility.

One who was relentless in the search for Nazi criminals was Dr. Fritz Bauer, the Attorney General of Hesse province. He was a Jew but, unlike other Jews who had returned to Germany after the war, he had become a politically conscious fighter for democracy and more specifically for the advancement of Social Democracy. The hunt for Adolf Eichmann was in his hands. Shortly after his death in Israel in July, 1968, it was disclosed that Bauer had, in fact, decisively shared in the discovery of the Nazi criminal. In 1958, he had informed Dr. Felix Shinnar of Eichmann's whereabouts in a Latin-American country, obviously apprehensive about the possibility of Eichmann escaping justice. Experience had taught him that Latin-American countries were most reluctant to extradite Nazi criminals wanted in Germany, so two days after this talk with Bauer, Dr. Shinnar traveled to Israel to convey the attorney's message. This was the beginning of the discovery and the eventual abduction of Adolf Eichmann to bring him to trial in Jerusalem.

Originally, the case against Eichmann was to be brought to justice in Vienna. On January 26, 1956, on request of Bonn's Minister of Justice, it was transferred to Germany on the grounds that German courts were already dealing with Eichmann's accomplices, former members of the *Reichssicherheitshauptamt Berlin,* so the entire complex should be coordinated. The Federal prosecution assigned the Eichmann investigations to the Frankfurt County Court. Once the investigations had started it did not take the Germans long to conclude that Eichmann might be responsible for thousands of murders and that there was need to issue an arrest warrant against him. This was done on November 24, 1956, by a Frankfurt court.[5] At this time, it seemed that Eichmann was in hiding.

Arab states in particular, with their hatred for Israel, as well as Latin-American countries with semi-Fascist governments, proved excellent hiding places for Nazi criminals. Not only did they give them sanctuary, well aware of their true identity, but they also gave them work and protected them against extradition to Germany. In some cases, no treaty with Germany existed, and often care was taken to see that none was drawn up. For instance, in Ghana, a concentration camp doctor, Horst Schumann, suspected of thousands of murders, lived under the Nkrumah regime, unmolested for many years, despite constant appeals of the German government. Sometimes the explanation was that extradition did not apply, according to their legal system. The likelihood that Eichmann would be found and put on trial seemed very remote, indeed.

Several months before Eichmann was captured (October, 1959), a news item that Eichmann was hiding in a Near East country caused excitement in Israel, mainly because it was feared that he, warned of being hunted, might now flee to another hiding place. Tuvia Friedmann, of the Institute for the Research of Nazi Crimes in Haifa,

[5] Information obtained from Frankfurt prosecution, November 24, 1967.

claimed that this bit of news came from Erwin Schuele, the chief of the office for the investigation of Nazi crimes in Ludwigsburg, Germany.[6]

Following this information, which turned out to have been entirely wrong—perhaps "planted" to make Eichmann feel safe in his hideout—Hesse's Attorney General announced that his office would renew its efforts to trace Eichmann. He stated that it seemed fairly certain now that Eichmann was an influential intermediary between German concerns and Kuweit as a member of the staff of the Sheik of Kuweit. Bauer added that, once the exact whereabouts were known, he would request the Bonn Ministries concerned to demand the extradition of Eichmann from Kuweit immediately.[7] The Federal Minister of Justice, Dr. Fritz Schaeffer, assured the *Bundestag* [8] one month after the announcement of Eichmann's capture—in reply to the question of the Social Democratic parliamentarian, Dr. Karl Mommer—that West German authorities had not known that Eichmann was hiding in the Argentine. According to rumors, the Federal German government had believed Eichmann to be in one of the Near East countries.

No wonder, then, that the name, "Adolf Eichmann," or the announcement that a certain Adolf Eichmann had fallen into the hands of Israeli justice meant nothing in Germany. However, the fact, that it was a German name made people feel uneasy. And, while the Germans still pondered, the world grasped the extraordinary contents of this news. The German reaction, once the news with all its implications had sunk in, was more instinctive than rational. The majority rejected the kidnapping. With a closed mind, they did not discuss the man, the crimes or the guilt. They concentrated on the act of kidnapping that gave them grounds for objections—generally not with malice but mainly in defense of their own actions and attitudes during that era.

Opinion polls [9] revealed this clearly. To be fair, however, it must be said that many Germans feared that by their approval of this case of kidnapping they would also have to sanction the abductions that had taken place in West Berlin in the years when the

[6] *Stuttgarter Zeitung,* October 13, 1959.
[7] *Stuttgarter Zeitung,* December 24, 1959.
[8] 118th Session, June 22, 1960.
[9] Elisabeth and Peter Noelle-Neumann, *The Germans, public opinion polls, 1947-1966,* p. 193, Verlag für Demoskopie, Allensbach, 1967.

East-West conflict had been hot in Germany. In any case, 48 percent of all men tested and 54 percent of all women declared this abduction of Eichmann unpermissible; 20 percent of all men and 22 percent of all women tested believed Eichmann's abduction had been an act of justice.

The reply of 32 percent of the men and 24 percent of the women that they had no opinion on this question of whether or not it had been right to kidnap Eichmann in order to bring him to justice discloses that, in reality, the number of Germans opposing the kidnapping was far greater than the 50 percent who expressed their opposition. Some of this was due to typical German uncommunicativeness and some to active fear of this trial, of this man Eichmann who could put before the entire world once again the facts about the crimes that Germans had committed and now would like to forget.

Official circles shared the fears of the people. Neither a statement nor a declaration was issued by the German government on the "abduction" of Eichmann and there is no doubt that this was deliberate. The German government did not feel free in this case to express its mind. With the legalistic approach to things (which is part of the German character), it could not have approved of the abduction. However, to denounce or to criticize it might have been misinterpreted abroad. Individual statements were made; for example, by Dr. Eugen Gerstenmaier, president of the *Bundestag*, who, having been involved in the abortive anti-Hitler *Putsch* of July 20, 1944, was above suspicion as far as his own past was concerned. Interviewed by the American Broadcasting Company (ABC),[10] he said: "Nobody can expect me to express pleasure at the manner in which he was caught. On the other hand, I by no means regret that Eichmann was captured and will be put on trial. . . ."

The German press, which so often differed from what is called public opinion in Germany, sided with the Israelis. What they generally expressed was that, from the legal point of view, the arrest of Eichmann was, plainly speaking, kidnapping and nothing but that, yet in view of this exceptional case the sympathy was with the kidnappers rather than with their victim.

The German Chancellor, Dr. Konrad Adenauer, with an excellent instinct for his people's feelings (the secret of his popularity), showed that he was equally worried over the consequences of an

[10] Bulletin of the *Bundesregierung*, April 8, 1961.

Eichmann trial when he said: ". . . The Eichmann trial worries me
—not the trial as such. . . . I have complete faith in Israel's administration of justice. But I am worried because of the repercussions it
will have and the judgment of the Germans, generally. . . ." [11] Dr.
Gerstenmaier, also expressed the fear that the trial would turn out to
be a heavy blow for German prestige abroad.

Clutching at another straw, the Germans joined in the international discussion as to whether or not Eichmann should be tried by
an Israeli court. Once they grew accustomed to the idea that Eichmann had been caught and would have to be tried, the wish to protect their own interests made many object to an Israeli court. Again,
not because they did not believe in the fairness of Israeli judges but
because any reference to the German people's guilt in this trial was
going to be noted by the entire world. The objection of a man like
Chief of Council Telford Taylor, the American representative for
prosecution of war criminals in the Nuremberg trials, to Eichmann's
being tried in Israel ("because he is no Israeli citizen nor was Israel
the place where he committed the crimes") [12] coincided with the
views of those who denied the Israelis the right to bring that man to
justice.

Only sixteen of one hundred Germans saw no harm in Eichmann
being tried in Israel; yet, the majority that was against Eichmann
being tried by an Israeli court was not united in pleading for an international or a German court to deal with Eichmann's crimes.
Those twenty-eight out of one hundred who suggested a German
court were, in all probability, either the more radical or the people
with the least scruples. They chose to disregard the embarrassment
that a German court might suffer at the evidence spread before it,
or they cared nothing about the world's reaction to a trial in Germany. But thirty out of one hundred thought that only an international court would be justifiable, basing their considerations on the
ground that an internationally composed court would certainly be
less biased against Germany than an Israeli one, if only for the international ties that linked the free world to the Federal Republic of
Germany. Again, a relatively substantial number of those questioned
—namely, twenty-four out of one hundred—expressed no opinion at
all on this matter which, this time, might not be a camouflage of

[11] Before the press in Bonn, March 10, 1961.
[12] *The New York Times Magazine,* January 22, 1961.

their feelings but a true inability to decide what would be more advantageous for Germany. Only two percent—obviously diehard Nazis—objected to Eichmann being put on trial at all.[13]

The question that remained unsolved till Eichmann's death was whether or not he was to be considered a German citizen; therefore, the obligation of the state to protect his legal rights became an advantage to the German authorities.[14] Eichmann had been born in Solingen, Germany, but in his early youth his father had moved to Austria where he had lived until he took over his functions in the Gestapo headquarters of Berlin. It was quite possible that his family had remained German citizens despite their move to Austria, or he might have become a German citizen after the *Anschluss* of Austria in 1938. This citizenship he would have lost again with the restoration of a separate Austrian state in 1945, had he not taken on an assumed identity by then. In addition to these doubts, there was no extradition treaty between Israel and Germany, which made it easy for the German authorities to decide that they would not and could not apply for Eichmann's extradition.[15]

Dr. Adenauer solved the issue in his own way. Questioned on his feelings with regard to the Eichmann controversy on NBC's "Meet the Press" on April 16, 1961, he made a clean sweep of the matter, saying: "Eichmann is no German citizen and we have no obligations toward Eichmann."

There was a German minority, however, that judged the situation differently. Attorney General Fritz Bauer believed that, although an application for the extradition of Eichmann to Germany surely would have been refused by the Israelis, the Federal German government should have applied for it as a demonstration to the world that it was ready to make every effort to deal with the problems of the past.[16] It is said that even in Israel legal circles there was surprise that Bonn did not request Eichmann's extradition, as Germany seemed the only country with some legal right to the man.

Bonn's Foreign Office left no doubt that it saw no benefit in such action and took none. Quite obviously, the German government felt it would not improve matters for itself if it set out to haggle with

[13] Elisabeth and Peter Noelle-Neumann, *Jahrbuch der öffentlichen Meinung, 1958-1964*, p. 225, Verlag für Demoskopie, Allensbach und Bonn.

[14] Foreign Office, Bonn, September 26, 1967.

[15] Foreign Office, Bonn, May 24, 1960. *United Press International.*

[16] *Stuttgarter Zeitung*, May 28, 1960.

Israel, of all countries, over this mass killer. Before Cologne's Administrative Court, with similar vehemence and with similar arguments, the German government's legal representative, Hans Freiherr von Gagern, rejected the claim of Eichmann's lawyer, Dr. Robert Servatius, that the German government had to grant legal aid to Eichmann. Servatius lost his case for reimbursement, which he intended to carry to the highest stage, the Federal Administrative Court in Berlin, even after Eichmann had been executed, but he had to give up for lack of money.

On the eve of the trial in April, 1961, Chancellor Adenauer once again became the "father figure" of the German nation, a role that had been greatly responsible for his election as postwar leader of the German people. He addressed the Germans several times and gave them to understand that the forthcoming trial might bring them into conflict, might hurt them, might treat them unjustly; that it would "stir up again all the horrors" of the Hitler era, and that it would be only natural for well-meaning people to recoil from the atrocities. At the same time, somewhat imploringly, he turned to the world and reminded it that there was not only a young German generation that had had nothing whatever to do with the crimes, who would soon be appalled, but also that there had been quite a number of Germans who had suffered under the Nazi regime. And again, in his typically simplistic manner, he said:

. . . One should not forget that here, in Germany, National Socialist Germans committed the same crimes against Germans as Eichmann had against Jews . . . most of the Germans readily helped Jewish citizens wherever this was possible, and it would be unjust to condemn all Germans. . . .[17]

It is futile to discuss whether or not Dr. Adenauer truly believed what he said. For although Germans—predominantly Social Democrats and Communists, though in no comparable number to the Jews —had suffered in concentration camps, there is certainly no analogy between the German plight and the Eichmann crimes with the institution of the superbly organized machine of murder for the Jews built up in Auschwitz. Nor could anyone uphold that "most of the Germans" had gladly been ready to help Jewish citizens although it would have been right to say that there had been some ready to do so, and to do so at the risk of their lives. But Dr. Adenauer never forgot his role and his political purpose which was to remain in

[17] Before the press in Bonn, March 10, 1961.

power and to do this by pleasing the people. And what could be more pleasing to the Germans than to hear that they were not as bad as the world made them appear to be?

The Social Democrats were infected by this. After all, general elections were ahead in Germany in the autumn of 1961. The clever election strategist, Herbert Wehner, the party's Vice-Chairman, advised Social Democratic editors and journalists (much to the disgust of a number of them) to refrain as much as possible from commenting on Eichmann and his trial. He did so, obviously, to avoid offending sections of the population whose votes he was after, like any other politician. Wehner, a militant Communist until World War II, was known to be free of any Nazi tendencies.

Adenauer also appealed to the Israelis, utilizing the German mass media. He told them that he had not only complete confidence in the manner in which they would handle the trial, but also in their objectivity, in their code of justice. Yet, he felt the need to remind the Israelis of what Germany had done for them. West Germany, he said, had always been generous towards Israel as far as finances were concerned and added "good will must be mutual." It was an obvious attempt on his part to counteract any hint during the trial that Eichmann might be identified with postwar Germany (particularly since the Adenauer government had not refrained from employing former Nazi officials in its administrations), and thus destroy all the German Chancellor's efforts to regain the world's confidence in his people.

Adenauer also appealed to his "friend," Ben-Gurion, and said before the press in Bonn on March 10, 1961:

I should like to mention my excellent contacts with Ben-Gurion, also. And if Mr. Ben-Gurion honors the Chancellor of this country with his friendship . . . then, please consider this as another proof of a very generous character. But, also consider it as a judgment of the German people as a whole.

Rumors persisted in Germany that Adenauer had begged Ben-Gurion to see to it that Eichmann would not be compelled by the Israeli court to say anything about the role of Adenauer's Secretary of State, Dr. Hans Globke, who had been Ministerial Councillor in Hitler's Ministry of the Interior, in which capacity he had written one of the four commentaries on the Nuremberg Racial Laws of 1935.

According to the chief of the delegation sent by the German government to the trial to observe it and to report from there, no such instructions were given by Foreign Minister Heinrich von Brentano.[18] Baron Gerhard von Preuschen, a lawyer in Wiesbaden, had been selected, and, with regard to his past, was above reproach. He had been connected with the abortive July, 1944, anti-Hitler *Putsch*.

Actually, the German government had not easily made a choice of the person to send to Israel, for it was obvious that he would not merely be an observer at the trial, in the strictest sense of the word. He would be, after all, the first German official delegate to be sent to Israel since the birth of the two states, and, inevitably, he would be invited, if only indirectly, to political talks with the leaders of the state of Israel. Therefore, he had to be able to diplomatically present the German case of the inability to establish diplomatic ties to Israel in order to maintain relations with the Arabs. As a close friend of Foreign Minister Heinrich von Brentano (at whose suggestion von Preuschen had been chosen), his authority seemed assured. At the same time, the German government made it clear that, with this choice of a man who was neither a politician nor a diplomat, it had no intention of "supervising" the legal proceedings of the Jerusalem court, nor could the selection be interpreted as the German government's consent to the abduction.

Baron von Preuschen himself termed this mission "most tricky." [19] He was to create friendship and understanding but he was not to go too far in his promises with reference to the future relations between the two countries. A delegation of officials and technical staff from the press and Information Ministry, as well as from the Foreign Office, accompanied Baron von Preuschen to look after the big contingent of German journalists during the trial and to make sure of proficient contact between Jerusalem and Bonn. The delegation was given every kind of protection against possible assaults and enjoyed diplomatic status in the sense that they could avail themselves of diplomatic facilities when they were in need of them.

The nearer the date of the trial came, the more realistic the Germans became. They realized that the trial was no bad dream but reality and they had to face up to it. This, and the qualms that the

---

18 Conversation with the writer, 1967.
19 *Ibid.*

crimes caused some Germans, came through in statements on the eve of the trial.

"I expect the Eichmann trial to deliver a heavy blow to the German reputation throughout the world, and anticipate that in Germany it will bring back to our conscience the old, burning question: how could this have happened?" the president of the *Bundestag*, Dr. Eugen Gerstenmaier, said.[20] And, as if to prepare his country for what was ahead, Professor Heuss, President of the Federal Republic, said, "The Germans must never forget what was done by some of their fellow citizens." [21] A commentary in a German weekly [22] described the atmosphere on the eve of the Eichmann trial adequately: ". . . The Germany of today is already scared to the bone at the prospect of all the dirt that will be churned up again. We have to swallow this great bitterness like men, and as befits Germans who are no cowards."

[20] American Broadcasting Company, published in bulletin of the Bundesregierung, April 4, 1961.

[21] *Westfälische Rundschau*, April 9, 1961.

[22] *Die Zeit*, March 16, 1961. Reprinted in *The New York Times*, April 4, 1961.

8
The Incomprehensible Trial

On April 11, 1961, the eyes of the whole world were on the bulletproof glass cage in Jerusalem's *Beth Ha'am* (People's House). Yet, for most of the world, when Adolf Eichmann, the former head of the "Jewish Department" of the *Reichssicherheitshauptamt* (Head Office for Reich Security of the SS, the RSHA), was led into it, this ended a startling episode which had begun with the daring abduction and transportation of Eichmann from the Argentine to Israel. The rest—the trial and the verdict—would have their sensational aspects, no doubt. This would be a chronicle of horror for all who wanted to listen, but it would not affect most nations to any greater extent than had the facts of Nazi persecution and torture methods revealed to the world after the war. It was bound to be different with the Jews, of whom six million had been murdered, and the Germans, the nation linked with that crime.

Until the day Adolf Eichmann appeared in the glass cage to be tried by Jewish judges as "Criminal Case No. 40-61" in the District Court of Jerusalem, the average Israeli had not quite grasped what was ahead of him in emotional strains and stresses. The fact that Jews had managed to capture the man whose name had become synonymous with the execution of the Nazi crimes had elated them perhaps as much as a war won.

Professor Heuss, who had been in Israel at the time, reviewed the situation in his book, "To say that it attracted attention is too weak an expression. It was a sensation—an explosive one." [1]

It was one of those events that gave the Jewish people the feeling of nationhood, of having overcome two thousand years of exile and the complexes that life as an often unwanted minority among other nations had instilled in them. That Jewish judges should impose the verdict added to their elation and their pride. Doubts as to the justification of abducting Eichmann, or of trying him in Israel—questions being raised then by practically the whole world—did not make the slightest impact on them.

Prime Minister Ben-Gurion explained to the world at large why he thought it absolutely necessary to try Adolf Eichmann in Jerusalem. And, no doubt he expressed the conviction of every Jew that no court in the world was more entitled to uncover the full historical truth about the mass murders than an Israeli one. Furthermore, this trial could serve an educational purpose. It could demonstrate to the world what might be the consequences if a people, any people, succumbed to the rule of a totalitarian regime. It also seemed to Ben-Gurion that it was the psychological moment to remind the world of the crimes against the Jewish people, for numerous Germans, in the pay of antagonistic Arab states, were known to be participants in a plan for the extinction of Israel. But, most important of all, the youth of Israel, the new generation, should learn the full extent of the crimes, if only to establish the right insight into their parents' past, for their own as well as for history's sake.

As a matter of fact, the young people of Israel often had asked their elders how such a thing had been possible. Judging from their own new world and the spirit with which it was imbued, the young Jews could not understand why their parents had accepted their fate lying down, and had allowed the Germans to massacre their people without fighting against it. Their judgement about the past and about the generation preceding them had come about from what they could read. For very few of the survivors were ready to talk at length or in detail about what they had suffered; to explain why they had allowed the Germans to lead them like sheep to the slaughter, or had failed to pass judgment on their former leaders in the *Diaspora* who had fallen short of encouraging them to fight for their lives, to any greater extent. What had been terrible reality for

---

[1] Theodor Heuss, *Staat und Volk im Werden*, p. 71, Ner Tamid Verlag, Munich, 1960.

their parents was abstract history to the young. The trial was to
bring to life what happened to a degree that, up to now, had not
been possible.

While the younger generation may have looked at the glass cage
at first with curiosity, the older generations from Europe viewed it
with fright. With Adolf Eichmann suddenly before them, flesh and
blood, the past came to life too vividly. In the recital of the horrors,
the cases of cruelty, they experienced all over again the fear, the
pains, the immeasurable suffering. Pictures of Auschwitz, Treblinka
and Sobibor vividly returned to mind, where, in the healing of time,
they had lain dormant. They again suffered the agonies caused by
the losses of their families, their parents, their relatives.

But Adolf Eichmann was also the catalyst that the Israelis needed
for confrontation with Germany and the German people. They
were forced to relate not to Eichmann alone, but also to the country that continued to exist in Europe and play an ever increasing
role there and to its people. "We must beware of any kind of racial
theory," Israel's Prime Minister warned in this connection. "There is
no doubt that before the Nazis came to power there was another
Germany. And there is another Germany *after* the Nazis . . ." [2]

The young Israelis might never have thought about Germany,
postwar or prewar. Due to reluctance on both sides to encourage
trips to Israel, they hardly had had a chance to meet a German unless they had sought the contact, and few had done so up to then.
For the older Jews from Poland, Hungary or Czechoslovakia, this
void was welcome. They had known the Germans as persecutors,
only; they had never known them in a different guise. Consequently, their judgment seemed inexorable. But to the Jews from
the Orient, all that had happened to Jewry in Europe was unreal,
and they were not too concerned about the trial, Germany or the
Germans.

Former German Jews suffered perhaps more than Jews of other
origin, from the pragmatic point of view. Once practically the most
assimilated of Jewry scattered all over the world—often more conservative and nationalistic than many Germans—for them, the man
in the glass cage not only brought back their sufferings and the shattering of a world that they had believed they had shared with equal
rights, but it also produced some kind of humiliation for the colossal
mistake they had made in their trust of Germans.

This man in the glass cage, now appearing servile and rather cow-

---

[2] *Allgemeine Sonntagszeitung*, April 16, 1961.

ardly, once had been master over life and death of millions of Jews. It seemed unreal, untrue—impossible that this small figure with the face of a middleclass bourgeois, with the demeanor of an accountant of limited intelligence, had organized the annihilation of human beings with a dedicated passion. The indictment charging him with the worst of crimes against humanity seemed to bear no relation to this man with the bird-like head and the twitching mouth. Yet, it was a fact that Eichmann had been in command of the "Jewish Department"—"IV B 4" it had been called in the language of bureaucracy—which had planned and executed the annihilation of European Jewry. He had been zealous, industrious and eager, as he might have been in any other post. Whenever he had encountered difficulties which seemed to delay the "Final Solution," he had done all in his power, despite all odds, to get the trains moving to the death camps of Auschwitz, Maidanek, Treblinka, Belzec and Sobibor. If his henchmen had trouble with the machinery of murder, he had seen to it that it was "oiled" to assure smooth execution of his calculations and orders. His powers seemed in no way to tally with his appearance.

But Adolf Eichmann was more than a mass murderer on trial. He was a symbol of Nazism, the evil that had managed to corrupt almost an entire nation, to degrade it and to make it capable of wholesale murder. He became a symbol of the type of person on whom Nazism could rely; ready to go the whole way, without scruples, even to mass murder. How it had been possible for Nazism to incite people to commit such crimes against humanity would not be solved by the Eichmann trial, nor was that its purpose. Eichmann, as the personification of the German who had been dough to mold into a ready murderer in the hands of Nazism, was, in fact, what the trial laid bare, more or less by accident.

It did it in an unexpected and unusual manner. It was the horrifying language, the inhuman use of words with which Adolf Eichmann tried to defend himself against what the indictment bill called "crimes against the Jewish people, crimes against humanity, and war crimes" that depicted the degree of dehumanization which had taken place in Germany under Nazism. Eichmann spoke a jargon, *the* jargon of the Nazi Reich to perfection, despite the fact that he had lived "in exile" for so many years. The words that came out of his mouth were just dead letters, instruments manufactured from his activities as a murderer of humanity, devoid of human feelings and aspirations.

"Administrative language is my only language," Adolf Eichmann replied when the Court's chairman, himself a native of Germany, failed to understand his way of expressing himself. Joachim Schwelien, reporting from Jerusalem for the well-known German daily, *Frankfurter Allgemeine Zeitung*, called Eichmann's language a "jargon of violence" [3]—a language which every totalitarian state created to camouflage and cover up and give a directive to something that would otherwise be meaningless or, in the case of the Nazis, to hide their acts of murder. The "Final Solution," which actually meant the plain murder of European Jewry, is such a case in point; or, "action," which was the camouflage expression of the Nazis for the rounding up of the Jews for deportation. Adolf Eichmann still spoke this language when he found himself in that glass cage, expressive of what he was—a man without respect for other men: ". . . I had orders. Whether they were to be killed, or not, they had to be carried out. It (the gunning of a transport) had been dealt with by administrative means. I had very little to do with it. . . ." What counted for Eichmann was "order" and "obedience."

"My guilt is obedience", he said, and it was clear that he actually did not repent of this "obedience" which for him, seemed to be the basis of life, and the basis of a state. His lament was, "my position is similar to that of millions of others who were forced to obey. The only difference is that I had much more difficult orders to execute." To prove his "humanity," he said: "By no means did I order about the Jewish functionaries. Cooperation was fair and correct on both sides." A "cooperation," enforced by him or other Nazis, which was to bring death to six million Jews as speedily as possible. The Israeli public listened to it and was puzzled. It seemed too incredible for words that men of Adolf Eichmann's ilk could have grown to such power among the Germans—once a nation that had produced humanitarians, thinkers and poets—and could have gained the upper hand, only to have helped to bring the German nation to ruin.

The trial brought a great number of German journalists to Israel. Almost all of the important German papers were represented in Jerusalem. Of course, even before the trial Germans had traveled in Israel, though in small numbers, and more or less unobtrusively; avoiding, if possible, an argument with Israelis unless they themselves had suffered at the hands of the Nazis. At the Eichmann trial, German journalists could not avoid the limelight, and could not resist defending their country and their countrymen, in spite of the

[3] *Von Gestern zum Morgen, zeitge Schriftenreihe*, vol. 14, p. 5, Ner Tamid Verlag, Frankfurt, 1961.

difficult task of having to listen to the testimonies of horror and report them in a manner that would make an impact on the Germans.

Albert Wucher, in the *Sueddeutsche Zeitung*, May 25, 1961,
reported from meetings and conversations in Jerusalem: ". . . I
anticipated that it would be a difficult mission, but I did not realize
how difficult. . . ." If the prophecies had proved right, there would
have been reservation and hostility towards Germans. Instead, there
was emphatic friendliness and constant readiness to help: ". . . Yet
I realized from the first minute that the magnanimity of the hosts
could be no certification that the problems between Jews and Germans were solved . . . How could they be—only sixteen years
after? . . . ."

The writer added that the majority of the Israelis who demonstrated their readiness to help and offered their friendship admitted
later how much they had been afraid of this encounter with Germans. And not only those forced to speak to Germans for reasons of
hospitality or duty, but others, also: "They spoke to the Germans,
predominantly with Germans, as if under some mysterious spell.
. . . Perhaps there was that mysterious compulsion which leads the
criminal back to the scene of the crime; that union through a common fate of victim and persecutor."

Wucher reported a conversation with a young student who had
served as a telephone operator in the course of the trial:

You don't know what this trial means to us . . . I don't sleep any more,
I am completely finished. For me, the Germans are a nation of murderers.
They have executed the 'Final Solution.' I have never heard anything
else. I know only people who suffered in Germany, whose parents, sisters and brothers and relatives have been murdered by Germans . . .
And now you come here to Israel . . . we speak to each other, and
sometimes we even laugh together. The German reporters are no different from the other foreigners; perhaps they are bit more conventional,
more formal, more quiet. We find them likable. And they are also Germans? You will understand . . . I am quite confused now . . .

All conversations, Wucher reported, led to the same question:
how had it been possible? How could it happen that a people so
fond of music and animals, so diligent, so efficient, so zealous, so
correct, could have committed one of the worst crimes in the history of the human race or, at least, could have permitted such things
to happen? And the more direct question was: "Are you, who appear likable to me, also able, under certain conditions, to persecute

and to murder?" Often I was told: "We do not say Eichmann is Germany; also, not all Germans are Eichmanns. But we ask, is Eichmann typically German; is not something of Eichmann inherent in all Germans? . . . is evil slumbering only because of the economic prosperity? Or, can a nation that has committed such crimes against humanity regain its integrity that very instant when it changes its constitution?" These were questions that, at the first encounters between Germans and Israelis, could not be answered. And most certainly not on occasions when emotions ran high.

Albert Wucher and his colleagues were touched, moved and upset by the trial. It is reflected in their reports from Jerusalem. And they reached their public. It was as if, for the first time, the Germans began to realize what and how the Jews had had to suffer at the hands of their countrymen. For the first time, they listened attentively to the tales of woe. Shortly after the war, when the Nuremberg trials or those dealing with the crimes committed in some of the concentration camps had taken place, the Germans had been too preoccupied with their own fate and with the problems that beset them right after the war, to listen. There was, also, an inner resistance against the accusation of guilt for the crimes, for the war, for Hitler.

Dr. Ernst Wilm, member of the Council of the Protestant churches, explained this at the time of the Eichmann trial:

. . . We did not want to see the horrors which came to light. To those who said anything about it, we replied that this was not true, that it was enemy propaganda. . . . In Nuremberg, the victors simply called the vanquished guilty, to force us to our knees. Or, when we could no more deny it, we explained that one did not talk about such things. . . .[4]

Meanwhile, the Germans, with remarkable zeal, had rebuilt their country, had acquired wealth and stability and had become respected members of international bodies. Perhaps now they were ready to listen: now that they no longer could avoid the facts. With the whole world watching—watching the man in his bulletproof cage and them—no longer was there any excuse for evading the issue. Of course, there was fear of a possible collective charge of the German nation at the trial, and a certain curiosity as to how the Jews would deal with the situation.

A German opinion poll disclosed that 26 percent of a representa-

[4] *Kirche und Mann*, April, 1961.

tive number of Germans read every single dispatch that was written about the trial from Jerusalem.[5] Considering that the hearing of the trial, in which the awful details were revealed, lasted from April 11 till August 14, 1961—with 114 sessions and, consequently, 114 reports—this figure indicates considerable interest. Every second or third report, or just haphazard reading of one or the other, was reported by 48 percent. That 22 percent of the people admitted not reading a single report could be misleading, considering the great number of people who watched the television broadcasts from Jerusalem, called, "A Period on Trial." These TV features, which did not spare the Germans the shocking details, were beamed out at a popular time, immediately after the 8 p.m. newscast. An analysis [6] showed that, on the average, about 50 percent of the general television audience watched and listened to these reports; even 60 percent to the first four reports from the trial.

It would be difficult to name any other event that had caught the interest of the Germans in a comparable manner and had held it for that length of time. It was, of course, extremely difficult to assess their reaction at first; the Germans were as if paralyzed by the revelation of what they had not wanted to admit for so long.

A more detailed analysis showed that the main viewers of the trial coverage on television were the fifteen to thirty-four year-old Germans who had not experienced the Third Reich. They wanted to learn, they said, about the "unbelievable happenings"; "to see how the trial was conducted"; and "to watch the reaction among the people in Israel and in the whole world." They said, "We know so little about it, and it is so important for us young people to hear as much as possible about it."

The interest among those whose ages ranged between forty-five and sixty-four—those who had been very much involved at that time when Eichmann and his men were "at work"—was almost as high. Asked why they showed this particular interest in the Jerusalem trial, they said they welcomed the opportunity "to see the period in a different light" from the way it had presented itself to them before (which, however, does not necessarily indicate an immediate readiness for a change of mind).

The least interest was registered among those over sixty-five years

---

[5] Elisabeth and Peter Noelle-Neumann, *Jahrbuch der öffentlichen Meinung, 1958-1964*, p. 226, Verlag für Demoskopie, Allensbach, 1965.
[6] Compiled by Infratest G.m.b.H., Munich.

of age who had spent the best part of their lives in the era of the Third Reich. They just wanted to forget. They explained to questioners that they felt they "could not burden themselves with all this again." Taking all age groups, 11 percent resented the reports from Jerusalem, saying that, in their opinion, television not only overdid its reporting from the trial but also had seized the opportunity to introduce Israel to German viewers.[7]

The German papers repeatedly published excerpts of letters written by their readers to the editor. A former sergeant major in the *Luftwaffe* wrote to *Die Welt:*

I just had to write this to you. I can't help it! I must say aloud what I felt and feel when I read your reports on the Eichmann trial. I feel ashamed, and nothing but wild, uncontrollable shame. I am ashamed because I am a German and was once compelled to wear that uniform. An incredible accident of fate saved me from joining the commandos who were ordered to commit such atrocities. Horrified, I ask myself, again and again, What I would have done if I had been ordered to perpetrate such crimes. Would I have had enough character or humaneness to swing my weapon around and shoot those who dragged children from their mothers and simply gunned them down? Would I have shown the same evilness of character to fire on wounded women and children who, with great effort and pain, had worked their way out of a mountain of corpses? My God! It is terrible! I just don't know. I cannot say. . . .[8]

Readers of the tabloid paper, *Bildzeitung*, with its three to four million circulation also expressed their feelings in letters to the editor:

. . . That they take so much trouble over this beast! . . .
I hope Israel passes the death sentence on the mass murderer Eichmann. . . .
Our youth will learn from this trial the meaning of a dictatorship. . . .
Your Eichmann trial reports should be posted at each board. . . .
There is too much talk about Eichmann. He should be hanged. . . .
Today, it is easy to be moved! . . .
I myself have rejected an order by Himmler to shoot a whole village for partisan warfare. Each dictatorship would be finished if it would not find so many assistants. . . .[9]

[7] Compiled by Infratest G.m.b.H., Munich.
[8] *Die Welt*, May 17, 1961.
[9] Hans Lamm, *Der Eichmann-Prozess in der deutschen offentlichen Meinung, eine Dokumentensammlung*, Ner Tamid Verlag, Frankfurt, 1961.

Foreign journalists described their impressions of the German people's reactions, too.

An elderly man, perhaps sixty, and obviously the worse for too much beer, stood in one of Bonn's bus stations and shouted to the long queue: "And you want to be Germans. This Eichmann, he killed six million Jews and you dare to smile!" Some people laughed at the man. Others paid no attention.

Three soldiers in a jeep . . . what did they think about it? One said: "No punishment can be made to fit his crime. We Germans are ashamed of ourselves." Another said: "Orders are orders." The third: "I have not thought about it much."

When a film on the life of Eichmann—including the first showing of pictures taken of mass executions of Jews in Eastern Europe by SS extermination squads—was over, a German woman was crying. "I did not know, how could I know?" she said, over and over again.[10]

It is difficult to say how many Germans echoed these sentiments. But it is perfectly correct to say that the feeling of despair and shame was widespread in Germany in the first weeks of the Eichmann trial. It was honest and genuine. Similarly, when the Anne Frank story had broken several years before, a wave of compassion had swept over Germany concerning the suffering of an adolescent girl who had been able to articulate her pains of persecution. This girl's words had caught the imagination of the people. She had done more to elicit sympathy for the mental suffering of those hunted than the figure of six million murdered had been able to conjure up. Now, at the Eichmann trial, some of those who had suffered the physical pains of inconceivable crimes spoke up—although overcome by the memory of what they themselves had gone through or witnessed—in words often primitive and inadequate. The crimes no longer remained unreal. They came to life, they acquired voice, they could be identified with persons; they could not be swept aside as something too dreadful to be true. There remained, of course, what may be called a "lunatic fringe" who continued to say that the only thing Hitler had done wrong was to lose the war and prevent the completion of the "Final Solution." And there were those who may not have dared to speak their true feeling, having been a cog in the machinery of murder themselves, and now were afraid of being mentioned in Jerusalem through some misfortune.

But the general impression remained that the majority of Germans

10 *The New York Times, International Edition,* Monday, April 17, 1961.

did not stay unmoved by what could be learned from Jerusalem; not necessarily that the German people were ready to accept any guilt or responsibility. In answer to the question of whether or not they felt guilty of having a share in the annihilation of the Jews, 88 percent said "no." And 50 percent said they read the reports because of "general interest," not because Germans had committed these crimes. Only 27 percent were ready to admit any feeling of national responsibility.[11]

Again, to admit guilt is certainly not easy for the majority of any people and this applies more in this case, considering the enormity of the crime. So it is doubtful whether the figures do give a correct picture.

But, as the trial progressed, most Germans recovered from their first shock. They did not question the trial, or the witnesses' stories; they found another means to "protect" themselves. They began to identify the crimes with the man in the dock in Jerusalem. For them, Eichmann became the personification of the crimes; the man who, with his accomplices, had planned and executed them all. They separated themselves from him. He and his coterie had lived aloof, away from them; had been different; murderers in somebody's name but most certainly not in theirs. Eichmann was Eichmann, was Himmler, was, perhaps, also Bormann, but certainly not Germany—not the Germans.

In a way, they did what Eichmann had done when he denied any guilt of murder, yet admitted having been responsible for the victims' transportation to the camps. In the same measure, the Germans could not deny the existence of Hitler, yet they refused to admit any knowledge of his crimes. Once the Germans had found a scapegoat which had no resemblance to any one of them, they were themselves again. Having reached that stage, it was not difficult to look into the eyes of the Jews—with pity, perhaps, for what they had suffered, but with no change of attitude.

At the time of the Eichmann trial the Divo-Institute in Frankfurt [12] put the following question to a representative number of Germans: "Would you have any reservations if Jews should occupy government posts?" Of those asked, 18 percent had "strong reservations" against such ideas, 23 percent just recorded their "reservations" which added up to 41 percent of the German population objecting to Jews taking an active part in the running of their state.

[11] Elisabeth and Peter Noelle-Neumann, *The Germans, public opinion polls, 1947-1966*, p. 187, Verlag für Demoskopie, Allensbach, 1966.
[12] Published August, 1961.

Moreover, 26 percent failed to answer at all, indicating that at least half of them, if not more, did not dare to speak their mind on the matter. The very same people, also questioned on Eichmann, confirmed the impact of the Eichmann trial on Germans, for 59 percent were convinced of Eichmann's guilt and responsibility for the murder of the six million Jews, but only 12 percent spoke out in positive terms.

Premier David Ben-Gurion, to a great extent responsible for the holding of the Eichmann trial in Jerusalem, at the end of the hearing in August, 1961, said that all the crimes of the Germans which the trial had laid bare could not change his mind: "My views about present-day Germany are unchanged. There is no Nazi Germany any more." [13]

No doubt, Ben-Gurion was sincere when he spoke these words. By then he had met Dr. Adenauer for whom he had developed a great deal of respect, even liking. He was, therefore, convinced that this man, Adenauer, had built up a different Germany, different from the one under Hitler. But, surely he did not speak in this vein simply to please the Germans. Such a pronouncement on the part of the Israeli leader was, of course, gratifying to the Germans who were fully aware of the usefulness of it for their world image, but his words would also set the trend for his own people's feelings at this moment.

The trial was not yet over. But what was still to come—the pleas of the defense and the general attorney and the verdict—would not upset the people as much as the hearing had done. For some, it had been a psychological relief that everything had been uncovered. For others, it had created a hell and caused them to live the abominations all over again. To the young, it had, indeed, shown the vast and expert machinery of murder set up by a ruthless dictatorship from which escape was immensely difficult, if not impossible for great numbers of people. Undoubtedly, the hearing had stirred up emotions and feelings in Israel, though this may not have been evident at first glance.

Ben-Gurion's words surely were aimed at preventing a new hatred of Germans and Germany. Ever since he and his government had accepted restitution from the Germans, at the time of need, the policy towards Germany had been cooperation with a country that had assumed a role again in international politics, a country that it

[13] Bulletin of the Federal Government, No. 162, August 31, 1961, reprinted from the *Deutsche Zeitung und Wirtschaftzeitung*.

would be unwise to ignore with Israel in need of friends in its precarious situation. It had not been easy to get the Israeli public to accept this course; many Jews have not done so to this day. The Eichmann trial was not to disturb this strategy.

When Ben-Gurion spoke these words he may have wanted to make sure that nothing would endanger his policy. From his point of view, it was the opportune moment; the Israeli public had not yet fully recovered from shock and had not yet been able to define its individual approach to Germany after learning, in detail, the crimes that had been committed by Germans. But, more there was the chance that Ben-Gurion's words would sink, as if into a vacuum.

9
Eichmann's Death— Germany's Resurrection

The people did not care two hoots about Eichmann, the man; the sooner dead, the better. This was the attitude of the majority of Germans after the hearing of the Jerusalem trial ended on August 14, 1961. And this view was shared not only by those who themselves had been cogs in the machinery of murder and were afraid that, by a stroke of bad luck they, too, might be mentioned in the trial, but even by those who, conscience stricken, claimed the crimes were, without exception, Eichmann's responsibility. With Eichmann at the gallows, a chapter—an unpleasant one for many—would be closed and the more quickly they could forget what they had heard.

Soon after the start of the trial in April, 1961, and after the first crimes had been bared, opinion polls tested the Germans as to what measure of punishment they would believe adequate for Adolf Eichmann, the executioner of Hitler's policy. The death sentence was demanded by 35 percent of those persons questioned. Another 31 percent expressed themselves in favor of the "highest possible sentence," adding that "usually" they were opposed to capital punishment; which could well mean that, in the Eichmann case, this principle did not apply. There is no doubt that this feeling that Eichmann should die persisted throughout the hearing. Only 15 percent called for leniency on the part of the court, making allowances for the fact that Eichmann had acted in accordance with the spirit of his time, while 13 percent were undecided—or claimed to have no opinion on Eichmann—and 4 percent said they had not heard of the trial at all.[1] That Eichmann would be sentenced to death seemed fairly certain to the Germans after all that had been heard in the course of the trial.

However, the resumption of the trial of Adolf Eichmann on December 11, 1961, did not attract much attention in Germany. Only a few German national papers sent their reporters to Jerusalem this time, a tip-off that the forthcoming verdict would be no great matter of interest to their German readers. However, this might be attributed to the fact that another severe Berlin crisis[2] understandably diverted the attention of the Germans.

The Attorney General actually requested the death sentence and on December 15, 1961, the court found Eichmann guilty on all points of the indictment bill. He was sentenced to death. Nobody in Germany expressed any surprise; nobody disputed it. It was argued that another verdict would have refuted the verdicts of Nuremberg. Israeli judges had no reason to do so. And the Germans were aware of the difficulties that would have arisen, had Eichmann been given a life sentence or a limited prison sentence. Where could he have served it; where would his life have been safe?

On December 16, before the international press, in Bonn, the government spokesman, Secretary of State Felix von Eckardt, explained that the trial had proven Eichmann guilty of millions of murders and that the review proceedings before the Court of Appeal, Israel's Supreme Court, could not change the judgment. The Christian Democratic politician, Chairman of the Parliamentary Legal Affairs Commission Matthias Hoogen, remarked that no one in Germany who, throughout the years of injustice, had preserved a healthy and conscientious belief in guilt and atonement would consider the Jerusalem verdict unfair. All Germans were convinced that anywhere else in the world where law and justice prevailed the same verdict would have been the outcome.[3] Even the strongest opponents of the death sentence would consider this verdict fair, the Free Democratic Party commented, adding that even the execution of Eichmann did not compensate for all crimes committed by Himmler and his men against the Jews.

Despite the Berlin crisis, German papers then dealt at length with the verdict. The *Sueddeutsche Zeitung* wrote that the death penalty

[1] Elisabeth and Peter Noelle-Neumann, *The Germans, public opinion polls, 1947-1966*, p. 193, Verlag für Demoskopie, Allensbach, 1965.
[2] The temporary Autobahn crisis.
[3] *Deutschland-Union-Dienst*, December 16, 1961.

never had been so justified; whether or not Eichmann actually would hang was irrelevant. The *Stuttgarter Zeitung* described the sentence as a valid verdict against the man, but not an atonement for the crimes. Eichmann knew that he had sent people to their deaths and thus his responsibility, legal and moral, was just as great as that of men who, with their own hands, had led the victims into the gas chambers. The *Frankfurter Allgemeine Zeitung* believed that actually there was no adequate punishment for Eichmann. *Die Welt*, on December 16, said it sounded like irony of history that the Jerusalem verdict tallied with present sentiments of justice in Germany.

Then, no doubt provoked by a discussion in Israel, suddenly some Germans had second thoughts on whether or not it was right to hang Adolf Eichmann. The Germans, like those Israelis who had campaigned against the execution, did not revise their attitude as to the justice of the verdict, but, somewhat gladly, they, too, began to doubt the wisdom of executing Eichmann. Two reasons may be offered for their action. They remembered that during the Hitler era the life of a human being had been of little consequence. The death sentence had been passed and executed without much concern. They felt as if they, too, sanctioned this attitude when they now called for Eichmann's death. But even more significantly, perhaps, many Germans felt in their heart of hearts that they, too, were guilty; less guilty than Eichmann, of course, yet guilty by having offered little or no resistance to these murders.

Arguments could be heard, like ". . . Eichmann has died several deaths since his arrest . . ." or: "He lived like a hunted deer those many years after the war." Some also spoke of a "generosity" on the part of the Jewish people that would prove true greatness if they spared Eichmann. Others even believed that commutation of the death sentence would help to do away with anti-Semitism in the world.

The German press took up the discussion (which incidentally did not take place in the less sophisticated echelons) with varying arguments.[4] The *Koelner Stadtanzeiger* commented that it was almost easier to pass judgment on Eichmann than, actually, to lead him to his death. The penny paper, *Abendpost*, wrote that the death sentence, even in the case of Eichmann, was a step backwards. The *Stuttgarter Zeitung* expressed the fear that Eichmann's death might lead to the wrong conclusion that, with his hanging, the crimes had

[4] March 22, 1962.

been atoned for. The hanging of a mere subordinate bureaucrat of the annihilation might minimize the Jewish suffering. *Die Welt* suggested, in view of the discussion in Israel on this issue, that the Federal Republic, as an example of courageous and ethical restitution, should take Eichmann and keep him in a German jail until the end of his days. This would free Israel from a great headache.

But the fact was that the number of people in Israel who opposed the hanging of Eichmann was comparatively small. The controversy attracted attention throughout the world as it was led by the reputed philosopher, Martin Buber. Reasoning was based solely on ethical viewpoints. But even in this discussion on the execution of the death sentence, Adolf Eichmann, the man, was of no interest to the Germans.

Eichmann's comment on the verdict to Police Colonel Leo Koppel, responsible for Eichmann's safety, was reported in the *Bildzeitung:* "I am stunned. I never expected this. In twenty months of imprisonment, I had thought of many things. I felt morally guilty for many things, but I never thought that I should be called guilty on all points."

Yet, what Eichmann said, in all seriousness, had absolutely no impact on the Germans and did not, in any way, influence the discussion. The story published (not sympathetically but ironically) in the penny paper *Der Mittag* of Duesseldorf that Mrs. Eichmann was heading for a breakdown, not knowing what was to become of her and her four children, did not impress people much. Even die-hard Nazis seemed to have lost patience with Eichmann. Those who had spoken up in favor of him at the beginning and in the course of the trial had nothing more to say about this man who had shown so little courage during the trial and who had not even stood up for his convictions. To this day, the Neo-Nazis in Germany never mention Eichmann although they frequently refer to other Nazi leaders.

Eventually, the review proceedings passed. On May 29, 1962, the Supreme Court confirmed the verdict pronounced by the Jerusalem court. The President of Israel also rejected mercy on May 30. On June 1, 1962, a few minutes after midnight, Adolf Eichmann, fifty-six years old, guilty of millions of cases of murder, was executed. In Germany the consensus was that he had deserved his lot. The *Bonner Rundschau* wrote, "There can be little doubt that Eichmann's verdict was justified." *Frankfurter Abendpost:* "Eichmann, and this was proven by his trial, was a murderer." *Westfaelische Rundschau:* "That Eichmann did not find mercy is understandable in view of the enormity of his crimes against the Jews." *Rheinische Post:* "Eichmann deserved it (the death)."

With similar emphasis, German papers pointed out that Eichmann had died without showing the slightest remorse. The *Rheinische Post,* June 3, 1962, reported: "Not a word of compassion came from his thin lips; no feeling of repentance was discernible in him . . . Thus he died as he had lived, cold, without emotions; an administrator of death, and he has left us with the repentance and shame." [5]

"Eichmann is dead. Will his name be forgotten?" This question was voiced in Israel, in Germany, in all circles that had taken a deep interest in the Jerusalem proceedings.

There can be no doubt that the Eichmann trial had made an enormous impact on the Germans. For the first time, they had taken the trouble to learn more about the Nazi crimes. And they did not doubt for one minute that what they had learned from the trial was correct. The trial and the court had impressed them; more so since their apprehensions had turned out to be unjustified. The abduction of Adolf Eichmann, generally considered illegal in Germany, though not necessarily condemned, had roused fears that the trial would be one of vengeance; that the Jewish judges, in an understandable fury at seeing before them the man responsible for the murder of millions of their brethren, would not adhere to the common code of justice.

"You will notice that the methods of the Gestapo are not applied here. If you don't want to reply, you do not need to." This admonition addressed to Eichmann by one of the judges could be taken as a description of the conduct of the trial, one of the German reporters wrote. "It (the trial) has the atmosphere of a seminar dealing with legal questions." [6] The fact that two years had passed from Eichmann's arrest to the day of his condemnation proved, *Sueddeutsche Zeitung* wrote, that he had not fallen into the hands of revenging furies who would make short work of him. He had had a fair trial and ample opportunity to defend himself. Israeli justice had proven to be no different from justice in democratic countries. *Koelner Stadtanzeiger* commented that, after all, it did not really matter where genocide was put on trial as long as this was done in conformity with international justice.

The Germans became angry when Eichmann's defense attorney,

[5] June 3, 1962.
[6] *Sieben Sagen Aus* (Seven Testimonies), edited by Dr. Dov B. Schmorak, p. viii, Arani Verlag, Berlin, 1962.

Dr. Robert Servatius, called the Jerusalem trial a mock trial. Much to the disgust of some three hundred listeners in the Catholic Academy in Munich, he had said shortly before the verdict. "Nobody knows what political murder actually is; and not those in Jerusalem." He offended the Germans even more when he said that every German could have found himself in Eichmann's situation.[7] In general, they disliked the man who had so eagerly offered to present Eichmann's case before the Israeli court. Although they realized that any mass murderer had the right to be defended in court, they assumed that the volunteer from Cologne had only his own publicity in mind as there was no financial benefit to be derived. The Eichmann family had no financial means worth speaking of. Servatius was the assigned counsel paid for by the state of Israel.

Long before the start of the trial, there had been apprehension in Germany that, along with Adolf Eichmann, postwar Germany and the Germans would be in the dock. After all, the postwar West German state had not chased former Nazis out of their posts. Though none of the actual murderers had been placed in high positions knowingly, now, helping to build up a democratic Germany, were those to whom the term "accomplices in the persecution of the Jews" could be applied.

At the end of the trial, there was a sigh of relief that it had not done harm to Germany's standing in the world. The court and the judges were highly praised: their conduct of the trial, it was said in Germany, had avoided unnecessary polemics to the detriment of postwar Germany. Matthias Hoogen expressed the opinion that the reason the German name had not suffered because of the Eichmann trial, to a great extent, was due to the perfect trial procedure to which the court adhered.[8]

As the conduct of the trial had been watched in Germany with great respect, the Germans were much more prepared to accept what had been said in Jerusalem. The conscience of most Germans had been awakened for the first time since the Hitler era had ended. They could no longer plead ignorance. The fact that German justice appeared to hunt down the Nazi criminals with new vigor may be called one reaction to the trial of Jerusalem. Another was the law passed by the *Bundestag* in the course of the hearing in Jerusalem in June, 1961. It called for prosecutors and judges connected with any

---

[7] *Stuttgarter Zeitung,* November 20, 1961.
[8] *Deutschland-Union-Dienst,* May 29, 1962.

of the Nazi verdicts passed during the Hitler regime to quit their services. (According to the German Constitution, judges cannot be dismissed against their will, so the *Bundestag* saw no other way to rid itself of former Nazi judges.)

In the opinion of millions of Germans, and from the technical point of view, Adolf Eichmann had been the most efficient, the most perfect murderer in the history of mass murder. He had become more of a symbol of the carnage than his superiors, Hitler and Himmler, who had actually ordered the crimes but had not executed them. It was a reminder of what Germans used to say during those dark years in Germany—that surely the Führer would not approve of the crimes if he knew of them. But many people could not deny that they had helped to vote Hitler into power. To accept Eichmann's crimes as part of Hitler's policy would have made them feel somehow guilty. Eichmann's crimes, in the eyes of most Germans, were of a criminal rather than a political nature.

So, it may be doubted that the Eichmann trial helped to sharpen the Germans' instincts for dangers which might once again threaten their state from dictatorships or from parties of a totalitarian character. The division of Germany, the isolated position of Berlin, the expulsion of Germans from the territories behind the Oder-Neisse Line, the destruction of their cities—all this was hardly ascribed to Hitler and his men any more. They blamed the Russians for most of the aftermath of the war. Considering this, Eichmann did not appeal to them to be identical with the Nazis—at least to the older generations.

However, apart from those who had opposed Hitler all along, others may have recognized their mistakes in the course of time. But they had hardly turned out to be active exponents of democracy. Disappointed and disgruntled, they would not participate in its life; they would rather devote their energies to their one, impressive achievement after the war that had left their country in shambles— the amassment of wealth. Others, under the embarrassment of the Eichmann trial revelations, may have admitted their guilt if only to salve their consciences. But they would neither make a contribution to democratic life, nor help to strengthen the new system considerably, except, perhaps, by casting a vote every four years to elect a new Parliament.

It would be hard to find a separation as great as the one between the generations in postwar Germany. For the German youth, the Eichmann trial was of great significance. The trial had given them, in detail, what they had often vainly asked to hear from both their parents and their teachers. Most of the older people, guilty or not guilty, had been reluctant to tell them about the past—for reasons of their own or because it was all so very difficult to explain. The Jerusalem trial had carried details about the past into every home. The truth about the older generation, about their own parents, may have been hard for the young to stomach, but now they knew the truth. The question of how it was possible for the older generation to turn a blind eye to Eichmann's crimes remained on their lips—unanswered. Nevertheless, the trial was a milestone in their education, although it may have increased the gap between the generations, may have caused this new generation to turn away in disgust from the many self-satisfied and self-righteous Germans of the postwar decades believing in nothing but money. It may have been one of the contributing causes of the revolt of youth in the later years.

The Eichmann trial had yet another effect. Through it the Germans discovered Israel; Israel, not as a refuge for the Jews persecuted throughout the centuries in many parts of the world, but as a country like any other: a state which had developed its own structure, its own institutions, its own characteristics. And the German reporters deserve credit for this revelation. Israel and Germany could not ignore each other in a world which, thanks to technical inventions, had grown smaller and had made its members more dependent on one another. The two governments had long recognized this, although the people had remained averse to admitting it. The Israeli people were not ready to meet the murderers and their accomplices; the Germans were afraid, rightly or wrongly, of being charged with the crimes of the past.

The Eichmann trial had changed this a good deal. It had forced the Israelis to take a stand towards postwar Germany. At the end of the trial, it was one of reluctant curiosity. The reaction of the Germans to the trial, the German journalists' behavior at the trial and, finally, the testimony of Propst Heinrich Grueber had impressed them. Grueber had suffered at the hands of the Nazis for his courageous aid to Jews during those years of persecution. He had taken the German anti-Nazi element, which most Israelis had not known or had not wanted to know, to Jerusalem. Now the Israelis doubted whether their sweeping statements on Germany were justified. However, their reactions did not go beyond doubts.

It was different with the Germans. For the older ones, who believed that with Eichmann's death all their sins had died away, it was suddenly much easier to talk about Israel, to put it on the map of their world. Inhibitions disappeared. Israel, the state of the Jews, became a topic of conversation in German society. It was easy to face the Israelis, easier than to face the Jewish people in Germany with whom one had to live side by side. Israel was far away. One could admire it without hesitation. It became the fashion to admire it, to be stunned by its achievements and to permit, even to urge the rising generation to visit it. But, the young people went there for different reasons. They wanted to learn something of the spirit that was inherent in this state of the Jews that had made its people victorious against their enemies, although far outnumbered and which had enabled them to capture Adolf Eichmann in his secluded retreat, while engaged in their own search for ideals, for an ideology worth striving for.

It may sound very strange, indeed, but the Eichmann trial did a good deal towards the *rapprochement* of Germans and Israelis.

10
Unofficial Relations Begin

Advertisements appeared in German newspapers at the end of 1961 inviting Germans to travel to Israel, "the land of the Bible." El Al Israel Airlines, promised the German tourist "traditional Oriental hospitality." Its business managers shrewdly estimated that there was a reservoir of likely customers to be tapped. Until then, there had been an understandable reluctance on the part of the Germans to travel to Israel. In Israel, the unwillingness to receive Germans was just as great. Therefore, El Al's invitation to German tourists was hotly debated. Fear grew that Germans, any Germans, might swamp the country, just as if it were Italy or Spain.

Most travelers from Germany, up to that time, had been persons with a blameless past and an anti-Hitler record. Nevertheless, even Germans in this category were advised by the Israeli authorities to travel under an assumed name—and this as recently as the mid-fifties. There was still reason to fear for their security.

One of the very first German guests to travel in disguise on a government invitation was Professor Franz Böhm who had helped to conclude the Luxembourg Treaty. And, as "Julius Bermann," (a Belgian Jew) Erich Lüth, the initiator of the "We beg Israel for peace" movement, was invited to Israel in spring, 1953 [1] (as he put it), to discuss the proposal of some Israeli officials to "take first

---

[1] Erich Lüth, *Viel Steine lagen am Weg*, p. 279, Marion v. Schröder Verlag, Hamburg, 1966.

steps to a normalization of relations with the Federal Republic."
Shortly before his departure, he was asked to postpone it because
there had been serious incidents in Israel in opposition to the ratification of the Luxembourg Treaty. He finally made it a secret expe-
dition.

As a matter of fact, so tight a rein was kept on visitors that when,
in 1954, two young German girls from an anti-Fascist family ven-
tured a tour of Israel on their own, the authorities begged them to
leave (which, incidentally, they did not do, expressing their confidence that they would be perfectly safe.)

The attitude of the Israeli citizens towards Germans changed considerably after the Sinai campaign in 1956 when Bonn continued restitution payments in face of Arab threats and impending economic
sanctions of the United Nations against Israel. This meant that German politicians now could travel to Israel on government invitation
without hiding their faces. Erich Ollenhauer, Chairman of the Social
Democratic Party, traveled to Israel with a small delegation in April,
1957. He was the first German to address an Israeli audience at a
public rally. Mayor Willy Brandt of West Berlin visited Israel in
November, 1960, as president of the *Deutscher Städtetag* (German
Towns) conference, to attend the Congress of the International
Union of Local Authorities (IULA). Invitations to German states-
men included one to State President Professor Theodor Heuss in
May, 1960, who lectured in German at the Hebrew University of
Jerusalem, as did the leading Social Democratic politician, Professor
Carlo Schmid. The first German politician to travel to Israel when
still in office was the president of the *Bundestag*, Dr. Eugen Gersten-
maier, in 1962. These guests had been carefully chosen.

Gradually, Germans curious to know more about Israel undertook
the trip; first hesitatingly, then more frequently. In 1955, Israel had
497 visitors with German passports, 1,516 in 1958 and 4,450 in
1960.[2] These figures included Jews of German nationality, for about
23,000 were living in the Federal Republic then.

To prevent entry of "undesirable" Germans in tourist disguise,
visas were issued only if proof could be furnished—with the help of
de-Nazification papers or similar documentation—that they had not
been active Nazis. This regulation was by no means foolproof.
Three million refugees from East Germany, who could hardly produce any documents at all, let alone such documents, had come to

---

[2] Figures from the Israeli Consulate in Bad Godesberg.

live in West Germany. Nor could this be expected from people who had been driven from Polish-occupied territories at the end of the war and who preferred to let the past remain a personal secret. Above all, this procedure, to which every German was subjected, was not exactly in line with the spirit of the El Al advertisement. To inquire about a person's past scarcely seems "traditional Oriental hospitality." But El Al was obviously motivated in its efforts to increase its numbers of passengers by the fact that, by now, German tourists were welcome the world over. Due to the "economic miracle," they had hard currency to spend. And, after having been confined for so long in Hitler's Germany, they were eager to see the world.

A great deal of German interest in Israel had been stimulated during the Eichmann trial when, for the first time, the German public had had more than a glimpse of that country. German journalists, there to cover the trial, "discovered" Israel, the beauty of its landscape and its people. Practically every paper in Germany at the time published, along with the Eichmann trial news, reports and articles about every phase of life in Israel. Yet, the ordinary German's reluctance to go there for a holiday persisted. A German student of theology expressed it in a letter to *Die Welt*, in December, 1961: "One cannot just go there with German money and German song. One has to be accompanied by one's conscience . . . whoever does not want to bear this burden must remain at home." Of course, he said, one could tour Israel, passing from one hotel to the next, just spending the wanted foreign currency. But, then, one must expect to be despised.

Following El Al's inducements in 1962, the German share of Israel's tourist trade was a mere 3.6 percent. In 1963, it rose to 5 percent and maintained its upward spiral in the years to come—7,650 German travelers in 1963 and 12,921 in 1965.[3] At all times, the majority of travelers were young people. *They* were not plagued by the past.

The first group of pupils and their teachers set out from Munich for Israel in 1957. After a three-weeks' trip they were welcomed home by the mayor, which indicates that they were considered pioneers in their field. This first visit started a youth exchange program (which had been discussed in 1950) by the leaders of the two countries' youth hostel associations. But there had been unwilling-

[3] Figures from the Israeli Consulate in Bad Godesberg.

ness on the Israeli part to assume responsibility for young Germans as there were groups in Israel not ready to make a distinction between Germans or, for that matter, between the different generations.

Gradually, the visits of German youth groups became a regular feature. The city of Cologne made it an annual event, starting in 1960. A certain number of pupils of Cologne schools, well prepared by lectures and through the study of background material, traveled to Israel every year. Often the number of applications exceeded that of available accommodations. In 1963, the City Council issued 25,000 copies of a book [4] on Israel—distributed to pupils on leaving school. About the same time, the province of Lower Saxony organized group travels through its semiofficial organization for political education. As early as 1956, some German students visited their Israeli colleagues. This was followed, in 1957, by the founding of a German-Israeli study group (DIS) at the Free University of West Berlin on the initiative of Professor Dr. Hellmut Gollwitzer. Students from practically all West German universities followed the example. In 1961, the Federal Association of German-Israel Study Groups (BDIS) was founded. The purpose of this organization was to spread and obtain information on Israel and as an exchange agency for Israeli and German students. For quite some years—actually until well after the establishment of diplomatic relations—these regular contacts remained unofficial and the Israeli students organization held to reservations concerning German colleagues. German students organized camps and seminars in which young Israelis participated. Discussions often were vivid criticism, not easy for the Germans to stand up to when called upon to account for past and present shortcomings in their country.

In 1958, the *Aktion Sühnezeichen* (Penance Corps Organization) was founded in Germany by Protestant Pastor Kreyssig. The idea was that young Germans would undertake projects of reconstruction in countries where crimes had been committed in the name of Germany. One of their first projects was the completion of an institute for blind people in Israel. The youth groups of political parties, churches, trade unions and sports clubs soon caught the fever, quickly spreading among youngsters, to see Israel.

There were just a few "test groups" in 1959; forty, in 1960; sixty,

---

[4] Johannes Giesberts, *Auf dem Weg nach Israel*, p. 117, Elgad, Ltd., Tel Aviv, 1963.

in 1961; forty-two years later. In all, between 1959 and 1965 more than twenty thousand young Germans became acquainted with the Jewish state.[5] They could have numbered even more, had there been sufficient places for them to stay in Israel. It had become the custom to put the youth groups up in communal settlements (*kibbutzim*), and for them to work there for a time. This was both practical and instructive. Yet, not many *kibbutzim* were ready to accommodate Germans. Even as late as 1964 there were only about twelve *kibbutzim* (of about 230) whose inhabitants were ready to live with Germans, even for a short time. There were, of course, some which, for lack of space, could not take in guests or share work with this sort of unskilled, young labor.

It may be called a bit schizophrenic that these very same *kibbutzim* accepted machines and tools from Germany, stemming from the Luxembourg Treaty, as a kind of effort to make up for the material losses of the Jewish people.

The German government soon realized that their youngsters made a favorable impression. Uninhibited and full of interest in the experiment of a young state, they turned out to be excellent ambassadors, so the government began to support the trips to Israel, financially and otherwise. In 1963, the Federal Youth Plan stipulated that the financial means at its disposal should be used for meetings between Israeli and German youth; that the young people to travel to Israel should be selected; that they should not be under eighteen years of age (preferably above twenty-one); that they should be instructed in seminars and courses about the history of the Jewish people and the state of Israel; that such trips should always be connected with a period of work in a *kibbutz* or a similar institution.

In August, 1963, on German television, Prime Minister Eshkol applauded the fact that so many young Gemans were visiting Israel: "I assume that these young people feel burdened by what their fathers' generation did and that they want to get to know the Jewish people and, the most important work of our generation, the state of Israel."

Yet, there were practically no young Israeli visitors to Germany and just a sprinkling of Israeli students in German universities. In 1958, they numbered 125. Some of them were children of parents who had returned from Israel to live in the country of their birth— which meant that these young people had not gone to Germany of

---

[5] Rolf Vogel, *Deutschlands Weg nach Israel*, p. 117, Seewald Verlag, Stuttgart, 1967. (These figures could not be confirmed by the Israeli Consulate).

their own volition. While the state of Israel encouraged the visits of young Germans to Israel, it did not support visits of their own children to Germany. Obviously, it was more acceptable to receive the German younger generation in Israel than to permit the Israeli younger generation to go to the country in which their relatives had been murdered and where some murderers were still at large. The fact that the Federal Republic had refused, so far, to extend diplomatic relations to Israel increased the disinclination to visit Germany, whose political preference for the Arabs failed to be understood.

However, the economic exchange between Israel and Germany was a mutual affair and began to develop in a manner that is normal between countries.

In the first few years of its existence as a state, Israel certainly had not much to offer in the way of products. Exports to Germany amounted to no more than $18,570 in 1950, one year after the armistice. Due to economic difficulties and the influx of refugees, monetary returns went down even further in 1951 and 1952 (to $9,050 and $6,428, respectively.) Shipments consisted mainly of oranges, which did not need any introduction to the German market. On the other hand, Israel, in need of working places for its incoming population, bought machinery, tools and so forth from Germany worth $4,153,800 and $5,438,570 in Germany in those two years. Israel soon realized that it had to increase its exports to pay for those purchases. The Arab countries, Israel's natural marketplace, refused to trade with Israel. Trade with Europe was therefore essential if Israel wanted to remain competitive in the European market, even though it involved difficult transport and increased costs which could not be applied to Israeli goods.

Trade with Germany took on a character of its own after the Luxembourg Treaty had been concluded. In the first two years of German deliveries, Israel's purchases in Germany naturally dropped to its lowest ever (in 1954 to $1,830,000 and in 1955 to $1,086,000).[6] After all, German deliveries made up 20 to 30 percent of the country's imports. Exports to Germany those two years together exceeded its imports from there for the first time. But then, due to the Luxembourg Treaty, German business concerns automatically obtained a market in Israel. For, Israeli firms were forced to turn for spare parts to those German companies which had delivered the ma-

[6] All figures from the Ministry of Economic Affairs, Bonn.

chinery originally. It was only natural, if a factory had been equipped with German machinery due to the restitution agreement, that it purchase the new consignment from the same source.

Consequently, in 1956, Israeli purchases in West Germany rose again to $8,385,000; in 1957, to $8,734,000. Dr. Shinnar estimated that purchases of spare parts and the like from Germany would amount to $25,000,000 per annum.[7] In both years, Israeli exports to Germany lagged behind imports yet the figures show that the Israelis made an extra effort to pay for their imports with exports.

In 1950, oranges made up one-third of Israel's exports to Germany; in 1951, almost 90 percent. Apart from Israeli citrus fruit, known in Germany from before the war, the introduction of all other Israeli products called for hard work. They were looked at, in the beginning, with a bit of suspicion in Germany, if for nothing else but for the fact that they were goods from a state with a new and inexperienced industry. It is not wrong to say that the first German purchases were made in Israel solely with the feeling of wanting to help the young state to progress and not because its goods were considered of particularly good quality or because of any special interest of German customers. The big German store, Kaufhof, was one of the first to buy Israeli goods in greater quantities. When the first batch of buyers returned from Israel they reported that the products, mainly foodstuffs, were good and up to standard.

In many ways, though, there had to be improvements: exports had to be adapted to European tastes, or the manner of packing had to be made more attractive. Starting in 1960, Israel participated in a number of fairs in West Germany (food, textiles, handicrafts, books, and so forth) to win over a wider section of the German public. In general, the Israeli stalls caused a great deal of interest. People were very curious to see how the new state managed to compete with the experienced countries in the world. In later years, Israel introduced and popularized a number of fruits in Germany, among them the avocado.

In 1961, the Federal Republic was the second biggest customer of Israeli goods, with Great Britain leading. Within ten years, Israel's exports to Germany jumped from $18,570 to $24,113,000.[8]

In 1963, $55,832,000 worth of exports to Germany were reached, though this figure remained unique until the end of 1965. The rea-

[7] *Jedioth Chadashoth*, Tel Aviv, October, 1960.
[8] All figures from the Ministry of Economic Affairs, Bonn.

son for this enormous increase is to be found in Israel's sales to the German army. This included submachine guns (Uzis) and clothing such as shirts, haversacks and coats. The purchases made by the German Defense Ministry, excluding arms and ammunition, although exact figures were not disclosed, were estimated at $2,000,000. And other goods found customers in Germany. While in 1953, 1954 and 1955 Germany had sold foodstuffs to Israel, in 1957, Israel began to supply the German market increasingly with vegetables and fruit other than oranges. Jewelry, cut diamonds and tires came into the picture, too. Israel's efforts were greatly helped by a devaluation of the Israel pound in February, 1961. It is worth noting, for example, that the sale of cut diamonds to Germany rose from $2,754,000 in 1961 to $4,254,000 in 1962; raw cotton (a relatively new venture in Israel) from $49,000 to $500,000, tires from $200,000 to $600,000, and so on. In other words, Israel was now perfectly able to tally its imports with its exports. Bad weather could, of course, influence its crops and, consequently, its exports: that was another reason why Israel was so keen to step up its industrial exports. In this endeavor, and to assure full employment, an experiment—which later fell prey to the regulations of the European Economic Community (EEC)— was made in the field of textiles. West German firms sent cloth to Israel for the manufacture of thirty thousand dresses. This solved the dilemma for German firms with orders on their hands which they could not handle due to lack of manpower.

Purchases in Germany increased in 1963 and continued to rise steadily in the following years. This indicates that the deliveries derived from the Luxembourg Treaty had decreased. Though the treaty extended to 1966, by advance orders for ships, and so on, Israel had practically used up the amount due by 1962. Trade between Israel and West Germany began to take on the same character as other countries' trade relations only then.

But this development was unsettled by the growing activities of the European Economic Community. The imposition of increased import taxes for goods coming in from third countries was to prove a particular burden to Israel whose exports to EEC countries amounted to 30 percent of its total exports. The enormous costs of transport, the refrigerator ships and, in some cases, even air transportation, left Israeli exporters with the smallest possible margin of profit. The EEC taxes were bound to stop the sale of at least some Israeli goods in European member states. This applied to Israeli chickens, eggs and edible oils. In 1961, Israel had sold eggs in Germany to the amount of $1,240,000 and oils worth $1,407,000. In 1962,[9] the sales dropped to $80,000 and $695,000, respectively. At the end of 1962 it was practically impossible to sell eggs from Israel on the German market. Israel was made to feel that, in other fields also, its prices were now 3 to 4 percent too high in comparison to German figures. For example, in 1964, Israel vainly competed for the first time for a deal with the *Bundeswehr*, which had once again invited bidders for the manufacture of the German soldiers' accouterment. It was different with Israeli citrus fruits. Although they, too, had increased in price in EEC member states—tariffs on them having been raised from 10 to 15 and, eventually, to 20 percent—they could still be sold on the German market and this in ever increasing quantities.

In this case, as in others, the quality was what mattered to the German housewife more than the price. Although this was pleasing to the Israeli supplier, just how long the economic miracle in the Federal Republic would allow the German housewife to spend a little more for quality goods was open to doubt.

The Germans, too, were truly concerned about this development. They had often stated that they did not want the European Economic Community to become an exclusive club whose members would be restricted in the choice of countries from which to buy their supplies. Therefore, the support that the Federal Republic gave to Israel's request to achieve some form of contact with the EEC, preferably association (as had been granted to former French colonies), was well defined, although in 1961, German industries, afraid of losing the Arab customers, temporarily exerted pressure successfully on the German government to stop its active support of Israel. It needed representation on the part of the Israeli government to be reassured of German assistance.

The Germans then worked out several plans for putting European-Israel trade relations on a firm basis, finally resulting in a trade treaty which turned out to be most unsatisfactory for Israel. Italy and France were just as earnest in not wanting Israel to have the benefits of the Community—particularly for the citrus fruits—afraid of the competition for their products in this field and mindful of Israel's development plans in this category.

In order to assist Israel economically, Germans and German institutions began to buy Israel state bonds, although the rate of interest

[9] All figures from the Ministry of Economic Affairs, Bonn.

and other benefits were well below what a German investor could obtain in Germany (the rate of interest for Israel state bonds, 4 percent, while comparable German investments started with 6 percent). German municipalities, counties, industries, banks, insurance companies, and so on, had purchased $4,000,000 worth of bonds by 1963. In 1959, the bonds' negotiators had taken up work in Germany, selling, at first, predominantly to Jews; later, to banks and insurance companies, also. In 1960, they approached the *Städtetag* and German mayors to persuade them to subscribe to the bonds. In general, German municipalities do not engage in financial activities of this kind. But, in this case, they made an exception. The *Städtetag* even recommended the state of Israel bonds to their 135 townships and 300 local governments. The fact that quite a few did subscribe must be rated very highly, for towns and municipalities were still engaged in the reconstruction of their bombed cities.

The trade union bank in Frankfurt (*Bank für Gemeinwirtschaft*) started a new venture in 1961 when it bought shares to the amount of $1,300,000 from the Israeli trade union's industrial concern, Koor. It continued to do this more frequently in later years. Another relationship in the financial area was established by the Feuchtwanger Bank in Munich in association with a bank of the same name in Israel, obtaining loans in Germany for Israeli firms and undertakings. It would be unfair not to stress that all these business transactions were made despite the fact that they would give benefit solely to the Israeli recipient.

The German government was no less active in this field. For instance, there was cooperation between West Germany and Israel in development projects in some new states of Africa and Asia where Israel had earned a great deal of credit due to its introduction of excellent practices in keeping with the technical age. Israel, however, lacked the finances to carry out projects to any greater extent. The Germans, often looked upon as "imperialists," or at least friends of the former colonial powers, failed to make such easy contact. In the hope that these new states would not turn Communist, the Germans supported such Israeli activities. There is no reliable information as to the extent of this Israeli-German cooperation.

Nevertheless, it can be assumed that an even closer cooperation was established between Israeli and German scientists in 1958. In a mixed commission, consisting of four German and four Israeli scientists headed by Dr. Wolfgang Gentner, Professor of Nuclear Physics in Heidelberg, joint research projects were undertaken. The

Weizmann Institute in Rechowoth and the Max-Planck-Gesellschaft in the Federal Republic became the centers of this partnership in the fields of physics, nuclear physics and biology, which led Israel's and Germany's enemies to protest, from time to time, that the Germans were helping Israel to develop atom bombs. The West German government subsidized these projects considerably, and from 1960 to 1965 donated about $5,000,000 to the development of the Weizmann Institute and its research projects. The *Volkswagen Stiftung*, a foundation for the sponsoring of scientific research, also chose the Weizmann Institute and Israeli research scholars for donations and scholarships to the value of $925,000 from 1963 to 1965, inclusive. Other academic institutions, like the *Deutsch Akademischer Austauschdienst* (German Academic Exchange Service) or the Friedrich-Ebert Foundation, and so forth, helped with scholarships for Israeli students.

From the German angle, it appeared as if cultural relations between the two nations would develop in a similar vein. In 1960, when youth exchanges and economic contacts became a permanent feature, the first exhibitions of Israeli arts and crafts were shown in West Germany. Since no official cultural ties existed, they were organized by private enterprise. Individual Germans with a flair for art and inspired by the special characteristics of Israeli culture, saw to it that such exhibitions came about. The first exhibition took place in Munich, in July, under the auspices of the Bavarian Chamber of Handicrafts. The Bavarian Prime Minister, Dr. Hans Ehard, spoke at the festive opening ceremony. At the same time, two exhibitions of contemporary paintings from Israel were shown in Marl and Cologne. All three exhibitions roused great interest among the German people, obviously curious to see the new state's development in this special sphere. Such exhibitions were continuously shown in Germany until early 1962.

Since no organization, no treaty and no program appeared to regulate cultural relations, some Israeli artists came to Germany on their own to offer their art to the Germans. With a little moral pressure—which was not difficult to exert—more than a few Germans felt it impossible to refuse a suggestion for an exhibition or for purchases from an Israeli artist. Consequently, some Israeli artists, hardly known in their own country and who did not deserve recognition, were sponsored in Germany. Even German critics did not dare to condemn their artistic qualifications as this was "not done" in the case of a Jew.

Yet, the Israeli public was not ready for a closer view of Germany, which cultural relations would have implied. Economic relations were a necessity; visits of young Germans were pleasing. They showed the new generation's interest in the Jewish people and their state. German arts and crafts, as well as German artists and craftsmen, would have given an insight into Germany, but the Israelis showed no interest.

Above all, German artists had allowed themselves to be used and abused during the Nazi regime. Films like *Jud Suess,* produced on orders of Goebbels, the Nazi Propaganda Minister, starring some of the greatest German actors, and the defamation of Jewish artists, like Elisabeth Bergner, through the Nazis and their German colleagues, were by no means forgotten. The antagonism against German culture reached the peak when performances of works in Israel by composers like Richard Wagner, reputed to have had anti-Semitic leanings, were banned. When the Israeli Philharmonic Orchestra celebrated its twenty-fifth anniversary in December, 1961, with a performance of Beethoven's *Ninth,* the vocal parts were sung in English—a ridiculous decision from the artistic point of view, though necessary from the emotional one.

According to a regulation, the showing of German films was prohibited in Israel unless they were co-productions. Around 1956, German-speaking films from Switzerland and Austria had flooded the country. Following public protests, the regulation came into being. A film censor board, its members appointed by the Ministry of the Interior, watched that this regulation was rigidly observed. This applied to any German film, even those which were critical of Germany and of the Nazis who had managed to return to leading positions in the government. A special government exemption in 1960 allowed a documentary on Israel to be shown in the country. *Paradies und Feurofen,* produced in 1958 by a German team with the permission of the Israeli government and the military establishment, was shown with dialogue in Hebrew. The Israeli government later obtained the English and the French translations—six duplicates each—for their public relations work abroad.[10]

Even German scientific books, which formerly had played an important part in the education and training of scientists the world over, were overshadowed in Israel by those published in English or Russian. Some private contact between the Jerusalem University Li-

[10] Rolf Vogel, *Deutschlands Weg nach Israel,* p. 300, Seewald Verlag, Stuttgart, 1967.

brary and the German publishing houses, the Book Dealers Association, and so on, had existed since 1952 (though on a very small scale) mainly due to personal connections with former German Jews.

The only, cautious attempt to lay a foundation for future cultural relations was undertaken by the setting up of a library of German books in Tel Aviv shortly after the Eichmann trial. It was done almost clandestinely. A former German Jew, Walter Hirsch, presented his thousands of books to this library. The Federal Press Office in Bonn supported it financially and by supplying it with modern German literature. It was frequented a great deal by German-speaking Jews who were able to overcome their prejudices, simply because they still preferred German to Hebrew for reading.

Undoubtedly, the political strain between Israel and West Germany played a vital part in curtailing efforts to improve the cultural relations. There was no intention at the time on the part of the German government to stabilize diplomatic relations with Israel. The work of German rocket experts in Egypt to set up a rocket industry for Nasser was just becoming known in Israel. The public outcry in October, 1961, against the Ramat Gan Orchestra accepting a German engagement was, unquestionably, a consequence. The Israeli Chamber Orchestra was forced to cancel this concert tour which had been arranged to the last detail by its impresario. The German authorities had planned to pay a considerable amount towards the orchestra's expenses and a gala performance had been prepared for Bonn. It had taken the manager in Munich four years to make the orchestra amenable to the idea.

The visit of a young German Protestant pastor to a Jerusalem secondary school only one month later aroused a national outcry. Pastor Dieckmann had made it his task to spread knowledge about the crimes committed against the Jews in Germany. His feelings towards Israel could not have been more honest. Therefore, the Israel Mission in Cologne as well as the Western European section of the Jerusalem Foreign Office supported the Reverend Mr. Dieckmann's request for a visit to an Israeli school. The Ministry of Education also saw no reason to object to it. The excitement over Pastor Dieckmann's visit to the school spread in particular because he had asked Israeli pupils to correspond with German children after he had entered into a discussion with the children and the teachers about Germany and the relation between Jews and Germans.

Abba Eban, Minister of Education, declared in the subsequent *Knesset* debate that he had understood, when he granted the permission, that the young man belonged to that breed of men like Dr. Grueber,[11] whom Jews would respect. He saw nothing wrong in discussing questions of common interest with a man like this who personally bore no responsibility for the past happenings.[12]

Yet, it was this incident which not only sparked an excited debate in the House and in the country but also caused directives to be drafted that were to control cultural and social relations with Germany. The debate in the *Knesset* was initiated by Raziel Naor of the right-wing *Heruth* opposition party, expressing disgust at the visit of a German teacher to an Israeli school. Her party's attacks against the Minister of Education were undoubtedly influenced by party political motives, meaning that *Heruth* knew only too well that it could gain in popularity with anti-German moves. But it could not be denied that there was a great deal of genuine feeling in the reactions of those unequivocally rejecting any contact with any German.

The Minister of Education expressed his understanding at the end of the lively debate, saying: "For a long time, all contact between those two peoples will remain in the shadow of their memories. It is impossible to isolate the holocaust within its narrow, historical limits." [13] Yet, Eban concluded, despite this, no one had spoken in the debate in favor of an absolute and general ban of these contacts based on a definition of race, and on the premise that all contact with Germans—even those who could in no way be called responsible for the catastrophe—should be ruled out. Consequently, the procedure was to be under a certain control for which a committee of Ministers sponsored by the government had set forth the directives. The committee consisted of the Foreign Minister, the Minister of Justice, the Minister of Development, the Minister of Transport, the Minister of Social Affairs and the Minister of Education, representing the three coalition parties—*Mapai,* National Religious and *Achdut Ha'avoda.*

Participation of Israelis in international events in Germany and participation of Germans in such events in Israel would be permitted. Visits by Germans, particularly young people—pupils, students, young workers and professional men—for the purpose of acquainting themselves with Israel's achievements also would be permitted.

A ministerial committee would choose suitable Israelis, in consul-

---

[11] Probst Heinrich Grueber, who tried to save numerous Jews from persecution.

[12] Abba Eban's speech in the *Knesset* on January 9, 1962.

[13] *Ibid.*

tation with institutions of higher learning, for informative activities in Germany. The same committee would decide on invitations for participation by any Israeli body in artistic events (noncommercial Israeli exhibitions) in Germany. No Germans would be permitted to perform in Israel without the permission of the government.

Young people would not be encouraged to study at German schools or universities and would not be granted foreign exchange for this purpose, nor would German scholarships be accepted. Permission would be given, however, for advanced studies in German universities or other scientific institutions where such subjects were vital to the state, or for study by workers or technicians in German plants when this was connected with the operation or maintenance of equipment bought in Germany.

German institutions, companies or organizations would not be allowed to establish branches in Israel, but this rule would not apply in cases of contributions to philanthropic institutions. But this did not entitle the contributors to take part in the management of these institutions.

Public organizations and institutions invited to send delegations to Germany, or wishing to invite delegations of parallel institutions in Germany to visit Israel, should request the advice of the government.

The Minister pointed out that, from these directives, one could see that not all was permitted but not everything was forbidden. He added: "We stand between the past and the future. We are not free to ignore the one or the other. The fact that certain restrictions exist proves that, at this moment, the present is nearer to the past than the future." He expressed the belief that these directives were an honorable and honest reaction to a situation which no other state in the world ever had had to face. The Motion of the *Heruth* Party, calling upon the government to discontinue all cultural and educational relations with Germany, was defeated by thirty-seven to twenty-five votes; the motion of the left-wing *Mapam*, calling on the government to prevent visits to Germany by Israeli teachers, by thirty-six to twenty-one. Finally the *Knesset*, by a large majority, adopted the governmental directives limiting and controlling the cultural and social relations between Israel and Germany.

The German press tried to make the German people understand the Israeli attitude. "We Germans should regard the directives for cultural relations as a sign of a generous and a realistic approach," the *Frankfurter Allgemeine Zeitung* wrote on January 13, 1962—a reminder that many Israelis (no members of *Heruth*) harbored the same feelings towards Germany without always expressing them. The *Knesset,* at least, had not decided on discontinuation of the contacts, the *Sueddeutsche Zeitung* stated, taking into account the unhappy past. The *Koelner Stadtanzeiger* added that the debate had shown that the change of heart, the repentance and the shame felt by the German people was understood in Israel. Considering the directives, this was a generous gesture. The majority of papers argued that any deterioration in the contacts with Israel and the development in cultural relations was due, to a great extent, to the lack of diplomatic relations and the way the German government had handled the situation.

The directives were left in the hands of a committee of three Ministers—the Minister of Foreign Affairs (*Mapai*), the Minister of Education (*Mapai*) and the Minister of Transport (*Achduth Ha'avoda*). The selection shows the deliberate inclusion of a representative of a party which opposed relations with Germany in general. This committee, however, met very rarely as its decisions were seldom requested. The directives had, in fact, their loopholes which individuals took advantage of to evade an official decision, especially in later years. For example, a German painter who did not want to seek permission could still exhibit his work in Israel provided he found a private gallery ready to assist him in this. Admittedly, this was difficult—at least in the first years after the *Knesset* decision. An Israeli artist could go to Germany any time to perform there without his government's consent provided he had been booked. He was then certainly condemned by a great many of his countrymen but, if he stayed on long enough and made his way in other European countries, criticism of him subsided as he aggrandized the reputation of Israel. Israeli students did not really need to be discouraged from studying in Germany. Yet, if they were offered a scholarship in Germany, they could accept without government permission once they were there.

Nevertheless, in view of the situation, the directives served their purpose. They pacified the Israeli people, while they did not rebuff the Germans entirely as this was not in line with Israeli general policy. But it showed the Germans that they could not hope for a normal development of relationship (as the economic contacts and tourism might have suggested) for some time to come. And, most certainly not without extending the diplomatic relations which the Germans had withheld from Israel for so long for fear of losing favor with the Arab world.

11
Two Governments Versus Public Opinion

On Platform 5, at Cologne Station, a group of German youngsters danced the hora (the Israeli folk dance) and sang Hebrew songs. The parents there to collect their children after a short stay in Israel, were amused, but also a bit embarrassed at this unusual performance at a railway station with lots of onlookers. The German organizers were pleased. Was it not the best sign that the experiment to acquaint German youths with Israel and with Jews in order to overcome old prejudices had succeeded? Nowhere else was there a better opportunity for intuitive learning than in Israel, Werner Bockelmann the Mayor of Frankfurt said, promoting trips to the state of the Jews. Arguments, common in Nazi Germany and still believed by some Germans, that Jews were exploiters, racketeers who shirked manual labor or cowards were so easily disproved in Israel. Not only the struggle for survival but also the achievements in the reconstruction of the country were striking examples to the contrary. The German youngsters, practically without exception, returned fascinated by the new state, its idealism, its spirit, its experiments. And they did not keep silent on what they had learned there.

Willy Brandt, Mayor of West Berlin, spoke about the young Germans' reaction to Israel: "The admiration for the pioneering, for the determination of survival, but also the recognition that Israel is in the same camp as we are . . . all these factors play a part in sympathy for the young state." [1] And he called it remarkable that this generation looked at the state of Israel with such respect and interest —a response shown to few other countries. The young people in his country, he explained, were generally critical, unemotional, to a great extent without illusions and unfortunately, very much impressed by material values.

It was often a bit difficult for the rising generation to convince their parents and their relatives of what they had seen in Israel. Some of the older people remained skeptical. But worse for some who had spent a few months in Israel was the readjustment to German life. They had grown to know a country where its people improvised, established new values and laid down new rules. This was so much in contrast to the staleness and stuffiness of German society, regimented by religious ties and social traditions and reluctant to accept new modes and ways of life. They were often laughed at, or dismissed with, "You and your Israel!" But that stay in Israel remained in their memory as an even more wonderful experience.

German parents, in general, had no objection to their children's desire to see Israel. Many of them, too, praised Israel, its people's virtues, the country's achievements. It was easy to do; easier than to be friends with Jews who lived next door. Israel was far away and its inhabitants no longer caused a problem to the Germans. At least, not the exact problems that living in the same society had presented to them for several centuries. And on top of it, they realized that a spoiled child, used to being waited on, would learn something about work and the need for it in a *kibbutz,* the institution, which had been greatly responsible for Israel's reconstruction. Children who were somewhat difficult or restless were sent there to see that life could have a purpose. In a way, the *kibbutz* became the substitute for army training, irrespective of the fact that it was a Socialist institution which was not appreciated in Germany. In the past, the German army had been thought of as the place where sons would be taught discipline, would be put on the right road and where the strict way of life would build character. Moreover, to allow one's child to visit Israel was modern and fashionable. For some parents, it was a kind of recompense.

In Israel, young Germans were welcome for more than one reason. For some time, farsighted politicians had realized that they

1 Herzl-Institute, New York, March 19, 1961.
   Reprinted in *Deutschland, Israel und die Juden,* p. 6, published by press and information service of Land West Berlin, 1961.

could not ignore West Germany, a political factor in Europe. To maintain contact with the older generation of Germans was not always easy for Israeli politicians, but a new generation would soon take the place of the one which had been associated with the Nazi crimes. Israel had to show that it was able to distinguish between Germans, and between the Germany of the past and the present. To quote Zeev Shek, in charge of the Western European desk in Jerusalem's Foreign Office from 1963 to 1967: "We have to fight all people who want to forget the past. But we must help those elements in Germany who are honest in their feelings towards us. This is not only in our interest; it is also a moral obligation. There are Nazis still, but there is also a new generation. . . ."

On January 29, 1964, Ben-Gurion (who, more than anybody else, was responsible for this strategy) in a conversation with German visitors, said: "Please, say at home that more young people should come as visitors, as pilgrims, as tourists to Israel. We should like them to see our country and to tell their countrymen of our young state of Israel." [2]

Ben-Gurion, and those who agreed with his policy towards Germany, requested the Israeli people to overcome understandable emotions by way of rational thinking. But this was asking a lot. Golda Meir, on a visit to Japan in January, 1962, said that one of the most painful problems of her nation was to arrive at a compromise between not being able to forget the horrors of the Hitler regime and adopting the view that Germans should not be despised because they were Germans. It was asking too much, she thought, to expect parents to forgive and forget, who, only a few years before, had been forced to watch how their children, torn from them, had been thrown into the fire or beaten to death against a wall.

Many former German Jews adopted a role of mediation. The correct compensation payments made by the German government for their material losses had done a lot to influence their attitude toward postwar Germany. And, they still had a strong attachment to German culture which was, perhaps, greater in their circles than in comparable ones in Germany, due to the fact that they lived cut off from their roots. But their political influence was almost nil [3] and their somewhat lenient attitude towards postwar Germany did not carry much weight. Pinchas Rosen, Minister of Justice until 1963,

[2] *Deutsche Presse-Agentur.*

[3] Report on a study-tour of Israel by young lawyers from Bonn and Freiburg, March to April, 1962, *Mitteilungen der List-Gesellschaft*, January, 1963.

(he, Perez Naftali, Giora Josephtal and Shlomo Yosef Burg were the only former German Jews ever to reach Cabinet rank) and Chairman of the Independent Liberal Party vowed that he never would step on German soil again.

Yet, at the same time, he rejected the idea of making the Germans go about wearing a hair shirt all their lives.[4] This attitude towards Germany was shared by the majority of German Jews. Edmund Duda, Secretary of the Trade Union Youth Movement, on his return after a three-week stay, reported: "The older generation, which still recalls the Germany before 1933, is prepared to forget . . . while the young Israelis look upon the Federal Republic of Germany with a great deal of suspicion . . ." At least three generations would have to pass until the good relationship that had existed between Jews and Germans before 1933 could be restored.[5]

Of course, not all trips to Israel passed without incidents. Young Germans did not always know the answer to tricky questions such as why the new Germany employed Nazis in high positions or why did they not fight this development and what had they learned in school about the past. German youngsters were heard singing songs they had been taught in postwar German schools which the Jews had been forced to sing in concentration camps. Some young sailors, going ashore in Haifa (surely out of sheer mischief), greeted people with "Heil Hitler" or sang Nazi songs when they were drunk. Such incidents were, understandably, magnified in Israel, particularly by the right-wing *Heruth* that ruled out contacts with Germany "for the next century."

But these are not the reasons why young Germans found it difficult to make contact with Israeli youngsters of comparable age. In general, the Israeli younger generation was not especially eager to meet Germans. Apart from the suspicions, they did not understand them. An Israeli youngster is proud of his country, it means everything to him and he is ready to fight for it. In a way, it seems to him the most important part of the world—which is, perhaps, not the very best approach to the world at large. German youth betrayed no such pride in their own country. They made it clear that they felt more at home in Israel than in Germany. They complained about the old Nazis still in office and the old style of life. The Israeli youngster could not understand why the German young person did

[4] Felix E. Shinnar, *Bericht eines Beauftragten,* p. 112, Rainer Wunderlich Verlag, Tübingen, 1967.
[5] *Deutsche Presse-Agentur,* March 6, 1961.

not fight for a change and did not do all to have reason to be proud of his country, too. In other words, there was no common language between the two younger generations fostered in such different environments. And this could be taken literally as unfamiliarity with the German language (not taught in Israeli schools) added to the difficulties.

The early history of the relations between the students movements of the two countries disclosed this plainly. The Israelis should be held mainly responsible, for there was a time when they even rejected contact with the German-Israel Study Groups (BDIS), a small but active group of Germans pledged to create understanding of Israel at German universities. Unofficial contacts between the students existed all the time, yet the majority of the National Union of Israeli Students (NUIS) refused to make them official until well after diplomatic relations had been established between the two countries. The National Congress, in February, 1963, did not oppose getting in touch with "anti-Fascist, pro-Israeli students organizations" in Germany, yet did nothing to sponsor them. On the contrary, when some Israeli students accepted an invitation of the German-Israel Students Organization to attend a seminar at Tutzing, Bavaria, in the summer of 1963, as "private individuals," they had to account for it on their return.

In an opinion poll among students of Haifa Technical College in spring, 1963, 51 percent of all those questioned rejected communicating with German students; 41 percent had no objections. In a plebiscite at the beginning of 1964, Haifa students decided to sever all existing connections with German student organizations. The students of Tel Aviv firmly opposed contacts in 1964, while the majority of the students of the Hebrew University in Jerusalem, voted in favor of them. However, nothing materialized as the National Union of Israeli Students arrived at different decisions.

The annual congress of NUIS of 1964–1965 resolved that questions concerning overtures to German student organizations should be determined by unanimous vote. Every functionary was threatened with the loss of his mandate, should he dicker with a German student representative.[6]

---

[6] Peter Müller, *Die Beziehungen der deutschen Studentenschaft zu den Studenten Israels,* published in *Diskussion,* journal for problems of society and German-Israel relations, Berlin, April, 1965.
Ulrich Kusche, *Die deutsch-israelischen Studentenbeziehungen, Diskussen,* February, 1967.

This was certain deterioration of earlier developments. At first, Israeli students had done nothing to impair contacts. They had even helped to make the visits of the first German youth groups a success. Two meetings of German and Israeli students in Germany on how to improve on and spread the knowledge of Jewish history were organized by the German Students Federation in November, 1957, and in October, 1959. This seemed a modest but hopeful beginning of closer relationship and plans were made for conferences of experts. Such conferences actually took place in September, 1960, under the auspices of the German Students Federation (VDS), the *Friedrich-Ebert-Stiftung*, the International Schoolbook Institute, Brunswick, and the Institute for International Encounters.

The reason for a refusal of the Israeli students, in 1963, to continue on this road was due to a great extent to the unsatisfactory development of German-Israel relations in general. The German government's failure to extend diplomatic relations added to the news about German scientists' activities in Nasser's pay caused criticism, if not anger. Every symptom of nationalistic tendencies, of Nazist and anti-Semitic trends in Germany was watched closely in Israel.

Israeli students, at that time, were far more politically minded than German youth. And even the few who were not, disliked Germany. Only a small percentage of German students took an interest in politics—at least until the mid-sixties. It was a general complaint in the country that they cared for their own education and careers and nothing else beyond that. Those who were organized did not do much to improve their position with Israeli students. The Students Federation, in fact, pursued a kind of "Hallstein Doctrine" of its own. It was eager to establish good relations with the Arab students in order to prevent East German student organizations from gaining a foothold in Arab countries. This, they thought, ruled out the possibility of closer relations with Israel at the same time. The VDS, until 1964, had a kind of ambassador in Cairo, an "overseas commissioner" who supported the aims of the Arab students organization and, in particular, the General Union of Palestine Students (GUPS). In resolutions passed in meetings, in 1962 and 1963, the Federation of German Students Organizations even resolved to "assure the Arabs from Palestine full rights of citizenship in their homeland." This changed only when the German students sensed the futility of their efforts to influence the Arab students and the hostile reaction of Israeli students to the German activities in Cairo.

In 1964, the Federation of German Students Organizations tried to improve on the situation, exhorting its executives to make efforts for normal relations with NUIS. But the policy of past years and the 1964–1965 political tension existing between Israel and West Germany did not make this any easier. Support of Israel's demand by German students at an international congress at Christchurch, New Zealand, in 1964, led to renewed contacts which were followed by an offer of the Federation of German Students to improve conditions. The reply was an invitation for a delegation of German students to Israel. The visit came about in February, 1965. The crisis in general relations between Germany and Israel had just then reached a climax. It is not difficult to gather that the visit produced no results.[7]

It must not be overlooked that German-Israel relations were influenced, held up or slowed down by events in Germany. For example, the 1959 vandalism at the Cologne synagogue, had been followed by a sweeping anti-Semitic campaign focusing world attention on Germany again, and had spread to other European countries.

Some of this probably had been due to the imitative instinct, the urge to cause trouble and to be mentioned in the press or on the radio. Slogans like "Out with the Jews" or "Death to the Jews," desecrations of cemeteries and threatening letters to Jewish people in Germany were the features of this sudden outbreak which had not been equaled in postwar years. It is perfectly true that the outbreak of this anti-Jewish campaign disturbed the German people deeply. Whatever their feelings, they had learned to dislike this kind of action and were fully aware of the repercussions abroad. But few, analyzing the reasons for the outbreak, dared to mention, in public, that the lack of political education of the young people of Germany and the former Nazis in government positions had anything to do with it.

A flood of assurances on the part of the government and German officials followed to repair the damage done to postwar Germany's reputation by this sort of thing. Dr. Gerhard Schroeder, then Minister of the Interior, said on television, December 30:

We are not at the beginning of a new seizure of power by an anti-Semitic group . . . we rather have to ask what else we can do to eradicate some dark prejudices which still exist in some people's minds and, after all, also infect some younger ones. . . .

[7] Peter Müller, *Die Beziehungen der deutschen Studentenschaft zu den Studenten Israels*, published in *Diskussion*, Berlin, April, 1965.

On January 6, 1960, the Cabinet had requested the *Bundestag* to pass the bill introduced in March, 1959, against racial discrimination as speedily as possible. This would make anti-Semitic remarks and actions punishable and would turn the Jewish community in Germany into a community protected by law. Federal President Heinrich Luebke assured the Jewish community that he shared the people's "deep disgust" about the incidents. On January 16, on German radio and television, Chancellor Adenauer said that present-day Germany rejected anti-Semitism outright: "In Germany, neither National Socialism nor anti-Semitism has any roots and the few incorrigible ones will not do any harm; I guarantee this." [8] His appeal to his fellow citizens to give "a sound thrashing" to any one caught daubing caused amusement rather than disgust because of its naïveté. A "white book" on anti-Semitic and Nazist incidents from December 25, 1959 to January 28, 1960, compiled by the Ministry of the Interior, concluded that the investigations had not produced any evidence that considerable sections of the population harbored anti-Semitic feelings.[9] The Minister's hint at Communist participation in the anti-Semitic campaigns in order to discredit the Federal Republic was not taken seriously, not even in Bonn.

On February 2, Dr. Adenauer went on a pilgrimage to the concentration camp, Bergen-Belsen, where with the Jewish leader, Dr. Nahum Goldmann, he spoke in honor of the murdered and said, "Germany of today respects all races, all nations." [10]

Although the Israeli public and the government were deeply disturbed by what had happened in Germany, nobody questioned the existing contacts with Germany. On January 5, the *Knesset* had enjoined its committee on Foreign and Security Affairs to issue a warning to the world regarding the dangers of anti-Semitism. A note had been handed to the Bonn Government on January 11, in which it had been emphatically stated that Israel was aware that "symptons of racial hatred (in Germany) do not express the opinion of the government nor of the educated people, but history teaches that these appearances must be fought from the beginning with all means possible."

A week later, without any further reproach, in reply to a ques-

[8] Joachim Kreysler and Klaus Jungfer, *Deutsche Israel Politik*, p 70, Wolf von Tucher Verlag G.m.b.H., Diessen-Ammersee, 1965.
[9] Joachim Kreysler and Klaus Jungfer, *Deutsche Israel Politik*, p. 71, Wolf von Tucher Verlag G.m.b.H., Diessen-Ammersee, 1965.
[10] *Deutsche Presse-Agentur*, February 2, 1960.

tion, Ben-Gurion said, "Israel must acquire the friendship of the new Germany just as it should avail itself of the friendship of any other people."

Of course, there had been contacts between German and Israeli politicians since the inception of the Luxembourg Treaty in 1953. Since 1955, Ben-Gurion and his followers had held to the line that good relations with the Federal Republic were essential for Israel. But, in a case of a serious recurrence of anti-Semitism in Germany, this policy surely would have been dropped, whatever the consequences for Israel. Therefore, the Israeli leaders did accept interpretations of the German situation and the German people's general attitude by "politically reliable" Germans. It may be concluded from this that meetings between Germans and Israelis plus the correct restitution payments did help to create some trust in each other.

The very first meeting (which received hardly any publicity) took place as early as February, 1953. In Hattenheim, a small, wine-producing village in the Rhineland, economists, journalists, a few politicians and members of the clergy of both denominations sat down with two Israeli diplomats of the Mission in Cologne and a Jewish publicist. The *Wirtschaftspolitische Gesellschaft von 1947* (Political Economic Society of 1947) was the organizer of this unofficial meeting to review the situation between Jews and Germans.[11]

Otto Klepper, former Finance Minister in Prussia during the Weimar Republic, took the chair. The meeting was of little political importance; it was more of a sentimental nature. The two Israelis, Dr. Chaim Yahil and Dr. Uri Naor, spoke in harsh terms of the German guilt. The German participants, deeply moved by it, assured the Jews that there was no opposition in the country against compensating them for their material losses, the majority of Germans being aware of their nation's guilt. The Israelis conceded that anti-Semitism was no specifically "German" phenomenon, although the Germans had failed to take it seriously or to combat it when there was still time. The "collective guilt theory," to which many Israelis adhered, was more one of collective pain, of collective suffering which constituted an enormous force in the life of a nation. Jews are bad haters.

Meetings between Germans and Israeli politicians had taken place

---

[11] Bulletin No. 26, July-August, 1953, of the *Wirtschaftspolitische Gesellschaft von 1947.*

with a certain regularity since the signing of the Luxembourg Treaty, usually on Israeli soil. Despite the Israeli reluctance to travel to Germany, the impression could be gained that everything was fine and normal with regard to the development of relations between Germany and Israel. There were, first and foremost, the contacts between the Social Democratic Party of Germany and the *Mapai*, the Israeli Labor Party. Both parties adhered to the principles of democratic Socialism and were members of the Socialist International. The German party had been readmitted to the International Socialist movement in November, 1947,[12] after the parties from Eastern Europe had given up their opposition. (A few months later, these parties either left or were made to leave the International Socialist movement as they were found to be infiltrated by Communists).

Some of the leading members of the German Social Democratic Party had also suffered at the hands of the Nazis, so *Mapai* leaders had little, if any, reservation against the German Socialist members. Erich Ollenhauer, Chairman of the SPD, had gone to Israel in 1957. As early as 1958, *Mapai*—for the first time—had dispatched a delegate to the biannual congress of the SPD held in Stuttgart. Herzl Berger, an executive member of the *Mapai*, had addressed the Congress and had been wildly cheered by the German Socialists. But while the *Mapai* had been in power ever since the creation of the state of Israel, the Social Democrats had remained in opposition in Germany during all those crucial years.

This meant, in practice, that the German Social Democrats had exclusive contact with the Israeli government. However, their influence on the German government was practically nil. Thus, their favorable reaction to Israel, the country and the numerous Socialist institutions—virtually unique in the world—had only a limited effect. No matter how vocal they were on the need of extending diplomatic relations to Israel, their voice was not decisive. Nevertheless, the value of their constant appeals to the government for action and their dissemination of information about Israel should not be underestimated. Certainly, they helped to prepare the ground for many sections of the German population to pressure the government on establishing diplomatic relations. The Israeli government was quick

---

[12] Comisco (Committee of the International Socialist Conference). The Socialist International was reestablished in Frankfurt, in 1951.

to grasp this and began to be very generous with invitations to German public figures from all walks of life.

Members of the Christian Democratic Party and the Free Democratic Party also traveled to Israel, but in much smaller numbers. This was as much due to embarrassment because their government had allowed itself to be intimidated by the Arabs as to relations with Israel in the past. To avoid an unfriendly reaction from the Arab side, German Ministers and State Secretaries from the ruling parties, though grateful for the invitations from Dr. Shinnar, refused to go there as long as they were in office.

Minister of Economic Cooperation Walter Scheel, a leading member of the Free Democrats, is a good example. He had accepted an invitation tendered to him in the summer of 1964, and he had planned the visit to Israel in connection with a trip to Ankara. Suddenly he canceled it, apparently having been told to do so by Bonn's Foreign Office. According to the Foreign Office in Jerusalem,[13] Scheel wrote a letter of apology to Dr. Shinnar, claiming to have business to attend to in Cameroun immediately after Ankara. He postponed the visit, indefinitely. Dr. Eugen Gerstenmaier, the president of the *Bundestag*, was an exception to this rule, perhaps because he felt a special allegiance to the Jewish people, having been in jail in connection with the abortive anti-Hitler *Putsch* of July 20, 1944.

But German politicians had no reservations about traveling to the Arab world. Israel had no objection to this, but the Israelis regretted this state of affairs. Nevertheless, they could do nothing except hope that, by their attitude, a change of mind would gradually take place in Germany.

Once German statesmen were out of office, they visited Israel without hesitation; Professor Heuss, the Federal Republic's first President, for instance, and Franz-Josef Strauss, Defense Minister until the end of 1962. Irrespective of political creed, the opinion of visitors was practically one and the same. Professor Carlo Schmid, a leading Social Democrat and one of the vice presidents of the *Bundestag*, said, after his return December, 1959: "The impressions are overpowering . . . To see what man can make of himself if he devotes his life entirely and without reservations . . . to an idea. . . ." Werner Bockelmann, Mayor of Frankfurt, admired the willpower that had been required to build up the country, and said: ". . .

[13] *Jedioth Chadashoth,* July 12, 1963.

Hatred is despised in Israel. People greet each other in the streets with 'Shalom.' Also, the Israeli is more reserved than unforgiving towards the Germans." Theo Burauen, Mayor of Cologne, stressed the tension under which the Israelis had been forced to live: ". . . yet worked unrelentingly for the future." [14] From Helmut Gollwitzer, a theologian of repute: ". . . We encountered no hatred in Israel, despite everything. Whoever does not speak Hebrew and whose English is bad will manage easily with German and will never experience nasty reactions." [15] And, Professor Franz Böhm: "Those Jews who now devote their lives to the proud work of reconstructing their state are far from feeling inextinguishable hatred for every German or harboring the thought of some kind of retaliation." [16]

This discovery on the part of the Germans was not of particular interest to the Israelis, although they realized that a good impression of their country would increase the moral pressure on responsible Germans for concerning themselves with diplomatic effort.

In 1963, Dr. Thomas Dehler, also one of the vice presidents of the *Bundestag* and leading member of the Free Democrats, said that he favored a German initiative for negotiating diplomatic ties between Bonn and Jerusalem, " . . . and I am ready to accept possibly negative reactions on the part of the Arab states." Dr. Dehler's support was a very personal one as his party, a junior member of the coalition in this period, had failed to make a committing statement on Israel. It was, however, opposed to the Hallstein Doctrine in general, considering it a stumbling block in the path of improvement of accord with the Communist states.

Professor Böhm, CDU, was of the opinion that Arab pressure no longer existed to such a degree that further capitulation could be justified. But he felt that Israel could judge a further delay of such an offer as "an offensive unfriendliness." Ernst Mueller-Herrmann, also of the CDU, said that the Federal Republic had reason to feel able to cope with the Arab states so that "it can also exercise justice towards the state of Israel."

Gerhard Jahn of the Social Democratic Party believed that the existing good diplomatic and economic relations were reason enough for the Arab states to beware of overhasty and rash steps and that

---

[14] On returning from the YULA Congress in Tel Aviv, November 16-23, 1960.
[15] Helmut Gollwitzer, *Israel und Wir*, Lettner Verlag, Berlin, 1958.
[16] *Frankfurter Hefte No. 10, 1956*, pp. 715-727, *Das jüdische Friedenswerk inmitten der arabischen Welt*.

the Federal Republic's attitude of resignation was completely un-called for.[17]

Perhaps the statement of Dr. Gerstenmaier, the most important official to visit Israel, should be considered of more significance than others. On his return, December 1, 1962, he said: "The extension of diplomatic relations between the Federal Republic and Israel is an important task on the road to the normalization of relations between the two states. Germany's hesitation is interpreted by many Israelis as a discrimination." [18] Gerstenmaier held talks with Ben-Gurion and the issue evidently figured largely in their conversation. The fact that the two already had discussed details gave rise to the im-pression that diplomatic accord was not so far off. After all that fol-lowed, it must be concluded that Gerstenmaier acted on his own ini-tiative, assuming—no doubt, rightly—that he had the sanction of Dr. Adenauer. After all, Adenauer, as well as his first Foreign Minister, Dr. von Brentano, had assured Dr. Shinnar that diplomatic relations were only a question of timing.[19]

In this conversation, Ben-Gurion suggested that West Germany should inform the Israeli government unofficially about it as soon as the time was ripe. He would then probe his Cabinet's view on the matter and make sure that he would get the majority of the *Knesset* to agree. He was not formally obliged to do so, but he did want to put the matter to the vote in Parliament for the sake of a broad basis of consent on this delicate issue. Only then would he ask the Ger-man government to make it an official request.[20]

According to *Agence France Press* November 30, 1962, Ben-Gur-ion referred to his talk with Gerstenmaier, saying that Israel would not request diplomatic connections with Germany, but should such initiative be taken by the Germans, he would do all in his power to see to it that conformation met with the request.

Dr. Gerstenmaier's visit to Israel was disturbed by demonstrations of protest, particularly when he appeared before the *Knesset*—a very high honor to be bestowed on a German. Reference was made to the issues standing between the two countries then: the Hallstein Doctrine that prevented the extension of diplomatic relations and the work of German rocket experts for Nasser's rocket industry.

[17] Joachim Kreysler and Klaus Jungfer, *Deutsche Israel Politik*, p. 90, Wolf von Tucher Verlag G.m.b.H., Diessen-Ammersee, 1965.

[18] *Ibid.*

[19] Felix E. Shinnar, *Bericht eines Beauftragten*, p. 108, Rainer Wunderlich Ver-lag, Tübingen, 1967.

[20] *Jedioth Chadashoth*, December 4, 1962.

Dr. Gerstenmaier was hardly the right target for complaints. But, perhaps, he just interpreted these demonstrations as generally anti-German. Ben-Gurion, who felt embarrassed (as a host as much as a politician), criticized the Israeli protest movement: "I feel ashamed of these anti-German demonstrations. They smell of racial preju-dices. They are beneath our dignity." [21] Incidentally, it hardly can be called a coincidence that another vice president of the *Bundestag*, Richard Jaeger, CSU, journeyed to Egypt almost immediately after Gerstenmaier's return from Israel.

Franz-Josef Strauss experienced similar demonstrations when in Is-rael from May 26 to June 7, 1963. He was then not known by the general public as the man who had assisted Israel with supplies of arms. Anti-German circles saw in him simply a former German Minister who, on top of everything else, had shown in the Spiegel affair [22]—which had cost him his Minister's post—a lack of under-standing of the functioning of democracy.

As in other cases, the demonstrators were mainly from the right-wing *Heruth* party which was eager to incite antigovernment feel-ings (more than anti-German sentiments) for its own political benefits. When the *Heruth* leader, Menahem Begin, was informed by Deputy Defense Minister Shimon Peres of the secret arms sup-plies from Germany for which Strauss was mainly responsible, the demonstrations stopped.

The German politician (an intellectual rightly believed to have a future in German politics despite the odds against him), who was still the leader of the Christian Social Union, from all practical points of view a party separate from the CDU, was feted by the Is-raeli government as seldom any other guest from Germany ever had been. Moshe Dayan, then Minister of Agriculture (between 1953 and 1957, Chief of the General Staff), went to the airport to receive Strauss. His greeting was: "I have come to thank the man who stood by our nation in its most difficult hours." [23]

Interestingly enough, Strauss changed his mind within those few days spent in Israel regarding the type of contacts between his country and the state of the Jews. He declared afterwards that he "always had been of the opinion that relations between Israel and the Federal Republic should be formalized on the level of General Consulates. This could have led to a gradual recognition in the sense

21 *Deutsche Presse-Agentur,* November 18, 1962.
22 See page 267.
23 Rolf Vogel, *Deutschlands Weg nach Israel,* p. 144, Seewald Verlag, Stutt-gart, 1967.

of the establishment of diplomatic relations." But, after his talks in Israel, he was convinced that this was no longer the right path. Therefore, he had come to the conclusion that "full diplomatic relations with the exchange of diplomatic missions" should be undertaken.[24]

In a press conference in Bonn, on June 11, Strauss stressed that all *Kulturnationen* maintained diplomatic relations with Israel—which he called, "a political reality"—and he believed that such relations between Israel and the Federal Republic were an act of "historic restitution." He and his party would use their strength to bring about such relations, which would by no means unbalance the situation in the Near East, as had been stated so often by German government leaders. In a talk with the *Maariv* correspondent in Bonn, he even expressed the opinion that there was no reason to fear now that the Arab countries—being recipients of such generous aid from Bonn [25]—would recognize East Germany if the Federal Republic finalized relations with Israel.

Strauss's untiring support throughout the years to gain the advantages of diplomatic relations was of considerable importance as he greatly influenced nationalistic circles in Germany so far without contact with Israel. Those factions were, above all, the champions of Germany's inflexible foreign policy aimed at preventing any move that might improve Communist Germany's position in the world. The diplomatic recognition of Israel had appeared to them to be inherently dangerous; it might prompt the Arab states to establish diplomatic relations with East Germany.

A most important meeting between Finance Minister Levi Eshkol and the Minister of Economic Affairs, Professor Ludwig Erhard was secretly arranged. The two met in Brussels in early March, 1962. As at their first meeting in 1960, following the Adenauer-Ben-Gurion agreement of the Waldorf-Astoria, they had talked about Germany's loan to Israel. But the subject of Israel's connection with the European community played the more important part this time. At one stage, the Germans, pressed by German industries, had no longer actively supported Israel's request for an association, and in Israel there was fear that it would be dropped in favor of the Arab states.

On September 3, 1961, the Bonn correspondent of the *Sunday*

[24] *Allgemeine Wochenzeitung der Juden in Deutschland,* June 21, 1963.
[25] *Maariv,* June 12, 1963.

Telegraph wrote that relations between Israel and the Federal Republic had reached the "freezing point." A representative of the Foreign Office in Jerusalem stated that the report was "a little exaggerated, yet correct in its essence." [26] It was then that Levi Eshkol requested the meeting with Erhard, during which Erhard assured Eshkol of West Germany's support in something like a trade agreement between Israel and the EEC. The Germans seemed to have come to the conclusion that such active support in the European body would not be disadvantageous to them, economically or politically. After all, any Arab objection to an arrangement with Israel would not concern them alone. It was obvious, by then, that at least the Dutch would support Israel even if France still hesitated because of ties to the Maghreb countries. At any rate, the Federal Republic was not alone in its attitude towards Israel, even though the Egyptians immediately attacked the Germans for their pro-Israel stand. However, they did not comment at all on the following Franco-Israeli talks on the same subject.

The *Rheinische Merkur* was probably correct when, in its mid-March issue, it observed that the German government would lend a helping hand to achieve Israel's contact with the EEC but certainly would not stick out its neck to secure it. But the Germans ignored the Arab protests this time. In fact, a few months later (August, 1962), they informed the Jordanian government, on request, that they would sponsor a trade agreement between Israel and the EEC.

Fear that the Arab countries would recognize East Germany as an act of retaliation if the Federal Republic initiated official connections with Israel was less at this period than ever in the history of German-Israel negotiations. Chinese aggressions against India had ruled out the possibility that India or any other noncommitted country—the Arab states, for that matter—would recognize East Germany. The Eastern bloc seemed somewhat an entity then, and an action of China was interpreted as having the sanction of the entire Communist world.

Then, there was the fact that the task of the Israel Mission in Cologne (one of purchasing goods within the framework of the Luxembourg Treaty) would be completed soon. Although the Luxembourg Treaty would not expire until March, 1966, Israel had already spent the money to which it was entitled on long-range or-

[26] *Deutsche Presse-Agentur,* September 13, 1961.

ders—on ships and railways that take years to complete. For this reason, Dr. Shinnar accepted the role of chief of the Citrus Marketing Board on July 1, 1962, and was to continue in his post as head of the Mission only at irregular intervals. No doubt, his appointment was a sort of gesture on the part of the Israeli government.

By 1963, the Mission staff had been greatly reduced and the big house in Cologne that had been built with a view to serving as an Embassy sometime in the future, looked deserted with most of its windows shuttered. German circles began to realize that, once the Mission's work was done, there would be no more official Israeli representation in Germany except, perhaps, for a Consulate to issue visas, or a trade section to watch over the transactions between firms of the two countries.

It was known that Dr. Adenauer now considered German-Jewish reconciliation the second most important task of his life's work, by then having replaced the century-old Franco-German enmity with a pact of friendship. Knowing that he would not be in power much longer (his own party was pressing him to turn over the burden of government to younger hands), he informed Dr. Shinnar, in early summer of 1963, that he had decided "to conclude what he had begun with his declaration before the *Bundestag* on September 27, 1951, and with the conclusion of the Treaty of September 10, 1952." He finally intended to suggest the extension of diplomatic relations on condition that it would not be rejected by Israel. He would try to reduce the danger of an unfavorable Arab reaction to a minimum through adequate feelers, but the success of this attempt would not be a precondition of this offer. Adenauer suggested to Shinnar that he advise the Israeli government, for he wanted to be absolutely sure that a German offer would not meet with refusal.[27]

Shinnar reported that Ben-Gurion was certain that there would be a 60 to 70 percent majority in the *Knesset* in favor of the proposal, with definite votes from Ben-Gurion's *Mapai* and the Liberals.[28] But, when Dr. Shinnar returned to Bonn, he learned that Dr. Adenauer had once again bowed to his Foreign Minister. While on a holiday in Cadenabbia, Italy, in August, he had conferred with Dr. Schroeder about this matter. But Schroeder had strongly advised

---

[27] Felix E. Shinnar, *Bericht eines Beauftragten,* p. 123, Rainer Wunderlich Verlag, Tübingen, 1967.
[28] Felix E. Shinnar, *Bericht eines Beauftragten,* p. 124, Rainer Wunderlich Verlag, Tübingen, 1967.

him against it, giving the hazard of an adverse Arab reaction as the reason. He claimed to have relevant information—which he undoubtedly had—from German ambassadors in the region who were inclined to accept Arab threats at their face value.

Many political observers in Bonn were convinced that Schroeder was as much against Israel as he was in favor of the Arab countries. Schroeder had not been a Nazi in the serious sense of the word, although he had been a member of the NSDAP. But, in 1941, when he married Brigitte Landsberg, who was partly Jewish, he had resigned from the party—something that required courage at the time.

Schroeder could be termed a conservative with nationalistic sentiments. Though it would be unfair, perhaps, to stamp him an enemy of Israel and Strauss its declared friend—as was done by political observers in Germany as well as in Israel—Schroeder certainly was a friend of the Arab states. This may have been partly due to the old allegiance that nationalistic Germans felt for the Arab world and partly because of his advisors, so-called "Arab experts," many of whom had less than an unblemished past and who inspired the phrase, "the Arabs of the Koblenzer Strasse."

Interviewed by the *Sueddeutsche Zeitung* on December 4, 1964, Dr. Adenauer, spoke of "trends in the Foreign Office in opposition to relations with Israel." He is even said to have angrily accused Foreign Office officials of anti-Semitic leanings. Time and again, these officials expressed the fear (which of course, was nurtured by the Arabs) that the Arab states would surely recognize East Germany, once Bonn recognized Jerusalem officially. To apply the Hallstein Doctrine, would mean cutting the ties to the Arab states, and losing influence in other noncommitted countries. In the eyes of conservative politicians (who preferred the trodden path, however unjust, rather than a risk), the recognition of Israel, therefore, might play havoc with German foreign policy. Dr. Adenauer, contrary to his previous statement to Dr. Shinnar, now informed the Israel diplomat in late August that the Federal Republic had reason to fear hostile Arab reaction. Consultation with a friendly power had confirmed this. Quite obviously he referred to the Americans, said to be alarmed that Germany would lose these contacts since they themselves were not on such friendly terms with the Arabs.[29] Adenauer

---

[29] Rolf Vogel, *Deutschlands Weg nach Israel*, p. 176, wrote that on September 10, 1963, the American Ambassador to Bonn, George McGhee, on behalf

could not shoulder the responsibility for such a perilous policy, especially as he was about to turn over the office to someone else.

According to the Social Democratic news service of October 16, 1963,[30] the Foreign Office organized a trip to Arab countries for two parliamentarians of the CDU, Ernst Majonica and Dr. Berthold Martin, "to collect arguments against the taking up of relations and to sound out the attitude of the Arabs." After their return, Adenauer could see no possibility of forcing through his intention of taking the anticipated step, the Agency said. Majonica, the foreign political spokesman of his party, and Dr. Martin, a cultural expert, had visited Cairo and Damascus at the beginning of September. There, they had turned against the idea of diplomatic relations with Israel, saying that this was "not in the interest of peace and not in the interest of Germany."

Interviewed by the German press agency, *Deutsche Presse-Agentur*, on September 12, 1963, the two parliamentarians repeated their objections to establishing relations. This would prompt the Arabs to recognize the East German Communist state, they said, and would do infinite harm to the Federal Republic, cripple the country's efforts at reunification and, last but not least, would prove to be disadvantageous to the entire Western world.

In a German-Jewish weekly [31] interview, Majonica added that both his and Martin's declarations were also made in the interest of Israel, lest the diplomatic recognition lead to a new hate campaign of the Arabs against Israel—a veiled hint that, if Israeli relations produced problems for Germany, this might lead to anti-Semitic tendencies there. A flood of angry press comments followed these declarations in Germany. The commentator of Hesse radio characterized the behavior of the two politicians as "political narrow-mindedness and arrogance"; the Bavarian radio described it as similar to two bulls in a china shop; the West German radio suggested that parliamentarians "think twice before they make statements abroad"; the *Stuttgarter Zeitung* believed that the two politicians had disqualified themselves with their statements.

Professor Heuss's appeal to Dr. Adenauer at the end of September to effect diplomatic relations with Israel while he was still in government no longer could change the mind of the German Chan-

of his government, advised against the establishment of diplomatic relations ⟩ between the Federal Republic and Israel for the reasons given above.

[30] *Parlamentarisch-Politischer Pressedienst.*

[31] *Allgemeine Wochenzeitung der Juden in Deutschland*, October 4, 1963.

cellor. On September 28, a few weeks before his death, Heuss had written: "I personally have the feeling . . . that the time is overripe for the establishment of diplomatic relations . . . I should be very grateful to you if you would conclude this issue within your term of office. . . ." [32]

Professor Erhard, who took over the chancellorship in October, 1963, soon made it clear that his opinion differed in no way from his predecessor's views on Israel. He pledged the German people's responsibility towards and the readiness for assistance to the Jewish state, yet he declared that diplomatic relations really were of minor importance: "The question is not *whether* we engage in diplomatic relations but *when* we do so." He expressed the belief that Israel did understand West Germany's predicament in this regard. Asked when he expected the realization of diplomatic relations with Israel, he replied: "Not for the time being." [33]

A curious situation had evolved. In Israel, the general public lagged behind its government with regard to its views on postwar Germany; a good number cared little about Germany and thought that the problem would solve itself if they ignored it. Many people did not really understand their government's policy towards West Germany. Had it not been for the prestige of Ben-Gurion as a leader of the nation, the Israeli government's policy might not have been accepted as it was, with relatively little protest. But, at times the true feelings broke out, often caused by a small incident. The revolt of workers at the ATA textile factories against having to sew uniforms for the German army is such a case. The ATA (Coordinating Council for Christian-Jewish Cooperation) factories prepared ten thousand uniforms, an order which (as was learned from government sources) had been first received in the name of the NATO army. On July 30, 1962, Minister of Trade and Commerce Sapir rejecting criticism, particularly from the Communists and the right-wing *Heruth*, confirmed the order in the *Knesset*. He considered this part of Israel's export drive and efforts to assure full employment. Sixty women were engaged for this work. The difficulties arose when some of them (former concentration camp inmates who had been forced to sew uniforms there) refused to carry out this order. Pressure was brought to bear at first and, stupidly enough, they were threatened with dismissal. It took some time to pacify

[32] *Stuttgarter Zeitung*, courtesy of Dr. Ernst-Ludwig Heuss, late son of Professor Heuss.
[33] Press Conference, Bonn, December 3, 1963.

them (and the country, which also was up in arms), some because of the order accepted by Israel, others because of the threat of dismissal and still others because of both aspects. The workers who objected to working on the uniforms were finally given a different task and the excitement gradually subsided.

In Germany, it was exactly the opposite. Public opinion demanded diplomatic harmony with Israel, calling it shabby and beyond any decent person's understanding that the government should refrain from effecting it. Time and again, in fact, at any possible opportunity, the press of practically all dimensions demanded that the government at last solidify relations which usually were withheld from a country only when at war—with Israel—.

"The Arabs surely will not have a higher estimation of our friendship because we allow ourselves to be put under pressure by them and let Israel wait. It is morally right that, after the material compensation, we also make a decision in favor of the normalization of political relations," the CDU weekly, *Rheinische Merkur*, published on January 8, 1960. Other papers wrote in a similar vein, not only papers reflecting Social Democratic opinion but traditional government supporters as well. Student and youth organizations, Social Democratic Party sections, CDU youth groups, trade unions, clerical and professional organizations of all kinds tried their best, with the help of resolutions and appeals, to force action from the government. It was a protest against only the Jewish state being deprived of what was normal among nations; above all, because the government, with the help of the Hallstein Doctrine, had allowed itself to be blackmailed, by the Arab states; by which improper tactics, the Jewish state became a victim of this doctrine.

There were German ambassadors in Cairo and Damascus, but none in Jerusalem. The government's arguments that it was due only to the Hallstein Doctrine that the Arab states had not granted official recognition to the East German Communist state was shared by few. But even they thought that it was necessary to take a risk in this case. The fact remained that it gave the Arabs every opportunity to exert pressure on Germany at their whim—whether it concerned development aid in their direction, or aid or a friendly gesture towards Israel. The people in Germany were aware of the immorality of this policy. Moreover, they detested the Arab countries for their attitude, which was that of humiliating Germany. The lack of friendly feeling towards the Arabs—also, accused of squandering German aid—certainly exceeded anti-Jewish tendencies any of them might still nurture. Interviews and articles by leading Arabs in the radical right-wing *Deutsche Nationalzeitung und Soldatenzeitung* did not add to their popularity.

In August, 1964, the trade union movement, headed by a German Jew together with the Council for Christian-Jewish Cooperation, finally organized a campaign. They asked their six million members, and anybody else ready to do so, to sign a petition for the extension of diplomatic relations to Israel. This campaign was not too successful—it produced only seventy thousand signatures within three months.[34] However, this was not necessarily due to political opinions. Petitions are an unfamiliar practice in Germany and ever since the Nazi regime, Germans are averse to signing anything in fear of their name being used for something beyond their control. Furthermore, trade unions normally refrain from political actions except in the interest of working and social conditions. Also, some employers with business interests in the Arab countries, or fearful of the Arab boycott, did not allow the signing of the petition to take place on their premises. Under the pretext that signing of petitions at places of work was contrary to constitutional law, the Federal Employers Association instigated this opposition—of course, afraid of the Arab lobby.

The opponents of German-Israeli diplomatic relations were not only among the conservative politicians but just as strong, perhaps, in industrial circles that also influenced the government. The manager of the German Chamber of Commerce and Industries, Dr. Düren, came to the point on April 3, 1964, in a television program called: *Why No Ambassador to Israel?* He said that diplomatic relations with Israel would mean a change of the balance in the Near East as the Arab states then would engage in diplomatic relations with East Germany: "It goes without saying that the responsibility for sixteen million Germans in the Zone must be just as near to our heart as the situation of the state of Israel." He then spoke of the "probably strong repercussions" which, from the point of view of the businessman, could only be regretted and he pointed to the good market in Arab states for German goods. In the same television spot, the government spokesman, Karl Guenther von Hase, repeated the hackneyed statement that relations with Israel were genuine without the exchange of ambassadors.[35]

[34] Representative of the trade union movement (DGB), November 24, 1964.
[35] Joachim Kreysler and Klaus Jungfer, *Deutsche Israel Politik*, p. 94, Wolf von Tucher Verlag G.m.b.H., Diessen-Ammersee, 1965.

The Social Democratic Party never stopped thinking of means to achieve what they thought was not only normal between peoples but also a moral obligation.[36] The idea of a motion from the floor of the *Bundestag* for diplomatic relation came from their ranks. They believed it could win sufficient votes—a view which, incidentally, was shared by Dr. Gerstenmaier. In June, 1963, on a visit to the United Nations in New York he expressed the conviction that a majority of votes could be raised in the *Bundestag* for an exchange of ambassadors with Israel.[37] Why this suggestion never was put forward is inexplicable. Another proposal worked out by the Social Democratic Parliamentary Party was a program of technical and economic aid to be given to Israel as well as to the Arab states. Such aid would be one means of establishing peace in that region, since it often had been said that social inequality between the Arab world and Israel was the source of all the evil and the enmity. This aid program, then, would help to improve the standard of living in Arab countries and enable Israel to take in more immigrants and provide them with employment.

The only real concession the Social Democrats extracted from the government was the setting up of the Near East Subcommittee as part of the Parliamentary Foreign Affairs Committee following a proposal made by Fritz Erler, the late Social Democratic Floor Leader, in reply to Professor Erhard's government declaration of October 24, 1963.

Erler said then that restitution payments alone would not improve the relations between Jews and Germans; also, that conflicting statements, constantly made by German politicians regarding the German attitude towards the Near East should be avoided.[38] The appointment of a subcommittee out of the Foreign Affairs Committee is very rare in German Parliament and done in principle in order to discuss subjects privately. The subcommittee was composed of three members of each of the two big parties—the CDU and the SPD—and one member of the Free Democrats and it was under the chairmanship of Herman Kopf, CDU. The manner in which it was manoeuvered made it clear that the CDU and FDP were not at all

[36] At its biannual congress in Karlsruhe, on November 28, 1964, twelve draft resolutions out of 140 dealt with a request for diplomatic relations with Israel.

[37] *Allgemeine Wochenzeitung der Juden in Deutschland*, June 21, 1963.

[38] Minutes of the *Bundestag*, vol. 53, p. 4272.

interested in arriving at a solution which would bring about diplomatic relations between Israel and Germany.

After eight meetings in which Foreign Office officials had presented reports on the situation in the Near East (the first one on January 9; the last one, on June 9, 1964), the Social Democrats tabled a motion which included the demand for diplomatic recognition of Israel. This motion was rejected and the CDU, shortly before the summer recess, declared that it, too, would now present a motion. It took until November 12 to complete it. It was now the turn of the Free Democrats to announce that they intended to put forward another motion, shortly. In the meeting on December 16, 1964, it was decided to combine the three drafts in one resolution. By then, the Committee's composition had been changed to give the CDU five seats, the SPD, four and the FDP, one. But the two meetings following did not bring any results, either. It would seem that the Committee had flogged a dead horse.[39] With the same noncommittal attitude, Chancellor Erhard said on October 15, 1964, in the Parliament's budget debate: "Our relationship to the state of Israel is not guided by political considerations. It cannot be freed from the burden imposed on it by National Socialism." [40]

This remark meant nothing. Israel was gradually losing patience with the Federal Republic. Premier Levi Eshkol replied to Erhard in the *Knesset* on October 19:

. . . It is not for us to beg the Federal Republic to renounce its strange isolation (of Israel) among the states of Europe regarding the question of diplomatic relations. The fact that Germany did not consider it right in those many years to take a step in this direction deprives its policy of that particular moral basis of which Professor Erhard has spoken.[41]

On November 4, 1964, parliamentarians debated the government's Near East policy in question hour. The dilemma of the government with regard to its policy was quite evident since it required this kind of debate to answer a simple question.

Dr. Friedensburg, CDU, started the ball rolling when he asked whether the Federal government would, at last, give in to the pressure of many citizens and extend diplomatic relations to Israel, "in

---

[39] Information obtained from SPD parliamentarian Fritz Sänger.
[40] Minutes of the *Bundestag*, vol. 56, p. 6778.
[41] Information Bulletin of the Israel Mission, Cologne, November, 1964

view of the special moral obligation of the German people." Dr. Carstens, State Secretary of the Foreign Office, who worked hand in glove with Dr. Schroeder, replied that this was not intended for the time being. When pressed again by Dr. Friedensburg, Carstens replied that, apart from the moral aspect mentioned by the CDU parliamentarian, there were other contentions which had to be taken into account. Dr. Carstens wriggled like an eel under the barrage of questions and implored the parliamentarians to refer the matter to the Foreign Affairs Commission where he could speak more freely. When he was asked by Dr. Mommer, SPD, whether he agreed that special responsibility toward Israel and the people's feelings in favor of diplomatic relations were important factors to be taken into consideration, Dr. Carstens coolly said that the issue had to be judged first from a "foreign" political point of view.[42] Only a month later, the issue was again a topic of parliamentary question hour. It was then that Dr. Schroeder held out a solution which was "under one hundred percent" but which, to his mind, still could be satisfactory.

From this remark it became evident that Schroeder hoped to deal with the pressure by offering a kind of German Mission to be set up in Israel with consular tasks and an ambassador at the head.[43] It was a trick similar to the one practiced by the GDR: setting up Consulate Generals in noncommitted countries when diplomatic relations were not granted to them. But what Dr. Schroeder did not disclose was that he was perfectly aware of the fact that Israel no longer was ready to accept such a shabby solution. Its politicians had said so, time and again. What had been negotiable in 1956, could no longer be considered an object of negotiations with Israel. Schroeder most likely expected that, once Germany had shown its "generosity" towards Israel, the German public would consider the rejection of even this minimum offer ungrateful, and would turn against Israel. But Dr. Schroeder totally miscalculated the situation, public sentiment and the generally weak standing of the Bonn government.

[42] Joachim Kreysler and Klaus Jungfer, *Deutsche Israel Politik*, p. 108, Wolf von Tucher Verlag G.m.b.H., Diessen-Ammersee, 1965.
[43] *Der Spiegel*, November, 1964.

12
The "Socialist" Germans and Israel

Until January, 1953, Julius Meyer had waited and had maintained hopes. He could not believe that, once again, he would have to escape, to take refuge somewhere where anti-Semitism was not part of a political program. Then he fled to save his skin, leaving most of his newly acquired belongings behind.

As Chairman of the Jewish communities in the Russian-occupied zone of Germany, Meyer had trusted the first pledges of the East German Communist rulers that once and for all Jews could live in peace in the "first German Socialist state." He and the other Jews had had good reason to believe. In the beginning, the Jewish communities in the Russian occupied zone had received financial and other support from the state to rebuild their religious and cultural institutions which had been destroyed or neglected during the Nazi Reich. The few Jews who had returned from concentration camps to settle in Eastern Germany practiced their religion, taught their children the Old Testament and received economic assistance from relatives abroad. Practically none registered with a Jewish community had political ties.

The number was fewer than that of the Jews who had decided to live in the West. Communism and the leadership of the Russians did not inspire confidence in all. Some of them went there because of past ties or out of sympathy with their liberators. As so-called "victims of Fascism," Jews had certain privileges, like all those who had suffered at the hands of the Nazis for political reasons. The Communists assured the Jews, and the world, that a revival of Fascism, Nazism or anti-Semitism would be totally excluded in Eastern Germany as long as the Socialists were in power, and that all would be done to guarantee that they could remain there.

This was the era, also, during which the Russians, the masters of Communist policy and their satellite states, appeared to have made their peace with the existence of the Jews as a separate entity. It was the time when they also voted in the United Nations to help found the state of Israel. This attitude was unique, considering later history. At that time, the Russians blamed the Germans for the genocide of European Jewry, as did most of the world. They could not have acted hostile to Jewry then. But a more important, political calculation, might have been the fact that by founding the state of Israel, the British lost yet another foothold in the Middle East where the Russians had always been eager to be represented. And, the Arab states had offered no partnership to the Russians, yet. Most of them were feudal societies and had no reason to hope for a Socialist system to replace them. Above all, a change of the political setup in the Near East promised more chances of influence than a stalemate.

The East German stooges of Moscow were bound to pursue a similar line of policy, as did all satellite states. They did not have voice in international politics and, therefore, could not vote on a state of Israel. But they tried to treat the Jews, within their realm of power, in a human fashion, indicating that they would take into account what the victims had suffered. There was, in fact, an offer from Otto Grotewohl—then Chairman of the Socialist Unity Party (SED), later the first Prime Minister of the GDR—to help Israel in gathering its immigrants. This was in April, 1948, when he met with Dr. Yachil, Consul in Munich, and Dr. Livneh, the Jewish agency representative in West Berlin. The meeting had been initiated by Dr. Yachil. The Arabs had already converged on what was to be the Jewish state; there had been heavy fighting in Palestine ever since the middle of February, 1948. At the end of March, the Americans no longer appeared ready to back up the partitioning of Palestine, making it a Jewish and an Arab state according to the United Nations' decision. There was talk of an international trusteeship of Palestine as a transitory solution, which was bound to be unacceptable to the Jews. It was up to Dr. Yachil [1] to solve the problem of what to do with the DPs in the camps of Western Germany waiting to be

[1] Dr. Haim Yachil, in conversation with the writer, May 20, 1969.

taken to Palestine. It was unthinkable to leave them in Germany until, or if ever, the state came into being, *de facto*. Worse still was the thought that a war would stop immigration altogether and the Jews would have to remain in Germany.

Dr. Yachil, who no longer had any contact with his government due to the fighting,[2] wondered whether there might be any support forthcoming from the Russians if the Americans failed them. Perhaps a route could be opened to Palestine for the emigrees by way of Eastern Europe. Yachil and Livneh asked Julius Meyer to contact Otto Grotewohl, as a direct approach to the Russians was impossible.

A meeting was arranged. In a private flat in East Berlin, Grotewohl, Dr. Yachil, Dr. Livneh, and Julius Meyer met and the talk (which for Dr. Yachil, curiously enough, remained the only one held with a German politician during his term of office in Germany from 1945 to 1949) lasted three hours. Grotewohl at once pledged his own and his party's solidarity with the Jews and with their fight for the state of Israel.

Dr. Yachil outlined his problems and inquired whether Russian aid could be expected for the immigration of the DPs to Palestine should the Americans fail to assist them. Grotewohl expressed the conviction that this was likely. He offered to take Dr. Yachil to Marshal Sokolowski, the Commander General of the Russian-occupied zone of Germany. Yachil, having no authorization from his government, declined for the time being. Then, Grotewohl offered restitution to Israel. Owing to the destruction and the great amount of unclaimed property, he suggested no individual compensation but a lump sum for the state of Israel. He said he preferred not to wait until Israel had actually come into being but would like to give something immediately, as a symbol of his state's support. There was, for example, the Jewish hospital in Leipzig. It had not been destroyed, but there were no Jews there. Therefore, he suggested, as a gesture and as compensation for the hospital a ship or ships that would help to transport the immigrants to Israel as soon as this was feasible—"as a symbol of making amends to the Jewish state."

Grotewohl and his Jewish interlocutors agreed to keep in touch with one another. Dr. Yachil told Grotewohl that there would be no backing down for the Jews from their demands, even if this

[2] At the beginning of April, 1948, traffic on the main road between Jerusalem and Tel Aviv was no longer possible and the outskirts of Jerusalem were being attacked by guerilla troops.

meant their destruction. "If we survive, we shall return," he said to Grotewohl. Many months later, Dr. Yachil was able to report this conversation to Foreign Minister Moshe Sharett. But, by then no contact could be made with East Germany.

Dr. Grotewohl, a former Social Democratic leader, who had succumbed to Russian pressure to merge his party with the Communists in the Russian-occupied zone in 1946 doubtlessly had spoken without authorization. For the East German government at no time showed any readiness to compensate the Jews or any other victims of Fascism for their material losses. But, again, the East Germans copied the Soviet Union which had failed to react from the very start to any similar request from Israel or World Jewry. They never replied to any of the notes from Israel addressed to the Four Powers requesting compensation from Germany. The Soviet Union, and subsequently the GDR, had reasons of their own for not paying any attention to the justified Jewish claims. One was that, if the East German government accepted them from its Jewish population or from those who had once lived there, the governments of Hungary, Bulgaria and Rumania, whose wartime governments had collaborated with Hitler, would hardly be able to repudiate them.[3]

But, the Communists had confiscated the Jewish property stolen by the Nazis, and had turned it into national property. They were not interested in restoring it to its rightful owners in accordance with their policy of state ownership. The official statement gave a different reason. East Germany, the Communists explained to the world, had no need to pay compensation to the Jews as, contrary to Bonn, it had eradicated Fascism in its part of the world. A new society was in the making there. This was a great achievement and assurance to former victims of Fascism that they could live in the GDR without fear. This was more important than any material sacrifices which the Jews demanded from the Germans.[4]

From the end of the war until his escape from the GDR, Julius Meyer and his executive board members had led a desperate but hopeless fight for the return of private Jewish property. In a few cases where Jewish property was still in private hands, legal proceedings for return only led to a speeding up of its confiscation. But, apart from this, the Jews in the GDR could live there without being molested until 1952. And this applied to those who had re-

[3] Kurt R. Grossmann, "Germany's Moral Debt," p. 30, *Public Affairs Press,* Washington, D.C.

[4] Albert Norden, in press conference, February 2, 1960.

nounced their Jewish origin. They did not sign up with the Jewish communities and, in compliance with their politics, they called themselves atheists. Among them were lifelong Communists who had suffered under Hitler for their creed rather than for any "racial" reasons. They played a part in the running of the state and accepted the rules laid down by Communism as gospel truth. They felt no allegiance to Jewry.

The attitude towards the Jews in the GDR changed drastically at the beginning of the fifties. Again, it was a perfect imitation of what went on within most of the Communist world by then. In the Soviet Union, a new wave of terror was directed against doctors and persons in economic life. These people were charged with anti-Russian activities or, more precisely, with having contacts with the "hostile" West. There were many Jews in these professions who consequently became victims of the new purges. The so-called "conspiracy" of some doctors against the life of Stalin and the arrest, trial and subsequent execution of the Jewish Communist Party Secretary, Rudolf Slansky, in Czechoslovakia—accused of high treason, espionage, sabotage and participation in an alleged Jewish plot to overthrow the government—are examples of this period.

East Germany did not lag behind in adopting this new line. In January, 1952, the Secretary of State of the Ministry for State Security, Mielke, gave orders to all branch offices throughout the country to watch the Jews and to register whether or with what groups they met regularly.[5] An East German security officer, who later escaped to the West, stated that it was marked on index cards whether or not a person was Jewish or partly Jewish. Who (of the Jewish population) received parcels from the American welfare organization, the American Joint Distribution Committee, was also noted, as well as which Jewish citizens of the GDR met in West Berlin's Café Wien, much frequented by Jews from the West.

In February, 1952, Jewish communities were requested under a certain, plausible pretext to supply the government authorities with membership lists, giving details about the person's place of residence during the war.

All this indicated that the charge of contacts with the "hostile" West was to be pursued. Censorship offices were advised to tap the telephones and control the mail of Jewish citizens. Once the Slansky trial had taken place in Czechoslovakia, the dismissal of Jewish em-

[5] *Die Neue Zeitung*, April 7, 1953.

ployees from municipalities and other government administrations became a matter of course. Notice was given by the Party Secretariats verbally, and, in case of inquiries as to the reason, the Slansky trial was given as a "lesson."

Subsidies to Jewish communities no longer were paid. Religious instructions and all cultural events were not permitted to take place any more. The escape of Julius Meyer led to several arrests of Jews serving in the Foreign Office. The offices of Jewish communities were raided and searched for "material." Jews were interrogated as to their contacts abroad. Most Jews left the GDR hurriedly, which was still fairly easy. However, they could not leave officially; this might have led to their immediate arrest as no freedom of movement exists in Communist countries. But, it was still possible to reach West Berlin, without belongings and using public conveyances connecting the Eastern and the Western part of the city. In the end, 1,500 Jews remained in the entire country, including East Berlin— about five thousand had settled there by 1947.

A correspondent of the Israeli paper, *Ha'aretz*, who traveled in East Germany reported the situation in detail.[6] Of the total population of seventeen million, there were about 1,500 Jews in East Germany, mostly old people living on pensions of some kind. There were eight Jewish communities: East Berlin had eight hundred Jews; Leipzig, 140; Chemnitz, together with Zwickau, thirty to forty. One hundred Jews lived in Magdeburg; in Dresden and surrounding areas, one hundred Jews were registered. About fifty lived in Halle and another fifty in Schwein-Rostock. A few Jews could be found in other small places. The Jews of East Berlin had no contact with those of the Western part of the city. They knew only what the papers published, which was usually unfriendly propaganda. There were 120 Jewish cemeteries in East Berlin which were cared for by the government. Generally speaking, the synagogues, cemeteries, community centers, orphanages and old-age homes were looked after with great care. Obviously, the synagogues were practically empty—including the one in Leipzig toward which the government contributed for reconstruction.

"There is no anti-Semitism in the Eastern Zone of Germany," the journalist was told, "but there are anti-Semites." Since Ulbricht did not depend on the people's likes or dislikes, his government, at first, conducted a relatively lenient policy towards the Jews.

[6] Reprinted in *Aufbau*, September 7, 1962.

The GDR, in its eagerness to be good followers of the leadership in Moscow, also produced its "Slansky." Paul Merker, a lifelong Communist and important member of the Communist hierarchy, was arrested in December, 1952. For him and for those who had shed their Jewish belief, and had lived and struggled for Communism, only, it meant a shattering of their world when they were suddenly accused of treason. Merker was expelled from the party on the grounds that, when still in exile during the war, he had demanded the return of Jewish property to its former owners. The Central Committee of the East German Communist Party (SED), called him a "subject of American finance oligarchy, who demanded compensation for Jewish property only to enable American capital to intrude upon Germany . . ." [7]

What Merker called Jewish property, the Communists said, was what monopoly capitalists had squeezed out of German and foreign workers. When this was taken from the Jews it was merely passed on to their "Aryan" counterparts.

A few days after Merker's arrest, other Jewish Communists of long standing were ousted from the Party for the same or similar reasons which, in the Communist setup, is equal to economic ruin, as there is no way to obtain employment other than through government or party authorities. The official version read that those persons had to be expelled from the party because, "on behalf of world Jewry, they had made a deal with their accomplices . . ." (meaning the capitalists). [8] Other Communists of Jewish stock who were not expelled were isolated and ignored.

The word "anti-Semitism" or "Jews," was never uttered in the GDR. No doubt, this was to make it appear to the outside world that Jews in the GDR were citizens like any others, and perfectly safe. Though in its application the anti-Jewish actions may have appeared similar to some introduced by the Nazis, the East German campaign against the Jews was not based on similar arguments. The Jews—as in the Soviet Union, also—became the scapegoat needed by any dictatorial regime at one time or another. They had preserved a unique solidarity and had remained a religious group, appearing at the time the only one which Communism had failed to break up and to subjugate, both politically and ideologically. This was difficult for the Communist leaders to take and, whenever needed, they

[7] *SBZ-Biographie, Bundesministerium fur gesamtdeutsche Fragen,* p. 232, Bonn, 1966.
[8] *SBZ von A bis Z,* p. 221, Bonn, 1963.

vented their wrath on the Jews. The worldwide contacts of Jewry made the Communists suspicious. They interpreted the hostility of the free world against their system as an intention to deal a death blow to it.

Israel was held responsible for the Jews remaining a separate entity. Zionism strengthened the bonds between them, the Communists said. It also distracted the Jewish workers from the class struggle. Therefore, the founding of the state of Israel had caused this special Jewish patriotism to become increasingly dangerous.[9] One of the many charges against Paul Merker and his colleagues in East Germany was that they were "Zionists." In the article written in his Mexican refuge, Merker had pleaded for the creation of a Jewish state and for the assistance to all those Jews who wanted to emigrate to it or to any other state of their choice. The Communists described Israel as a capitalist state in sympathy and close cooperation with America. The Jews in the GDR who admitted to being Zionists had to expect to be looked upon as "enemies of the state."

Political changes in the Arab world in the beginning of the fifties made the Communists also aware of the Arab prospects ripe for Communism. Their anti-Israel attitude began to serve an additional political purpose. The East Germans added to this the hope that the Arab world might be able to help them to win international recognition. If only one such state would extend diplomatic relations to them, they reckoned, other noncommitted countries might follow suit. Thus, the road would be prepared for an international acceptance of a second German state. The Luxembourg Treaty between Israel and West Germany offered an excellent opportunity for the East German Communists to prove to the Arabs that, contrary to Bonn, they were with them in their struggle against Israel.

On November 25, 1951—two months after Dr. Adenauer had indicated in a declaration before the *Bundestag* that Bonn would favorably consider the Jewish requests for compensation—*Neues Deutschland*, the East German Communist party organ, called this a business deal "between West German and Israeli big capitalists." It said that German capitalists had secured for themselves a market and high profits for years to come; the same imperialist criminals of German industries who had benefited from the murder of millions of Jews profited now for a second time from these crimes. The paper continued, those who benefited from the deal were those "damned" Is-

9 *Ibid.*

raeli capitalists and the chief profit was cashed in by "the initiators of the deal," the American imperialists who wanted to strengthen their own position in the Near East opposite the Arab states and England.

The slogan, "axis of revanchism," was born and harped on continually in the attempt to convince those Arab states calling themselves "Socialist" of East German friendship, in contrast to Bonn, still holding up ties to Israel. Eventually, the East German Communists made West German restitution payments appear to be nothing but a deliberate, hostile act against the Arab world. On November 2, 1956, Prime Minister Otto Grotewohl, in a government statement, denounced restitution as "so-called reparations of which Israel made use in its struggle against the Near East peoples' independence movements." He appealed to Bonn to stop every kind of aid to Israel at once.[10] This statement was made at the time of the Suez conflict which served the East German Communists in their wooing of Arab countries. They called Israel "an American agency," "an aggressive military outpost" and "a constant troublemaker in the Near East." Like all other Communist countries, East Germany, with furious charges against the West and Israel, tried at the same time to distract the attention of the noncommitted countries from the Russian intervention in Hungary.

In April, 1957, Grotewohl, in another government declaration, repeated this theme: "Irrespective of Israel's aggressive acts towards the Arab peoples, the Bonn government have continued to pay reparations to Israel, which are used for arming against the Arab peoples." [11] On October 27, 1958, Gerhard Weiss, Deputy Minister of Foreign Trade, said before the press in Baghdad, as chief of a trade delegation: "While the GDR, as you probably know, has no relations with Israel, the Bonn government contributes greatly through so-called reparation payments to the material and moral strengthening of Israel, whose role in the imperialist policy of hostility towards the Arabs has become repeatedly clear." [12]

When Dr. Adenauer and David Ben-Gurion met in New York in March, 1960, the Foreign Ministry in East Berlin termed it, "One cold warrior pays his tribute to the other." [13] In the Communists' opinion, Dr. Adenauer wanted to retain West Berlin as a center of

[10] *Neues Deutschland*, November 3, 1956.
[11] *Neues Deutschland*, April 4, 1957.
[12] *Deutsche Presse-Agentur*, October 27, 1958.
[13] Statement of the GDR Foreign Ministry, March 17, 1960.

trouble against peace in Europe, and Ben-Gurion was seeking support for Israel's policy of endangering peace in the Near East, to the detriment of the Arab world.

The East German regime, however, were in a quandary over the Eichmann capture. They could not actually condemn Israel for having caught one of the men responsible for the mass murder of the Jews. Therefore, they managed another lie. They claimed that Israel had known of Eichmann's hiding place in Buenos Aires since 1953. Professor Friedrich Kaul, a Jew (who appeared as defense counsel before West German courts), in his book, *Der Fall Eichmann*,[14] quotes Simon Wiesenthal, the noted hunter of Nazis in Vienna, as having learned this from a friend. Kaul reasoned that Israel had to leave Eichmann in his hiding place because of the trouble with Kastner. The Hungarian Jewish leader had been accused in Israel of collusion with the Nazis in Hungary in 1944; with Eichmann, in particular, over the exclusion of six hundred Hungarian Jews—mainly friends and members of Kastner's family—from deportation.

In a trial in Israel, starting in May, 1953, the alleged guilt of Dr. Israel Kastner was confirmed. Kaul wrongly alleges in his book that Kastner was a high-ranking official of the Israeli state and a leading member of the ruling party, the *Mapai*. As the trial and the verdict against Kastner were most embarrassing to the Israeli government, Kaul claims that Eichmann had to be left in his South American refuge to avoid embarrassing the government: Eichmann could have revealed the full truth about Dr. Kastner's collaboration with the Nazis. Nevertheless, a higher court, four years later, did not uphold the former verdict. Two months later, in March, 1957, Kastner was murdered in a street of Tel Aviv by a Hungarian fanatic.

Despite this, Kaul went to Israel for the Eichmann trial and made efforts to be admitted as representative of East German co-plaintiffs, with the obvious intention of using the Israeli court as a platform against West Germany and the "Eichmanns" in office there. Since Israel's legal system recognizes the institution of co-plaintiffs for civil suits, only, Professor Kaul was forced to carry out his activities (with little success) aside from the Jerusalem court.

But, in order to influence people still harboring sympathy for the Jewish state—especially in the wake of the daring abduction of Adolf Eichmann—the East German authorities published a special

[14] Published by *Das Neue Berlin*, p. 91, 1963.

booklet directed against Israel.[15] This booklet concluded with the statements that: Israel was a breeding place of national suppression and of national discrimination; that the disgrace of *Mapai*, the leading party, was its racialist policy towards the Arab minority; that the country's inhabitants were compelled to live under a racialist Fascist regime mindful of Verwoerd [16] in South Africa; that the entire legal and executive power lay in the hands of a small group of leaders of bourgeois nationalist organizations which were in closest contact with the American monopolies and societies; that the mixture of Turkish, English and old Jewish legislation, contradicting one another, and often reactionary and outdated, suited the Israeli administration well. Israel, in this booklet, was called "a paradise for crooks" and "a place where the masses lived under unimaginable want"; where hundreds of thousands led an abominably poor life so that most of the immigrants from Socialist countries, virtually from the day of their arrival, could hardly wait for a speedy return, and the ruling circles were on the side of the worst enemies of freedom.

The few Jews who had remained in East Germany and whose fate had improved with the end of Stalinism in the GDR (hesitatingly, but not as drastically as in some other Communist states) constantly issued declarations. They were directed either against Israel or against the revival of Nazism, militarism or anti-Semitism in the Federal Republic of Germany. These declarations and statements were obviously ordered and appeared on "suitable occasions."

On January 11, 1960, a memorandum signed by all chairmen of the Jewish communities in the GDR was sent to the Four Powers, protesting the "revival of anti-Semitism, militarism and Nazism in the Federal Republic." On November 4, 1963, on the occasion of the twenty-fifth anniversary of the *Reichskristallnacht* (November 9, 1938, the beginning of organized persecution of Jews in Germany), the executive of the Jewish communities in the GDR declared that "the murderers of six million Jews were employed in state and economy of Western Germany."

The Jews seemed to be the most striking witnesses against the Jewish state, although the GDR citizens could learn the truth from West German television and radio, as well as from West German

---

[15] *Der Staat Israel—Situation und Politik*, (a translation from the Russian), Dietz Verlag, Berlin, 1961.

[16] Hendrik Frensch Verwoerd, South African political leader, Prime Minister, 1958-1966.

newspapers obtainable in West Berlin until the erection of the Wall in 1961. Since the signatories were generally from leading Communists who had obeyed such orders all their lives, this was nothing exceptional, nor did it seem in any way painful to them.

The disclosure, in 1964, that Bonn was aiding Israel with arms caused an uproar in East Germany. Once again, the East Germans explained that this was precisely the reason why they had not paid any compensation to the Jews—this would only have enabled them to conclude an arms deal with Bonn. While the West German government, feeling a moral obligation, extended this military aid to assure the Jewish state's survival against all odds, the East Germans charged that, by this arms deal, Israel proved its purpose of being an imperialist bulwark in the Middle East with the intention of suppressing, at all costs, the freedom struggle of the Arab peoples. They alleged that the West Germans also assisted Israel with atomic and nuclear arms as they hoped by doing so that they, too, would become eligible for the possession of this type of armament one day.

On November 19, 1964, the Deputy Foreign Minister of the GDR, Dr. Wolfgang Kiesewetter, declared in the *Volkskammer* (Parliament): ". . . the West German pledges of friendship towards them (the Jews) were nothing else but the hypocritical double game, and solely served the purpose of diverting attention from the fact of the West German assistance for Israel's atomic rearmament. The GDR government evaluates the cooperation of the Federal Republic with Israel as part of the efforts of the West German generals of Hitler to obtain for themselves, by hook or by crook, the power of disposition over nuclear arms and other means of mass annihilation." [17]

The East Germans' painting of this particularly grim picture surely served the double purpose of appearing to be the guardians of the Arabs as well as calming their own people who could not all have felt entirely free from a certain responsibility towards the Jews.

While the Federal Republic of Germany paid compensation to Israel, and to the Jews who had once possessed property in Germany, and while a certain relationship developed between the two countries in the course of time, the GDR and Israel had no contact,

---

[17] ADN (*Allgemeine Deutsche Nachrichten*), East Germany news agency, November 19, 1964.

whatsoever. The GDR pretended to feel absolutely no need to make up for anything to the people who had suffered most at the hands of the Germans. After 1952, Israel, realizing the futility, no longer made any requests to the GDR for compensation. Somehow, the East Germans behaved as if they were not Germans; as if they were in no way related to or accountable for, the Germany of the past. The East Germans implied that they had created a new country; a healthy mutation of the stale, ailing parent-nation in the West.

The West Germans struggled with the past, they discussed it, they worried about it, they tried to understand how it all had happened—particularly their young people. Some never got away from it; others suppressed it. But, in reality, it was always with them in some form.

In East Germany, no one found it necessary to rake over the past. Pointing to the West and the efforts there to winnow this past, visitors were told that these were consequences of "capitalism," which never would recur in East Germany. *They* were building a Socialist state with a wonderful future, to which, unlike West Germany, the Nazis and Nazism would never have access. Pupils in schools learned about Hitler as about Frederick the Great, and whenever there were hints of Fascists or Nazis, they were told that they were "on the other side." It must be assumed that this appealed to the East Germans, who, like the West Germans, always showed gratitude for any kind of absolution.[18]

Thus, the East Germans felt no moral pangs about Israel or the state of the Jewish survivors of the German massacre. Moreover, under East German dictatorship, public pressure would not be tolerated. The East German government could, therefore, use Israel as a pawn in a political game along the lines of their Russian masters. Moscow wanted a foothold in the Middle East, even if the people there could not be converted to Communism. Israel, with all its ties to the West, and a well-established democracy, did not promise success. So, it could be only the Arab states that offered the Russians the advantage of playing a part in the noncommitted world—an indication of why, from the Russian point of view, the Near East conflict must persist.

The East Germans could do their share to achieve this by placat-

---

[18] Amos Elon, *In einem heimgesuchten Land*, p. 181, Kindler Verlag, Munich, 1966.

ing the Arabs with an anti-Israel policy and by aiding them in their limited way. But, apart from this, the East Germans kept hoping that the Arab states, in "brotherhood and friendship," would extend diplomatic relations so that not only the Federal Republic but East Germany, too, would find international recognition. That the Arabs withhold this diplomatic relationship to this day (even after they severed ties to West Germany in 1965) is probably due to practical sense: the East Germans could not offer as much as Bonn. Nasser, the undisputed leader of the Arab world, until after the Arab defeat in 1967, tried hard, though ineffectively, not to become totally dependent on the Communist world.

East Germany has remained the only Communist country that never had any contact with Israel in the course of the past twenty years. Intermittently, diplomatic relations have been maintained with other Eastern bloc states. Jewish nationals of these countries have been given rare opportunities to visit Israel and their relations there. The frontiers of East Germany have remained absolutely tight since the Wall was erected in Berlin, in 1961, to stop people from escaping from the East German "workers and peasants" state. Only old-age pensioners were permitted to leave, at a later stage. Israel's Communists, their number minute, were allowed into this Communist people's state to dutifully deliver the pledges to Socialism and unfriendly statements against their own country. Israel, a democratic state, had no means to stop them from doing so.

Israel, the Jewish state, with quite a number of functioning Socialist institutions, and the GDR, the East German state, allegedly Socialist, yet being totalitarian in the extreme, are totally alien to one another. Israel and the Federal Republic of Germany have struggled for a basis on which to found a relationship after the bitter past. It is not a relationship of cordiality—perhaps, for many people on the Jewish side, rather one of necessity in view of the West German state's influence in Europe. But, it *is* a basis, however shaky at the present moment, wherein new generations may find a different approach to one another.

The East Germans have a lot to explain and to account for, if ever the political regime allows contacts with the state of Israel. Although it was not easy for Israel to eventually accept the West German advances, it seems almost out of the question that Israel should ever cooperate with East Germany, considering the postwar attitude and the fact that Germans who failed to make amends for the Nazi past remain there.

13
Two States in a Fix

Strangers embraced each other, fellaheen danced, when, to the tune of a specially composed hymn of jubilation, Egypt's first rockets were paraded past them through the streets of Cairo. That July 23, 1962 (the tenth anniversary of the successful revolt of Egyptian officers against the monarchy, marked each year by a military parade) was, for Egypt, a day especially memorable. The rockets—which experts had considered merely empty shells—were constructed to reach even "south of Beirut," Nasser proudly threatened. A special Egyptian postage stamp was to announce this "feat" to the whole world.

In Israel (obviously the target), the new menace caused concern. The country had no weapons with which to defend itself against rockets. It might not have taken this new threat from Egypt so seriously, had it not been that German scientists and experts had had a major share in the construction of the Egyptian weapons. Even though German rocket and space research was at a low ebb at the time and could not pride itself on international esteem, the fact remained that Germans had produced V-rockets causing considerable damage to England during the war. "If they construct these V-rockets for Egypt, Israel's security is undoubtedly threatened," Israeli military experts warned. And, in truth, some of Hitler's former rocket experts were members of the team of German scientists who had given a new stimulus to Egyptian war strategists.

Since 1960, a chartered plane had always been ready for instantaneous takeoff at Stuttgart's airport, *Echterdingen*, to fly Germany's No. 1 rocket expert, Dr. Eugen Saenger, or any of his staff to Cairo. Professor Saenger, by then chief of *Strahlenantrieb*, the Stuttgart research institute for physics of jet power, had been a member of Hitler's favorite rocket development team. In 1933, he had published his first book on rockets which had become the standard textbook for all German rocket researchers in Hitler's service.[1] Saenger had been given all-out support to develop missiles for military purposes. In 1936, he had founded a modern institute in the secluded area of the Lüneburger Heide, camouflaged as an aviation testing ground. In 1943, when Saenger announced that he could execute his task of developing missiles for the purpose of hitting far distant targets (such as New York) in about ten years' time, he had been transferred to Peenemünde, Hitler's rocket laboratory on the Baltic Sea, to help there with the construction of V-weapons.

Like practically all German scientists who went abroad in 1945 (some voluntarily, the majority forced), Saenger had joined the French research team at that time. When he returned in 1954—some people say because he had not produced a single new idea since the Hitler Reich's collapse, and had proved of little international market value—it had prompted the Germans to found the Stuttgart research institute to catch up with international development in the field of space research, dormant since the war. Fifteen industrial firms, including Daimler-Benz, technical colleges and the Land government of Baden-Wuerttemberg, supported the Stuttgart headquarters. The Bonn Ministry of Transport saw to it that it was supplied with research projects which included the development of planes, such as increasing their starting speed, and so forth.

Surely the ambitious researchers of Stuttgart were dissatisfied with their limited tasks, for they were not permitted to construct rockets. According to the armistice agreement, Germany was not to touch such projects, having misused them for military and destructive purposes. When Professor Wolfgang Pilz, one of Saenger's colleagues, offered the German government a blueprint for the construction of a three-phase rocket with which a German satellite could be shot out into space, he did not even receive a reply.

Consequently, in 1960, Assam Mahmoud from the National Research Center in Cairo found eager volunteers in Stuttgart for part-time work on Cairo's "space research rocket for meteorological pur-

---

[1] E. Saenger, *Raketenflugtechnik*, 1933.

poses." Nasser put *Heliopolis,* the Egyptian testing ground, at the disposal of the German team. When the German government nervously reproached Saenger, he claimed that the only time he had spent in Nasser's research laboratories or lecturing to aspiring Egyptian scientists had been forty-eight of the seventy-two holidays due him. According to the scientists, the German government had been told of their scientific "sideline" and had raised no objections. On the contrary, every assistance given by Germans to Egypt was considered a strengthening of the bonds between Egypt, an influential development country, and the Federal Republic, handicapped by the East-West conflict. Yet, when diplomats from both Israel and France came to draw Bonn's attention to the activities of the German rocket researchers in Egypt, the West German government pleaded complete ignorance and promised immediate action. All those connected with the Egyptian enterprise were turned out of the Stuttgart institute at once. The German authorities were disgusted at the German scientists' behavior, considered it a breach of the confidence placed in them, and charged Saenger and his colleagues with having betrayed research secrets to another country. Professor Saenger, often called "the fool of science" for his political ignorance, hastily gave notice to his Egyptian employers. His colleagues, however, annoyed and hurt and weighing the advantages for themselves, decided to go over entirely to the Egyptian side. The most prominent among them was Professor Wolfgang Pilz, a veteran of the Nazi wartime rocket development team, but, according to Wernher von Braun (also an associate), not one of the more important researchers. Still, Pilz had worked from 1943 to 1945 in the production center for V weapons and it is said that his work from 1946 to 1957 had been decisive in the construction of the French rocket, "Véronique." [2] He had then replaced Saenger as head of the team on the Nile.

Professor Paul Goercke, an electronics guidance expert, was also an old hand at Peenemünde and France's postwar rocket research. Dr. Hans Kleinwaechter, another electronics expert (too young to have had Peenemünde experience), had come to appreciate his connection with the Saenger team in the Stuttgart research institute. Dr. Heinz Krug, the manager, remained in Germany to found the Intra Trading Company—first in Stuttgart, later on Munich's Schillerstrasse—which was to provide material and spare parts for Egypt's

[2] *Der Spiegel,* No. 19, 1963.

rocket research. Professors Pilz and Goercke became his partners in a business which turned out to be most prosperous: Krug prided himself on being so successful that he could have lived on the refunding of the export turnover tax. They encountered no difficulties in obtaining export licenses from the German government as separate parts could not be easily recognized as contributory elements to military production.

In Munich, as in Stuttgart, the offices of the company were set up in the same house with the United Arab Airlines of which, eventually, Dr. Krug also became the manager. The introduction of a weekly flight directly from Munich to Cairo assured perfect accommodations for material and men destined for Cairo.

The two rockets, *El Kahir* (The Conqueror), with an alleged range of 360 km., and *El Safir* (The Victor), with an alleged range of 280 km. (which were paraded through Cairo two years after the Saenger team had begun its work in Egypt), showed a striking resemblance to the French "Véronique" in the construction of which at least some of the German researchers had had a share.

The Israelis, pleased in 1961 when the German government took such immediate action against the Stuttgart part-timers, had not wanted and certainly had not expected that these German experts would now put their knowledge entirely at the disposal of President Nasser. None of the men could have been an expert of international renown, which may be ascertained by the fact that they had not received offers of posts in more advanced and wealthier countries, as had some of their compatriots. But they were, no doubt, proficient enough to produce a weapon that could spark the precarious Near East situation. Nasser, in his excitement over such success and in the hope that, at last, he had found a weapon which would tip the scales in his country's favor, might well risk a military confrontation with Israel.

True, the Saenger rocket team had not been the first German one to help develop Nasser's war industry and army. In 1950, German technicians and master minds already had taken up their positions in Egypt. Former officers of Hitler's *Wehrmacht*, under General Wilhelm Fahrmbacher, had undertaken to train the Egyptian army while Captain von Bechtolsheim concentrated on the Egyptian navy. According to Fahrmbacher, the Bonn Ministry of Economic Affairs had sanctioned this work.[3] A group of fellow researchers and technicians, under the leadership of Dr. Wilhelm Voss, were charged

[3] *Der Spiegel*, No. 19, 1963.

with the organization of an arms industry including the first attempts at rocket building for Egypt. These were also men tainted with a Nazi past who no longer felt "at home" in postwar Germany and for whose technical ambitions there were no longer any possibilities.

This contribution to the Egyptian war machine was still insignificant, partly due to the Egyptian government which, up to that time, had not invested too much energy and effort in the project of rocket building. It hoped to obtain decisive aid in this field from Russia or Western countries competing for Egypt's favors, but the contribution of Germans had turned out to be more important in the development of the Egyptian plane industry. Professor Willy Messerschmitt, a pioneer of Hitler's aviation industry, sold Egypt the right to copy his supersonic jet fighter, HA-200, developed in Spain. A former Austrian, Ferdinand Brandner—according to his own words, "an idealist and a fanatic of technique" [4]—was put in charge of the Egyptian aviation industry. He was soon joined by Austrians and Germans, making up a team of about two hundred who, with the assistance of several thousand Egyptians, helped to establish the two military factories "36" and "135" in Helwan. German industries, big and small, seeing nothing but their business profits in such deals, supplied the parts needed for the plane production.

All looked bright for the future of the German experts and technicians near the pyramids. They felt as if they were in paradise. Their salaries, paid partly in Swiss francs and partly in Egyptian pounds, were far above any payment they could have obtained in Europe. Their contracts entitled them to all the luxuries that are often part of the rumuneration to lure people into service abroad.

This lavish living was due to a certain Hassan Sayed Kamil, a former Egyptian-Swiss engineer and trader in jewelry and armaments, who then lived in Basle, later in Zurich. In 1952, he, together with the Egyptian War Ministry, had set up the MECO (Mechanical Corporation) and, in 1960, the MTP (Machines, Turbines, Pumps). The two firms were to assure material and experts for Nasser's aviation industry, also, later on, for the rocket production. [5] In large advertisements placed in West German newspapers, Kamil had worded it: "Experts of every kind wanted by aviation industry in

[4] *Ibid.*
[5] *Sueddeutsche Zeitung*, April 5, 1963.
  Joachim Kreysler and Klaus Jungfer, *Deutsche Israel Politik*, p. 79, Wolf von Tucher Verlag G.m.b.H., Diessen-Ammersee, 1965.

North Africa." By not naming the exact country, he showed that he was fully aware of what he was doing. The German government which, at a later date, objected strongly to this manner of enticing Germans into foreign service, did not appear to take any notice of Kamil's activities.

In 1960, Nasser decided to give priority to rocket construction at home. His relationship with the West, following the Suez conflict in 1956, seldom had been so strained. No support for his ambitious plans would be forthcoming from there. Despite all assistance from Moscow, he still hoped to steer clear of too much Russian dominance. Money was no object in his eagerness to make his dreams come true. Looking around in the world for experts, he found, for the most part, Germans, available and ready. His and his country's affinity for Germans, was of long standing, anyhow. A good number of former Nazis had found a comfortable refuge in Egypt and had become respectable citizens there, ready at any time to work against the Jews.

Restricted in their fields of work in Germany, German rocket experts had been lured to the Nile quite easily; generous working compensation and attractive living conditions had served their purpose. Two years later, the first products of their efforts filled every Egyptian's heart with unbounded joy. Now, at last, they would be able to deal the decisive blow to their enemies. The respect of the whole world for their achievement was within sight. No doubt the complexes of an underdeveloped country denied equality had influenced their thinking. However, the hope that now they would be able to eliminate Israel was paramount in their consideration.

The Israelis' uneasiness over Nasser's rocket feat was not immediately shared by their American friends. They even belittled the danger. "Don't take it too seriously," they advised the Israelis. "What they produce in Cairo are no more than toys." But this did not convince the Israelis; on the contrary, it angered them. After all, it was easy for the Americans to talk like that, living miles away from the threat. Worse still, the Americans did not seem to mind that these experts with a destructive task were Germans. They, in fact, preferred them to the Russians, convinced that they would have jumped into the breach if the Germans had not come. It was quite true that the qualifications of men like Pilz could be disputed. The West German Minister of Defense and declared friend of Israel, Franz-Josef Strauss, told Israeli government officials that he had tried to work with Pilz, only to find him absolutely below the current standard in his field.

But, for Israel, the fact remained that Pilz and his crew—however little they could match their knowledge with that of postwar rocket scientists—could still construct arms against which Israel possessed no adequate defense. Moreover, it was an unbearable thought for Israel that Germans, of all peoples, once again were contributing to the planned destruction of the Jewish state. For, Nasser never had left any doubt as to the purpose of the rockets he was building in the military factory "333." The Egyptian chief had stated the purpose repeatedly. Even if those German scientists worked in Egypt solely to make money, or because they had no field in Germany or did not measure up to the United States' space and rocket program, they could not have been unaware of the project to which they applied their knowledge. It surely is not wrong to assume that some were Nazis still, possibly because their dreams of a happy past were connected with that regime, while postwar Germany had nothing to offer them or their ambitions. Others might have cherished anti-Semitic feelings and would not have minded using the Jews once again as guinea pigs for their experiments. Incidentally, the senior medical officer of the team was the notorious Hans Eisele, who had conducted medical experiments on prisoners in the concentration camp of Buchenwald. During his trial in Germany, he had managed to escape to Egypt where he had been welcomed into the fold of the German colony in and around Cairo.

Israel rightly speculated that all of those scientists or experts who went to Egypt for work were bound to return to Germany with anti-Israel feelings. With their work concentrated on only one purpose, they were bound, as time passed, to accept the slogans and ideas that were the basis of Nasser's military schemes. With life in Egypt such a boon to them, other Germans could have been tempted to join the Egyptian teams, only to return to Germany eventually, convinced of the righteousness of Arab plans. And, last but not least, the Germans might have made the Arabs "science conscious"; an attainment to the good of the people in any other part of the world, but, in the Arab world, charged with the danger that such knowledge would be employed solely for military advantages. The Israeli fears were very real and by no means construed for political ends as some people—especially in Germany—believed likely.

Although the German experts in Egypt had gone there without

the explicit backing of the German government, Israeli public opinion, in the first place, turned against Bonn's political leadership.

"Does Bonn not know of German scientists and technicians in Egypt?" *Maariv* asked in an editorial on August 8, 1962. The government should point out to the Germans, the paper insisted, that Israel was not going to accept this policy; flirting with Israel while, at the same time, helping the Egyptian war machinery. Although the Israeli government fully realized that the German government could not be made responsible for German citizens' support of Nasser's ambitious plans, it turned to this subject one month after the rockets had been paraded through Cairo streets, when Deputy Minister of Defense Shimon Peres, in a detailed report to the German government, declared his government's concern over the work of German scientists in Egypt. Dr. Shinnar retraced in his book [6] the Germans' full understanding of the Israeli fears and their promise to do all in their power to see that no German citizen would be connected with Nasser's plans to destroy the state of Israel. Exactly what they could do to stop them they were unable to say right then.

When Professor Franz Böhm paid a visit to Israel as a guest of the government to mark the tenth anniversary of the signing of the Luxembourg Treaty, Foreign Minister Golda Meir stressed the fact that the Israeli concern was by no means a matter of "political" expediency. The problem must have given the German authorities a headache, for in a democracy every citizen has the right to freedom of movement. As postwar Germany tried its utmost to perfect its democratic system, the German government's dilemma was how to solve this problem.

When, on July 7, 1962, Hassan Sayed Kamil's German wife, Helene, Duchess of Mecklenburg, was blown to bits by a bomb in a plane over Germany, the circumstances of the accident were considered very mysterious. The fact that Kamil himself—head of MECO and MTP which supplied the Egyptian rocket industry with material and manpower—was to have been on the plane, but had changed his mind at the last minute, gave rise to the suspicion that the bomb had been intended for him.

On September 11, 1962, Dr. Heinz Krug, the top man of the Intra-Trading Society dealing in military hardware for Egypt, disappeared under equally mysterious circumstances. All that became

---

[6] Felix E. Shinnar, *Bericht eines Beauftragten*, p. 135, Rainer Wunderlich Verlag, Tübingen, 1967.

known was that Krug, on the evening before his disappearance, had been introduced to a swarthy gentleman calling himself "Saleh" (through a letter allegedly written by the Egyptian Colonel Nadim in charge of Egypt's rocket development) and had driven with him to Munich's suburb, Solln. Dr. Krug never returned. His locked Mercedes was found, three days later, in a street of Solln.

The suspicion grew that, while the German authorities still considered countermeasures, the Israeli Secret Service had taken the matter into its own hands—probably not convinced that the German government efforts would lead anywhere and worried that, meanwhile, the Egyptian rocket research might advance to perfection. The main purpose of its actions seemed to be to scare off the German experts and others who might have toyed with the idea of accepting a generous offer from Nasser's men.

The series of accidents continued. On November 27, an airmail parcel addressed to Wolfgang Pilz, the German rocket engineer in Egyptian service, blew up when opened in his "333" office in Heliopolis. It blinded and disfigured Pilz's German secretary, Hannelore Wende. A letter-bomb contained in a parcel of scientific books addressed to the Egyptian director of the rocket factory and handed in on November 28 to a Hamburg postoffice killed five Egyptians and injured six.

On February 20, 1963, Dr. Hans Kleinwaechter, by a miracle, escaped an attack on his life. Kleinwaechter, in his own laboratory in Loerrach, had undertaken research work for the Egyptian government which Professor Goercke—for lack of laboratories—could not do in Cairo. Driving home late at night another car obstructed the narrow road. While he was slowing down, a man came towards him as if he wanted to ask for something. As Kleinwaechter came to a stop, but before he was able to pull down the window, the man fired a shot through it. However, the bullet was deflected and caught by Kleinwaechter's woolen scarf. The gun jammed and, however much the attacker pulled the trigger, a second shot never was fired. The man fled in the waiting car. Kleinwaechter started up in hot pursuit but eventually lost sight of the car. The police later found it to be a hired vehicle containing identification papers issued in the names of three Egyptians and one German, all allegedly residing in Vienna.

On March 2, Israeli agents tried to "convince" Professor Paul Goercke's daughter and son, both in their twenties, that it would be better for their father to abandon his work in Cairo. Dr. Otto Joklik phoned the young persons in their Freiburg home and arranged a meeting with them to take place in the Hotel Drei Koenige in Basle. He persuaded them to cross from the South German town of Freiburg to Switzerland, apparently not wanting to risk arrest in Germany. "If he does not come back, he will be killed," the two agents threatened. Although Goercke was involved in the construction of rockets for use against Israel, "they wanted to give him a chance" because "he was not a Nazi," unlike Pilz, who was "a Nazi and a criminal" and would not be spared.

At the request of the West German authorities (who had been informed by the Goercke daughter and son), Swiss detectives eavesdropped on the meeting in Basle when the two men attempted to compel Heidi Goercke to travel to Egypt to induce her father to return home. Two weeks after this meeting, March 19, it was officially announced in Basle that two Israeli agents, Dr. Otto Joklik, an Austrian nuclear scientist, and Josef Ben-Gal, an Israeli citizen, had been arrested on the charges of "attempted coercion."

Dr. Joklik's name, it appeared, had also been mentioned in connection with the Munich disappearance of Dr. Krug. It was alleged that he had accompanied the foreign-looking "Saleh" in whose company Krug had been last seen. The scientist had originally worked in Egypt's pay but had changed sides for reasons of conscience, he maintained. Before the court, he testified that Egypt was also preparing ABC weapons against Israel. His defense counsel submitted documents said to be facsimiles of orders for Cobalt 60 made by the UAR, and declared the amount could "contaminate the atmosphere above Israel for years with fifty times the maximum genetically tolerable amount."

Joklik and Ben-Gal were also to face trial [7] for the attempted murder of Dr. Kleinwaechter, although no evidence was available. The West German legal authorities were of the opinion that the two agents had also been connected with this case. The Swiss Department of Justice refused to extradite the two men. On June 12, the accused were found guilty of attempted coercion and were sentenced to two months' imprisonment. Since the sentences were dated from their arrest on March 2, both were released immediately.

After the arrest of the two agents, the Israeli government, taking advantage of the reaction in Europe against actions aimed at contaminating human beings, stepped up their political campaign.

---

[7] During this entire trial, Ben-Gal managed to keep his face averted from the public and became known as "the man without a face."

Foreign Minister Golda Meir officially announced in the *Knesset*, on March 20, that German scientists and technicians in the UAR (whom she branded "an evil crew") were helping to develop offensive missiles and "armaments banned by international law" for use against Israel. She said: "A number of German scientists and hundreds of technicians are helping to develop offensive missiles and arms, the production of which is prohibited by international law." She indicated that, with the help of Germans, Egypt was preparing for atomic, biological and chemical warfare to wipe out the Jewish state. Egypt was "endeavoring to obtain these types of weapons which other powers are not prepared to supply through a group of scientists without conscience. . . ." There was no doubt about their motives: "On one hand, lust for gain and on the other, a Nazi inclination to hatred of Israel and the destruction of Jews." She demanded that the German government put a stop to the activities of these scientists who were, after all, its citizens. "If legislative or other measures are required for the purpose, we demand that such measures be taken at once." The accusation that Germans participated in the preparation of ABC weapons was new, but no details were given.

In a special meeting on March 19, the Israeli government had already hinted at these dangerous weapons when it had announced that it "would make disclosures of the most horrible nature about the participation of foreign experts in the development of most dangerous arms" if its agents captured in Switzerland were to be sentenced.[8] Yigal Allon, Minister of Works, was equally outspoken when he threatened: "The survivors of the death camps will not look on passively while German Neo-Nazis in the services of the Cairo Dictator prepare the destruction of Israel." [9]

The Israeli press was no less violent in its comments on Germans lending a helping hand in the preparations for annihilating Israel. "The Germans must recognize," the *Jerusalem Post* wrote, "that Israel cannot watch silently how Germans construct rockets for Nasser destined for the destruction of Israel.[10] The *Ha'aretz* wrote [11] that, actually, the responsibility lay with the Federal Republic should Israel be forced to employ "unconventional means to defend

[8] *Der Spiegel*, No. 13, 1963.
[9] Joachim Kreysler and Klaus Jungfer, *Deutsche Israel Politik*, p. 82, Wolf von Tucher Verlag G.m.b.H., Diessen-Ammersee, 1965.
[10] *Der Spiegel*, No. 13, 1963.
[11] Joachim Kreysler and Klaus Jungfer, *Deutsche Israel Politik*, p. 83, Wolf von Tucher Verlag G.m.b.H., Diessen-Ammersee, 1965.

itself against the threat with unconventional and cruel weapons." The *Maariv* charged the German government with having failed, to date, to condemn the working of German scientists for Cairo. It described the behavior of the Swiss authorities (putting the Israeli agents in jail) as most annoying and the behavior of the German authorities as criminal.[12] This anti-German tenor found a great amount of support in Israel. Even moderate politicians, ready for accord with Germany despite the past, believed that Israel had the right to censure the German government and to demand action, just because of the past.

In a resolution, the *Knesset* denounced the activities of scientists and experts working in the arms industry of Egypt which meant grave danger for the security of Israel and its citizens. It said,

The German people cannot deny its responsibility for this continued criminal activity. It is the duty of the German government to put a stop to these activities at once. . . and to take steps necessary to prevent the cooperation between these people and the Egyptian government.

The resolution was carried unanimously except for the abstention of the Communist members who stayed in line with Moscow's pro-Arab policy. On March 21, the resolution was handed to the Bonn government, which evoked an immediate promise to investigate whether or not it had means at its disposal to stop Germans from assisting in military preparations.

On the same day, Dr. Abdul Kader Hatem, the Egyptian Minister of Information, denied that Germans were engaged in the manufacture of nuclear weapons. The German Embassy in Cairo, which had held friendly contacts with the German expert teams (seeing in them, no doubt, propagandists for the German cause), confirmed the Egyptian Minister's statement. A government spokesman in Bonn indicated, on March 22, that the Israeli government had exaggerated the situation. He said that, according to his information, a maximum of eleven German experts were working on missile development in the UAR. Nevertheless, he added, the government disapproved of Germans engaging in such activities in areas of tension, but that it had no means of preventing it after their departure, unless these German citizens had violated the laws of Germany or of their host countries. Nor could the government take measures which would contravene the freedom of movement guaranteed under the Federal Constitution.

On March 27, the German Federal government, following inquir-

12 *Ibid.*, p. 85.

ies by the German Embassy in Cairo, stated that there was no evidence of Germans in the UAR being engaged in the production of atomic, biological or chemical weapons. Experts in Germany were rather surprised at this immediate assertion on the part of the German government. It was known that Egypt had approached a number of countries in the past for aid in building up its atomic reactor for the purpose of constructing an atom bomb. UAR Vice President Boghdadi had expressed this desire when he had paid his visit to Germany in 1961, but had dropped the subject when Professor Erhard, Minister of Economic Affairs, had promptly refused any such aid. Observers wondered whether the German government's statement was made in good faith or without giving much thought to the matter. After all, how could the German Embassy in Cairo know exactly what each German was doing in Egypt's employment? It is, however, correct to say that there was little need for European experts to help prepare bacteriological and chemical warfare as this could easily have been done by the Egyptians themselves.[13]

The German government added, in its declaration of March 27, that it would endeavor to bring about the return of German citizens whose activities abroad might contribute to an increase of political tension, and that it was investigating whether such activities could be effectively hindered by further legislation or administrative measures. Radical circles in Israel, with an undiminished hatred for Germans and Germany, construed this to mean that the Bonn government was well able to recall the scientists but would not do so. They used this issue to attack their government on its policy of establishing more conciliatory relations with Germany.

It was felt in Germany that Dr. Adenauer understood the Israeli grievances and his government's statement was interpreted as a definite attempt to take the matter seriously. Obviously, he had a sincere desire to remain on good terms with Israel. A crisis in the relationship—which had shown an upward trend since his meeting with Ben-Gurion in 1960—would not be to his country's advantage. Adenauer's views were shared by Bonn's politicians. On April 2, members of all three parties in the *Bundestag* demanded the recall of all German scientists and technicians working in the UAR on rocket development and aircraft production and pledged that they would introduce legislation to forbid such activities.

SPD leader Carlo Schmid questioned the government's stand that

[13] *Sueddeutsche Zeitung*, April 5, 1963.

the scientists' activities were not illegal. Schmid said that the Arab states were known to be unreconciled to the existence of Israel so whoever worked on rockets in the UAR increased the risk of war. Cooperation of German technicians in Egyptian rocket research, therefore, was contrary to Article 26 of the Federal Constitution which stated that: "Activities tending to disturb the peaceful relations between nations, and especially preparing for aggressive war" were unconstitutional and subject to punishment. However, he condemned the Israeli Secret Service activities on German soil and said that the government should make it clear to Israel that such activities were incompatible with the respect for the German government.[14]

Schmid expressed what many felt in Germany, and which was consistent with the German press reaction. The German papers called Israel's condemnation of the German scientists justified, but did not conceal their strong objections to the activities of the Israeli Secret Service. The German people's reaction was no different. What definitely had caused an additional loss of sympathy in Germany for Israel was the fact that the Israeli government had failed, up to then, to base its charges of German participation in the manufacture of ABC weapons on the publication of facts. Doubts mounted in Germany as to the existence of such evidence.

However, the activities ascribed to the Israeli Secret Service coupled with the political and press campaign produced results in the sense that German scientists in Egypt began to fear for their lives. Special provisions were made to protect them.[15]

In Cairo's central postoffice, specialists of the Egyptian security services x-rayed each parcel posted in Europe to trace explosives. Some of the experts, believing in self-protection, acquired firearms which they always kept on hand. Others, including Professor Pilz, changed residence every few months and never appeared in public.

"I have nothing whatever to do with the construction of military rockets, as can easily be proven," Professor Goercke swore. Professor Pilz made a similar statement.[16]

On March 26, the Germans on the right bank of the Nile issued a declaration, calling the reports that they were working on the development of nuclear and bacteriological weapons "a blatant lie"; their

[14] Statement before the press in Bonn, published in the newssheet of the SPD parliamentary party, June 26, 1964.
[15] Sueddeutsche Zeitung, April 5, 1963.
[16] Der Spiegel, No. 19, 1963.

work was restricted to training Egyptian engineers in rocket techniques, they said. They and their families were being threatened in a criminal and most evil way and fabrications about their work were being used "to justify these criminal acts." Thanks to their work in Egypt, the country had been able on its own strength to join the states doing space research and the results of such research could be decisive for the development of a number of industries.[17]

Professor Saenger, lecturer at the Technical University of West Berlin—no doubt pleased at his timely withdrawal—told a reporter of Israel's newspaper, *Maariv*, in April, 1963, that, according to his knowledge, the development of Egyptian military missiles would be completed by 1964, provided that the present speed of work could be maintained.[18] He announced that Nasser had given high priority to the rocket construction and that the German scientists, Goercke and Pilz, were assured of all-out support. However, Saenger disclosed, the German scientists were unhappy in Cairo. But they had such excellent working conditions that they would return to Germany only if they could be assured of similar work opportunities.

What Professor Saenger evidently did not know was that some of the German experts had already discussed the possibility of giving up their excellent posts in view of the risks now involved in their work. The first to return was the physicist, Dr. Karl-Heinz Gronau. For thirty months, he had been employed in fuel research for rockets in Egypt. He had left in March, he stated, because his contract had expired. Later on, he blamed the German authorities for misleading the German experts in Egypt. When in summer, 1962, Gronau had read in an Egyptian newspaper that Nasser threatened to destroy Israel, he and two others had asked for advice from the German Embassy in Cairo as they did not want to be charged with having participated in Egyptian production for war with Israel. The Embassy's military attaché, Kriebel—earlier accused in the Israeli press of having been an active Nazi—had advised him and his two colleagues to remain in Egypt as the Federal government and, more particularly, Defense Minister Strauss, were in favor of it and wanted to avoid the occupation of these posts by Russians, at all cost.[19] Hermann Hoecherl, Minister of the Interior, denied later that his Ministry had ever issued a written or verbal declaration authorizing German citizens to work for technical development in

[17] *Deutsche Presse-Agentur*, March 26, 1963.
[18] Reprinted in *Parlamentarisch-Politischer-Pressedienst*, April 2, 1963.
[19] *Welt der Arbeit*, April 8, 1964.

Egypt. He based this on the fact that no German needed a permit to work abroad.

Isser Harel, Israel's Security Chief, could report to his superior, the Prime Minister, that his combined actions had produced results. The German government had been alerted and now was resolved to introduce legislation to stop Germans from working on armaments in areas of tension. The German scientists showed signs of wanting to quit their dangerous posts. But, to his surprise, Ben-Gurion's reaction was one of fury; what Harel did not know was that, meanwhile, Ben-Gurion had changed his mind. Of course, Ben-Gurion was also concerned that German scientists were lending a helping hand to Nasser's plans to destroy Israel. Reports had it that Volkmar Hopf conveyed hints from Defense Minister Franz-Josef Strauss to the Israeli government that its violent anti-German campaign might endanger the secret deals between the two countries.

Hopf, State Secretary to Bonn's Defense Ministry, was in Israel when the propaganda against Germany began to run at top speed, and this was surely not accidental. He conferred with Ben-Gurion at his holiday resort in Tiberias; twice he met with Foreign Minister Mrs. Meir. The danger seemed to the Germans that Nasser, who was undoubtedly aware of the secret deals between Israel and Germany, would find this moment auspicious enough for his purposes to reveal them to the world, or that German politicians also in the know and uneasy about it would also lose patience with Israel. It is a bit difficult to understand why Ben-Gurion did not make use of his excellent contacts with Adenauer to make the German Chancellor act before the campaign against the scientists was set in motion and political control over it was lost. Possibly he did not mind the campaign against the scientists as long as he was unaware that this might have repercussions on his policy towards Germany. He then showed particular anger that the worldwide press attacks tried to place the blame on the Adenauer government for condoning a Nazi-like effort to help Nasser. Harel, who had the Eichmann capture to his credit, resigned on March 25 when Ben-Gurion told him that he could not accept "his political evaluation" and that he should stop his activities against the German scientists, at once. Ben-Gurion asked now about his attitude then, simply replied: "I was not convinced of the evidence." [20] This, no doubt, mainly concerned the charges that Germans assisted in the preparation of chemical, bacter-

[20] Interview with the writer, Haifa, August 7, 1968.

iological and atomic warheads which never were based on direct disclosures.

Ben-Gurion's attitude caused a political crisis in Israel. Rumors had it that he was displeased by Mrs. Meir's references to the West German government in her statement before the *Knesset*. This, however, was officially denied and backed up with the argument that Ben-Gurion had received the text of her statement in his holiday resort in advance and had approved its contents. However, Ben-Gurion tried hard to make the *Knesset* reverse its decision of March 20, in which it had called it the duty of the German government to put a stop to the scientists' activities in Egypt. He found very limited support among government members. Moshe Dayan, then Minister of Agriculture, shared Ben-Gurion's views. He wrote in *Maariv:*

One must never identify the German rocket research team with the German people and its government . . . It is not the German people who turn against us, but the Egyptian Dictator. And there is no talk about the German *Bundeswehr*, but there is about the Egyptian army which is assisted by a group of foreigners, Germans and others.[21]

But Ben-Gurion gained no agreement from his Foreign Minister.

A special session of the *Knesset* was held on April 7, at the request of the *Mapam*, the Liberal, the Communist and the *Heruth* parties to discuss motions demanding a full debate on the Prime Minister's attitude concerning the question of the German scientists and the resignation of the Security Chief. To opposition allegations that he had suppressed documents on the extent of the work of German scientists for Nasser's destructive projects and had caused the campaign against the Federal government to be toned down, Ben-Gurion replied: "Our grave concern over the design of the Egyptian Dictator to destroy Israel and the assistance he is receiving from German and other scientists and technicians should not throw us off our balance."

Ben-Gurion quite obviously wanted to reduce the tension that had developed due to the propaganda drumming against Germany. Not only did he fear for his policy, but he also did not wish to endanger the various secret aid measures for Israel on the part of the German government. He urged the *Knesset* to resume a responsible

21 Joachim Kreysler and Klaus Jungfer, *Deutsche Israel Politik*, p. 85, Wolf von Tucher Verlag, G.m.b.H., Diessen-Ammersee, 1965.

attitude and allow the committees concerned to deal with the issue:
". . . for obvious reasons, that discussion should take place there,
for, there are numerous things which cannot be spoken of here." A
motion against Ben-Gurion's handling of the matter was defeated—
sixty-seven to forty-two votes. Nevertheless, the rift between him
and his government members (for example, Foreign Minister Golda
Meir) persisted. His resignation on June 16, 1963, reflected this,
though it was by no means the main reason. Still, to this day, he is
not ready to talk about the affair in detail.

Anyhow, Ben-Gurion had achieved what he wanted. The issue
remained on the table but it was discussed without hysterics. In the
Bundestag, efforts were under way to find legal means to call a halt
to German scientists working on arms in another country. Nobody
could envisage then that it would become a long struggle for the
Germans, with legal and political considerations taking preference
over moral obligations towards Israel.

An inter-party committee presided over by Professor Franz
Boehm (CDU), one of Israel's best friends, assisted by representatives of the Ministry of Justice, was formed to find legal means to
stop the rocket experts in Egypt. By the beginning of May, they
had completed a draft bill that was to make work on ABC weapons
and rockets abroad dependent on permission from the Foreign Office. Whoever failed to obtain it would be liable to punishment.
Those already abroad and working on rocket projects would be
forced to apply within six months for this permit. Failing this, legal
proceedings would be started, in which case the person concerned
would be arrested on entering the Federal Republic.

This draft did not get very far. It foundered on the objections in
the Christian Democratic parliamentary party, officially claiming
that the provisions in the draft bill were not sufficiently extensive.
Some objections stemmed, however, from consideration that the bill
infringed upon the citizens' right to freedom of movement. Others
were just worried that such a law would antagonize the Arab states.
Since the committee did not know how to improve on the draft, it
was simply shelved. Instead, a motion was prepared by all three parties represented in the *Bundestag*, now charging the government
with the presentation of a bill that would rule out the participation
of Germans in the production of ABC weapons and rockets abroad.
The motion was passed unanimously on June 28, 1963, three months
after the idea of introducing legislation had been conceived. Bonn's
parliamentarians went into their summer recess with this political

gesture towards Israel, committing themselves to action against the German scientists in Egypt. Israel was disappointed. Foreign Minister Golda Meir expressed this shortly afterwards in the *Knesset*, remarking: "It was to be hoped that the Federal government would act faster on this issue. . . ." But, she was fair enough to stress that the Germans had shown understanding for the Israeli grievances.

An Inter-Ministerial Commission now set to work (consisting of representatives of the Foreign Offices, the Ministries of Justice, of the Interior, of Economic Affairs and of Economic Cooperation) but soon came up against problems similar to those of the Inter-Party Commission. They concluded that whatever they suggested was bound to clash with the citizens' right to freedom of movement guaranteed in the German Constitution. Were they to draw up a bill with similar contents as the Inter-Party Commission—and there appeared to be little alternative—it would have little practical result. A German scientist could do without the permission from a Bonn Ministry if he were to travel to an Arab country from another European state. He could also adopt the citizenship of an Arab state in order to evade punishment in Germany. And, the Commission found it very difficult to determine exactly what was a contribution to a military project; where, for example, to differentiate between atomic research for peaceful or for military ends. It might be assumed that Goercke and Pilz would not feel compelled to return even after the introduction of such a law, but it might convince young German scientists that they had not only a scientific but also a political and a moral responsibility, as in this particular case.

Appearing on German television, August 16, 1963, Israel's Prime Minister Eshkol reminded the Germans of this, saying that whoever had helped the enemies of Israel to realize their plans of annihilating other states had become guilty of a crime: "If sons of the German people who are burdened with the murder of six million Jews do so, then the crime is infinitely greater. . . ."

Eventually, the Inter-Ministerial Commission did produce two suggestions: a law forbidding work of Germans abroad should the final product be of a military character; an amendment to the passport laws according to which passports of German citizens working abroad on military projects would be confiscated.

On December 11, the West German Cabinet saw a good way out in the second suggestion and decided to ask the Minister of the Interior to draft such amendments to the passport laws. This draft contained the "right of recall," or a time limit within which persons known to participate in the construction of military projects must return; otherwise, they would forfeit German citizenship and would be liable to punishment. But this came under the same fire of criticism as the previous attempts. For, the longer the deliberations over this law lasted, the more active the Arab lobby became.

The most powerful pro-Arab pressure group represented West German heavy industries fearing for their business relations with the Arab world.[22] The Foreign Office, always mindful of German relations with the Arabs, also opposed the bill. Chancellor Erhard declared before the press on December 3, that, though the activities of the German scientists were "undesirable," they were not such as to warrant "political action." Large sections of the CDU and a majority in the Free Democratic Party also joined the opposition. The Social Democrats, who had been the most active party to see such legislation through, objected to this draft, fearing that it might, one day, be abused by a government recalling political opponents from abroad. The bill was changed again, deleting the "right of recall." On April 22, the Cabinet rejected the draft on the grounds that it infringed upon the citizens' right to freedom of movement. Thirteen months after the decision to consider such legislation, Minister of the Interior Hoecherl announced in Parliament that it could not be presented as there were legal difficulties. Specifically, the question defining the term "aggressive wars" had held up the deliberations and solution. The draft had contained a clause forbidding German scientists to help prepare "aggressive wars." The bill was turned back to the committees.[23]

On June 15, 1964, the Social Democrats made a third attempt. They tabled a draft bill to amend the section of the Constitution that dealt with the relations between peoples. According to this bill, it was to be forbidden to Germans abroad to develop, produce or assist in the production or distribution of certain arms designed for warfare. Exceptions were to be conceded by way of permits to be valid only for countries which were partners in the same defense treaty as the Federal Republic. Such exceptions were not to be granted should there be reason to assume that it would do harm to the Federal Republic's international obligations.[24] The bill passed the first reading on June 25, though hardly any parliamentarians believed that this one would see "the light of day" as it differed little

[22] *The Guardian*, May 5, 1964.
[23] Minutes of the *Bundestag*, vol. 55, p. 5963, April 29, 1964.
[24] Draft bill submitted by the SPD parliamentary party, IV-2355.

from the very first draft bill that had been rejected. And, indeed, the bill got sidetracked in the *Bundestag* committees. The problem of how to prove that German scientists worked on military projects caused the dead end. The bill never reappeared.

Chancellor Erhard announced in a press conference on September 25, 1964, that he had no hope for the introduction of an effective bill: ". . . and to produce a law for show only, is, to my mind, a bad thing." Only three weeks later, in the *Bundestag*,[25] Erhard assured Israel that the Federal Republic would do all in its power to allay the feeling of the Israeli people of being threatened by Germans. He did not divulge how this was to be done.

The Chancellor's message to Israel had been preceded by a "reminder" from Levi Eshkol on October 12. In the *Knesset*, Eshkol had taken up Erhard's pessimistic views on legislation regarding the scientists. Expressing his appreciation that the Chancellor and the Germans widely opposed the scientists' work in Egypt's pay, he had deplored the apparent inability of "a great state to find legal and concrete means to express its declared negative attitude towards the activities of the scientists."

The *Jerusalem Post* (often referred to as a semiofficial paper), on October 11, had maintained that the German attitude towards the problem of the German scientists in Nasser's services was one of "double dealing." German assurances that something would be done were followed by hints that legal difficulties existed. When, at last, there was a draft bill the Chancellor declared that any type of legislation would be useless.

Chancellor Erhard, in a general government statement on October 15, reiterated his government's regret and its disapproval of the work of Germans abroad endangering peace, but he had nothing else to offer. Social Democratic Floor Leader Fritz Erler urged the government, in the ensuing debate, not to leave the matter at that. The government must make it clear that the participation of Germans in the arms production against Israel was incompatible with the interests of the German people.[26] Deputy Herbert Wehner condemned the manner in which the affair had been handled in harsh words. He called the information (given by the Minister of the Interior) that positions had been offered to the scientists with higher pay to "lure" them from Egypt, "an inadequate manner to deal with

[25] Minutes of the *Bundestag,* vol. 56, p. 6778, October 15, 1964.
[26] Minutes of the *Bundestag,* vol. 56, p. 6778, October 15, 1964.

the disgusting problem; especially not to be able to say more to a people to whom we have done so much harm, than that we have tried to place them somewhere else but that they did not accept it." [27]

What Wehner hinted at already had been mentioned on August 2, 1963, in the Berlin *Tagesspiegel*. It said that "other means" had been found to solve the problem of the German scientists. The Ministry of Science and Research pressed the plan to coax these men back to Germany. The idea was to offer them high-salaried posts and excellent working and living conditions. Spokesmen of the Ministry hailed (*sub rosa*), as a first success of such efforts, Dr. Karl-Heinz Gronau's return to accept a post in a semiofficial research institute in Bad Godesberg. Gronau himself, however, claimed that he had come back because his contract had expired.[28] Naturally, the Germans wanted such a campaign to be kept secret, or at least to be played down as much as possible so that the Arabs would not be offended. Minister of the Interior Hoecherl hewed to the line when, before the press, in Bonn, he said that efforts were being made by many sides to bring about the return of German scientists, but, "with very limited results."

At the end of October, the Foreign Office in Bonn announced that hundreds of Germans were leaving Egypt to take up work in Germany.[29] Egypt had let them go for lack of finances, it was said. German industries, short of trained men, offered them good salaries, excellent prospects and, the rumor went, a more secure life than that in the posh suburbs of Cairo.

When Walter Schuran, a test engineer, and five other technicians left Egypt it was explained that their contracts had run out. They accepted positions with the firm of Boelkow in Munich, financed by the government and engaged in development of planes and rockets in Germany. Then talk was that Professor Paul Goercke, also, had returned to work at the Messerschmitt firm in Augsburg, though, for a long time, it was not known if this was merely a business trip. However, Professor Pilz requested an exorbitant salary when he came to Germany to hear what the government had to offer him, the Ministry of Science and Research complained. He asked, too, for assurance of security measures by the government against possible Israeli assaults. The government felt no obligation to give such

[27] Minutes of the *Bundestag*, vol 56, p. 6880, October 16, 1964.
[28] *Maariv*, April 9, 1964.
[29] Statement on request of *Maariv* correspondent in Bonn, November, 1964.

assurances. News of successful efforts to entice German scientists to leave the shores of the Nile was bound to influence the discussion in Bonn on legal means to prevent Germans from working abroad on military projects. Opposition circles in Bonn expressed surprise that such news recurred, with boring uniformity, whenever these legal provisions were under consideration in the Cabinet or in Parliament. In any case, the Social Democrats announced that they would insist on such legislation, if only to stop other scientists from ever considering the idea of entering into employment of countries preparing for war. In fact, the Social Democrats never stopped reminding the government of its commitment toward Israel. But, to no avail.

The problem about the German scientists was then overshadowed by the rumors about secret Germans arms deliveries to Israel and the ensuing public debate about them.

On January 5, 1965, Premier Eshkol brought it up again and declared, in an interview on the West Berlin radio (SFB) that the Federal government had made little effort to actually effect the return of the rocket scientists from Egypt. "Where there is a will, there is a way," he said. Then he proposed that the scientists be put before some sort of commission: ". . . to explain to them the whole complex of the political and moral relations . . . If Germany is serious about it—and I address these words to the German people—a way will be found."

On May 12, 1965, when the Prime Ministers of Israel and the Federal Republic of Germany exchanged letters which were to confirm their intention to enter into diplomatic relations, the subject of the scientists was raised, too, as it had been part of the negotiations between the two countries on the establishment of diplomatic relations. Professor Erhard told Prime Minister Eshkol: "In recent months, many of the German scientists, technicians and experts who had been working on military projects in countries outside NATO have returned to Germany. The Federal government has reason to assume that some of the experts who remained abroad, particularly those engaged in rocket construction, also intend to return to Germany in the near future." The Chancellor promised that legal action would be taken against any person who tried to encourage Germans to take up scientific, technical or expert activities in the military field abroad.[30]

In his reply, Levi Eshkol expressed the hope that, "the attitude

---

[30] Government communiqué, May 12, 1965, published by the Government Press and Information Office.

and intentions set out in your letter (about the scientists) . . . will speedily dispose of this affair." [31]

Thus, ended a chapter in which both countries failed to cut a good figure: the Israelis, with their allegations which they could only partly prove, and with a hysterical campaign that was stopped in midstream and for which they paid with a government crisis; the Germans, with their clumsy and vain efforts to introduce legislation to which they had committed themselves only because legal considerations were given preference over moral and political values.

[31] *Ibid.*

14
A German Compromise

The parliamentarians of Bonn's two big parties were on their way to the Plenary Hall that morning of March 25, 1965, when they were suddenly called to their respective rooms. What they were told there left them stunned.

Rainer Barzel, the Floor Leader of the Christian Democratic Union, announced that the Social Democrats no longer intended to support the bill put forward by Ernst Benda to abolish the statute of limitations for murder and genocide. The CDU parliamentarian, Benda, who had been in contact with the Social Democrats constantly, was taken completely by surprise. He had been given reason to assume that, supported by fifty parliamentarians of his party and the entire Social Democratic parliamentary party, the *Bundestag* would carry his bill. At the very same moment, Fritz Erler, Floor Leader of the opposition, the Social Democratic party, announced before his equally surprised parliamentary group that Ernst Benda would withdraw his bill, so a compromise now had to be sought.

Benda, looking back,[1] remarked that before the meeting Barzel had asked him to withdraw his motion. But Benda had refused, being certain that his bill would be carried. He then went to the meeting to hear that the Social Democrats no longer would back him up. He felt sure that the two parliamentary leaders had arranged this "little trick" among themselves, afraid of the repercus-

[1] Conversation with the writer, April 23, 1968.

sions, should his bill be put to Parliament. It might have produced a debate on the *pro et contra* of the statute, revealing views that could have been interpreted abroad as a reversion into Nazism.

The Social Democrats had no need to fear this for themselves, as such views were not indicated within their ranks. But they, too, were apprehensive of the electorate, fully aware of the unpopularity of Nazi criminal trials in the Federal Republic. With this "little trick," the two parliamentary leaders paved the way for a development that solved the problem temporarily, only; a problem which, in the mid-fifties appeared to have lost its sting, and which many Germans had so often vainly hoped would solve itself. But it was not to be so.

Before the assizes in Ulm in 1956, a man accused of having shot Jews denied the charge, claiming that they were not Jews but partisans and, in doing so, he merely would have executed a sentence passed by a drumhead courtmartial. But, since he had belonged to a fighting unit which had been ordered out summarily, they had left without carrying out the sentence.[2] Ordinarily, the court would have had to believe every word of the man's allegations, for who could have proved that the accused lied? As so often in cases of Nazi crimes, the victims were dead, there were no survivors and there were few witnesses except those who had had a part in the crime. But the prosecutor also had been a soldier. He suddenly remembered that, in compliance with international law, partisans were executed without a court decision. It was evident that the accused lied.

It was no different regarding the crimes committed in the notorious Auschwitz camps. Nobody knew too much about them. The survivors—few in number compared to those murdered there—did not want to keep the wound open, or knew just that tiny bit about the crimes that they had been able to witness at the risk of their lives, and often without knowing names, persons or details. A former German soldier, sifting through his war souvenirs about ten years after the war had ended, discovered a few documents he remembered having picked up in the streets of Breslau in the days of chaos. They contained reports of executions carried out in one of the Auschwitz camps. They later became the basic material for the prosecution to delve deeper into the complexity of Auschwitz.

Since fifteen years or more had passed since the crimes had been perpetrated, German justice realized that it had to work more sys-

[2] Inge Deutschkron, *Abrechnung mit Naziverbrechern*, p. 24, Geist und Tat, 1960.

tematically than before if it truly wanted to reveal the crimes committed in the German name and make those guilty pay for them. It was soon found that foreign countries—especially those which had been under German occupation—would not allow the Germans to pass over this period lightly. In 1958, therefore, a decision was reached on establishing a central office in Ludwigsburg for the investigation of Nazi crimes, with the Conference of the Ministers of Justice [3] assigned to prepare the background material for Nazi criminal trials. The incident before the assizes in Ulm became the determining factor. Erwin Schuele, the prosecutor of Ulm who had made the decisive discovery was chosen the first chief. The systematic hunt for the Nazi criminals was on.

It would not be fair to give the impression that German justice ignored the Nazi crimes altogether in those years prior to the founding of the Ludwigsburg Office. Since 1949, when German justice had been permitted to function independently again, hundreds of cases had been dealt with before German courts.[4] But, those cases had come to the knowledge of German prosecutors, more or less by accident. There had been no particular eagerness on the part of German courts to deal with the Nazi period. Judges themselves had often been involved in crimes, predominantly as members of "special courts." [5]

It was not easy to hear about the most horrifying crimes which could have stemmed only from perverse or sadistic brains. Prosecution of these outrages was made more complicated by the fact that more than ten thousand German prisoners of war had been held in Russia until 1955—among them many Nazi criminals, as a larger number of the crimes had been committed in the East. A still greater handicap proved to be that most of the documents which could have given detailed information about the crimes committed had been taken away by the masters of the situation and had only partly been returned to West Germany in the mid-fifties. The bulk

[3] The Conference of the Ministers of Justice is composed of ten ministers of the German states making up the federation, the Senator of Justice of West Berlin and the Federal Minister of Justice in Bonn.

[4] German courts were restricted to dealing with civil suits after 1945 and until 1949. Courts set up by the three Allies handled Nazi crime cases. Up to 1949, 5,025 Nazi war criminals had been sentenced. Of them, 806 had been sentenced to death; 486 actually executed; the remainder, reprieved.

[5] As a judge in Germany cannot be dismissed, the German Parliament could only "request" those who had served under the Nazi rule to retire voluntarily.

of them remained in the document centers of the victors; in Alexandria (Virginia), in Moscow, in Warsaw or in Prague. A good deal of material also had been retained in East Berlin, and had been found in the archives of former Nazi Ministries situated there. The Communist rulers refused to release it unless the West German government addressed its request to the respective East German Ministries. Bonn interpreted this as another attempt on the part of the East Germans to attain recognition of their state so they did not enter, at first, into any negotiations over these records.

However, documents made available had to be sifted, studied, copied and analyzed. Only an organization like the Ludwigsburg Office could take over this task which was soon found to be too formidable to be handled by just a few prosecutors.

In the first few years of its existence, the Ludwigsburg Office staff of eleven prosecutors studied literature, documents and background material in English, Russian, Polish, Yiddish, Hebrew and German and dealt almost exclusively with research. Still, after about one year, they were able to pass on to German justice names of culprits for prosecution—an almost impossible task in a country where hundreds of thousands had died at the front and in the bombing, or had been driven from their previous homes. And it was not always carried out with the necessary cooperation. Policemen charged with this task often were unwilling to hunt those criminals, due, mostly, to a false conception of the meaning of comradeship, for frequently, the officer had served in the East, too, as a police official or as a soldier. He remembered that he, also, had had to execute orders which were harsh and inhuman—in short, in the spirit of the Nazi occupation of Poland and Russia. This discovery was soon made by the Ludwigsburg prosecutors, who personally had no executive powers.[6] Yet, German courts, from the beginning of the sixties, were virtually flooded with Nazi crime trials. A belated expiation had begun.

In 1960, the statute of limitations prevailed for the crime of manslaughter. According to the German penal code, dating back to 1871 and still valid, manslaughter could be prosecuted within a period of fifteen years, and murder, twenty years, beginning with the date of the commitment of the crime.[7] A tussle set in among political par-

[6] Stated by Prosecutor Barbara Just-Dahlmann at a conference of jurists. Published in *Rheinischer Merkur*, December 22, 1961.

[7] In the case of Nazi crimes, May 8, 1945, the day of the capitulation of the Nazi Reich, was chosen as the date from which the fifteen or twenty years' grace counted.

ties in Bonn as to whether or not, in view of the Nazi crimes now coming to light, one could allow manslaughter to be beyond punishment if not within the prescribed time limit.

The Social Democrats, having suffered at the hands of the Nazis (perhaps, for this reason, with the greatest compassion for the Nazi victims who sought punishment for their torturers), pleaded for an extension of the statute of limitation for manslaughter. Their spokesman pointed out that, in the first few years, no proper legal prosecution of Nazi culprits had been possible and that, by allowing the statute to stand, just these criminals would benefit. But neither the majority of the CDU nor of the FDP (both government parties) was ready for it.

In the *Bundestag's* debate on May 24, 1960, the Minister of Justice, Fritz Schaeffer said that manslaughter was the least of the crimes committed during that period; most were cases of plain murder and they could be prosecuted until 1965. And, he argued, most of the cases had been attended to, anyhow. In Parliament, that same month, against the votes of the Social Democrats, the statute of limitations was allowed to apply in the Federal Republic to all cases of manslaughter.

This was in fullest agreement with the majority of the German people. In 1958, 54 percent of all Germans tested had agreed with the statement: "I feel we should cease trying now for crimes committed many years ago. It would be a good thing to draw a line concerning the past, once and for all." This was countered by 34 percent who said: "I do not see why anyone who has tortured or killed others should go scot-free." And 12 percent were "undecided." [8]

It surely was in concurrence with this public feeling that some courts proved to be very lenient in their treatment of Nazi criminals. Although often charged with any number of odious crimes, the accused still were allowed to be free men in the course of their trials. Their sentences were often unusually low and in no comparison to what any other species of murderer would have to suffer for a single crime. Statistics were compiled by some German papers. Of the sentences passed, a sixteen minutes' jail sentence was the punishment that a German court apparently considered adequate for one murder in Hitler's concentration camps. There was a warning of this development by politicians and individuals. Ernst Benda, in

[8] Elisabeth and Peter Noelle-Neumann, *The Germans, public opinion polls, 1947-1966,* p. 316, Verlag für Demoskopie, Allensbach, 1967.

1958, had spoken of "verdicts passed by German courts which fill all of us, I believe, with concern and alarm . . ." [9]

The Council for Christian-Jewish Cooperation expressed fear that the generally lax tendency among the people was supported and that Nazi crimes were made to appear harmless. Also, there was the danger, the Council said, that the average man would come to think that the crime committed on behalf of the state was no real crime, and that the murder ordered or approved of by the state was less than murder. The sentences with regard to Nazi crimes may have been the result of the judges' own political involvement during the Nazi era, and the negative attitude of the public toward these trials may have had their influence on them, too. The feeling prevailed that soon these crimes would cease to be punishable.

But this is precisely where the German people were mistaken. Foreign countries watched developments far more closely than anybody in Germany had assumed. And the eyes of those nations, once victimized by Germans, were particularly watchful with regard to the treatment of seasoned Nazis in postwar democratic Germany. They were the first to complain about murders committed during the Nazi era no longer being punishable beyond May 8, 1965, viewing with alarm that, from that date, no more Nazi criminals—unknown to the authorities until then—could be brought to justice. However, the German authorities emphasized, time and again, that trials of Nazi criminals would not cease with May 8, 1965. In all cases where the criminals were known, yet not apprehended for some reason or other, the time limit for the prosecution of their crimes would be suspended by judicial action. This had been done even in the cases of Hitler, of Bormann and the like, whose deaths were presumed, so that if, indeed, any of them was to reappear one day, he could still be brought to trial. But German authorities expressed their firm conviction that no unknown criminals or crimes would materialize after the eighth of May to embarrass the German government.

Schuele, the chief of the Ludwigsburg Office was looked upon as *the* authority in this respect. At the time when the discussion of Nazi crimes had been rekindled, he had expressed the conviction that there were no more loopholes for Nazi criminals to slip through; the Ludwigsburg Office had worked so systematically that, with the help of documentation often found (thanks to German

[9] *Bundestag* protocol, vol. 40, p. 1577, May 8, 1958.

thoroughness) and witnessed evidence, hardly any crime or criminal would remain in the dark after May 8, 1965. He was modest enough, however, to admit that an occasional criminal might be overlooked, yet, these would be few and their crimes by no means the most serious. This, he observed, was the case, also, with ordinary crimes. Schuele emphatically opposed legislation for the purpose of abolishing the statute of limitations for murder, insisting that a democratic state should not resort to the methods used by the totalitarian state. "Special laws and special courts are Nazi inventions," he said.[10] No doubt his words carried weight. Schuele, whose work as hunter of Nazi criminals was beyond reproach, later was found to have been a member of the NSDAP. An allegation by the Russians that he also had committed war crimes failed to be proven.

The discussion of whether or not to abolish the statute of limitations began to rage with all vehemence in autumn, 1964. The reaction abroad at the thought that Nazi criminals might go unpunished was influential. Delegations appeared in Bonn from organizations representing victims of Fascism to influence the politicians by lobbying. They warned that even in the archives of Western countries there was still a plethora of incriminating evidence that had not been sifted—not to speak of that in the Eastern world, the content of which was practically unknown. Dr. Nahum Goldmann, the Jewish leader, respected in Bonn since his part in the negotiations for the Luxembourg Treaty, claimed this to be the case, extending even to the American archives in Alexandria, Virginia. Yet, the Bonn government, in autumn of 1964, seemed more inclined to retain the statute than to abolish it.

The reasons were evident: trials of Nazi and war criminals were most unpopular in the country; they stirred up a past that the majority of the people wanted to forget; they were a reminder of guilt, and the fact remained that there was no way in which one actually could atone for past crimes and individual deficiencies.

General elections were looming up in Germany. None of the government parties wanted to be connected with such an unpopular move as the abolition of the statute of limitations and the subsequent continuation of Nazi criminal trials. Government circles tried to dismiss the question with the allegation that the abolition of the statute would be no more than a political demonstration without any practical value since the number of Nazi criminals to escape justice

10 Government Press and Information Office, Bulletin No. 74, May 5, 1964.

would be infinitely small. Experts like prosecutor Erwin Schuele had given them the cue to uphold this argument.

Chancellor Erhard was not as determined on this question as the majority of his party and the government he led. In a press conference on September 25, 1964, he replied to a relevant question: "For me, it would be an unbearable thought if such brutal and beastly mass murderers no longer could be punished." The Chancellor also hinted at the political consequences for his country, saying that he would not rule out that the GDR—which, so far, had failed to cooperate with the Federal Republic in the hunt for Nazi criminals—would publish documents incriminating citizens of the Federal Republic after May 8, 1965, in order to embarrass his state if the Bonn government allowed the statute of limitations to stand. In a statement on October 15, the West German Chancellor held out hope that a way would be found to exclude Nazi crimes from the application of statute of limitations. He asked what would happen if such criminals were discovered in trials after May 8, 1965? The termination of the statute would exclude the possibility of opening proceedings against them: "We, therefore, hope that a way will be found to exclude the crimes of the Nazis from the application of Article 103 (the statute of limitations) of the West German Basic Law." [11]

Despite the fact that the majority of the executive branch of the government had taken a firm view against changing the existing law, three suggestions were still under consideration: to abolish the statute altogether and so conform with the rules of a number of other countries (but, this seemed to have the least chance of being accepted as it would be so in the lex-Nazi, a law especially compiled for the prosecution of certain criminals that it would find little or no popular support); to extend the statute by ten years so that the time limit for the prosecution of murder would be raised from twenty to thirty years—since the statute of limitations had been passed in 1871, when life expectancy had been far below the present standard—some justification could be found for such a ruling (the suggestion to extend the statute by ten years for all kinds of murder already had been submitted in connection with a general penal code reform which was under discussion in parliamentary bodies); lastly, there was the proposal, favored by former Chancellor Adenauer, to postpone the expiration of the statute of limitations to 1969 on the grounds that German justice had not functioned independently be-

[11] Keesing's Contemporary Archives, 1965, p. 20512.

fore 1949—the law had been in the hands of the Allies from 1945 to 1949. Dr. Adenauer opposed a proper extension of the statute as this, he believed, conflicted with the German Constitution. Postponement of the expiry of the statute to 1969, for the reasons mentioned, could be defended on legal and political grounds and would also influence public opinion.

The proposal did not find many supporters, at first. The opponents of the statute of limitations were still eager to enact, through Parliament, a drastic measure that would either abolish or extend the statute. But the discussions continuing in all quarters made it quite evident that the last word had not been spoken on the issue.

Understandably, the thought that Nazi criminals might escape their deserved punishment was unbearable—particularly for the Jewish people. This was the feeling in the United States as well as in Israel. German Ambassador Knappstein, in Washington, made the statement, totally inconsistent with his government, that the statute of limitations should be abolished at all costs.

On October 12, Prime Minister Eshkol (referring to Chancellor Erhard's opinion, voiced on various occasions) said before the *Knesset*, that he hoped the Chancellor's opinion would gain ground in Germany; this kind of crime did not superannuate with the calendar. If the Germans wanted the chapter to be treated as past, then it was up to them to see to it that criminals of this type did not benefit from the statute of limitations . . . "The nation should be allowed to hope; not the criminals."

The Israeli Parliament passed a resolution [12] on October 19, emphatically stating that these crimes should not be allowed to go unpunished. *Knesset* members appealed to all states in which Nazi atrocities had been committed and, in particular to the Federal Government, to prevent Nazi criminals from benefiting from the statute of limitations. A note submitted by the Government of Israel to the Federal government on October 20, 1964, read: "It is the view of the government of Israel that, in regard to the crimes in question which are without parallel in human history, it is permissible, necessary and essential to extend the period of prescription and then regard this as a measure for the protection of morality and justice."

But, the German government was not swayed by Israel's or any other foreign objection. It announced its decision on November 11. Under the statute of limitations, the twenty-year period for bring-

[12] Fifty-one votes in favor, two against, thirty-three abstentions.

ing to trial those implicated in crimes of murder by Nazis between 1933 and 1945 would expire throughout West Germany on July 1, 1965. This, in accordance with Article 103 of the German Constitution: "An act can be punished only if it was a punishable offense by law before the act was committed."

This meant that, should evidence of murder committed before 1945 be uncovered subsequently, proceedings could not be instituted against the accused from May 8, 1965, in the former British and French zones, and from July 1, 1965, in the former American occupation zone.

The decision had been made in a meeting of the Federal Cabinet on November 5, "after lengthy discussion." It seems that Chancellor Erhard, known to favor an extension, had been outvoted. The government spokesman, Von Hase, explained that this conclusion had been reached in compliance with the long recognized legal principle of *nulla poena sine lege*. It had been the aim of the government to make sure, at all costs, that this very important question would not lead to a controversial debate in Parliament. The Federal Minister of Justice, therefore, had attempted to discuss the matter with parliamentary parties in view of announcing the Federal government's attitude in Parliament and supporting it with a declaration of the three parties. This possibility was frustrated by the Social Democrats and a small group of CDU parliamentarians, led by Ernst Benda, opposing the statute.

To make sure that evidence from any place on earth would come to the knowledge of German justice, the government spokesman announced an appeal to the world asking for the divulgence of any evidence still existing which had not yet led to judicial action suspending the time limit. This attitude proved, as Von Hase put it, the political importance attached to the question by the Federal government. Actually, the appeal was made on November 20, to governments, private organizations and individuals throughout the world, with mention that, in the German government's opinion, the majority of crimes had been disposed of by Allied and German courts. Yet, several countries and some German cliques demanded the extention of the statute of limitations by at least ten years, or until 1975.[13] The American government had refused to intervene in the tussle. An applicable letter had been written by Undersecretary of State Robert Lee to Congressman Leonhard Farbstein who had requested that Secretary of State Dean Rusk appeal to the German government to voice its objections.

[13] Keesing's Archiv der Gegenwart, 1964, p. 11503.

The Federal Minister of Justice, Ewald Bucher, known for his opposition to the abolition of the statute, stressed again that the statute of limitations would apply only to crimes which had remained unknown until May, 1965. In the case of all other known crimes, and of crimes where legal proceedings had already begun, prosecution would continue.

This meant that the statute would not apply to approximately 750 cases of suspected war crimes still pending in West Germany which were not expected to be disposed of until 1970, at the earliest. Statistics published by his Ministry on November 13, revealed that inquiries had been made by the German authorities with regard to thirty thousand persons up to the beginning of 1964. Since 1949, West German courts had preferred charges against 12,862 persons. Of these, 5,445 had been found guilty—most of them of brutality, but 172 of murder and 248 of manslaughter. More than four thousand had been found not guilty and, in 2,500 other cases the courts had decided to stop the proceedings for lack of evidence.[14]

The Ministry assured the public and the government that 99 percent of all Nazi criminals would have been tried, acquitted or punished by judicial action before May 8. It rejected outright the possibility that documents discovered then or after that date would give them additional information. Even the masses of material produced at the Eichmann trial in Jerusalem had not disclosed anything new to the German authorities, it was said.

Deputy Prime Minister Abba Eban, in the Israeli Parliament on November 18, expressed "disappointment and indignation" at the West German government's refusal to extend the statute of limitations beyond 1965. While recognizing that the principle of *praescription* was generally embodied in the legal systems of free governments, Eban emphasized that the "campaign of slaughter and torture perpetrated by the vile Nazi government" was unique in the annals of criminality, as recognized at the Nuremberg trials and in the UN Genocide Act. Denouncing the "abominable deeds of which there is no parallel or precedent in history of human society," he declared: "Anyone who attempts to compare these crimes with ordinary ones belittles the significance of the most appalling chapter of brutality ever recorded in the annals of mankind."

Eban also showed that he was unconvinced of the accuracy of the figures on convictions produced by the German government, time and again, to prove its actions against Nazi criminals. He said: "The figures . . . in comparison with the extent and scope of the holo-

14 *Ibid.*, p. 11522.

caust that Nazi Germany inflicted on the world, leave no room for doubt that many criminals of this type are still at large in many countries; and if the period of prescription were extended there would still be some possibility of apprehending them and bringing them to justice."

In the *Knesset* debate on this subject, the spokesmen of political parties demanded a global action that would make Bonn revoke its decision. This suggestion was passed on to the *Knesset's* Foreign Political Committee for consideration. Parliamentarians debated, noting that Bonn's refusal to extend the statute of limitations could be interpreted as a "re-Nazification and a remilitarization of Germany." The reaction of the Israeli public did not differ at all from that of their political representatives.

Federal Minister of Justice Ewald Bucher disliked the comments from abroad which were no more favorable than from anywhere else in the world. He belonged to the Free Democrats, a party that was united against any changes to be made with regard to the statute. Some people believed that this was due to the fact that former Nazis played a prominent part in the leadership of the party. But, it was perhaps more that the forthcoming general elections influenced the party's decision. Considering the unpopularity of Nazi war crime trials, they could expect only to lose votes if a representative of their party became instrumental in abolishing or extending the statute.

The Minister threatened to resign should the statute of limitations be tampered with. He rejected all suggestions that assured the prosecution of Nazi criminals beyond May 8, 1965, calling this illegal and unjustifiable. He made no bones about his true feelings on this issue. Before a selected group of journalists, he warned the Jewish people to stop sending delegations or *aide-mémoirs* to Bonn, saying: "We cannot give the impression that we allow ourselves to be put under pressure in this matter." He added, in explanation of his attitude, that the subject was not at all popular. "People dislike it," he said in all honesty, "and don't want these Nazi trials." [15]

It was not easy to go against the grain of public opinion. Bucher also raised the matter of the difficulties encountered in trying to clear up Nazi crimes after so many years had elapsed between the crime and the prosecution. It was, according to his way of thinking,

[15] Bonn, November 12, 1964.

the fate of the German nation to tolerate the "Kaduks" [16] in its society, and "to live with murderers." [17]

The Minister confided to the Bonn correspondent of Israel's *Maariv*, that, in his heart of hearts, however, he also favored the extension or the abolition of the statute of limitations. But, as so often is the case in Germany, he put legal grounds before moral ones, saying that, being a lawyer by profession, legal reasons for May 8 as the date of expiry of the statute had to take precedence. A democratic state, he contended, ought not to pass laws which are contrary to legality. And, he begged to consider that it was not really fair to punish criminals twenty or thirty years after their crimes had been committed. Finally, the Minister was sure that the "big" Nazi criminals already had been punished and had long been reintegrated into German society; any extension of the statute would concern the "small" criminal only, the one who executed the orders given to him by the "big" ones, often very lightly penalized by Allied courts.[18]

According to the German Treaty, no criminal tried by Allied courts could be retried by a German one unless new, incriminating evidence could be produced. But, the appeal of the government to the world to hand in all documentation about Nazis and war criminals hardly could have been issued by Bonn with the expectation that it would bring results. Rather, it was meant to prove Bonn's good will and to show the world that the little material forthcoming would not warrant such an important action as the extension of the statute. Western countries had cooperated with the Ludwigsburg Office from the start, therefore not much additional material could be expected from them. Latin-American countries, often enough, proved a haven for Nazi criminals, and the Eastern bloc states were not at all interested in passing information in their possession over to the West German state. For them, it was bound to be of far greater political benefit if they could embarrass the German government after the eighth of May with the disclosure of relevant material. With this appeal, Bonn, obviously hoped to close the discussion on the subject, and most certainly, before the election campaign was in full swing.

[16] Oswald Kaduk was one of the worst killers and torturers in Auschwitz. He was sentenced to life imprisonment by the Frankfurt assizes in August, 1965.

[17] *Die Welt*, November 14, 1964.

[18] November 15, 1964.

Of all Germans tested, 60 percent favored applying the statute to war crimes just as was prescribed by law. "We should not requite injustice with further injustice," they said. Only 29 percent opposed the expiry of the statute and 11 percent remained undecided.[19] The Free Democratic party knew perfectly well why they were solidly against the extension. In the case of the CDU, it was equally clear that the majority was afraid of facing the electorate on this issue. Only the Social Democrats felt that they could not make a decision in the light of electoral advantages.

But, the government's efforts to close the subject failed: the world would not allow it. Worldwide public opinion was united in its disgust that Nazi criminals might go scot-free after the expiry of the statute.

Dr. Nahum Goldmann, the world Jewish leader, came to Bonn at the end of November in an attempt to persuade the Federal government to prolong the statute in the case of Nazi and war criminals. He said, "What is involved is not a political offense but the murder of millions of human beings on a scale unprecedented in human history. Elementary justice demands that the perpetrators of these monstrous crimes should not go unpunished because of legal and technical restrictions." [20] Dr. Goldmann saw Chancellor Erhard and former Chancellor Dr. Adenauer as well as party leaders. Both, Adenauer and Erhard, showed the fullest understanding of Goldmann's arguments, and he repeated that American archives were still to be tapped for material.

At last, the Social Democrats managed to force the government— undoubtedly impressed by world reaction—to postpone a final decision until after March 1, 1965, the date which had been set for foreign countries and other sources to supply so far unknown material on Nazi crimes. They recommended that an office be set up with the utmost speed, to investigate all Nazi institutions in the Reich, as the Ludwigsburg Office was responsible only for the clarification of crimes committed beyond the German frontiers in occupied territories. This new institution should concentrate mainly on Hitler's Ministries which had been responsible for the smooth running of all operations connected with the extermination of the Jews: for example, the Ministry of Transport which had put the trains at the dis-

[19] Elisabeth and Peter Noelle-Neumann, *The Germans, public opinion polls, 1947-1966*, p. 316, Verlag für Demoskopie, Allensbach, 1967.
[20] Keesing's Contemporary Archives, 1965, p. 20512.

posal of the Gestapo and the SS to ship the Jews to the annihilation camps, or the Ministry in charge of the occupied territories in the East. But very few of the so-called "desk-murderers" (those who had given the orders but personally had never done any physical harm to anyone) had been brought to trial.

The Social Democrats suggested that the government report to Parliament, in detail, the findings of this institution up to March 1, 1965. Only then should the decision be made on whether or not to abolish the statute of limitations.

The Social Democrats presented this as a motion to the *Bundestag,* but before doing so they tried to obtain the support of the other two parties. They found only the CDU ready to agree—a decisive change of mind. In compliance, the government also dropped its previous, usual argument that the extension was in conflict with the Constitution. The government spokesman said before the press, on December 7, that should it be found that material concerning Nazi criminals could not be investigated before May 8, the government would consider an extension of the statute, after all. It appears that mounting pressure at home and abroad had begun to have its effect. The joint motion put forward by CDU and SPD was approved by a large majority in Parliament on December 9, with the proviso that a centralized effort be made by the German Länder to utilize whatever information available on such crimes, whether through the Federal government, worldwide appeal or otherwise, and that account should be taken, in particular, of heretofore uninvestigated incriminating material in Eastern Europe and the Soviet zone of Germany.

The motion also specified that the Federal Minister of Justice report results of these investigations to Parliament by the first of March, and state whether the Federal government was prepared to examine the question of extending the time limit before its expiration, in cooperation with the *Bundestag*—if it came to the conclusion that the prosecution of such murders could not be guaranteed in any other way.[21]

The acceptance of the motion promptly opened a way to an extension of the statute which the Federal government had rejected only four weeks before. The Minister of Justice (a member of the FDP, which opposed the motion), voted with the government but

[21] Minutes of the *Bundestag,* vol. 56, p. 7458, December 9, 1964.

he tried to dissuade parliamentarians from voting affirmatively, once again listing the achievements regarding the hunt for Nazi criminals up to then.[22]

To the surprise of the authorities, background material on Nazi crimes yet to be prosecuted began to pour in to Bonn from Eastern as well as from Western countries. By mid-January, six weeks before the Minister of Justice had to present his report to Parliament, it became quite clear that Bonn could not uphold the opinion that new criminals and crimes would not become documented after May 8, 1965. Prosecutors of the Ludwigsburg Office, meanwhile, had been allowed to dig into the archives in Warsaw and had come to realize that the examination of the vast amount of material on record there would be beyond their capacity before the May eighth deadline. There was no doubt that the Eastern bloc states had every means to embarrass the Bonn government by releasing information on Nazi criminals at their whim, if, indeed, Bonn allowed the statute to be proscribed on that date.

The majority of the government was finally convinced of the need to "provide a means for justice to be done." [23] The decision was made to support the efforts of parliamentarians to find ways and means to see that Nazi criminals did not escape justice through the operation of the statute, but fear of a coalition crisis prevented the government itself from suggesting a solution. The Free Democrats, the junior coalition partner of the CDU, felt that they could not change their opinion. Nevertheless, the government's decision was a complete reversal of previous policy which had been based on legal and political considerations. The legal aspect could hardly be upheld after prominent German legal experts had declared publicly that no legal grounds stood in the way of an extension of the statute.[24] The political stand was shaken to a great extent by reaction from abroad. The Federal Republic could not afford to defy public opinion in countries from which it needed support in the struggle for the reunification of Germany. Government spokesman Von Hase still insisted that the decision to back up Parliament's efforts to find ways and means to extend the statute was no policy revision on the part of the government. It was merely that a new situation had arisen which warranted a new approach.

[22] *Ibid.*
[23] Meeting on February 24, 1965.
[24] Ernst Benda, in his speech in Parliament on March 10, 1965, quoted from the appeal of seventy-six professors of law to extend the statute.

As if to confirm the situation confronting Germany, a newly discovered document forced Judge Carl Creifelds to seek a premature retirement. It was found that he had been in charge of legislation for Poland in Hitler's Ministry of Justice and, therefore, had helped to lay the legal basis for numerous crimes. The judge, fifty-seven years old, in charge of the Penal Code Department of the Ministry of Justice in West Berlin, had just been suggested for the post of judge at Germany's Supreme Court in Karlsruhe. Of course, the Federal President refused to sign his nomination papers when his past became known.

That Nazi murderers of the worst sort were still at large came to light in the mysterious murder of Herbert Cukurs in Montevideo at the end of February. Cukurs had been the head of the special department for Jews in the Latvian Police Force, and was believed to have been guilty of supervising the extermination of over thirty thousand Jews during 1940–1941, which included the massacre of Riga ghetto inhabitants. It was said that he, personally, had displayed extreme brutality—beating men, women and children to death. This was stated in an anonymous letter, which reached various news agencies in Bonn, announcing that Cukurs "had been executed" by "those who can never forget February 23, 1965." The corpse of the murdered Herbert Cukurs was found at the Montevideo address given in the letter. Investigation of this case never was conclusive. It was once again assumed that the Israeli Secret Service had had a hand in the murder.

Parliamentarians now left to take the initiative presented two bills to Parliament for debate on March 10. Ernst Benda had prepared a bill to extend the statute of limitations from twenty to thirty years for all cases of murder while Social Democrat Gerhard Jahn, on behalf of his party, wanted Parliament to abolish the statute of limitations altogether. There was now no doubt that, on May 8, the statute would not be allowed to follow the course that had been prescribed and confirmed by the government in November, 1964.

Even Nazi circles seemed to realize that the government was now serious in its intentions. On the eve of the parliamentary debate, members of Parliament and journalists in Bonn received threatening letters decorated with the swastika, saying: "Parliamentarians who are bondsmen of Tel Aviv and New York and who voted in favor of the abolition of the statute for 'so-called Nazi crimes' are legally condemned to death!" The letter was signed *OBF* (*Oberbrigade-führer*) *vom Schutzbereich III*. Only two days after the letters had been received in Bonn, the police arrested two men, below 30 years of age, found with more of these leaflets in their home.

On March 10, the *Bundestag* decided in favor of extending the statute of limitations beyond May 8, 1965. It referred all suggestions and motions put to the parliamentary legal committee to a single bill that was to be debated by the House in second and third reading at the end of March. The decision was carried by the CDU and the SPD while the FDP and the CSU, the Bavarian branch of the Christian Democrats, opposed it.

The debate, lasting seven hours, became impassioned at times. It began with the report of the Minister of Justice who stated that, since 1945, the Federal Republic investigation files had been opened against 61,000 persons in connection with Nazi crimes. Of these, 6,-100 had been sentenced, and proceedings were continuing against 14,000 persons. Apart from 6,100 persons sentenced in the Federal Republic and those 5,000 condemned by Allied courts, 12,000 persons had received verdicts by East German courts, at least 17,000 by Polish courts, 24,000 Germans by Russian courts, 16,000 Germans by Czech courts and an unknown number of Germans by courts of various other countries. This added up to figures of over 80,000 Germans who had been punished for Nazi crimes; a figure which seemed to rule out that tens of thousands of Nazi criminals were still at large, as had been suggested abroad. In view of the amount of material still lying untouched in the American National archives, a German judge had been sent to the United States to examine it.

East German General Attorney Streit had offered no material, the Minister of Justice stated, but had suggested the formation of a commission consisting of representatives of Justice of both parts of Germany to study the material available in East German archives.

The Bonn Minister saw in this an attempt on the part of the East Germans to obtain diplomatic recognition and did not acknowledge it. An offer made by the Ludwigsburg Office to send a representative to East Germany was rejected by the East German authorities, insisting on this all-German commission. Material obtained in the Warsaw Archives had offered a number of clues. The CSSR had sent copies of original documents preserved in their archives. But, in all, one could say that a great part of the crimes had been cleared up. Yet, the Minister admitted that it still could not be excluded that after the statute had run its course new crimes and criminals might become known, as it seemed impossible to shift all the material available, particularly in the Eastern bloc states.[25]

[25] Minutes of the *Bundestag*, vol. 57, p. 8516, March 10, 1965.

Contrary to his original intentions, Christian Democrat Ernst Benda presented a bill in which he asked Parliament to abolish the statute of limitations for murder and genocide. He shelved his motion to extend it from twenty to thirty years and was thus in line with the Social Democrats, who, from the beginning, had campaigned for the abolition. Benda said it was right to say that the Germans were under pressure from abroad on this issue but they were also under pressure from their own conscience. And, extension of the statute would not be a victory due to foreign pressure, but a victory of the principle of the search for the truth.

Benda was booed by the Free Democrats when he told the House of a letter in which an ordinary man had told him that he could no longer understand justice if a boy was sent to prison for stealing while murderers walked about freely. Benda added that there were some people in his party who spoke of pardon in connection with the statute but, in his opinion, "pardon can only be granted by the victims." Germany was not a nation of murderers; that was why the German people must not allow themselves to be identified with them, but, rather had to rid itself of them.[26] Christian Democratic Floor Leader Rainer Barzel turned to the people, saying that the statute concerned criminals' delicts, only, and not "political mistakes" which were also permissible when it concerned Nazism.

Minister Bucher took the floor as parliamentarian again and pleaded with the House to consider that, due to the lapse of time marring the ability to memorize events, courts could no longer deal with these crimes properly; he wanted only to prevent courts being overburdened with difficulties when he opposed an extension of the statute.

Social Democrat Gerhard Jahn accused the government of not having done enough about these crimes years before. The prosecutors dealing with the crimes committed in Auschwitz had been forced to inspect the Auschwitz camps during their holidays because the government had refused them permission to visit Poland, he said.

Free Democrat Dr. Thomas Dehler made use of his rhetorical eloquence to prevent abolition of the statute. He even quoted Hannah Arendt, referring to Nazi crimes as "banality of evil"; except for sadists, criminals were just stupid men living in exceptional times. It had been the state that had formulated the crimes and had carried them out, Dr. Dehler said, implying that the people were free from any blame.

[26] Minutes of the *Bundestag*, vol. 57, p. 8517, March 10, 1965.

Adolf Arndt (SPD) roused the house to violent applause and to excited booing when he said that the Germans had known of the crimes, and added: "I am guilty, for, you see, I did not go on the street to protest when they carried off the Jews, lorrywise. I did not put on the yellow star and I did not say, 'I, too.'" He also blamed the foreign countries which had closed their frontiers to the German Jews when they were on the run from Hitler, and told the young people that they could not simply say that this heritage did not concern them: "We have to do justice to the victims by saying that this is murder . . ."

Arndt, in fact, had opposed an extension or an abolition of the statute in the early stages of the controversy. He and other legal experts were of the opinion that in post-Hitler Germany the law should not be tampered with. The Social Democratic party then suggested the Benda Bill be made an amendment to the Constitution as this would reduce the danger of manipulation in the future.[27]

All seemed set for Parliament's final decision on March 25, 1965. Everybody expected a close vote on the issue. Nobody quite understood what was going on behind the scenes when it was announced that the beginning of the debate would be postponed. It seemed very mysterious when it became known that the parliamentary parties of the SPD and CDU were deliberating again. It was then that the bill to abolish the statute of limitation was killed by the floor leaders, apparently for purely electoral considerations.

It was suggested that a bill should be presented to the House which would postpone the date of expiry of the statute to 1969 on the grounds that German justice had only been able to function independently starting with the year 1949; the suggestion originally made by Chancellor Adenauer. This compromise was arrived at by the two floor leaders on the eve of the *Bundestag's* debate.

To start the twenty years' grace from May 8, 1945, had been a mistake, Richard Jaeger, CSU, argued in support of the new motion: "It was a mistake because on May 9, 1945, there was not a single German court which functioned. . . ."

This bill finally was passed by the House—344 votes against 96. The Free Democrats battled for six hours, even against this compromise bill, sending speaker after speaker to the rostrum with varying arguments. The evening after the debate, Minister of Justice Ewald Bucher resigned, saying that he disagreed with the decision and that he would be unable to affix his signature to it.

[27] Minutes of the *Bundestag*, vol. 57, p. 8526, March 10, 1965.

The bill became law on April 13. Most German parliamentarians were convinced that they had found an excellent compromise, contrary to opinion in Israel where there was general disgust at the tame adjustment. The Germans were quite sure that the problem was solved and never would plague them again. Few expected that, in 1969, parliamentarians would be beset with the same question. At the same time, Parliament felt certain that it had solved the problem in such a manner that it did not antagonize the German voters who were so clearly against all extensions of the statute concerning Nazi crimes. But, in reality, the "little trick" by the party strategists had not been good enough. They had forced the same, painful issue on the people for the second time.

15
The Secret Deal

Thick fog reduced the visibility on the German *autobahn* beyond the French border. It was a dark night in December, 1957, and bitterly cold. The road was treacherous beneath a frosting of snow and ice. Three men sped along in a car with a French license plate. They traveled by car, despite the weather, because they were on a secret mission. Rounding a bend, the car suddenly came to a stop in a snow drift.

The man at the wheel, Asher Ben-Nathan, the representative of the Israeli Defense Ministry for Western Europe and chief of the purchasing mission in France, was unprepared for it. He was not used to driving under these conditions, nor were the other passengers, Shimon Peres, Director General of the Israeli Defense Ministry and General Haim Laskow of the Israeli army. However Ben-Nathan tried, he could not make the wheels get a grip on the ground. The three men were furious and shivered with the cold. What if they were discovered here on the German *autobahn;* how could they explain it at home, after all the excitement and the consequent Cabinet crisis over Ben-Gurion's announcement that he considered purchasing arms in Germany, and the disclosure that a "high-ranking personality" was to go to Germany for this purpose? In despair, Ben-Nathan tried again, this time shifting the gear to reverse and pressing his foot firmly on the accelerator. The car jerked back and, over the roar of the engine, Ben-Nathan heard a shout. Laskow, who had stepped outside when the driver had been too busy to notice it, managed to escape being run down in the very last second. Recovering from this, the three men continued on to their destination, the home of Franz-Josef Strauss, West Germany's Defense Minister, in Rott am Inn, Bavaria.

It was Shimon Peres' second visit to Strauss. He had seen him a few months earlier in his Bonn office. It had been a conversation lasting five hours, as Peres looked back on it: [1] "We talked about everything concerning our two peoples. German-Israel relations, the situation in the Near East, the Jewish problem." Then Peres said to Strauss: "Kind words, even money, won't help us to overcome the past and secure our future. I did not come for that. I want to pave the way for a different policy. Israel needs practical aid for defense and for contacts with the European powers. Germany should do all in its power to assure Israel's security." Peres said, "Strauss understood me at once and responded favorably."

It was agreed to meet again in order to discuss details. That being the case, Peres brought Laskow to the Rott am Inn meeting to give a detailed account of Israel's military situation: ". . . of a country against thirteen hostile states; of two and a half million people against sixty million."

These first contacts were the basis of a very important relationship—no doubt *the* most important one, pending establishment of diplomatic connections; a relationship, in fact, that represented the first political decision of the Federal Republic of Germany in favor of Israel.

Shimon Peres' decision, authorized by Ben-Gurion, to establish contacts with West Germany for the purpose of arms aid was not accidental. It was the result of careful consideration. The military threat to Israel was a salient point. The Arabs' arsenal was enormous. "Nasser can order practically all his arms by telephone from Russia," Peres said,[2] adding that there were only a few countries to which Israel could turn for arms and, in fact, not all of those could deliver anything to Israel: "There are actually very few states with a modern army that can help! Germany is among those that can."

Besides, Israel had to become more independent of the United States, remembering America's cessation of arms delivery to Israel during the Sinai campaign of 1956, and its insistence on Israel adhering to previously designated armistice lines. It was then that Is-

[1] Conversation with the writer, July 30, 1968.
[2] *Der Spiegel*, No. 9, February 24, 1965.

raeli politicians agreed that their policy had been too circumscribed. There was need to strengthen the ties to Europe, as much in the interest of Israel's efforts to improve on security as on trade. Israel urgently wanted some form of relations with the European Economic Community, being cut off and greatly dependent on trade with Europe; France's cooperation, also Italy's, was excellent already. Peres recalled a conversation with Jean Monnet, one of the creators of the European Community, in which the politician, understanding Israel's need for European support, asked what was Israel's relationship to Germany, "which is, after all, one of the six member-states of the European Community."

So, from two points of view, it seemed that contacts with Germany were essential. And there was the moral aspect, also. A member of the *Knesset* had given Peres an idea. He had remarked that the Germans should add a clause to their Constitution binding them to responsibility for Israel's security.[3]

The Defense Minister in France at the time, Jacques Chaban-Delmas, happened to be on very good terms with Strauss. It was through him that Peres put out the first feelers. Strauss agreed at once to see Peres, probably flattered at having been chosen the second leading German politician to meet an Israeli statesman, and this at the latter's request.[4] At that time, this made an impression in German politics, and he must have anticipated that he was about to do something of historic significance for his country. After Shimon Peres had requested and obtained Ben-Gurion's consent, Colonel Avigdor Tal, of the army's planning department, was sent to Cologne to inform Dr. Shinnar. A letter of introduction was handed to Strauss signed by Ben-Gurion. Everything was set for the first meeting to take place.

Of course, haphazard contacts had existed before. In summer, 1955, an Israeli purchasing delegation stationed in France had come to Germany to order chains for half-tracks. Until then they had bought them in France (although a German product), at a far higher price.

After the Sinai campaign, in 1956, Strauss, as well as all other NATO Defense Ministers, had received from Israel samples of Rus-

---

[3] Peres, in conversation with the writer, July 30, 1968.

[4] The first meeting had been the one which had taken place between Chancellor Adenauer and Foreign Minister Moshe Sharett at the signing of the Luxembourg Treaty, September, 1952.

sian arms and equipment—booty from that war.[5] In June, 1957, Peres had instructed Dr. Shinnar to acquaint Strauss with the Israeli Uzi, which eventually led to an introduction of this machine gun in the *Bundeswehr*. As spokesman for Ben-Gurion, Dr. Giora Josephtal, General Secretary of *Mapai*, had talked to Dr. Adenauer about what Germany could do for Israel's security in early December, 1957. This led to the mention of the possibility of obtaining arms from Germany in the *Knesset* debate of December 24, 1957. But, until Peres and Strauss reached an agreement, this particular relationship lacked the political premise.

In Germany, Strauss was considered a very controversial politician. He had more enemies than friends, particularly among the Social Democrats, the counterpart of Peres' *Mapai* party in Israel.

Nobody denied his intellectual qualities. Just because of them, many people attached importance to his statements and declarations. And in them, he had often betrayed a nationalistic tendency which caused people at home and abroad to see in him a dangerous man for Germany and its development as a democracy. Strauss gave the impression of a reactionary, aggressive German who, although without Nazi taint, seemed to be the image of an "incurable" German.

The German postwar situation, the divided country and Adenauer's policy of ignoring the Communist states supplied him with ample opportunities to create this image of himself. Above all, Strauss, a Bavarian, with the temperament and the impulsiveness of people of this origin, was all but a diplomat. The "Spiegel affair" of autumn, 1962, in which he ordered the arrest of a journalist vacationing abroad and a Gestapo-like raid on the journal's offices colored the impressions about Strauss.

Shimon Peres got to know a different Strauss. To him, he seemed to be a man with vision, a politician who wanted his country to play a role again and to pursue a policy of its own.

Strauss saw Israel as part of the Western world that should not be forsaken. Peres quoted Strauss as saying that it was not enough for Europe to defend its front door but there was need, also, to watch over the rear door.[6] Interviewed ten years later,[7] Strauss showed

[5] Rolf Vogel, *Deutschlands Weg nach Israel*, p. 137, Seewald Verlag, Stuttgart, 1967.

[6] Peres, in conversation with the writer, July 30, 1968.

[7] Rolf Vogel, *Deutschlands Weg nach Israel*, p. 139, Seewald Verlag, Stuttgart, 1967.

that he also saw the implications of the Near East conflict in the greater perspective of the East-West issue. In the case of an Israeli-Arab conflict, there was the danger of a military confrontation of the Big Powers. Germany, the place where the two power blocs were in direct confrontation, had every reason to fear such a clash, wherever it might occur. To arm Israel, it appeared to him, would reduce tensions in the Near East and with it, in the world. This could be only in the interest of Germany. He was sure that Israel would not use arms to start up a war as that would endanger its very existence.

But, apart from the political issue, Strauss offered some more reasons why he thought arms for Israel were the most logical conclusion for Germany: ". . . millions of Jews have been murdered as a consequence of a criminal German policy through German arms." It was not for Germany to judge whether or not the United Nations' decision to found the state had been properly implemented. "It (the state) exists," Strauss continued, "and in it a fraction of the Jews of the world had found a home and done admirable work of reconstruction. Threats are uttered frequently against this state and its inhabitants, threats from a hostile world around it to conquer this state and to annihilate its inhabitants. If, then, the Federal Republic makes a modest contribution towards the preservation of peace in the Near East . . . then it is some kind of compensation in the field in which there had been so much sin in the German name." He frankly added that aid to Israel, apart from being a contribution towards reconciliation, would also further Germany's readmittance into the family of nations. "So, this policy appeared to us—to Dr. Adenauer and myself—as a contribution to compensation and something having the way to assure peace." [8]

Strauss surely would not have recommended arms aid to Israel had he not had complete faith in and respect for the Israeli army. Being a man of action himself, he was no doubt impressed by its victories, its fighting spirit, its morale. Peres was the personification of this Israel unknown to him and to most Germans. The two men became friends as time passed, something that was virtually essential in view of their clandestine cooperation. There had to be complete trust in each other since not one of the agreements was in writing.

Strauss informed the Chancellor of all his moves on the matter. He gave him the "yellow light"—as Peres put it—"neither green, nor

[8] Rolf Vogel, *Deutschlands Weg nach Israel*, p. 140, Seewald Verlag, Stuttgart, 1967.

red." In other words, Adenauer did not object to the idea, but he did not express explicit consent. His silent acknowledgment was sufficient for Strauss to proceed with his scheme, despite the warnings of the Foreign Minister, Dr. von Brentano, in a letter to the Chancellor. Brentano's successor, Dr. Gerhard Schroeder, repeated these warnings, both afraid of the political repercussions in case the secret deal with Israel should be revealed. Adenauer's favorable attitude may have been motivated by feeling handicapped, or even guilty, on the question of diplomatic relations with Israel. Nevertheless, Strauss insisted that Adenauer share the responsibility.

Dr. Shinnar recalled in his memoirs on this issue that, although Adenauer had agreed to a certain consignment to be shipped to Israel, Strauss would not carry it out before he had the Chancellor's signature for it. Over and above everything, the arms were forwarded without payment. "America gave us money; France, arms for money; Germany, arms without money," Shimon Peres acknowledged.[9]

The secret deliveries began in 1959; they reached Israel via France. This was material "on loan," therefore it did not have to be registered anywhere. It was surplus material—something that "moved," was not "fired," Peres recalled, explaining that Israel needed something to improve the army's mobility. When the two premiers—David Ben-Gurion and Dr. Konrad Adenauer—had met in New York in 1960, the Israeli statesman had wanted Adenauer's explicit consent for Strauss's initiative.

In reply, Adenauer had said of Strauss, ". . . He is all right, he thinks as I do. . . ." and had left no doubt that he agreed to the secret deal. Later in the year, Adenauer told Strauss to go ahead with the planning of the scheme. Until then, the deliveries had been fairly small; more or less, test cases. At the end of 1961, the deliveries had reached the amount of $5,000,000 [10]—a relatively small sum compared to later years.

In June, 1961, Strauss, on Peres' suggestion, met Ben-Gurion when the latter was on a state visit to Paris. It was meant to be an honor for Strauss. But it made impact on Ben-Gurion, too, to meet a German who had gone out of his way to help Israel in such a decisive manner. Strauss's recollection was that the meeting took place in the private home of an Israeli. In a three-hour conversation, he once

[9] Conversation with the writer, July 30, 1968.
[10] *Der Spiegel,* February 24, 1965.

again elaborated on his views regarding the German-Israel relations and the special German obligation for Israel's security: "With this conversation, the personal contact between Ben-Gurion and myself began . . . this friendship was preserved throughout the following years. . . ." [11]

At the beginning of 1962, an item appeared for the first time in the budget of the Federal Republic called "aid, in form of equipment" for which the government put down an estimate of $60,-000,000 and which, according to Strauss, was to be spread over five years.[12] This figure was the result of negotiations between Strauss and Peres who had once again come to Germany for this purpose. ("I came to Germany four or five times a year but I never stayed more than twelve hours.") [13] On this occasion, Peres, who had been promoted to Deputy Defense Minister in 1959, met Adenauer for the first time. He conveyed a letter from Ben-Gurion. Peres recalled how Adenauer, eighty-six years old by then, read the letter without glasses. On seeing Peres smile, Adenauer asked: "Young man, why do you smile?" [14] The two men had a two-hour conversation in the presence of Dr. Shinnar. Adenauer consented to authorize Strauss to aid Israel to the Federal Republic's greatest ability.

According to Dr. Shinnar's memoirs, in doing so, he exercised the rights as Chancellor to determine the policy because he was convinced that it would serve in the preservation of peace which was the highest political obligation. Adenauer wrote in reply to Ben-Gurion, making no commitment regarding the arms deal. He just mentioned that Ben-Gurion's Deputy Defense Minister had made a good impression on him. But, no doubt his talk with Peres definitely strengthened Strauss's aid projects.

The estimate of $60,000,000 was to cover delivery (mainly from German army surplus) of fifty planes, among them Noratlas, Dorniers 27 and Fouga Magister, jet trainers, helicopters, lorries, ambulances, automatic 4-cm antiaircraft guns with electronic installations, 36 howitzers and steerable antitank rockets of the German Cobra type. The training of Israeli officers in the Air Force training camp of Rendsburg and in the school for combat troops in Mun-

[11] Rolf Vogel, *Deutschlands Weg nach Israel*, p. 140, Seewald Verlag, Stuttgart, 1967.
[12] *Quick Illustrated*, February 17, 1965.
[13] Conversation with writer, July 30, 1968.
[14] *Ibid.*

sterlager was included in the bill. It was to introduce the Israeli army to the handling of newly acquired equipment.

The delivery of the arms, being the result of a secret deal, was not so easy and was close to smuggling. Both sides were eager to conceal it from Israel's enemies. This became the task of some of Israel's military personnel in a number of countries. Various methods were applied. Often the contents of the crates did not tally with the declarations made on the accompanying documents. Captains of freighters had no idea of what was actually in the load. Sometimes arms, which were bought in other countries, were shipped straight to Israel while the bills were sent to Bonn.

This was the case with helicopters from France, antiaircraft guns from Sweden and two, modernized 1,280 ton submarines from Great Britain. The practice developed of addressing the cargo to another country first, where it would be unloaded at once and readdressed to Israel.[15]

All this needed a master plan to work. But it had its loopholes. On one occasion, a ship loaded with arms for Israel landed in Genoa at the wrong quay. The contents (instead of being shifted to a waiting boat beside it, as was the practice) were unloaded and opened. Italian press photographers interpreted this as new supplies for the Italian army. The next day, pictures appeared in the Italian newspapers of arms of which the Italian general staff was not even aware. The incident called for some elucidation that would satisfy the Italian authorities. But, Israelis connected with the physical part of the deliveries still are quick to contend that the deal was not revealed because of a failure on their part.

Meanwhile, German parliamentary parties had an inkling that something was going on that was not under their control. Erich Ollenhauer, Chairman of the Social Democratic Party, requested information from Adenauer in a letter written in June, 1961. Adenauer must have realized that the deal, which was to increase in volume, no longer could be concealed. He then informed the chairmen of the three political factions in the *Bundestag*, Dr. Heinrich von Brentano of the Christian Democratic Union, Erich Mende of the Free Democratic Party and Erich Ollenhauer of the Social Democratic Party. The three politicians decided to form a small committee—two of each faction that should be kept posted about the arms aid

[15] *Frankfurter Allgemeine Zeitung*, February 20, 1965.

scheme. On March 28, 1962, the parliamentary Budget Committee agreed that, before each new aid project was undertaken, the Defense Ministry should inform the two parliamentarians of each party. The representatives of the factions' chairmen (Dr. Georg Kliesing and Heinrich Draeger of the CDU, Fritz Erler and Bruno Diekmann of the SPD, and Fritz-Rudolf Schultz of the FDP) met with members of the Defense Ministry on June 28, 1962. The final nominations for this committee were made later in letters from the respective parties. It was this committee which was then told of all the arms deliveries to Israel.[16]

The Committee, of course, was pledged to secrecy. And so were the high-ranking German officers who, in the course of time, paid visits to the Israeli army in disguise. Not even Germany's present allies knew much about the scheme; least of all, America. Due to pressure on the part of the Social Democratic leader, Fritz Erler, who wanted the consent of the Americans for the scheme, Shimon Peres had casually talked to President Kennedy about it at the beginning of 1963. The President did not see any reason to object to it but he must not have paid much attention to the question. For, in November, 1963, George Ball, the United States Undersecretary of State, protested to Germany against "an unauthorized resale" of American helicopters which had appeared in Israel. According to NATO rules, every country is obliged to obtain the consent of the manufacturer state in the case of an intended resale. It was only then that the Germans informed the Americans more fully of the secret deal. There can be no better proof that there was no outside pressure to induce the Germans to deliver arms to Israel.

When Strauss was forced to quit his post in November, 1962, his successor, Kai-Uwe von Hassel, continued the operation without any fuss. After his resignation, Strauss was invited and actually went to Israel in June, 1963. There, he was feted as hardly any other German visitor before. After all, the government and the *Knesset's* parliamentary committees on defense and foreign affairs were informed

[16] The Committee finally consisted of Dr. Georg Kliesing and Albert Leicht (CDU), Dr. Karl Mommer and Dr. Friedrich Schäfer (SPD). Dr. Thomas Dehler and Dr. Hans-Georg Emde (FDP). In June, 1964, the Committee was increased by one of each party—Dr. Richard Jaeger (CSU), Hans-Juergen Wischnewski (SPD), Klaus Freiherr von Muehlen (FDP). They met for information about the projects on December 13, 1962; February 5, 1963; February 10, 1964; June 30, 1964; October 7, 1964 and February 10, 1965. This information was given by Chancellor Erhard in a speech before the *Bundestag*, February 17, 1965.

of the arms deal. Even the leader of the opposition was finally told in order to make him stop the demonstrations against Strauss. In the end, Strauss could appear in public without incidents. He lectured to Israeli officers and gave a press conference. Interviewed by the daily *Ha'aretz*, on June 2, 1963, Strauss hinted at the secret deal when he spoke of "reciprocal arrangements between Israel and Germany about which it was better not to speak openly."

On June 15, 1963, the general public learned something about the German military aid to Israel for the first time. Hans Merten, an SPD parliamentarian and Deputy Chairman of the parliamentary Defense Committee in Bonn, said, when interviewed by the *Neue Rhein Zeitung*, "We give training to Israeli soldiers here in the Federal Republic in the use of modern arms." The reason for the disclosure might only be found in Merten's desire for personal publicity.

The revelation caused excitement in Germany. Strauss was promptly named the initiator of the plan affording fourteen Israeli officers a six-months course in the Rendsburg Air Force training camp. He denied all knowledge of such an arrangement when he was asked a relevant question in a press conference. The parliamentary Defense Committee (which Merten said had agreed to the publication of this fact) declared it never had heard of such a project. The government spokesman also tried to give the impression that this was a "fairy tale" when he deliberately omitted Israel as one of the countries on a list receiving military aid from Germany. The spokesman of the Defense Ministry refused to comment, though he did say that, "If, indeed, it happened that Israeli soldiers were trained by the *Bundeswehr* (which would be a matter for the *Bundeswehr* to speak about) it was part of restitution and not of military aid." He rightly contended that there were no Israeli soldiers on German soil at that moment, as it goes without saying that those in Germany at the time of the disclosure left quickly.

A protest from the Arab countries, announced with the usual verbosity, never was received in Bonn. It was later stated that forty-five Israeli officers and corporals had attended a course in the school for combat troops in Munsterlager, November through December, 1964.[17]

The second phase in the arms deal started in the beginning of the summer of 1964. It came about through American pressure. The reason was that the Americans had delivered Hawk antiaircraft mis-

17 *Der Spiegel*, February 6, 1965.

siles to Israel in 1963 and had also trained the personnel for it. The Arab states had protested vigorously against it which did cause some concern in America, where there was the intention to preserve what was left of American influence in the Arab world. When Khrushchev, in May, 1964, assured Egypt of new arms, Israel once again turned to America for aid. Prime Minister Eshkol put the request to the American President, in Washington, in May. But America hesitated. Though it wished to lend support to Israel's military position, the Americans did not want to ship any arms to Israel in view of a deterioration of relations with Cairo.

When Chancellor Erhard paid a visit to President Johnson in June, 1964, he and McNamara suggested to him that Germany deliver some of the obsolete American and German arms to Israel. Erhard was for it in principle—saying, as he looked back on it,[18] "We wanted to help Israel."

About this time, Israel requested 150 American M-48 tanks from Bonn. In 1963, Germany had already delivered some American tanks to Israel, but Israel needed more since its neighbor, Jordan, had received such tanks from the United States. Shortly after Erhard's return, McNamara, on a European trip, made a detour to Bonn to urge the Germans to deliver the tanks which the Americans were ready to pay for. The United States State Department disclosed in February, 1965, that it had approved the transfer of American-built M-48 tanks to Israel by the Federal Republic. The spokesman, Robert McCloskey, said that the United States had "made it clear to the Federal Republic that we favored the sale of tanks to Israel" for two reasons: to help restore the balance of power in the Middle East after the large-scale Communist arms deliveries to Egypt, and because Israel traditionally obtained weapons from Western Europe.[19] There was only one snag. Chancellor Erhard disliked the idea of being reduced to an "arms dealer."

The German government requested Shimon Peres to come to Bonn to discuss the problem about which American Ambassador McGhee was also informed. And Peres, who appreciated Erhard's viewpoint, conceived an idea which would embarrass neither the Germans nor the Americans. He arrived in Bonn on June 24, 1964. After a talk with the American Ambassador, who had asked to see him before he went to Erhard, he hurried to the Chancellory. It was afternoon and rush hour. Peres was delayed on the highway be-

[18] Erhard, in a conversation with the writer, July 11, 1968.
[19] Keesing's Contemporary Archives.

tween Bad Godesberg and Bonn. He reached the Chancellory thirty minutes after the appointed time. But nobody seemed to mind his tardiness. In fact, he was asked to wait. In an anteroom, he recognized a number of German Ministers standing around, appearing rather tense. Nobody spoke to him at first—"It seemed as if they did not even see me." Finally, he inquired about the reason for this unusual atmosphere. He was told that President de Gaulle was in the country to open the Moselle Canal, together with the Prime Minister of Luxembourg and the Saarland. A rumor had spread to Bonn that there had been an attack on President de Gaulle's life.

At last, Peres was asked to enter the Chancellor's room. There he found Erhard and Minister of Special Affairs Westrick in the same state of nervousness. Peres ignored it and began to speak about the Near East situation. He had the feeling that no one was listening. Suddenly, Westrick cut him short and said: "Let us talk about the tanks." Peres immediately presented his suggestion. Germany should deliver empty tank shells to Italy. There, they could be refitted with new American guns, engines and electronic equipment. After six months, they could be shipped to Israel without anybody knowing where they came from. The two German statesmen seemed relieved. They agreed instantly. Some doubts arose later in Peres' mind whether they would have agreed so easily, had they not been caught preoccupied with other problems.[20] The Italian consent for the unusual "transfer" was not difficult to obtain.

But this scheme also incurred its difficulties. Once, by mistake, twenty tanks had been sent from Germany as they were, with turrets, guns and engines. Due to the turrets, they were higher than expected and they got stuck in a tunnel right behind the Italian frontier. For some time, they blocked the traffic there for everybody to see and to wonder at, although Italian authorities had, by then, become accustomed to these German practices.

Up to the end of 1964, Israel had received equipment from Germany to the value of $45,000,000. The original agreement had been for $60,000,000 worth of aid. The agreement on the delivery of tanks increased the scheme to $80,000,000. First hints as to the arms deliveries to Israel were published in German papers in October, 1964, though not all corresponded to the facts. State Secretary Karl-Guenther von Hase, the government spokesman, denied on October 26, that such deliveries had taken place.

[20] Peres, in conversation with the writer, July 30, 1968.

Nevertheless, on November 1, *Al Gumhuriya*, the semiofficial Egyptian paper strongly condemned German military aid to Israel and the "conspiritative spirit in which the Bonn government practiced its relations with Israel behind the back of the Arabs. . . . the Arabs were today a big economic and military power which was not to be ignored." And, "The Bonn government, which has chosen the friendship of a handful of Zionists, cannot dream of Arab friendship."

The fact that something of the scheme leaked out was not really surprising. A considerable number of people knew about it. The parliamentary Budget Committee consisted of twenty-seven members. And there were the heads of the three parties and their representatives in the subcommittee that were kept informed about the various aid projects; then, the leader of the Defense Ministry, State Secretary Volkmar Hopf, was often in Israel for consultations—not to speak of the high-ranking officers of the German army who visited Israel.

It is hard to believe that the Arabs had not learned about the arms deal earlier. President Nasser claimed that he had received information about the German arms deliveries about 1963. [21] He knew no details then, and believed it concerned smaller weapons from Germany's own production. Much later he realized that the deliveries included tanks and planes. One can only speculate as to the reasons why the Arabs revealed the deal at the end of 1964, including the German plan (hinted at then, in public) to open a Diplomatic Mission in Israel with consular powers on April 1, 1965. But, that it was due to a German source was not excluded. There was a good deal of annoyance among German government officials about the constant Israeli pressure on Bonn concerning a recall of German scientists in Egypt.

On November 9, 1964, Cairo officially requested information from Bonn about the arms aid to Israel. A day later, a faction of the Christian Democratic Union decided to send Dr. Eugen Gerstenmaier, the president of the *Bundestag*, to Cairo for talks with Nasser. He had held an invitation to visit Egypt since April, the time when the Arabs had made special efforts to influence German politicians against Israel. The choice of Gerstenmaier was an ostensible indication that the German government wanted neither to offend nor to provoke Israel. Gerstenmaier was known as a friend of Israel and,

---

[21] *Sueddeutsche Zeitung*, February 17, 1965.

on various occasions, he had pleaded for the establishment of diplomatic relations even if this meant risking official Arab recognition of the East German GDR. As he explained later, he was intent on overcoming the barriers that had been erected by the Arabs against diplomatic connection with Israel. He was empowered to offer an "arrangement" ("which would not have been to the disadvantage of Israel") and to repeat the invitation to Nasser to come to Bonn for consultations with the German government which had been informally tendered by German officials.

When he met the Egyptian President on November 23, Nasser put before him papers that proved the arms deliveries to Israel which Gerstenmaier, when asked previously, had denied. And he continued to do so, even in view of the papers: "I denied the truth of the information contained therein." Gerstenmaier said he never had heard about such an agreement. When Nasser managed to convince him that such secret arms deliveries were taking place, he is reported to have said: "I cannot find any words to express my regret about the dilemma into which my government has manoeuvered itself." [22] Back in Bonn, he went straight to the Chancellor and learned the truth. He said: "I raised hell about it." To his mind, three men of each party faction could not bind Parliament on such an important decision.

But, again in Cairo he was faced with a situation which was allegedly new to him. Nasser was by no means as "pigheaded" as he had thought him to be. Gerstenmaier was convinced that, had there not been the arms deal, he could have reached an agreement with him which would have assured official ties to Israel without Arab retaliation. But now he had to combat the situation. He countered with the accusation that Nasser had obtained wagonloads of arms from the Russians, yet, if the Germans gave Israel a few old tanks he made a fuss about it. This was not fair.

Nasser retorted that Germany gave these arms to Israel for nothing while he had to pay the Russians. When Gerstenmaier asked him, with a bit of malice, with what he could possibly have paid the Russians, Nasser replied angrily, "With my best cotton."

Gerstenmaier, there and then, offered, on his own initiative the discontinuation of the arms deal with Israel and asked the Egyptian President to assent to, without retaliation (recognition of the

---

[22] Joachim Kreysler and Klaus Jungfer, *Deutsche Israel Politik*, p. 116, Wolf von Tucher Verlag G.m.b.H., Diessen-Ammersee, 1965.

GDR), German official ties to Israel. The German guest also emphasized that Nasser should be aware there would never be any German-Arab relations at the expense of Israel. Nasser pretended to be ready to consider the suggestion though he made it clear that he had to think of his position in the Arab world; he might risk the leadership and lose it to Algeria's Ben Bella. This could not be to the advantage of the Federal Republic which had better contacts with him than with Algeria. This remark may have induced the Germans to suggest merely the setting up of a Trade Mission plus German Consulate in Israel as Foreign Minister Schroeder hinted in Parliament on December 3, 1964.

On December 27, the Egyptian paper, *Al Achbar*, published details about the military aid treaty between Bonn and Jerusalem. According to its information, the aid treaty was controlled by a secret committee of the *Bundestag* which could ratify such secret military treaties without informing Parliament about it. The planes and tanks which the Federal government bought for Israel in the United States had been delivered there via Portugal. Whatever had leaked out about this "dilemma," had sufficed to inspire angry comments both among German politicians and the German press about a secret agreement that was bound to be disclosed one day. Rumors had it that the government would soon make a statement on it. And this could only be to the disadvantage of Germany and, in the long run, not of service to Israel, either.

This was watched in Israel with concern. Nobody there had any illusions about the effect of the press campaign in Germany—as well as in the Arab countries—on a weak government such as Erhard's. And were Germany to stop arms deliveries it would mean a capitulation before Arab threats to the detriment of Israel's interests. This was bound to be a new stumbling block in German-Israel relations.

On November 4, Dr. Shinnar [23] was told to go to Bonn to deliver a verbal message to Chancellor Erhard. In it, Prime Minister Eshkol expressed his concern that the Federal government intended to publish a declaration (it had been learned in Israel) in which the arms aid to Israel would be confirmed and in which it was to be announced that there was no intention of subscribing to any further agreements of this kind. Eshkol was chiefly concerned about the Federal government's intention to reveal and lay down its future

[23] Felix E. Shinnar, *Bericht eines Beauftragten*, p. 145, Rainer Wunderlich Verlag, Tübingen, 1967.

policy plans. Such a declaration would give the Arab states the sure feeling that this was the result of their pressure. It would also provoke a comparison between the success of Arab pressure and the failure of the German government to force German scientists to stop working for Nasser's arms industries. Eshkol pleaded with Erhard to drop at least the second part of the intended publication.

Shinnar remained in Germany ten days during which he met several times with Professor Erhard and Dr. Westrick who both showed understanding for Eshkol's arguments. Nevertheless, Erhard asked Shinnar to inquire whether, perhaps, his government would not consider the cancellation of the deal and accept money for the remainder.

Chancellor Erhard said, in review,[24] "From the beginning, I was in favor of giving the Israelis money. With the money, they could buy arms. This would annoy the Arabs far less, while we would not appear as arms dealers." It was on one of those occasions that Westrick said to Shinnar: "There is a price for everything," to which the Israeli diplomat replied: "Except for honor." Westrick agreed.[25] But Erhard and Westrick had to face the arguments of their Foreign Minister, Dr. Gerhard Schroeder, who with any improvement in the German-Israel relations saw a deterioration of Arab-German relations and an increasing influence of the Eastern bloc in the Arab world, both strategically and economically. The weakening of the Western position there could not possibly be in the interest of Israel, either.

At first, Schroeder was not ready, Shinnar reported,[26] to accept the Israeli suggestion to refrain from publishing the Federal government's intention not to deliver any arms to Israel in the future, but in the end, he gave in, at least for the moment. When Shinnar returned to Jerusalem, he pleaded with his government to accept the German suggestion to substitute money for arms, believing that this would curtail the crisis. This was quite contrary to what politicians in Jerusalem believed right, interpreting such a move as a concession and a political victory for the enemy. Shinnar was asked not to return to his post in Cologne. It was at this time that he offered to resign.[27] It was said that he disagreed with his government's policy

---

[24] Conversation with the writer, July 11, 1968.
[25] Felix E. Shinnar, *Bericht eines Beauftragten*, p. 149, Rainer Wunderlich Verlag, Tübingen, 1967.
[26] *Ibid.*
[27] Published in the Israeli press, January 5, 1965.

and argued in the early stages of this dispute that Israel should accept the German concession offer.

Meanwhile, the Arabs increased their propaganda fire against Bonn. In a conference, taking place in Cairo from January 9 to 12, the thirteen heads of the Arab states decided on a three-stage plan of action. First, in a common *démarche*, to demand the immediate stoppage of German military aid to Israel. If Bonn did not comply, to threaten the dissolution of relations and, thirdly, to leave it then to the individual Arab states to decide whether or not to establish diplomatic ties to East Germany.

This again roused the German press to angry comments. "The Arabs put German-Arab friendship to a hard test," Klaus Boelling commented on television on January 14, 1965, calling the Arabs' policy a very bad one. In categorical denial, he said, "We cannot bow to this policy of blackmail. It would be against our self-respect." The *Stuttgarter Zeitung* believed that: "The Arabs speak to us in this language only because the previous success of their policy of blackmail went to their heads," and, "It is about time to tell those gentlemen who are plagued by psychopathic nationalism and who lose patience with us so quickly that our patience with blackmailers is limited, also." The *Sueddeutsche Zeitung* called Cairo's attempt at intimidating Bonn stronger even than the Arab line against Israel. The *Frankfurter Rundschau* recommended telling the Arabs, once and for all, that German relationship to Israel was not to be determined either in Cairo or in Damascus: "Then, at least, the Arabs cannot accuse us of being dishonest with them." All papers, however, were once again unanimous in their condemnation of military aid to Israel. The German government failed to comment.

On January 20, 1965, Daniel Schorr, the Bonn correspondent of Columbia Broadcasting, reported German arms sales to Israel to the value of $80,000,000. All other publications had remained vague; this was the first more definite disclosure. The news item appeared a day later in *The New York Times* and in *France Soir*. Official Bonn was helpless and made no comment. The Foreign Office spokesman advised turning to the Defense Ministry for information. The Defense Ministry spokesman recommended the Foreign Office. The government Press Office finally announced—at 5 p.m.—that a statement would be made in an hour. It eventually came at 7 p.m. and simply said that all figures and facts mentioned in this news item were mere speculation. Who leaked the details to the American correspondent remained a secret. It is known that he did not obtain it directly from

German sources, which indicates that American circles had something to do with it. But this does not exclude the possibility that the original source was in Bonn's Foreign Office which, after all, had been frank about its opposition to this part of the policy towards Israel. Quite possibly, Foreign Minister Schroeder hoped for a de-escalation of anti-Bonn propaganda in the Arab states once the secret arms deal was out of the way.

As was to be expected, German press reaction was dead against the deal now out in the open. The *Koelner Stadtanzeiger* called it, "a capital mistake." The *Stuttgarter Zeitung* thought that what Adenauer and Ben-Gurion had arranged was not very clever. The basic mistake had been made by Adenauer, the *Frankfurter Allgemeine* said. *Die Welt* wrote on February 13, 1965, "There is no need to say much about this unholy heritage that Erhard took over. . . ."

Foreign Minister Dr. Schroeder called arms aid to Israel "foolishness" on the part of the former Chancellor: he always had been opposed to it.[28] But, when Strauss was questioned, he said that Adenauer's directives for the arms deal had not been against his conscience. Adenauer had told him to allocate something so that the Jews living in Israel could build up their state in peace and security. In a public meeting in Duesseldorf, on February 17, Strauss mentioned that the German arms aid to Israel had worked to the advantage of Germany. The general declarations in favor of Germany made by the Israeli Prime Minister Ben-Gurion and his successor, Levi Eshkol, were not accidental.

Strauss's statement certainly is correct. Strauss was the only German politician who acted logically. Every other German who wished Israel well but hesitated to help it with arms could only be called hypocritical, considering the military situation. This surely was the case when they condemned Strauss afterwards for having given the aid.

On January 31, 1965, Social Democrats and Free Democrats demanded in rather strong words, the immediate discontinuation of arms deliveries to Israel. This is the more surprising since their representatives had been on the subcommittee in control of the deal. Strauss had done more for German-Jewish reconciliation than any other German, with the exception of Professor Boehm, who had done such vital work to see the Luxembourg Treaty through. Shimon Peres confirmed this when he said, in a *Spiegel* interview, on

[28] *Quick Illustrated,* February 17, 1965.

February 24, that Strauss, acting on the German government's behalf, helped greatly to draft a concept for a better moral relationship between the two peoples: ". . . Although we talked about military affairs, the background was always political and moral."

Of course, the question can be asked why the Germans, as other
countries, did not enter into an open arms deal with Israel. German
politicians ruled this out for the same reason they gave for not entering into diplomatic relations with Israel; fear of the Arab reaction.
Once they had agreed to the deal being secret, there always was the
danger of it being revealed; but this was the problem for the Germans to solve. It was strange to see their helplessness when, at last, it
was disclosed. They were not prepared for it, yet they should have
calculated on this possibility. Apparently, they hoped that their deliberately generous economic aid to Egypt would keep Nasser from
using the arms deliveries to Israel as a pretext for recognizing the
GDR.

Surely it can be assumed that Adenauer never would have consented to the arms deal, had diplomatic relations existed. He, no
doubt, felt uneasy in denying just the Jewish state such accord, but
lacked the courage to insist on the establishment of diplomatic
connections, in view of the Arab policy of threats to cement relations with East Berlin. Therefore, he accepted the secret plan, clos-
ing his eyes and hoping for the best.

Shimon Peres put this into words when he said to Strauss in one
of their first meetings, "All right—you have the Hallstein Doctrine.
Therefore, we cannot take the first step (diplomatic relations). Let
us then take the second." [29] In the end, how much the situation
suited the Israelis can be judged from Peres' sentence in the *Spiegel*
interview: "I found security more important than diplomatic relations. Frontiers cannot be defended with ambassadors."

[29] Peres, in conversation with the writer, July 30, 1968.

16
From Ulbricht to Erhard

The conference hall of the CDU faction in the *Bundestag*, was virtually turned into a press camp on Friday afternoon, March 5, 1965—a time when, normally, political life stops in Bonn for the weekend recess. That afternoon, a press conference was called three times to inform about three hundred foreign and German journalists of a decision of the German Cabinet. Three times, it had to be postponed, again because the German Cabinet had failed to reach agreement. When it finally ended, the Cabinet had met for thirteen hours in two consecutive days. It had dealt with one subject: the crisis that had arisen between the Federal Republic and the Arab states and between the Federal Republic and Israel.

The announcement made by the government spokesman, at last, drew open laughter from the newsmen. The Cabinet had not made a decision yet because additional factors had just become known and still needed analyzing. A German reaction had been expected at least on the future relationship with the Arab states, and more particularly with Egypt, following the Cairo quasi-state visit of the East German Communist boss, Walter Ulbricht.

It seemed almost to symbolize the past relationship with the Near East countries that, even in face of a proper crisis, Bonn could not muster up a hard decision. The Germans had just postponed the problems that needed a solution long ago. This concerned Israel as much as the Arab states.

Legislation had not been passed to stop German scientists from working in Nasser's armament factories as had been promised two years before to pacify the Israelis alarmed by the German rocket production there. Nor had the Germans shown any readiness to extend or abolish the statute of limitations which in May, 1965, would stop the persecution of Nazi criminals. Instead, the Germans seemed intent on discontinuing their arms aid to Israel under Arab pressure. In recompense, and, at the same time, to solve the problem of how to preserve ties to Israel after the completion of the Luxembourg Treaty in 1966, they had suggested the setting up of a kind of "German Mission" with consular powers. Because of the Arabs they did not dare offer more. The opening of East German Consulates in Cairo and Alexandria gave them the feeling of having the right, at least, to do this.

The two heads of government had entered into a correspondence (which never was divulged) on the problems concerned. The time that it took Chancellor Erhard to reply to the letters from the Israeli Prime Minister and the efforts of writing and rewriting relevant drafts made it clear that Erhard just did not know how to cope with the conflict for which his predecessor was just as much to blame.

A suggestion for a meeting between the two men was contemplated. It seems to have been initiated by Eshkol.

In a *Maariv* interview on September 6, 1964, Eshkol remarked: "I think I shall meet with Chancellor Erhard." This was "noted" in Bonn "with interest," yet the Israeli Prime Minister's hint was called "still unfounded." Two months later (November 5), Erhard confirmed this hint on German television saying, "I shall, perhaps, meet with Eshkol within a measurable space of time."

The CDU parliamentarian, Erik Blumenfeld, announced in Washington on December 10, that a meeting between Erhard and Eshkol would take place some time in February. This was not confirmed in Bonn. At such a meeting, the Germans would have to offer something tangible. Erhard and his advisors knew only too well that for the Israelis—and the latter had left no doubts about it—there no longer existed an alternative to diplomatic relations. The difficulties that the Germans had with the Arabs did not interest them in the least. On German television, December 21, 1964, Eshkol said: "I presume the Germans understand that the relationship between Germany and Israel, in view of . . . the genocide . . . is a matter in which the interference of the Arabs cannot be tolerated."

The Arabs used the publication of German arms aid to Israel as a means of exerting new pressure on the West Germans, a policy of blackmail they had pursued ever since the reestablishment of diplomatic relations after World War II. As the Germans had responded to this policy in the manner the Arabs had anticipated, they felt perfectly within their rights to continue it. It certainly had prevented the establishment of diplomatic relations between Bonn and Jerusalem. Now, they demanded, categorically, the immediate stoppage of arms deliveries to Israel and threatened the rupture of diplomatic relations with Bonn, should the West Germans fail to comply with their request. Wherever and however possible, they implied that they might grant official recognition to the East German Communist state. They seemed to rule out an extension of diplomatic relations to Jerusalem on the part of Bonn, as all the suggestions made by leading German politicians until then had not gone beyond the establishment of consular relations. This was the state of affairs with which the Germans were faced at the turn of the year.

While the Germans still were deep "in thought" about their attitude to the new problems, the Arabs hinted at their "needs" which gave Bonn the feeling that there was still a means to bypass the situation. However, Bonn's generosity was limited by then, due to financial difficulties. On January 4, the government spokesman in Bonn told the Arabs point-blank that they had received a considerable share of Bonn's development aid. Bonn could not concentrate its aid on one part of the world, only. Latin-American states and countries of black Africa were just as much in need of development aid and now—for both political and economic reasons—Bonn had to grant them a share of its aid.

The Arab Prime Ministers' meeting in Cairo from January 9 to 12 resulted in a declaration that a common policy would be pursued against any state which sought to take up new relations with Israel, or which supported its aggressive aims.[1]

Syria's President Hafez threatened to sever the ties if Bonn failed to pay $87,500,000 for the construction of the Euphrates Dam, demanding Bonn's consent within six weeks. Before the press on January 16, 1965, government spokesman von Hase waived the Syrian request, saying Bonn would not allow itself to be put under pressure.

But the climax was reached when, on January 24, the Egyptian paper, *Al Ahram*, published the news that Nasser had invited Wal-

---

[1] Joachim Kreysler and Klaus Jungfer, *Deutsche Israel Politik*, p. 118, Wolf von Tucher Verlag G.m.b.H., Diessen-Ammersee, 1965.

ter Ulbricht, Chairman of the Council of Ministers of the GDR, to visit Egypt. The pretext was the signing of a $78,000,000 credit agreement between Egypt and the GDR. The East German news agency, ADN, confirmed it on January 27.

At first, the news produced the feeling in Bonn that Egypt wanted only to tighten the screws on Bonn a little more in order to make the Germans stop the military aid to Israel and, at the same time, force them to grant even more aid to Egyptian development projects. Officials, therefore, still hoped that it would be possible to dissuade Nasser from receiving Ulbricht in Egypt.

After a Cabinet meeting on January 27, the Bonn government spokesman expressed surprise at the sudden invitation. The German government reminded Nasser of his accepted invitation to Bonn and said that it hoped he would pay his visit "very soon." The spokesman went as far as saying that the preparations for this visit had reached a more developed stage than for the projected meeting between Erhard and Eshkol: while Nasser already had the invitation of the Federal President in his hands, there was no more than mutual agreement about an Eshkol-Erhard meeting. It was Bonn's attempt to nip in the bud the East German-Egyptian flirtation. "A sovereign state can invite whomever it wants, but our friends in Cairo must know how we rate this visit." Once again, Bonn reminded Nasser of its aid to his country. It was "rather considerable having reached $187,500,000." Von Hase did not add any threats or warnings, yet, as to what might happen if Ulbricht were to set foot on Egyptian soil.

It has often been alleged that Nasser's invitation to Ulbricht was an act of retaliation for Bonn's arms aid to Israel. But this seems far off the mark. Nasser had known about the arms deal, as he himself had admitted, for at least two years. He simply wanted to create this impression in order to cover up the true reasons for his inviting the East German Communist leader.

One was pressure from the Russians, who did all possible to make other states accept their theory of the existence of two German states. A Soviet delegation under the leadership of Alexander Shelepin had been in Cairo in December, 1964. The USSR took over the considerable financial commitment of aiding Nasser with $275,000,000 in the wake of this delegation's trip to Cairo. Nasser was in great financial trouble, then. His country's economy had been close to bankruptcy. The war in Yemen had eaten up a good deal of his country's meager resources. Egypt had suffered a food shortage.

The first five-year plan had been in jeopardy. The second, in the planning stage only, was to have been started in 1965. The country, not having the means to complete the first one, certainly could not embark on the second. $78,000,000 from East Germany was not much, but Nasser had been in need of every penny. Besides, he hoped that with it he could induce the West Germans to increase their aid contributions. Over and above this, he had had political difficulties. Arab unity was further away from realization than ever. The Syrians kept their distance from the Egyptians. In Iraq, the difficulties with the Kurds were obstacles on the road to Arab unity; Nasser's adventurous war in Yemen had increased the enmity of the Arabian kingdoms towards him. And only with Arab unity, would Nasser's leadership in the so-called third world be real and of significance. An anti-Israel and an anti-imperialist line had often helped to rally the Arabs behind the Egyptian dictator.

In the parliamentary question hour of January 29, Foreign Minister Dr. Gerhard Schroeder, for the first time, threatened the disruption of development aid for Egypt as a direct consequence of the invitation to Ulbricht. To a question put to him by the Social Democratic parliamentarian, Karl Mommer, as to whether he would agree that the House should not vote a penny of development aid to countries receiving Ulbricht, Schroeder, (to the applause of parliamentarians) replied: "I should say you are right there." [2]

Several suggestions were offered by West German politicians on how to deal with the situation: to apply the Hallstein Doctrine, in case Ulbricht was received in Cairo, i.e., to cut the ties to Egypt, was certainly the severest punishment and was demanded mainly by Christian Democratic politicians. They surely felt betrayed, as in all those past years everything had been done by their government representatives to please the Arabs. The Free Democrats—junior partners in the government coalition—warned of the application of the Hallstein Doctrine, as the visit of the East German chief to Egypt was not identical with the extension of diplomatic relations to East Germany for which the Hallstein Doctrine had been created. The passing of time brought an increase in the number of politicians—from both these parties—who preferred the discontinuation of all aid measures to Egypt as a punishment. The Social Democrats, the official opposition in Bonn, spoke of the need of taking strong action against Egypt, but without specifying what that might be. In addi-

[2] Minutes of the *Bundestag*, vol. 57, p. 8076.

tion, they suggested an entirely new Near East policy starting with the establishment of diplomatic relations with Israel. But all three parties were united in their support of government action because whoever received "the arch enemy of the reunification of Germany and the Moscow satellite" could not expect anything but harsh treatment.[3]

Nasser pretended to be unconcerned about the threats from Bonn. The account of his meeting with West German Ambassador Dr. Federer on January 31, as published in *Al Ahram*,[4] gives this impression. Federer, who had to wait all day to be received, asked Nasser to consider the serious effect on his government of the invitation to Ulbricht to visit Cairo. The opening of the Cairo doors to Ulbricht meant that the whole third-world bloc had opened its doors to East Germany. Nasser, making it clear that he would not cancel the invitation, and did not consider the East German Communist a mere tourist, said:

. . . Israel is a hundred times more dangerous to the Arab world than East Germany is to West Germany. You have not been content with everything you did to help Israel with reparations. Today, you are adding to it by the supply of an arms gift to our enemy. . . .

He continued that, apart from its danger to the entire Arab world, the treaty had been concluded in "a disgusting manner . . . and then the outcome [of the Waldorf-Astoria meeting] remains secret while we, unfortunately, believe your official assurances and your repeated public statements denying what happened."

When Federer wanted an assurance that Ulbricht's visit did not actually mean official recognition of the GDR, Nasser replied,

I am afraid I have to tell you that the situation may change . . . if the arms deal with Israel continues we shall reconsider our whole position and shall definitely recognize East Germany . . . everything depends on your actions. Please realize and convey to your government in Bonn that giving an arms gift to Israel is a matter of life and death for us.

When Nasser was reminded of the amount of aid he had received from Bonn, he said he would not consider this *aid*, as every penny of it had to be repaid with a high interest rate.[5]

Following this conversation with Nasser, Federer was called to

3 *Maariv*, February 13, 1965.
4 English translation published in *Guardian*, February 11.
5 *The Guardian*, February 11, 1965.

Bonn for reporting. There were hectic discussions and meetings between him and Bonn's leading politicians. Bonn also conferred with its allies and asked them to use their influence on Cairo to make Nasser change his mind. All other Arab states were informed, via their ambassadors to Bonn, of how the West German government would view a visit of Walter Ulbricht to Cairo, and that such a visit would have serious consequences for German relations with the Arabs.[6]

The Bonn Cabinet, in a special meeting on February 3, postponed making a decision as to political and economic consequences to be applied against Egypt until it was evident in what manner Ulbricht had been received in Cairo. They realized that they no longer could prevent the visit from taking place. Ambassador Federer was asked to remain in Bonn as a warning to Nasser.

At the same time, practically all Bonn politicians were agreed on the discontinuation of German arms aid to Israel and the conversion of the remainder of the agreement. Dr. Shinnar reported in his memoirs [7] that, at the end of January, he was called to Minister of Special Affairs Westrick, who told him that the Federal government saw no other means to prevent Ulbricht's visit to Cairo than to publish its intention not to deliver any more arms in areas of tension. This was by no means a surrender to Arab pressure and it was not to affect just Israel. Even when it was plain that the Ulbricht visit could no longer be prevented, the Germans stuck to this line. Dr. Gerstenmaier was the most outspoken opponent of military aid to other countries outside NATO because he thought that Germany should not be involved in armed conflicts under any circumstances, wherever they might be. He collected signatures to enable him to put a private members bill to Parliament to this effect. While Strauss, the initiator of the arms aid scheme, and Dr. Konrad Adenauer, the former Chancellor (responsible for its execution), belonged to a group within the CDU who felt that this was giving in to the blackmail of the Egyptians, the majority supported Gerstenmaier. The Free Democrats assured Gerstenmaier of their unconditional support practically daily after the disclosure of the arms aid. The Social Democrats were split on this issue. Most of them shared the view that Germany, of all countries, should give no arms aid to any country while Floor Leader Fritz Erler demanded assurance

[6] Von Hase, press conference, February 12, 1965.
[7] Felix E. Shinnar, *Bericht eines Beauftragten*, p. 149, Rainer Wunderlich Verlag, Tübingen, 1967.

that "the Israelis are not just slaughtered." Other Social Democrats thought that other ways and means ought to be sought to aid Israel. Gerstenmaier's bill had every chance of being accepted and of leading to regulations that, according to the government spokesman,[8] would in no way be "of a discriminatory nature." However, it was later dropped, due to developments.

A proper war of nerves now developed between Bonn and Cairo. Threats were used as ammunition and the aim seemed to be to wring from the opponent the highest possible concession. After Bonn had recalled its ambassador and made it manifest that it was not to be blackmailed, it was Cairo's turn to go for higher stakes. It did so on February 6, by threatening to recognize East Germany if Bonn did not decide on a discontinuation of military aid to Israel. Perhaps not to turn the screws too tightly, this was merely published in Egyptian newspapers. The Bonn government appeared to take it relatively calmly. The article was called "one-sided propaganda," using Israel as a pretext for distracting attention from the fact that Ulbricht had bought his Cairo trip with a $78,000,000 credit. Egyptian papers repeated their threat the following day. It was about the time when there were considerations in Bonn to cancel the arms deliveries to Israel.

While Bonn was in a fever of speculations, suggestions and statements (unknown to the public), a Spanish diplomat tried his hands at mediation. In his press conference of February 8, von Hase did not deny that the Director General of the Spanish Foreign Ministry had held talks on Bonn's behalf in Cairo. He called this a part of "efforts to regulate German relations with the Near East" in such a way that it was possible to continue bilateral relations with both sides there. Von Hase stated before the press on February 12, that the Federal government had approached the Spanish government asking it to exercise its influence in Egypt with the aim of preventing Ulbricht's visit to Cairo.[9] It was later mentioned that the Federal government had previously invoked Spanish mediation successfully in 1959, at the time of the Grotewohl visit to Cairo, when the UAR and the GDR entered into consular relations and when Egypt

[8] Before the press in Bonn, February 8, 1965.
[9] On February 15, the Foreign Ministry suddenly denied that the Marqués de Nerva had been asked to mediate by the German government. In February, 1969, a Foreign Ministry spokesman told the writer that the Spanish government had offered this service to Bonn.

officially declared (September 29, 1959), that this did not imply recognition of the GDR.[10]

Still, in Cairo, on February 8, the Marqués de Nerva announced, triumphantly, that he had been "successful." Two days later, Egyptian Prime Minister Ali Sabri announced in the National Assembly in Cairo that the German government had given assurance that it would: end arms supplies to Israel; insure that no arms shipments were in transit to that country; and would not supply arms, in the future, to any "areas of tension."

Ali Sabri made this statement after some members of the UAR National Assembly had called for the severing of ties with West Germany and for diplomatic recognition of Eastern Germany.[11] He claimed he had been given this piece of information by the Spanish diplomat. Bonn was greatly annoyed and did not confirm this news until two days later. The reason for this was simple. Dr. Shinnar had returned to Bonn on the ninth. He was to give the reply of his government to a suggestion which had been made by Minister Westrick at the end of January to convert the remainder of the arms deal into money. The fact that this should be published and be connected with a regulation that in future Bonn would not deliver any arms to areas of tension was unacceptable to Israel. The Jerusalem government could not allow this to appear as a victory of the Arabs and objected to being called an "area of tension." Israel was fighting for its existence which was something quite different. The term would apply far more to Germany, Israeli politicians remarked.

On the morning of the tenth, Dr. Shinnar saw State Secretary Carstens of the Foreign Office, and told of the Israeli government's objections. Carstens did not inform the Israeli diplomat that his government had already arrived at a decision, as de Nerva's statements implied. On the contrary. Carstens asked Shinnar to return home and convey to his government the suggestion that Bonn might consider passing a law according to which it would not deliver any arms to countries outside NATO, but this law would include a clause prohibiting German scientists from working in armaments factories abroad. No wonder Dr. Shinnar called it "incomprehensible" and "not understandable" when he was told later that same night of Ali Sabri's announcement in Cairo.

[10] Foreign Minister Schroeder on February 17, before Parliament.
[11] Keesing's Contemporary Archives, 1965, p. 20738.

Over and above this, the Spanish grandee had announced on Egyptian television that the Germans had given assurance to Egypt that they would not extend diplomatic relations to Israel. Who had given the Marqués the mandate to make such statements on behalf of the West German government never was clarified. There were some rumors in Bonn that de Nerva was keenly interested in preserving the ties between Bonn and Egypt. It was said that he was an agent of the German Messerschmitt manufacturing firm which had plants in Egypt, Spain and Germany, and that a rupture of ties between Bonn and Cairo would have impeded this business based on a three-country cooperation.[12]

Late in the night of the tenth, Dr. Gerstenmaier affirmed to foreign correspondents that Bonn had decided to stop arms deliveries to Israel. He told questioners that he had this news from a telephone conversation with the Foreign Minister. Dr. Schroeder, then, had outmanoeuvred all other political forces. It seemed that he had made a decision on his own initiative. Having a weak Chancellor at the helm of the state, he could well do so on the grounds that the situation, as it was, was untenable and called for some decisive action. Again no comments could be obtained. The government declared that it first wanted to hear the report of the Spanish mediator who, incidentally, continued to make statements in the same spirit as before, adding: "I am so happy to have been able to be of help to Germany." When the Marqués finally reached Bonn on the twelfth to make a report of his mission he was received by the State Secretary, only. Neither the Chancellor, nor the Foreign Minister found time to see the man responsible (with his public statements) for incriminating the Bonn government in such a manner.

Dr. Shinnar was received by the Chancellor in the afternoon of the eleventh. He allowed the Israeli diplomat to read the instructions given to the Spanish gentleman, which proved that de Nerva had either overstepped his powers or had not said what was attributed to him.[13] There was, of course, this other possibility which Erhard did not mention—that Schroeder had given the Spaniard a different set of instructions which appeared more "plausible" to the man. Chancellor Erhard then asked Dr. Shinnar to go home and put before his government the suggestion regarding the conversation of the arms agreement as discussed on the tenth with Carstens. In a letter to

---

[12] *Mainzer Allgemeine Zeitung*, February 13, 1965.

[13] Felix E. Shinnar, *Bericht eines Beauftragten*, p. 154, Rainer Wunderlich Verlag, Tübingen, 1967.

Eshkol, Erhard explained, in detail, his government's attitude which concerned solely the need to convert the arms deal.

An hour before Shinnar left for Israel, Egyptian Ambassador Gamal Eddine Mansour returned to Bonn and proudly announced that from then on the relations between Germany and his country were bound to improve. He referred to the alleged de Nerva statements that Germany would stop arms deliveries to Israel and also not conclude any diplomatic relations with the state of the Jews.

Despite the Bonn assurances that the Spaniard had not been entitled to make the statements [14] referred to, Israel felt that it had been "cheated." Premier Eshkol announced on the eleventh that, under the circumstances, he would reject meeting with Chancellor Erhard. A day later, the Germans solidified their decision. Government spokesman von Hase said, before the press, that the Federal government had decided not to enter into any new obligations for arms supplies in "areas of tension"; that it was also trying to suspend supplies of arms outstanding under earlier commitments (though it could not take a unilateral decision) and that it should be made clear that any threats on the part of the Arabs could only make the steps already initiated with this aim in mind more difficult.

Furthermore, the Egyptian government had been told (through the Spanish mediator and also through its ambassador to Bonn on February 13) that the Federal government could not accept Ulbricht's visit to Egypt under any circumstances and that the German people would react to such a visit "with deep indignation." Only a cancellation or indefinite deferment of the visit could avoid the "heavy damage" to German-Egyptian relations which otherwise would be created. Von Hase, defending these decisions, said that the Federal government, in order to regain its freedom of action, in the first place, had to justify its claim of being the sole representative of Germany, and must normalize its relations with the countries of the Near East. The decisions taken were in the German people's interest, which were bound to have priority over both Egyptian and Israeli interests. He appealed to the Israeli public to understand the German action which had to be taken as German concerns were at stake.[15]

Addressing foreign correspondents in Bonn on the same day, the

[14] Von Hase on February 12. On February 17, the State Secretary, Professor Carstens, stated in the *Bundestag's* question hour that de Nerva had assured him he never had made the alleged statements.

[15] Published by the Press and Information Ministry, February 12, 1965.

West German Chancellor confirmed that the Federal Cabinet had decided on the cessation of German arms deliveries to all Middle East countries. The government would not break its promises to Israel where existing commitments had not been met. It would seek other means of avoiding a breach of contract. Turning to Nasser, Erhard called the invitation to Ulbricht "a hostile act" which was pertinent to endangering and disturbing the relations between Egypt and the Federal Republic. He also hinted at the possibility of discontinuing German aid to Egypt, saying "The Federal Republic can reconsider her political and economic ties wherever and whenever hostile actions are committed which are contrary to the interests of the German people." [16]

On reaching Israel, Dr. Shinnar was immediately involved in a conference with government leaders which was to prepare Sunday morning's Cabinet meeting on this issue. The recommendations worked out by this meeting—in which the participants were Prime Minister Eshkol, his deputy, Abba Eban, Foreign Minister Golda Meir, State Secretary Shimon Peres of the Defense Ministry, Arye Levavi, General Director of the Foreign Office and his deputy, Ehud Avriel, as well as Israel's Ambassador to Paris, Walter Eytan —were a sharp rejection of Bonn's offers. Israel saw no means to accept the suggestions made by the Federal Republic as they constituted a capitulation before Arab blackmail at the expense of Israel. The one-sided cancellation of commitments concerning Israel's security under Arab pressure not only caused considerable damage to Israel but was also a political blow to it in its struggle with the Arab world which, by the action of the Federal Republic, had scored a victory. Israel refused to accept money for the outstanding arms and insisted on the completion of deliveries. Dr. Shinnar was asked to remain in Israel as a demonstration of protest.

In this spirit, Prime Minister Eshkol spoke to the *Knesset* on February 15. He said, with regard to the announced cancellation of the arms treaty:

> Germany's duty is to help Israel with the equipment necessary for her security, and no compensation or monetary substitutes can exempt Germany from this duty. We shall accept no compensation in return for the cancellation of the promised security aid . . . The German government must continue to observe its obligation to Israel in the spirit and the letter . . .

[16] Felix E. Shinnar, *Bericht eines Beauftragten*, p. 156, Rainer Wunderlich Verlag, Tübingen, 1967.

He angrily rejected the reason given for the German decision—that Israel was part of an "area of tension." It was strange that Western Germany, itself in an area of most delicate tension, should utilize this concept as a reason for the refusal to supply security aid to Israel: ". . . I cannot fail to point out the flagrant contrast between the Bonn government's haste in taking action to halt arms dispatches to 'areas of tension' and the sluggishness it has displayed in its response to Israel's demand for effective action for the withdrawal of the scientists from Egypt. The government of Israel cannot agree that any government should be entitled to halt its security aid to Israel or refrain from providing such aid on the grounds of Arab opposition to this assistance. Nor can Israel acquiesce in the prospect that it may be reduced to the status of a kind of currency with which other governments can purchase the satisfaction of their own aims." After a four-hour debate, the *Knesset* passed a resolution by fifty-four votes to twenty-six expressing "astonishment and indignation at the intention of the government of the German Federal Republic to stop the security aid promised to Israel." It stated that this intention, if carried out, would be, "a surrender to the Egyptian ruler's policy of hostility to Israel and an encouragement for its implementation." The resolution approved the Israeli government's decision ". . . to demand that the German government fulfill its obligations to Israel in the letter and the spirit and not accept any financial compensation as a substitute for the cancellation of the promised security aid." [17]

Von Hase called the *Knesset* resolution and Eshkol's speech "deeply disappointing," in reply to a question of the *Maariv* correspondent. He added. "We shall not be dissuaded in our efforts to find a basis on which to come to an agreement with Israel in this difficult question." He argued that he could not quite see why the conversion of the arms agreement was worse for Israel than Arab unity or the possibility that, with Ulbricht, a new Communist state might enter on the Near East scenery.[18]

In a press conference, two hours later, von Hase reiterated that a visit to Cairo by Ulbricht would be considered a "hostile act to the German people" and announced that the Federal Republic would cease its economic aid to the UAR if the visit should not be cancelled. This concerned all types of aid, von Hase said.[19] He implied

[17] *Sueddeutsche Zeitung*, February 16, 1965.
[18] *Maariv*, February 16, 1965.
[19] On February 20, Bonn published the figures of the aid Cairo had received in

that there would be more serious action in store but they would depend on the manner of Ulbricht's reception in Cairo. This was conveyed to the Egyptian government through its ambassador in Bonn and in a letter written by the Federal President to King Hussein of Jordan, asking the latter to use his influence to make Nasser change his mind regarding the Ulbricht visit.

The measure to stop aid to Egypt in case of Ulbricht's being received in Cairo was fully approved by the German people. In an opinion poll,[20] 56 percent of those questioned favored it, 18 percent were against it, while 26 percent gave no answer.

The Arab countries seemed totally unconcerned about Bonn's cancellation of the arms deliveries to Israel. Nor did they seem to worry about the threats addressed to them. At a mass meeting in Helwan, on February 19, Nasser shouted, "The Federal Republic of Germany betrays the Arabs and bleeds Egypt white." The Prime Minister of Iraq, Tahir Jahja, demanded over the radio that Bonn annul all its arrangements with Israel, including the restitution treaty. After the cessation of the arms aid to Israel, the Arabs could expect further steps in this direction.[21]

On February 17, the Bonn Parliament reviewed the government's Near East policy. Chancellor Erhard took the floor to explain that the Federal Republic, while desiring good relations with the Arabs, had a "debt of honor" towards Israel and the Jewish people; Germany still bore "the guilt imposed on it by the Third Reich."

The tension between the UAR and the Federal Republic did not develop because Germany supplied arms to Israel—aid which was on a much smaller scale than the massive arms deliveries to Egypt from Communist sources. It was caused because the Cairo government invited Ulbricht, described as "a puppet" of the Soviet Union. What

---

refutation of Nasser's assertion in *Der Spiegel* that he had not "received any aid or support from Germany; only loans or credit facilities which we repay—and on top pay 6 to 7 percent interest." Under protocol of April 3, 1963, the Federal Republic had provided economic aid to UAR totaling $202,000,000 of which $57,500,000 was in the form of capital-aid credits bearing interest at 2½ to 4 percent. An additional export guarantee amounting to $87,500,000 had been made available to the UAR under the agreement of March 7, 1958.

[20] Elisabeth and Peter Noelle-Neumann, *The Germans, public opinion polls, 1947-1966*, p. 570, Verlag für Demoskopie, Allensbach, 1967.

[21] Joachim Kreysler and Klaus Jungfer, *Deutsche Israel Politik*, p. 120, Wolf von Tucher Verlag G.m.b.H., Diessen-Ammersee, 1965.

the Arabs have done when inviting Ulbricht was to come to terms with those who divided the German people. That was a hostile act, Erhard said: "For, anyone who approved of the division of Germany cannot be a friend of the German people." However, the Chancellor added that German relations with the Arab states were based on a long tradition of unclouded friendship: "Our relations with Israel, on the other hand, were most severely strained. It would have rendered good services to peace had the Arab states . . . shown more understanding of the German nation's debt of honor vis-à-vis the Jews."

The Chancellor then said that he was disappointed at the Israel government's reaction to the German offer to convert the arms deal: "We have always regarded our services to Israel as a duty, but believed that after complying with this duty faithfully for more than a decade we were entitled to hope for recognition of our honest intentions in our actions." In his words, Germany did not withdraw unilaterally from an accepted obligation; all it did was to propose that, by mutual agreement, "we should be relieved of the final part of the obligation—without any material disadvantage to Israel. . . ." [22]

SPD Floor Leader Fritz Erler charged the government with "complete failure" in its Near East policy. He said that it must be Germany's concern to prevent a new massacre of part of those Jews who had survived the German regime of violence. Egypt's invitation to Ulbricht was an act of solidarity with the East German Communists. It destroyed the foundations for friendly and helpful cooperation with the German people and the Federal government. Erler believed that the Egyptian action had to be judged within the context of Soviet policy which had tried to set up a base in the Mediterranean area and in North Africa. The debate made it clear that the majority of the House was now behind the government when it viewed Ulbricht's invitation to Egypt as a hostile act. That one way out of the dilemma would be to stop military aid to Israel at once was accepted by everyone. And, so far as this suggestion was concerned, the politicians could also be sure of public support. Again, questioned as to whether or not they thought it was a good or bad policy to stop supplies of weapons to Israel, the greater majority of Germans approved of Government action. Sixty-four percent did

---

[22] Minutes of the *Bundestag*, vol. 57, p. 8103.

so, and only 11 percent thought it a bad policy. Twenty-five percent did not know what to answer.[23]

Annoyance began to spread in Germany at the fact that the Western Allies did not make the slightest move to help Germany out of its dilemma. Fritz Erler, in his speech before the *Bundestag* on February 17, had already maintained that the problem exceeded the strength of Germany and must be the subject of a joint Near East policy with Germany's current allies. The German press supported this view. *The Rheinische Post* complained angrily that, despite repeated requests from the Bonn government and an obvious responsibility for at least part of its difficulties, the Allies had taken no initiative to support the German position. That Bonn was angry because of the lack of support from the Allies—particularly from the Americans—was also reported in the *Frankfurter Neue Presse* and the *Frankfurter Allgemeine*. The near-Socialist *Neue Rhein Zeitung* suggested that the United States should be reminded of its pressure for German arms deliveries to Israel. Several papers ascribed this attitude of leaving Germany in the lurch to America's wish to see the Hallstein Doctrine removed, which might help to improve the relations of the West with the Soviet Union.

On February 16, Prime Minister Eshkol already had appealed to the Western Allies to help in the overcoming of the crisis. Speaking of an "alarming weakness" of the Federal government in Bonn, Eshkol addressed his appeal especially to the Americans. On February 20, before the press, von Hase criticized the Allies for their attitude. The United States government had very hesitatingly come around to admitting its participation in this arms deal with Israel. In England, German Ambassador von Etzdorf was said to have expressed Bonn's disappointment at the British passivity to Her Majesty's government. There was also concern about the French, now trying to expand their trade in the Arab states at the expense of the Germans. The German government also expressed this view to governments of the Allied Powers through their ambassadors in Bonn.[24]

Eventually, Averell Harriman, America's roving ambassador, went to Jerusalem to help straighten out the aftermath of the German-Israel deal for which his country had reason to feel partly responsible. The Bonn spokesman explained that Harriman's visit manifested America's efforts to exert its good offices on behalf of West Ger-

[23] Elisabeth and Peter Noelle-Neumann, *The Germans, public opinion polls, 1947-1966*, p. 570, Verlag für Demoskopie, Allensbach, 1967.
[24] *Maariv*, February 21, 1965.

many throughout the Middle East.[25] The Americans felt further encouraged to undertake this effort by the appeals sent to the West by Arab governments such as Saudi Arabia, Jordan and Lebanon, weighing the results for themselves of a Nasser triumph.

On February 21, Walter Ulbricht set out on his trip to Egypt—his first official visit to a state outside the Eastern bloc. Accompanied by his wife, Lotte, and a party of forty (which included Dr. Lothar Bolz, the East German Foreign Minister), he sailed from Dubrovnik on the East German ship, *Völkerfreundschaft* (Friendship between Peoples), to Alexandria. When interviewed by the Egyptian paper *Al Ahram,* before his arrival, he said that the GDR was opposed to all attempts by international monopoly capital to strengthen Israel as an imperialist advance post in the Arab sphere: "For this reason, we condemn the military cooperation of the West German Federal Republic with Israel. . . ."

On the twenty-fourth, Ulbricht was greeted in Alexandria with a 21-gun salute—an honor customarily reserved for heads of state—and a salute of the UAR Air Force. By special train, he then reached Cairo where President Nasser, the members of his Cabinet and the ambassadors of thirty Arab, African and Asian countries welcomed him. Thousands of East German and UAR flags flew at the Cairo station and in the streets and the crowd cheered the two leaders as they drove to the Koubbeh Palace, a former royal residence used to accommodate visiting heads of state. At a state banquet given in honor of the visiting East German Communist head, President Nasser made it very clear that he did not wish for a further deterioration in his country's relationship with West Germany. Referring to the "catastrophe" of Germany being a split nation, he said that Egypt had always tried to make its relations with "both sides . . . healthy and strong." Egypt had maintained excellent relations with the East German state but it was also anxious to assure good relations with West Germany: "I need not explain the regrettable and painful circumstances which have recently affected our relations with the Bonn government. Nevertheless, we sincerely intend to prevent a further deterioration. . . ." [26]

Ulbricht toured Egypt until March 2. A lengthy joint communiqué was issued on the eve of his departure. It contained the announcement that the GDR would participate in industrialization

[25] *Ibid.*
[26] Keesing's Archiv der Gegenwart, 1965, p. 11725.

projects under the UAR's second five-year plan and that agreements had been signed on economic and technical cooperation, scientific-technical relations, and cooperation in the spheres of culture, science and health. Agreement had also been reached on the setting up of a joint economic commission, a joint scientific commission and other bodies necessary for implementing the above agreements. Both sides had decided to conclude long-term trade and payment agreements covering the period 1966–1970. There was no mention of any political ties to be developed. Ulbricht gave assurance of his country's support for the right of the whole Arab world to liberty, development and prosperity. He recognized all the rights of the Arab people of Palestine and both countries condemned the aggressive plans of imperialism, "under which Israel had been created as a spearhead directed at the rights of the Arab people and their struggle for liberation and progress. . . ." Ulbricht invited Nasser to visit the GDR. Nasser expressed "sympathy for the German people" and re-affirmed the view that the question of German unity was a matter for the German people to decide.[27]

On the night of Ulbricht's arrival in Egypt, Ambassador Gamal Eddine Mansour was summoned to the Foreign Office in Bonn. Nothing was revealed about this talk but it was correctly assumed that Dr. Hermann Meyer-Lindenberg, the head of the Foreign Office's Political Department, informed the Egyptian diplomat that as Ulbricht had set foot on the Egyptian shores, there would be no more aid forthcoming from West Germany, as previously announced. The government spokesman added that his government would hold in reserve political steps against the UAR. The triumphant reception of the East German leader, the "state visit" treatment, and the refusal of the Egyptian government to allow ten West German journalists to cover the event had annoyed Bonn considerably. On the eve of the Cabinet meeting (which was to decide what measures were to be taken against the UAR), there was again an increasing tendency noticeable among Bonn politicians to punish the Arabs severely and break off relations. Even Professor Walter Hallstein, then president of the European Economic Community, is said to have intervened—something which he was not known to have done since he had held the Brussels post—and demanded strong action be taken against Egypt.[28]

[27] Keesing's Archiv der Gegenwart, 1965, p. 11725.
[28] Joachim Kreysler and Klaus Jungfer, *Deutsche-Israel Politik*, p. 122, Wolf von Tucher Verlag G.m.b.H., Diessen-Ammersee, 1965.

Franz-Josef Strauss (at the time, without ministerial post but still Chairman of the Christian Social Union), an influential politician, demanded both the application of the Hallstein Doctrine to Egypt and the establishment of diplomatic relations with Israel. In those days, the controversy with Israel had, in fact, been pushed into the background due to the struggle with Egypt although it had not been entirely overlooked. It was learned later that Erhard, on March 2, had already considered sending a special envoy to Israel to explain the German attitude. He had chosen the CDU parliamentarian, Dr. Kurt Birrenbach, hardly known by the German public but a man with good connections with international financial and economic circles. That Erhard gave preference to him rather than to someone like Professor Boehm (who had had amicable contacts with Israel since the signing of the Luxembourg Treaty), showed that, despite being the Chancellor, Erhard still had more trust in an economist. Also, he might have thought of the need to pacify American business factions that looked on the German treatment of Israel with misgivings. Birrenbach was, of course, an excellent choice. The parliamentarian was actually on a business trip in the United States when Chancellor Erhard called him and asked him to return for a special task.

Over and above the insult that Nasser had inflicted upon the West Germans when he had received Ulbricht in the manner of a state guest, he announced in an interview, published by the *Sueddeutsche Zeitung* on March 4, that he would establish a Consulate General in East Berlin. This persuaded some Ministers, who still had been undecided, of the need to sever the ties with Egypt so that there would be no doubt about the Bonn government's determination. While the majority of the Christian Democratic Ministers favored such action, Foreign Minister Schroeder opposed it strongly, and so did all the Ministers of the junior coalition party, the Free Democrats. Finally, eight Ministers were in favor, and eight against. This was the result of a five-hour Cabinet meeting on March 4, which ended without a decision.[29]

The majority of the German press generally supported strong action against Egypt. The Federal government would have to apply the Hallstein Doctrine now, the *Stuttgarter Nachrichten* wrote. *Die Welt* thought that stopping development aid could be only a frac-

---

[29] Joachim Kreysler and Klaus Jungfer, *Deutsche Israel Politik*, p. 122, Wolf von Tucher Verlag G.m.b.H., Diessen-Ammersee, 1965.

tion of the action that had to be taken against Egypt. If Bonn does not take strong measures, the dilemma of 1939 might repeat itself, the *Frankfurter Neue Presse* feared. *Handelsblatt*, the German businessman's daily, ironically commented that, if Bonn did not apply severe measures against Egypt, the world would interpret it as a new line of policy—that of enduring conditions made in Cairo.[30]

The day after the inconclusive meeting, Ambassador George McGhee of the United States and Great Britain's Ambassador, Sir Frank Roberts, asked to see the Chancellor and warned him against a rupture with Cairo. They again used the argument that the West had to remain in the Arab states at all costs; it should do nothing to reduce its influence. French Ambassador Francois Seydoux expressed the same view on the sixth, having received relevant instructions from his government. This caused some political leaders to have second thoughts on the issue. Erhard could not overlook the fact of a Cabinet crisis in store for him. "It was a terrible situation", the former Chancellor said.[31] "I was left quite alone." He called to mind that none of the three parliamentary parties had given him any guidance.

For a few hours on Friday morning, March 5, Bonn had reason to believe in a drastic decision. Chancellor Erhard seemed ready to resort to his right as Chancellor to determine the line of policy. Rumors had it that he was intent on severing the ties to Egypt. "Something has got to happen at last which is understood by the people and the world," he is said to have explained to his aides.[32] His press office had already requested radio and television stations to reserve time for an important announcement to be made by the Chancellor himself. But the warnings of the Allies had given new ammunition to the opponents of severing bonds with Egypt. Also, such an important politician as Dr. Rainer Barzel, Floor Leader of the CDU, began to have doubts again. He was in the United States at the time and kept in contact with the Chancellor by phone.

As a result of this, the Cabinet meeting on Friday afternoon, March 5, was again inconclusive and caused the press to wait for several hours in vain for a decision. "On Friday night, I realized that I had to take the initiative," Chancellor Erhard recollected.[33] It can hardly be assumed that Erhard then had thought of extending rela-

---

[30] All newspapers from March 3, 1965.
[31] Conversation with the writer, July 11, 1968.
[32] *Maariv*, March 7, 1965.
[33] Conversation of July 11, 1968.

tions to Israel. But, in the end, chance had its way. Dr. Barzel helped the Chancellor to arrive at a decision—who, incidentally, also met Israel's Deputy Prime Minister Abba Eban in the U.S.—confirmed over the phone from New York that the crisis between Bonn and the state of the Jews could have disastrous consequences for Germany. All the good will that Germany had managed to regain after the war had been squandered in the three weeks during which the Germans showed that they were willing to bow to Egypt's pressure and to stop the arms aid to Israel.

Several American companies were joining a move to curtail imports from Western Germany, protesting the German policy towards Israel.[34] Chairman Michael Daroff, president of Botany Industries and a diversified group of textile, clothing and retail concerns, ordered his buyers to take West Germany off their lists. The orders might have amounted to several hundred thousand dollars for the current year. The same policy spread throughout his group. "We will buy American sewing machines instead of Pfaff," others said, "We are not going to do business with anyone who lets himself be blackmailed by any dictator." The shirt makers refused to place orders in Germany. Jewish organizations like the B'nai B'rith and veterans' organizations began to set up a boycott of German goods. A German wholesale dealer visiting a big American chain store was told, "I don't buy German any more." Demonstrations encouraged this sort of action and Bonn watched this with concern. On February 20, the government spokesman criticized this attitude, reminding the Jews in America of all Germany had so far done for Israel.

Rainer Barzel returned from the United States on the fifth. Next morning, he saw Erhard and told him, again, of the impact of the crisis in America, adding: "We shall lose everything, our prestige, our honor." It was he, then, who suggested that the Federal Republic should take up diplomatic relations with Israel. He threatened Erhard saying that, if the Chancellor failed to make a decision, he would call the executive of the Christian Democrats and demand action. Erhard suggested asking Adenauer what he thought of the idea of making official overtures to Israel. But, Adenauer only smiled and said, "But I was always in favor of extending relations to Israel."

The deliberations on Saturday were disquieted by the presence of British Prime Minister Harold Wilson in Bonn. On Sunday morning, while Wilson was in Berlin, Chancellor Erhard made up his

34 *The New York Times*, February 17, 1965.

mind. Hastily, a press conference was called for Sunday afternoon, apparently not to give the impression that Wilson (who was to return to Bonn on Monday) had anything to do with the decision. It was done on such short notice that only a few journalists could be reached. Those who hurried there were sure that they would be told that the Federal Republic had decided to cut the ties to Egypt. But it was a very different story that von Hase had to announce to the public. It consisted of five points of which the most far reaching was the decision to strive for the establishment of diplomatic relations with Israel. It was announced that this step was taken to bring about a normalization of the situation. It was not directed against any Arab state. The government statement repeated that the Ulbricht visit to Egypt had caused the Federal government to cut off its economic aid to Egypt. West Germany would not contribute to Egypt's second five-year plan. It would grant no more capital aid to Egypt, nor give it any long-term, state-sponsored credits. The people in the Soviet-occupied zone of Germany had been deprived by a regime of terror of the right to self determination. An aggrandizement of that regime was considered "an unfriendly act" in the Federal Republic and was reacted to in an adequate manner. The Federal government's decision to deliver no more arms to Israel and to convert the remainder was an important contribution to a clear Near East policy. It was stressed, in this connection, that the government rejected every kind of influence on its policy in this region, especially concerning its relationship to Israel. Together with its allies, the Federal government by its presence there would continue to press for an easing of tension in the Near East.[35]

Never before in his career had Chancellor Erhard had such a good press as after his decision to recognize Israel—a decision, incidentally, which was to remain one of the very few he ever made during his term of government. *Die Welt* commented, jubilantly: "Erhard decided in the manner which German interests in the Near East afforded." The penny paper, *Bildzeitung*: "The Chancellor did the best he could do." The *Frankfurter Allgemeine* wrote, "At last we have clarity." And, "That is a decision with which we agree from the bottom of our heart." *Bonner Rundschau* reported that the government had acted with prudence and with firmness. The Chancellor's language in opposition to Nasser was good; it betrayed more

[35] Rolf Vogel, *Deutschlands Weg nach Israel,* p. 184, Seewald Verlag, Stuttgart, 1967.

power and a greater readiness for resistance than one could expect after the last Cabinet meetings, the *Stuttgarter Zeitung* said.[36]

In Israel, the country's famous satirist, Ephraim Kishon, and the cartoonist, Dosh, commented on the German decision with a cartoon showing "Conscience" in bed and dreaming. Conscience shows anger when it is disturbed by voices reminding it of the past and sleepily suggests dealing with the problem "tomorrow." It wakes up with a start when a voice tells it: "In Cairo, a 21-gun salute has been fired for Ulbricht." The figure staggers out of bed, spreads out its arms and calls: "Israel, here I come. . . ."[37]

[36] All newspapers from March 8, 1965.
[37] *Maariv*, March 8, 1965.

17
A Chapter is Closed

Lod Airport was crowded on Sunday night, March 7. A plane had just come in from Zurich. Faintly, one could hear the loudspeaker from which came the names of certain passengers who were wanted at the information desk, including a name that sounded vaguely like "Birrenbach." As nobody seemed to respond, the loudspeaker repeated the name more urgently, at intervals. Dr. Kurt Birrenbach, sitting in the VIP lounge, was puzzled. It seemed unlikely that there had been another passenger by the name of Birrenbach on the same plane. On the other hand, he had come to Israel on a secret mission; his name had not been entered on the passenger list. Therefore, he logically concluded, as did the Israeli gentlemen taking care of him, that this could not be a message for him.

Early next morning, Israeli officials came to meet Birrenbach in his suite of the Sharon Hotel in Herzlia-on-Sea. They were to take him to Deputy Defense Minister Shimon Peres, and, later in the day, depart for a first meeting with Premier Eshkol and Foreign Minister Golda Meir in Jerusalem.

Mentioning, in general terms, the tasks they had to solve, Birrenbach stated that some substitute had to be found for the arms deliveries and that arrangements should be made for consular relations—something of the kind that Foreign Minister Dr. Schroeder had had in mind before the crisis had reached its peak. The Israelis were flabbergasted. Only yesterday the German government had announced that it "strove" for diplomatic relations with Israel and here was the special emissary of this very same government offering much less. But, in the end, it was Dr. Birrenbach who was left gaping when he was shown the German government announcement of March 7. He had no choice but to believe it.

The facts were that as recently as Thursday, March 4, Professor Erhard had phoned Birrenbach in Washington, asking him to discontinue his American journey in order to take on a "special task." Birrenbach had hurried back and left Bonn for Israel on March 6, staying overnight in Zurich. In a long talk with the Chancellor and CDU Floor Leader Rainer Barzel, he had been instructed to counteract arms deliveries with an offer of consular relations. But, in the main, he had been told to "pacify" the Israelis as the conflict had begun to have an adverse effect on Germany's reputation abroad.

Dr. Birrenbach was helpless. Here he was, a special emissary of the German Chancellor, with the wrong instructions. On top of it all, he did not even have a means with which to consult his government in the manner that was usual for diplomats. This explained, then, why he had been called to the information desk in Lod when he had landed. The German government had tried to inform its emissary, via El Al, of a most important development. Since West Germany had no official representation in Israel, once he had left the airport it had lost all contact with him.

The Israeli officials, seeing Dr. Birrenbach's predicament, offered him assistance. In order to enable him to confer with his government, they gave him the use of the Israeli Foreign Office code. The question may well be asked how the German government could allow its special emissary to travel like this. The negotiations were delayed several hours until Dr. Birrenbach was brought up to date on the new situation which, literally speaking, had changed drastically overnight.

The news of Dr. Birrenbach's mission was confirmed in Germany one day after his arrival in Israel. The question was asked, Why just he? This parliamentarian of the CDU had not been an outstanding politician; his name was hardly known to the general public. Nor had he been connected with any law that was of particular advantage or interest to the world's Jewish population. Nevertheless, Professor Erhard's choice had not been accidental.

Birrenbach, who had studied law in Berlin, Paris, Munich and Geneva had emigrated in 1939 to Latin America, where, from 1939 to 1950, he had been the representative of General Motors. Married to a partly Jewish woman, he had had the courage to resign from the

NSDAP in 1934, after hardly a year's membership. On his return to Germany in 1954, this man with excellent international connections immediately was made the Chairman of the Board of the Thyssen works in Düsseldorf. Soon after his election to the *Bundestag* he had become a member of the Foreign Affairs Committee and had been nominated for the Montan Parliament in Luxembourg and the European Council in Strasbourg. His leanings towards international politics were evident from the start. His contacts with America, in the main (thanks to his business connections), were considered a great asset.

But, Dr. Birrenbach knew little, if anything, of the Middle East. He was truly perturbed when he was told of Israel's military position, Israeli officials recall. He was equally unprepared for the negotiations on which he was to embark. Although he had been told briefly, of previous agreements and arrangements between the Federal Republic and Israel, he hardly knew of the intricate details since most of them had been concluded in secret. In the few hours during which he had been briefed on the task ahead of him he had been told, repeatedly, of what seemed imperative to the Germans: to find a substitute arrangement for the arms deal. The curious thing about it all was that the people who guided him had scarcely been made aware of all the secret arrangements.

Strauss, who had effected the arms deal in the first place, was no longer in office, nor was State Secretary Volkmar Hopf who had done so much to speed it on its way. Nobody in the present administration had been present at Ben-Gurion's meeting with Adenauer in 1960 to interpret their agreements.

Birrenbach knew next to nothing about the Arab-German relations. The Middle East never had been his field and he knew about it only as any interested politician would. This became apparent in the course of the negotiations, for Birrenbach became dependent on instructions for every little detail. When he arrived in Israel, he gave the impression that he felt confident in making decisions although he had not the faintest idea of how to solve the complicated situation. An Israeli official described his appearance, at first, as that of a "paratrooper from a different planet." It didn't take him long to notice through negotiators, that he dealt with a type of people with which he was not familiar. Moreover, the whole arms deal was so unconventional and the agreement so vague, that it demanded an unusual approach, alien to a man who was more of an industrialist used to straightforward business.

Dr. Birrenbach, in the two days of his first stay, acquainted himself with the task with which he had been entrusted. Presenting his letter of introduction in Jerusalem, he got to know the Israeli leaders and the officials he was to deal with during the negotiations. Prime Minister Eshkol, Foreign Minister Golda Meir, Deputy Premier Abba Eban and Deputy Defense Minister Shimon Peres assisted by Israeli officials like Arye Levavi, Director General in the Foreign Office, Zeev Shek, head of the Western European desk and Dr. Shinnar, the head of the Israel Mission in Cologne were to become his discussion partners in long and arduous sessions.

During those first encounters, March 8–10 (in which everyone spoke English), Dr. Birrenbach presented the problems—as his government saw them—that stood in the way of future relations between the two countries. He explained that the crisis that had arisen between Bonn, the Arab states and Israel had had a bearing on the division of Germany and, whatever Bonn did, it had to take this fact into consideration in its contacts with Israel. In other words, Bonn wanted to avoid any further conflicts with the Arabs, who might very well take vengeance by granting official recognition to the East German Communist state. Therefore, the discontinuation of the arms deal was definite. He had come to discuss a conversion of the deal, as it still was incomplete. Offering money as a substitute, he gave the impression that the amount was no object as long as Bonn could rid itself of this incriminating arrangement. He was soon made to feel that his task was much bigger than he had anticipated. The Israelis did not spare harsh words. Premier Eshkol barked at him: "How can you offer me anything of this type in view of the requests of my Parliament?" [1] Mrs. Meir, who had often shown that she was emotionally opposed to Germany, bluntly revealed her feelings when she told Birrenbach her impression was that Israel had been made an object of trading betweeen Bonn and the Arab states.[2] Shimon Peres gave him to understand that, after all, an agreement existed which simply could not be terminated. Israel's defense depended on planning, just as that of every other country. And, above all, Israel could not just knock at another country's door and ask for the sale of arms.

---

[1] *Der Spiegel*, March 11, 1965. Eshkol referred to the decision of February 15 in which the *Knesset* had rejected a conversion and insisted on the completion of the arms deal.

[2] Felix E. Shinnar, *Bericht eines Beauftragten*, p. 159, Rainer Wunderlich Verlag, Tübingen, 1967.

The Israelis rejected the very principle on which the Germans based their decision to deliver no more arms to Israel. It was the argument that Israel represented an area of tension. The Germans had pledged not to sell arms to areas of tension, wherever they might be, believing that their past did not allow them to become involved in armed conflicts. Under no circumstances should postwar Germany give the impression that it once again wanted to play a part in international power politics. The negotiations reechoed what Premier Eshkol had already maintained in his speech before the *Knesset* on February 15—that Israel was no area of tension. Its very existence was threatened by the Arab states around it and this was a very different thing. Furthermore, Germany could not deny her special responsibility towards the state of the Jews.[3]

But, Dr. Birrenbach was not to be swayed on this subject of the arms deliveries. He emphasized, time and again, that no more arms would be forthcoming from Germany, however much the Israelis might press for them or point at existing agreements. The Germans were prepared to give money, only, for the remainder of the deal, though Birrenbach at first tried hard to make it plain that, in fact, it was not a "deal" in the proper sense of the word; there were legal rights to the delivery of the remainder. The Israelis said they could not accept this view. After all, they had relied on the word of the Germans for the prompt deliveries. And there was the resolution of the *Knesset* which forbade acceptance of any money in place of the arms still due. The standpoints appeared irreconcilable.

But, before Dr. Birrenbach could threaten breaking off the negotiations, a compromise came into view. And when Birrenbach had left, after two days of tough negotiations, it was agreed to sound out the Americans, or any other third state, on supplying the equipment that Israel had relied on receiving from Germany. After all, the Americans, to some extent, had had a hand in the evolution of the arms deal. This compromise would help both sides—the Germans could give the necessary financial aid as they had suggested doing, and the Israelis would get the arms to which they believed they were entitled according to the agreement.

Three other problems resulting from past unofficial relations were threshed out at the conference table, most of the time in the Ministry of Defense. The question of German economic aid to Israel, un-

---

[3] The information in this chapter on the Birrenbach talks was given to the writer by reliable sources.

like the 1960 Adenauer-Ben-Gurion agreement, was to be concluded in a proper contract without any more secrecies. In principle, the Germans wanted the new chapter of relations with Israel to be open to inspection by anyone.

Birrenbach was vague about it, however, speaking of the possibility of giving Israel "long-term loans with low interest rates"; this loan should include what was still "outstanding" from the Waldorf-Astoria agreement. When asked for details, he suggested a loan to run thirty or even forty years, at 2 1/2 percent interest. It could consist of capital aid as well as technical assistance in the form of grants. He made it appear that Bonn would be generous, though it never went beyond a mere conversation on this subject. That this issue was not without pitfalls soon became clear as, from the beginning, the two sides differed in their interpretation of the Adenauer-Ben-Gurion agreement.[4] Finally, it was left to a special conference to deal with on its assembly two or three months after the end of the present negotiations. The Federal Republic wanted some time to elapse to overcome the currently critical phase with the Arab states.

The question of the German scientists in Nasser's pay, which had caused a crisis between Germany and Israel in spring, 1963, was still "simmering." Dr. Birrenbach explained to the Israelis that the majority of experts, technicians and scientists had left the Nile as they had been offered posts at better pay in the Federal Republic. The others were about to do so, too, and the problem would shortly be settled. Three of the four leading scientists had definitely turned their backs on Egypt; the fourth, Professor Pilz, agreed in principle. His case was more complicated because of Hannelore Wende, his secretary, who had been maimed by a letter bomb addressed to the scientist. Provisions were being made to assure her of financial compensation.

Birrenbach pledged that the German authorities would do all they could to dissuade German subjects from working in Nasser's armament factories. However, legislation to prevent Germans from participating in such work, as had originally been envisaged and worked on by the *Bundestag* for almost two years, seemed out of the question. It was considered an infringement upon the German Constitution's guarantee of freedom of movement to every citizen.

But one issue that required immediate clarification was the announcement, on March 7, that the German government was striving

---

[4] In accordance with this agreement, Israel received loan payments on December 23, 1963, March 31, 1964 and September 10, 1964.

for diplomatic relations with Israel. Having some experience with German promises and diplomatic excuses during those many years of half-hearted relations, the Israelis demanded to know whether this was indeed an offer and, if so, why it was not said so definitely.

According to Dr. Shinnar's records, this query was answered in an exchange of telegrams between Bonn and Jerusalem on March 8 and 11.[5] The concrete offer was on the table and an equally concrete answer had to be given. Prime Minister Eshkol, like his predecessor, decided to put the issue not only to the Cabinet but also to the vote of the *Knesset*. He made it clear to Birrenbach that he was in favor of establishing diplomatic relations with West Germany and that he would lend his weight to effect them. Eshkol, as well as other politicians like Golda Meir, who were less inclined to accept the German offer, realized that Israel could hardly refuse it. It had come about as a consequence of Bonn's feud with Nasser over the quasi-state visit of Walter Ulbricht. To reject it would have meant a political victory for Nasser and would have ruled out diplomatic relations with the Federal Republic of Germany for a long time to come. Having recognized this, Eshkol wanted this issue settled, and as quickly as possible to avoid the possibility of the Germans having second thoughts on the matter. The fear was justified as, in Bonn, there were a number of opponents to cultivating diplomatic relations with Israel. They were bound to be strengthened, once the Arab fury set in. And it did, immediately after the Bonn decision had been made public.

Egypt's President Nasser used violent language against the Germans. He called them "the biggest liars," referring to the secret arms deal. In order to please the Communist bloc he also described the West Germans as "tools in the hands of the imperialists" and announced that, as West Germany had behaved like an imperialist country, Egypt intended to punish it. Iraqi Foreign Minister Talib denounced the Bonn decision as a "hostile act which is irreconcilable with the traditional friendship between the Arab and the German people." King Hassan II of Morocco cancelled his intended state visit to West Germany.[6]

At the request of Iraq, an emergency session of envoys of Arab heads of state was held in Cairo on March 9 to discuss West Ger-

[5] Felix E. Shinnar, *Bericht eines Beauftragten*, p. 130, Rainer Wunderlich Verlag, Tübingen, 1967.
[6] Joachim Kreysler and Klaus Jungfer, *Deutsche Israel Politik*, Wolf von Tucher Verlag G.m.b.H., Diessen-Ammersee, 1965.

many's decision to establish diplomatic relations with Israel. In Lower Egypt, on March 10, President Nasser announced that the Cairo meeting had adopted four resolutions which would be put before a special meeting of Arab Foreign Ministers: the immediate withdrawal of all Arab ambassadors from Bonn; the severing of diplomatic relations with Western Germany if, in fact, it recognized Israel; the breaking off of economic relations with Western Germany if that country persisted in its "hostile attitude" towards the UAR, including a boycott, nonpayment of credits, nondelivery of oil; a warning to the great powers supporting Israel that the Arab states would cease dealing with them if that attitude continued. Nasser further announced that if Western Germany recognized Israel, the UAR would recognize Eastern Germany and sequestrate all West German property in Egypt. The recall of the UAR ambassador from Bonn was announced in Cairo on the same day.[7]

But, before the Arab Foreign Ministers could arrive at a decision, Jerusalem took the initiative. Exactly one week after the Bonn intention had been made public, and only few days after the Germans had confirmed it to be a definite offer, the Israeli government, in a discussion lasting over four hours, decided in favor of accepting it. An Israeli government spokesman said afterwards that Eshkol had informed the Cabinet that he had "grounds to assume" that an agreement would be reached with Bonn on all "controversial questions."

Hardly twenty-four hours later, the German government spokesman informed the press in Bonn that his government had already been formally told of the Jerusalem decision through the Israel Mission in Cologne. "On behalf of the Federal government, I want to acknowledge this decision with satisfaction. . . ." Also, he wanted it to be put on record that the German public and all parties represented in the *Bundestag* had reacted very favorably to the government's decision to assume relations with Israel.

Turning to the Arab states, von Hase said the government would regret the rupture of relations or similar irreparable steps. Bonn was interested in a good relationship with all Arab states. With its decision to stop arms deliveries to Israel, Bonn was convinced that it had contributed to the easing of tension in the Near East which was also bound to be in the interest of the Arab states. Chancellor Erhard, only a few days earlier, had demonstrated strength when he said be-

---

[7] Keesing's Archiv der Gegenwart, 1965, p. 11801.

fore his parliamentary faction: "We do not allow the Arab states to make us nervous. We shall not go down on our knees before them."

The Foreign Ministers of the Arab League states met in Cairo on March 14 and 15 and arrived at only two decisions: to withdraw their ambassadors from Bonn immediately; to sever diplomatic relations with Western Germany if that country recognized Israel. According to conference sources, the second decision was arrived at by a majority vote and not unanimously. It was reported that Morocco, Tunisia, and Libya had expressed reservations.[8] The fact alone that Nasser's four-point resolution and all other threats failed to get the general support revealed clearly that a sharp difference of opinion existed among the Arab states and that Arab unity was a myth. It was learned that only six of thirteen countries—Egypt, Iraq, Yemen, Algeria, Sudan and Kuwait—were ready to recognize East Germany. Two—Iraq and Yemen—supported Egypt's demand for cutting economic relations with West Germany.

The fury, as much over the German attitude as over the disunity among themselves, expressed itself in terror against West German institutions. On March 16, over two thousand demonstrators—mostly students and youngsters—demolished the West German Embassy in Baghdad, setting fire to two floors of the building and hurling stones at it for several hours while the police looked on. The following day, the German Embassy in Taiz (Yemen) radioed a similar message to Bonn saying that its building had been destroyed, the flag torn down and work no longer was possible. Demonstrations of protest were also organized in Cairo, in Tripoli, Damascus and Beirut, but the police prevented acts of violence there. Nevertheless, in most cases, Bonn ordered its Embassy staffs to pack up and return.

It was an important day in the history of Israel when, on March 16, 1965, Levi Eshkol rose to explain to the *Knesset* what had motivated him and his government to favor the acceptance of the German offer. He called it a "proposal of double value." It was a remarkable example of resistance against attempted blackmail of Israel's neighbors—those who, in the years past, had managed to prevent the German government from extending diplomatic relations to Israel. The more the number of influential forces in Germany had grown, demanding to seek ways and means for an understanding with Israel, the more the Arab governments had increased their pressure to hinder the Germans from fulfilling their duty towards Israel and the Jewish people.

[8] Keesing's Archiv der Gegenwart, 1965, p. 11801.

The German suggestion could not be separated from the regional and international impact, and Eshkol pointed to Germany's strength and influence in Europe and reminded his listeners that Israel was also eager to strengthen its ties with this new Europe:

I am aware that the decision which we have to take today is no ordinary one. It is of a different nature than a decision of the establishment of diplomatic relations with any other state. We all are in a conflict between emotions and reasons.

But, over and above everything, there should be the consideration of wanting to strengthen the state of Israel, he said. "We have the sacred duty to assure a safe place for the state in the family of nations. . . . I am sure that, when weighing emotions and reason, the desire to strengthen the state and its prestige will be decisive."

With this appeal, the motion to accept the German proposal for the establishment of diplomatic relations was put to the House and carried by sixty-six against twenty-nine votes with ten abstentions. In view of the importance of the decision the vote was taken by roll call, on request of twenty-two members. The opposition votes came from the right-wing *Heruth*, the left-wing *Mapam* and the Communists. In the case of the latter two parties, it was obviously a political decision in compliance with Communist bloc policy against the Federal Republic of Germany. In the case of the *Heruth*, emotions were mixed with political considerations; namely, to gain popularity. The *Heruth* leader, Menahem Begin, said in the debate that mention had been made, time and again, of a different Germany: "Surely, this Germany is different from that of Hitler. It is divided and Treblinka and Auschwitz are no longer on Germany territory. . . ." His request to decide the issue through a plebiscite was rejected by eighty-three against sixteen votes before the House voted on the government motion to recognize West Germany. The *Achduth Ha'avoda*, a coalition partner, abstained. On this special issue, which was to put the relations between Germany and Israel on a new level, the party had no reason to fear a reprimand.

On March 17, the *Jerusalem Post* commented that, if indeed it was (as has been said), "a victory of reason over emotion," it was not an easy victory. From every practical or contemporary point of view, official relations with Germany were necessary for the strengthening of the state which could not prevail upon the rest of the world to quarantine Germany for another fifty years, or until the last of the Nazis of Hitler's day had died out. To sacrifice even a part of Israel's possible security and stability in order to be able to 'reject the Bonn proposal indicated more than anything else a false estimate of the nature of diplomatic relations. *Maariv*, which had been most critical of postwar Germany also had come to the conclusion that Israel could do nothing else but accept the German offer. Had Bonn offered the establishment of diplomatic relations in previous months,

before the situation in this area had become so involved, we would have said without hesitation: the time is not ripe yet. Germany has not paid her debts yet . . . Today . . . we tend to say, if our conditions in the negotiations with Bonn are fulfilled, that we should accept the German Chancellor's initiative. . . .

Thus, the ground was prepared for the exchange of ambassadors seventeen years after Israel had come into being.

Only a day after the *Knesset* vote, March 17, the German government welcomed the decisions of the Israeli government and the *Knesset* to accept the German proposal for the establishment of diplomatic relations. They indicated the wish to normalize the relationship between the two countries, the government spokesman said. The Federal government was eager to establish strong foundations for both the human relations and those between the two states. Once again, the spokesman, Karl-Guenther von Hase, appealed to the Arab states to understand the German action. Germany could not be refused what almost the entire world claimed to be entitled to—namely, diplomatic relations with Israel. Among those states having ties to Israel were some closely linked with the Arab world. Chancellor Erhard expressed his "deep satisfaction that the Israeli people, its government and its Parliament have accepted the hand stretched out by us. . . ." [9]

But, several German politicians, Foreign Minister Schroeder in particular, disliked the speed with which the Israelis reacted to the German offer of March 7. Ostensibly, this was deliberate. Israel had separated the issue of diplomatic relations from all other problems still to be settled between the two countries. No doubt, Israel now dictated the pace of developments, at least on this important issue, lest the Germans reconsider and delay the matter indefinitely as a consequence of unwelcome Arab reaction.

According to information obtained by the *Maariv* correspondent in Bonn, Schroeder expressed his anger before the CDU faction at 'this development which had taken the initiative completely out of

[9] At the opening of the International Handicraft Fair in Munich, March 18.

his hands and bound him, hand and foot. He even made it understood that the Israelis had broken an agreement between them and Birrenbach, according to which diplomatic relations were to crown the end of successful negotiations on all points to be settled between the two countries. Birrenbach himself expressed surprise at the speedy Israeli decision. In an exclusive interview with *Maariv* journalists on March 14 in his Düsseldorf home, he said: "I thought that they would postpone it until after my second mission."

Thus, Schroeder, whose policy had been overruled by the Erhard decision of March 7, had hoped at least to be able to delay the establishment of diplomatic relations with Israel until (with the help of some "diplomacy") the excitement in the Arab countries had subsided. Schroeder's outburst before his party's faction showed that the Cabinet was split on this question. Schroeder and the junior coalition partner, the Free Democrats, were eager to restore close rapport with the Arab countries, even at the expense of Israel, if necessary, and the majority of Ministers of the CDU, with Erhard at the head, supported by such important politicians as Dr. Konrad Adenauer, Franz-Josef Strauss and Rainer Barzel now wanted the ties to the state of Israel firmly and quickly established.

Through all those years and recent months of tension the German press had been in favor of diplomatic relations with Israel but now it was worried about the loss of influence in the Arab world as a consequence of ties to Israel. The *Frankfurter Allgemeine* warned the government not to accept conditions from Israel which might force all Arabs to rally around Nasser and to demonstrate this even by severing ties with Bonn. It would be regrettable, the *Rhein-Neckar Zeitung* wrote, if Israel should insist on the fulfillment of political conditions which were unacceptable to Bonn because of the possible repercussions in the Arab states. Some favored a delay in the establishment of the diplomatic relations. The first German ambassador must not travel to Tel Aviv in March, the *Mainzer Allgemeine* suggested. The later diplomatic relations were actually effected, the more hope remained that the excitement would die down in Arab world, the *Bonner Rundschau* thought.

Before Birrenbach left Israel to report back to Bonn he had signed a "memorandum of understanding" in which the suggestions for the arms conversion and the other points under discussion had been put down. When he returned on the eighteenth for a second round in the negotiations, Birrenbach went back on some of the points on which a principle agreement previously had been reached. It appeared that he had been given two kinds of instructions this time. Chancellor Erhard, proud of his decision to recognize Israel, wanted Birrenbach to continue in the matter of speedily bringing about the exchange of ambassadors. Foreign Minister Dr. Schroeder and State Secretary Professor Carstens seemed to have on their minds, first and foremost, the conflict with the Arab states which they wanted settled amicably, should this still be possible. A speedy agreement with Israel was no part of their policy. Dr. Birrenbach must have had sympathy for both lines of policy, otherwise, it would be hard to understand why he had undertaken the mission at all—an incumbency which was difficult in itself.

Dr. Birrenbach also understood Israel's case. On March 14, before his departure for the second time, he told *Maariv* reporters in his Düsseldorf home that he did appreciate Israel's standpoint, also the view of his own country. But the two were not identical. He further mentioned that he was aware of the Western Allies' attitude toward the whole conflict. The Western Allies, in particular the Americans, had not been very appreciative of the recent developments. They wanted the West Germans to remain in the Arab states as a moderating force—both to reduce Communist influence and to preserve the Western viewpoint which had been changeable and chronically anti-American since the Suez Canal war in 1956.

The German government through its ambassadors in Bonn, had kept its allies informed of all the developments in this connection. It may be remembered that British Prime Minister Harold Wilson was in the Federal Republic for consultations just when the crisis broke. In a Bonn press conference, March 8, he welcomed the West German plan to exchange ambassadors with Israel but would not say any more. The West German Ambassador to Washington, Heinrich Knappstein, consulted Undersecretary of State George Ball, on the arms issue following Birrenbach's return from his first trip. It is difficult to say whether the result of this conversation gave Dr. Birrenbach the feeling that he could tell Israeli reporters in Düsseldorf on March 14 that he hoped for an early understanding with Israel and that it would not take him long to return from his second trip. When he sat down again at the conference table he soon realized that an agreement was, by no means "around the corner."

The Israelis showed annoyance when they found that Birrenbach now had doubts on certain points put down in the memorandum of understanding of the first round of talks. They admitted, however, that could not be considered a commitment.

Difficulties showed up, particularly on the subject of the arms conversion. The Americans had declared readiness to deliver some of the arms against German payment (this applied to the remaining tanks), but only forty M-48 A2Cs out of the 150 ordered had reached Israel. Twenty had been held in Italy and now were to be shipped back, due to the crisis. Ninety had not been put on the road at all. In the course of the negotiations, it was found to have been a very vague promise; nothing definite had been arranged. The Americans had not yet been told, and consequently had not agreed, to the payment and mode of delivery of 110 tanks, still outstanding. After some debating it was agreed that both governments, German and the Israeli, would now contact the United States and arrange with them for the delivery of tanks straight to Israel.

Birrenbach was equally vague about the ordered Dornier planes. He said that they might be delivered as civil aircraft to assist the country's development via the German Ministry of Economic Cooperation; nothing could ever again be handled by the Ministry of Defense. This prompted the Israelis to express their readiness to accept six super Frelon helicopters in place of the planes which they could purchase in a third country if Germany undertook to pay for them. This, again, left Birrenbach in difficulties, unable to say anything definite. The question of two modernized submarines seemed the only one settled. They had already been paid for by the Germans under the British-German offset agreement which had forced the Federal Republic to purchase arms in Great Britain to ease the country's costs of stationing the Rhine Army in Germany. They would soon be delivered by the British.

The greatest difficulties arose about six speedboats to help guard Israel's coast. Israel had ordered a special design suited to the Mediterranean and its particular coast from a German shipyard. In this case, Birrenbach was at a loss. He could offer only money, instead, —for this and other military equipment of minor importance—to finish, once and for all, the secret agreements between the two countries. Faced with Israeli opposition, he promised once again to "search" for a solution. The Israelis declared that they would ask another government to undertake the construction of similar boats, the costs of which were to be borne by the Germans. It was thought that the Italians might be able to help out. But, as in the case of everything else, Birrenbach was not ready for concessions.

Birrenbach pleaded with the Israelis to understand the German position. Six Arab countries might very well recognize the GDR, among them Algeria. This would mean that Germany would have to veto the application for Algeria's association with the EEC which would turn the entire Maghreb against Bonn. And this, of course, would be against all French interests. Above all, there were fears that noncommitted countries such as India or Indonesia would feel encouraged by such a move on the part of the Arab countries with whom they were friendly and, in their turn, would initiate official connections with East Berlin. The existence of the Hallstein Doctrine had so far stopped them from doing so. Bonn dreaded the thought of having to apply it—of being compelled to sever relations in case they recognized East Berlin. Furthermore, Dr. Birrenbach explained, Bonn expected nine Arab countries to disassociate themselves from the Federal Republic without any move towards the East German Communist state; this might well mean a loss of markets for West Germany. Currently, 5 percent of the entire trade was conducted with the Arab states and there were prospects for an extension. This was the situation as it presented itself to his country. Under no circumstances could West Germany allow any further deterioration in the relationship with the Arab world.

The Israelis did not pay much attention to the German point of view as presented by Dr. Birrenbach. Prime Minister Eshkol, as well as Abba Eban, expressed the belief that the Germans saw the issue out of proportion. The Arab attitude towards Germany surely would not depend on past agreements. Dr. Birrenbach repeated—and he must have repeated it innumerable times in the course of the negotiations—no more arms, ever; development aid, at any time. But, he added, there would also be no arms for Israel's enemies. With equal monotony, Shimon Peres pointed out that Israel did not need development to the same extent that it needed security. In this, it differed basically from the new states of Asia and Africa. Aid for Israel should, therefore, be as close to arms as was possible.

Birrenbach was reminded of assurances given by Dr. Ludger Westrick, Minister of Special Affairs and Erhard's right-hand man. In a conversation with Dr. Shinnar on November 4, 1964, he had favored the fulfillment of existing agreements. Over and above this, there was the "special German responsibility" for the Jewish state, which the Israelis interpreted as reference to security, and on which former Chancellor Adenauer and his successor, Professor Erhard, had placed emphasis on various occasions. The negotiations, particularly of this second phase, were not without dramatic moments.

During six sessions, Dr. Birrenbach had often given the impression that he agreed up to a certain point. After adjournments, (during which he apparently informed his government and was given new instructions) he reneged. There were stages when agreement seemed far off, and when Birrenbach threatened to break off proceedings entirely. In his memoirs,[10] Dr. Shinnar wrote of a phone call from Dr. Birrenbach early on the morning of the twentieth to say that, as matters stood, he saw no way out but to leave. He asked Shinnar to intervene with the Premier to try to prevent the foundering of the negotiations. Eshkol saw Birrenbach, the deadlock was overcome and the negotiations continued.

Again, Birrenbach tried to connect the establishment of diplomatic relations with the arms conversion, just as Dr. Schroeder had wanted it. He explained that he saw the two issues as integral parts of a whole agreement, although the exchange of ambassadors had been accepted in Israel as a consequence of a German offer to this effect. Birrenbach was not ready to name a date for the exchange of ambassadors. The place where the German Embassy was to be located was also part of the controversy. The Israelis wanted it to be in Jerusalem, their official capital, with all their government institutions but the Germans dared not do this, fearing offence to the Arabs who did not recognize Jerusalem as part of Israel. The argument that thirteen out of sixteen Embassies which had been established since 1958 had set up offices in Jerusalem and incurred no trouble with the Arabs did not score. The Israelis later suggested a *pied-à-terre* in Jerusalem (as a concession), in addition to having the German Diplomatic Mission in Tel Aviv or one Chancellory in each of the two towns. This, they said, would create a great deal of good will for Germany. But this point also remained "on the table," as did a number of others.

Birrenbach decided that March 22 would be the last day of his second stay. It was evident that no final agreement could be reached. The German emissary insisted on a third round. The Israelis were furious. Birrenbach tried to pacify them saying that, looking at it realistically, there were no more real problems and an agreement was just "around the corner." It was simply that his Chancellor and his Foreign Minister wanted an "interim report" and to discuss the entire issue with him once again before he finalized an agreement. "We thought you were a plenipotentiary," Abba Eban

---

10 Felix E. Shinnar, *Bericht eines Beauftragten*, p. 161, Rainer Wunderlich Verlag, Tübingen, 1967.

said to the German, angrily. The Israelis were particularly annoyed as they had to face a foreign affairs debate on March 28, in the *Knesset*, during which details of an agreement with the Germans were expected. The world press already had spoken of "stalling" on the part of the Germans, eager to pacify the Arabs. Birrenbach was on the defensive. Once again, he asked to phone his government as he had done several times during the debate. Again he returned to say that he had been told to call back. It was, after all, a matter for the Cabinet to decide.

Again, the Israelis did not spare severe words. Eban expressed his indignation and called it "a crisis." Eshkol put Birrenbach to a hard test, reminding him of the offer of March 7 to establish diplomatic relations. An early reply had been requested of Israel. This had been answered promptly, but the German reaction was still missing. Again, Birrenbach told Bonn of the critical situation. But it was all of no avail. He was told to return, but to assure the Israelis that an agreement would be reached, shortly. To prevent further trouble, he added, that the coalition governments, such as the German one, needed longer to determine their stand. Unlike the first time, he refused (on instructions from Bonn) to sign or initial even the memorandum of understanding which had been drafted with difficulty but which contained points of agreement. He was worried lest he be taken up on the points mentioned therein, even though his signature did not commit him. This only showed how little power had been granted him.

The Israelis took the opportunity of the negotiations to express their misgivings about the solution that the Germans believed they had found in the case of the statute of limitations for murder. The Germans had decided to postpone the counting of the twenty-year statute from 1945 to 1949 on the grounds that German justice had not been able to work independently in the prosecution of Nazi murders until 1949. Dr. Birrenbach shared the Israeli view and said that the German government, too, was not happy about this solution. He hinted, however, at the forthcoming elections, that issue having been one of the obstacles in the rate of a more drastic decision. No party wanted to be connected with so unpopular an act. The Israelis also touched on the subject of their future contacts with the European Economic Community. They had applied for membership and wanted to assure themselves of the German support. Chancellor Erhard had written to Premier Eshkol on May 8, 1964, that he would do the "utmost to support Israel's justified claims to be an associate member to the European Market." Yet, Dr. Birrenbach, reminded of it, did not believe that association was likely to be achieved. He saw a trade treaty with the EEC as the only chance for Israel and was ready to express the assumption that Germany would support Israel's endeavor to reach a favorable trade arrangement with the European Market organization. The "all-out support" that Israel was after seemed unacceptable to Birrenbach; his country could not commit itself in such general terms.

A few hours after Dr. Birrenbach's return from his second trip, Chancellor Erhard told his parliamentary faction: "His mission was successful." Erhard expressed his satisfaction and added, "We shall assume diplomatic relations with Israel with neither exaggerated haste nor with any delay." He, together with the Foreign Minister, had heard Dr. Birrenbach's report right after the emissary's return. Dr. Birrenbach described his second visit as "very much better" than the first one for the basis of a success. He praised Israel's understanding of the difficulties of the Federal Republic in conjunction with the Near East countries, which was interpreted in Germany to mean that Israel had accepted the arms conversion. Nevertheless, Foreign Minister Golda Meir told the *Knesset*, on March 29, that there was hope for an agreement with the Federal Republic which would not entail an impairment of Israel's security, and it would also strengthen Israel, politically and economically. Interviewed by the German businessman's daily, *Handelsblatt*, Birrenbach described the negotiations as "not exactly a pleasure. They require much patience, tact and nerves. But the mutual respect, which could not be more pleasant, facilitates work very much."

While Birrenbach negotiated in Israel, Bonn had sent out a number of special emissaries to prevent the Arab states from reacting unfavorably to official German-Israel relations. The majority of Arab ambassadors to Bonn had been recalled after March 7 "for reporting," and were officially informed by State Secretary Carstens on March 8 of the German government's intention to exchange ambassadors with Israel. Nobody could say whether these Arab ambassadors would ever return. The German authorities felt that diplomatic relations with Israel, under the circumstances, would have not only political repercussions but also economic consequences. Iraq had already cancelled orders for the construction of television installations by West German firms. Saudi Arabia and Kuwait, also had abrogated orders for road constructions, machines, the building of a cement factory, and so forth.

German industries were very worried as they had just gained a foothold in these areas in competition with the Americans and the British. On March 6, Mannesmann A. G., one of West Germany's biggest steel combines, speaking for German industry, warned of the dissolution of diplomatic relations with the Arab countries, saying that this was bound to have serious economic consequences for all German industries. They were particularly afraid of a confiscation of industrial investments, apart from losing the markets. It was only natural that a number of promises were held out to the Arab governments in addition to making the attempt to explain why Bonn intended to recognize Israel.

The "ambassadors" were chosen according to their contacts with the Arab world. Rudolf Werner, a parliamentarian of the Christian Democratic party and an industrialist, was no stranger in Cairo. He had the toughest mission to fulfill as Nasser's decision would determine that of the other Arab countries, however much Bonn hoped to split up the Arab bloc. From Cairo, Werner appealed to Bonn for an assurance to serve as a basis for his talks signifying that an agreement on diplomatic relations between the Federal Republic and Israel would not impair Arab security or prestige. Werner (who claimed to have held talks "at the highest level" during his first 24-hour stay) was said to have promised that Bonn would neither discontinue technical aid projects nor disrupt economic aid plans in Egypt. Another lure dangled before Nasser is said to have been German economic aid for the country's five-year plan should he be ready for an early reestablishment of diplomatic relations with the Federal Republic, although having to sever them now to save his face. The fact that Werner returned to Cairo—in all, he traveled there four times during this critical phase—after reporting to the Chancellor and to the Foreign Minister in Bonn, left the impression that he had something definite to offer. "Money is no object," Rudolf Werner told the Foreign Affairs Working Committee of the CDU. But, it was all of no avail.

On March 22, the Bonn government spokesman confirmed the Federal Republic's readiness to give new economic aid to Egypt despite its announcement to the contrary at the time of Ulbricht's "state visit" there. He explained that Bonn felt compelled to explore all possibilities to restore German-Arab relations.

Several German newspapers criticized this announcement the following day. The *Stuttgarter Zeitung* called it "regrettable" that the government was not prepared to act according to the treatment it had received from Nasser. The *Frankfurter Neue Presse* feared that Bonn was again lending itself to a policy of blackmail if it offered a loan to Cairo. The *Frankfurter Allgemeine* called it "disgusting" that Bonn allowed itself to be pressured again.

Rudolf Werner's efforts were supported by the CDU parliamentarian, Heinrich Gewandt, Chairman of the Parliamentary Development Aid Commission, who also traveled to Cairo and Damascus. Hans Juergen Wischnewski, a social Democratic parliamentarian, was another emissary of the government, although he belonged to the opposition. Having supported the Algerian freedom fighters, he had excellent contacts with the new Algerian government. His appeal to Algeria differed little from that of other special emissaries. A possible rupture of relations with Bonn could hurt Algeria considerably. It could block Algeria's efforts for close ties to the European Common Market organization, quite apart from the fact that there would be a risk of losing German development aid.

On his return, Wischnewski said that Algeria felt very much indebted to Cairo and would follow Nasser's example. State Secretary Rolf Lahr of the Foreign Office flew to King Hussein with a special message from the Federal President, for the Jordanian King had been Heinrich Luebke's guest in Bonn in November, 1964, and then had shown understanding for the special German difficulties as a divided country. Therefore, it was believed that he would be able to understand why Bonn wanted to avoid, at all costs, the recognition of East Germany by the Arab states.

Dr. Lahr paid calls on the governments of Lebanon and Syria, also. His colleague in the Foreign Office, State Secretary Professor Carstens, saw King Feisal of Saudi-Arabia who, it was clear from the start, could not decide on anything that would increase his difficulties with Nasser due to their conflicting interests in Yemen. CDU parliamentarian, Dr. Gerhard Stoltenberg, visited the Sudan while Wilhelm Hartmann, the manager of one of the biggest industrial concerns, Hochtief, was delegated to Damascus having big business interests there. Morocco, Tunisia and Libya were not on the itinerary of special ambassadors as, from the start, they had given the impression that they would not take any drastic action against Bonn.

On April 6, Birrenbach departed for the third round with the remark, "It won't take long this time" implying that the agreement was about to be brought to a conclusion. But, once again, he had another week of solid, arduous negotiations ahead of him. This time he was accompanied by Dr. Rolf Pauls, a high-ranking Foreign Office official, head of the subsection development aid in the Ministry's Trade Political Department. The qualification for his participation was—aside from the lack of a Nazi past—the fact that he had some knowledge of Jewish affairs. As a young official, he had served State Secretary Hallstein in the Foreign Office as personal assistant in 1952, the time of the negotiations concerning the Luxembourg Treaty. In his later career he spent some time in the German Embassy in Washington as councilor for political affairs and had contacts with a number of Jewish organizations and circles. He would talk with some authority in these negotiations sanctioned by the foreign office, while Birrenbach was to be more of a political emissary. The presence of Pauls at this last conference was taken at once, both in Germany and in Israel, to mean a preparation for the diplomat to serve as the first German ambassador in Israel.

The fact that a fortnight had elapsed between the second and the third meeting—although Birrenbach had assured the Israelis that he would not be long in returning—created the impression in Germany as well as in Israel that the German government was playing for time; a period to allow German mediators in Arab countries to ward off the violent threats with reference to German diplomatic relations with Israel. In some of the Arab countries, the wanton destruction of German property that followed the German offer to Israel had both surprised and frightened the Germans. How much so was shown by Birrenbach's demand in the middle of the third session for a complete news blackout in the negotiations—for a few days at least —to allow the evacuation of German citizens from Arab countries to pass without incident.

The Israelis fully appreciated the Germans' concern about the Arab reaction. Arye Levavi expressed this in the course of the negotiations. He assured Birrenbach that the new phase of relations should be conducted with Germany causing as little trouble as possible with the Arab world. This was not only in Germany's but also in Israel's interest: ". . . the less violent and serious the Arab reactions the less it will frighten other countries." Israel was eager to achieve a situation where the Arab threats would be implemented only temporarily and would be very much reduced in extent.[11]

At the conference table at last, the greatest problem turned out to be that of the speedboats. The Israelis told Birrenbach that they had

---

[11] Felix E. Shinnar, *Bericht eines Beauftragten*, p. 164, Rainer Wunderlich Verlag, Tübingen, 1967.

investigated which of the countries could supply them. Italy and France were able to do so. The French boats would be preferable. The French were ready to construct the boats according to the German blueprints; German experts would have to advise and help to construct them. Birrenbach tried to sweep this off the table quickly, arguing that this would not remain secret and would appear as if the Germans were continuing to deliver arms to Israel. But Peres insisted, complaining that they had been negotiating for three years for the boats and they needed them badly for the defense of their coast. He insisted, also, on German engines for the boats and pacified Birrenbach by saying that these engines could be delivered to Israel State Railways which already used the same type of engine. But Birrenbach was furious, as it meant that his government had to do the negotiating which, he feared, would incriminate it again, apart from giving the money. He accused the Israelis of risking future relations because of six boats.

The Israelis drew up the bill that would have to be paid for the remaining arms. The tanks from America would cost $35,000,000. But there would be additional expenses due to the conversion. The forty tanks already in the country now needed spare parts different from the 110 tanks to arrive from America. In addition, there was a compensation to be paid for the cancellation of previous orders which meant that the whole business would involve additional expenditure. Birrenbach refused to go beyond $35,000,000. He was reminded again of the fact that it was not the Israelis who wanted the arms deliveries stopped.

The two factions diverted to side issues which capped the impression that this was a sort of complete "cleaning up" of long-standing problems between Israel and Germany. The Germans vigorously rejected an Israeli proposal to recognize the Oder-Neisse lien as the German-Polish frontier, calling it an unfriendly act. In addition to a true conviction on this point, the Israelis were eager to preserve their contacts with the Eastern bloc states, which explained their statement. Then there were the Arab boycott efforts to which some German firms had adhered and, consequently, did not trade with Israel. The AEG, one of Germany's biggest electrical companies, had sold installations to Israel for many years. Suddenly, the firms refused to continue to do so on the grounds that they were afraid of losing the Arab markets. In turn, Israel had boycotted German firms for having signed an Arab boycott request. It was agreed that the two governments would not encourage boycotts against each other.

After all, the Federal government had told the Arabs what they thought of this unfair practice.

Then the battle for the communique set in. It had hovered above the conference table all the time. Premier Eshkol suggested that it all be put into a "nice letter" from the German Chancellor. He could then reply and express his satisfaction about the agreement. It took some time before this point was reached. Dr. Birrenbach battled hard against including something about the "special position of Germans in relations towards Israel." He thought that this was implicit and needed no repetition. Besides, Germany had proved itself in deeds. The Arabs might request the same treatment of preference; they would not bother about the reasons—only about the facts. By now, there ought to be some trust among the two peoples. But the Israelis were insistent, and it was, in fact, the first item in the letter signed by the German Chancellor. This "special responsibility" was to include the Jews the world over. The Germans were eager to have this mentioned with an obvious side-glance at American Jewry. The Germans wanted the issue of the conversion of the arms deal to figure predominantly in the letter. The Israelis objected to the indication that money was a substitution. Both were agreed, then, that the true mode of solving this problem was still obscure.

The letter was to state the conclusion of full diplomatic relations to do away with all rumors that the Germans were still opposed to this type of relationship. The subject of the German scientists in Egypt was to be included in the letter at some length. The Germans pledged that they would prevent German citizens from assisting other countries in the production of weapons. The two countries would "shortly" enter into negotiations with Israel on further economic aid. Levi Eshkol confirmed the letter and its contents. He included a "reminder" about the statute of limitations, a subject which had not been mentioned in Erhard's letter, saying, ". . . this problem will understandably remain for us a matter of great concern. . . ."

Both added a few niceties. Erhard: "I hope that the decision taken by both our governments about the establishment of diplomatic relations will pave the way for a happier future relationship between our peoples." Eshkol: "The decision of our two governments was taken in view of a somber, historical background and a stormy political one. I share your hope that our mutual decision proves itself as an important step for a better future."

Thus, the letters were written. Yet, when Birrenbach and Pauls left, not all of the problems had been eliminated. It was decided to settle them in consultations between the two governments. Dr. Shinnar returned to Germany on May 3 for negotiations with the German government. He explained to press inquiries that only small matters still needed clarification.[12] But, he recalled, these "small" matters produced a few more headaches on both sides.

Shinnar held talks with the Chancellor, with his Minister of Special Affairs, Dr. Westrick, and also with Professor Carstens from the Foreign Office. They met four times in Bonn's Chancellory (on May 4, 6, 10 and 12) and there was an endless exchange of messages between Shinnar and his government. The chief obstacle turned out to be the consequences of the Waldorf-Astoria agreement between Adenauer and Ben-Gurion. The Germans wanted this agreement to be concluded and a new agreement arrived at in the negotiations on economic aid (as it had been envisaged by the two sides,) to take place two or three months after the establishment of diplomatic relations. The Israelis insisted that the agreement be continued and that the payments on this loan be made as before.

The outcome of this controversy was a note in which the differences of opinion of the two sides were recorded. The indication was that the forthcoming negotiations would be equally tough. But, at least the two sides agreed on not wanting the difficulties to delay the official relationship any further. The public in Germany and in Israel were annoyed at this delay and read all sorts of meanings into it. On April 27, the German spokesman hastened to assure all those inquiring that, "Nothing whatever can now prevent the agreement between Israel and the Federal Republic from being reached."

Negotiations officially began on May 12. Professor Erhard gave his letter written to Premier Eshkol to Dr. Shinnar; Shinnar then presented the German Chancellor with the Israeli Premier's reply. State Secretary Karl-Guenther von Hase of the Press and Information Office, State Secretary Rolf Lahr of the Foreign Office (in place of Foreign Minister Schroeder, who was absent because he had to participate in a NATO conference), Dr. Kurt Birrenbach, and Dr. Rolf Pauls (whose nomination as first ambassador to Israel was now an open secret) were witnesses to this ceremony. A day later the contents of the two letters were released to the press in Bonn. About four hundred journalists from Germany and abroad

---

[12] Felix E. Shinnar, *Bericht eines Beauftragten*, p. 167, Rainer Wunderlich Verlag, Tübingen, 1967.

awaited the publication of the agreements between Israel and the Federal Republic—the details on which they had speculated on so much in the last few weeks—with tension. And they showed annoyance when they became aware that the substitute for the remainder of the arms deal was to remain a secret. Once again, despite all assurances, there were secrets in the agreement, the majority of the German press complained. The *Rheinische Post* believed it knew the reason for it. It had been done out of consideration for Premier Eshkol who was bound by the *Knesset* decision not to accept any money. The *Frankfurter Rundschau* thought that the secrecy could not possibly be preserved for long. Radio Hesse called the secrecy "no good," but understandable.

The establishment of German-Israel relations was welcomed unanimously. The *Rheinische Post* referred to it as "a milestone" on the road to reconciliation with the Israeli people. This step had to be taken in view of Germany's special responsibility towards the Jewish people, the *Bonn General-Anzeiger* said. The *Sueddeutsche Zeitung* thought that the normalization of relations gave ample opportunity to do something for reconciliation. "At last," the *Badische Zeitung* editorialized, saying that these relations were long overdue. *Die Welt* believed that Germany could, at last, approach everybody without embarrassment. According to an opinion poll,[13] 56 percent of the population agreed with the establishment of diplomatic relations despite the Arab protests. Only 10 percent were in favor of acceding to Arab demands, 22 percent had no opinion at all and 11 percent declined to express it. Asked which of the two—Arabs or Israelites—they thought to be the more important partners for Germany, 35 percent named Israel and 29 percent, the Arab states.

On the evening of May 12, Iraq took the lead in cutting connections with the Federal Republic. It was now only a matter of hours for the other nine Arab states—UAR, Syria, Lebanon, Saudi Arabia, Jordan, Kuwait, Yemen, Algeria and Sudan—to do likewise. It seemed clear from the start that Morocco, Tunisia and Libya would not sever relations. In fact, they did not go beyond informing the German government of their disagreement with its step to recognize Israel. Chancellor Erhard had written a letter to all thirteen Arab states in which he reaffirmed the need for Arab-German friendship, and asserted that the Federal Republic would do all in its power to effect such friendly relations. Germany's hands remained stretched

[13] *Infas*, May 16, 1965.

out towards the Arab states, the government spokesman said on May 13, explaining that now, in all probability, the majority of Arab states would sever the ties in Bonn. He emphasized that economic aid would continue to flow to Arab states, with the exception of Egypt. Cultural and other economic ties would remain untouched. The Arab countries were also allowed to maintain Consulates in West Germany, if they so wished. Chancellor Erhard, in his press conference of May 15, called it "high time" for the normalization of relations with Israel. He expressed the opinion that the establishment of diplomatic relations coupled with the honest wish to maintain friendly relations with the Arab states constituted a stabilizing factor in the Near East; a cleavage between the Federal Republic and the Arab world was not to Israel's advantage. The allegation that Germany continued arms aid to Israel was emphatically rejected by Erhard as "malicious defamation."

Franz-Josef Strauss, who had been the architect of the secret arms deal, said to the *Maariv* correspondent on March 13: "Time is ripe for the establishment of normal relations . . . I have the firm hope that the decision arrived at by our two countries will have a stabilizing influence on the political situation within the Near East region and that it will also serve the security and prosperity of Israel."

The Social Democratic Floor Leader, Fritz Erler, called the establishment of relations with Israel "something special," saying: "Gratefully, we should accept the outstretched hand, knowing well that there is still much to do to achieve a true reconciliation." Dr. Konrad Adenauer, ill in bed, wrote to Dr. Shinnar: ". . . I am very satisfied that this entire issue, which caused us two a great deal of headache in the past years, now has finally been solved. . . ." Dr. Eugen Gerstenmaier, president of the *Bundestag* said:

that I am glad that what we talked about for years has finally become reality . . . But diplomatic relations will not be the instrument which eradicates the past, full of tragedy, pain, suffering and tears.[14]

Premier Eshkol addressed the *Knesset* on May 17, saying that Erhard's decision was an "important step" which had been well received in the world; the Arabs had been taught that blackmail did not pay. The world became a witness that there were differences of opinion also among the Arab states on this question. The East German Communist state, GDR, commented:

[14] *Maariv*, May 14, 1965.

The establishment of diplomatic relations between the West German Federal Republic and Israel constitutes the continuation of a long and secret cooperation between the ruling classes of Israel and the imperialistic and Neo-colonialist forces in West Germany in the military, political and economic fields. This step cannot be interpreted other than as a demonstrative support of the aggressive policy of the Israeli government, which is being abused as the imperialistic instrument against the Arab freedom movements. . . .

Thus ends a chapter in Germany's history which could be described only as an unfortunate one. For many years, the Germans withheld from the state of the Jews, and just from them, what was normal among nations. In this case, surely a risk would have been justified. In an earlier stage, it would have been considerably less dangerous, as the Arab-German controversy of 1952–53 (the time of the signing of the Luxembourg Treaty), proved.

That the Israelis—despite their awareness of having been treated solely from the point of view of power politics—still were open to acceptance when they finally were offered diplomatic recognition can be explained only by their dire need for contacts with Europe, or more precisely, with one of the strongest members of the European Community. More than anything else, the achievement of diplomatic relations with Israel became an important cornerstone in the reconciliation. That motion should have immediately been effected when Israel was ready for it.

18
A New Start

"Pauls, go home!" hundreds of demonstrators—young and old—shouted. Their eyes glowed with hatred as they threw themselves against the police barriers. Some waved placards urging the Jewish people never to forget the six million murdered. Empty bottles were hurled, stones were flung at the heavily guarded car of the first German Ambassador on his way to Jerusalem for the ceremony of presenting his credentials. Dr. Rolf Pauls' face was as tense and as pale as those of the police guards who had the difficult task of protecting him. But they had to charge at a crowd whose motives of opposition against Pauls originated in the suffering of their own people. And the demonstrators on that August 19, 1965, could no longer hinder the German standard from being hoisted in Israel, the chords of the German anthem from being played in public as part of the ceremony or Israeli soldiers from standing at attention in a guard of honor for a German—for the first time since the holocaust.

The rioting could be heard inside the President's house where the ceremony of presentation of credentials went on. It was formal and brief. Dr. Pauls, in a short speech in German (which was translated into Hebrew), assured his listeners that "the new Germany looked back on the horrible crimes of the national Socialist regime with grief and disgust. . . ." Since then, Dr. Pauls said, many people of good will on both sides had worked patiently to prepare the road for a new beginning of relations between both nations. "We hope that the exchange of ambassadors will contribute to its continuance along this road. . . ." [1] Israel's President Zalman Shazar replied in Hebrew, which was translated into English, that the presentation of credentials in Jerusalem proved that chaos did not persist forever, and that even the darkest of nights must end with the break of dawn: "And, just because of the lessons of the bitter past, we are obliged to concentrate our energies on the future so that those spreading hatred can be silenced, and so that the spirit of that terrible period can never again be revived. . . ." [2]

When, after tendering his letter of accreditation to the Israeli President and extending his courtesies to the members of the Israeli government, all lined up to receive the new diplomat to Jerusalem, Pauls braved a situation that was laden with emotions. With all the good will that may have existed among those Israelis present, the fact remained that Pauls represented a nation in whose name six million of their people had been slain. Even after twenty years, a handshake with an official of this nation was difficult, indeed, however little he himself may have had to do with it. Pauls was fully aware of this. It might be said that no German had been in a comparable situation. Above all, long before Pauls had stepped on Israeli soil, the entire country had hotly disputed the German choice of the first ambassador to Israel.

Although Dr. Pauls had been no member of the Nazi party or of any of its formations, he had been an officer in Hitler's army at the Eastern front, just where most of the crimes against humanity had been committed. This was exactly why the Israeli public objected to Pauls. The German people never quite understood this. The reason is simple. Except in documentation, the Germans never have publicly stated that the *Wehrmacht* had been involved in crimes. The SS, the Gestapo and the special execution squads are generally charged with them, yet, there is proof that the army cooperated, at least to some extent, with the murderers. It could base its actions on two criminal directives—the *Barbarossa-Befehl* and the *Kommissar-Befehl*.

The *Barbarossa-Befehl* was issued by the chief of the armed forces, Field Marshal Wilhelm Keitel on May 14, 1941 (following verbal instructions by Hitler), giving a free hand to every German officer to "deal" with the population under his occupation in the

[1] Rolf Vogel, *Deutschlands Weg nach Israel*, p. 190, Seewald Verlag, Stuttgart, 1967.
[2] Rolf Vogel, *Deutschlands Weg nach Israel*, p. 197, Seewald Verlag, Stuttgart, 1967.

East at his discretion and without the need for legal proceedings. The *Befehl* became the basis for the murder of civilians, particularly in areas where guerilla warfare was practiced. On June 6, 1941, the chief of the army, General Walther von Brauchitsch, issued the *Kommissar-Befehl* according to which all political commissars, Jews, and the like, whose existence "endangered" national socialism, could be executed. It became the pretext for the mass murder of Russian prisoners of war. The execution of these orders was mainly in the hands of the police and the security services, yet the cooperation of the armed forces was essential.[3] Moreover, the Jews recalled that German soldiers had fought doggedly, thus lengthening Hitler's criminal war and giving the executioners a prolonged opportunity to commit their crimes. The survivors never forgot that German soldiers marched past them and did not lift a finger to save them or help them in their plight.

Dr. Pauls was considered one of these. He had joined the German army in 1934, immediately after finishing school. Pauls had wanted to study history. But, he claims today that he wanted to avoid contact with the Nazis and thought it best to join the army, where party membership was not required. He had been a lieutenant when war broke out. He had fought in France and later in Russia where, after a few days in battle, he had lost his left arm. For a short while, he had served as an orderly officer with the military attaché in Turkey. But the German retreat in the East had thrust him into active duty again. When most of the leading officers were killed he had found himself in a senior position. Surrounded by the Russians, he is reported to have ordered the cutting of all telephone connections in order to avoid being given the usual Führer's orders, "to hold out to the last man." He had finally broken through the Russian lines with his unit and had been decorated for this brave action with the Knight's Cross. At the end of the war, he had been captured by American troops on German soil. Having no Nazi past, he had merely spent three months in a prisoner-of-war camp.

A civilian again at the age of twenty-nine, Pauls started his studies of law at Hamburg University. His thesis dealing with the new German Constitution and the working of the Federal Government brought him into contact with government officials. His first government appointment was that of a liaison officer of the Chancellor

[3] Reinhard Henkys: *Die nationalsozialistischen Gewaltverbrechen*, p. 261, Kreuz-Verlag, Stuttgart, 1964.

to the High Commissioner of Germany. From then on, it was a straight line for him in his diplomatic career.

For those in Israel who opposed the diplomatic relations with Germany in principle, the choice of Pauls was an additional point of controversy. Demonstrations of masses of people in the streets of Israel after he was nominated were ample proof of this. For others, who had accepted the relations with postwar Germany as something that could not be avoided, the appointment of the former officer seemed incredibly stupid. They were ready to believe, some from experiences of their own, that there were "good" Germans. They failed to understand why the first postwar German Ambassador had not been selected from among those who had opposed Hitler or who, at least, had done nothing that could be interpreted as an act in favor of the Nazis. Such a man would have been received immediately by the majority of the Israeli people. There were very few who shared the opinion that a man like Pauls was really much more fitting as the first German ambassador than a resistance fighter, since his record was typical of that of an average German of his time, and only he would be able to present a proper picture of the present Germany.

The controversy that raged in Israel over his appointment was also carried to Germany. There, many Germans accepted the Israeli objections and agreed that the first German Ambassador to Israel should not be one of Hitler's former officers. They were quite sure that, if only Foreign Minister Dr. Schroeder had wanted to, he could have given preference to a member of the former resistance movement. Some even interpreted this appointment as a kind of vengeance on the part of the Foreign Minister who had been against extension of diplomatic relations to Israel, fearing for the German-Arab relations. Foreign Office officials, however, pointed out that a career diplomat had been chosen deliberately, this being part of the policy to "normalize" relations with Israel. This term cannot be more contentious, as a "normalization" of relations between Germany and Israel (similar to links between Germany and Nigeria, for instance) seems hardly feasible in our lifetime. Were they to appoint a political figurehead with a perfect past for the post, German officials argued, they would once again make an exception to the rule and would have to continue doing this for the appointments of the next two or three German ambassadors to Israel.

However, the majority of the German public reacted with impatience to the dispute in Israel over Pauls. A question put by a correspondent of a well-known German daily in a government press conference in Bonn, June 9, 1965, revealed the general feeling: "Has it ever happened before that any government rejected a German diplomat as ambassador because he did no more than fulfill his duty as a soldier?" Hundreds of thousands of Germans had fought in the *Wehrmacht* and had seen no wrong in it until today.

The *Frankfurter Allgemeine Zeitung* wrote that the Chancellor could not allow himself to be impressed by Israel's arguments against Pauls. He had to uphold soldiers who did nothing but their duty. In a press conference (June 18, 1965), Erhard said, "If a German man became a soldier, there is no reason to discriminate against him . . . I reject the view that German soldiers who did nothing but their duty are to be looked down on."

And, even if there were sympathizers with Israeli uneasiness over Hitler's former officer for the post of ambassador in Tel Aviv, it would have cost the German government parties dearly, had they given in to Israel's objections with general elections only two months away.

It seems that the German government had first sounded the Israeli reaction before it requested the official agreement on Pauls. The Israeli government took quite some time considering it. According to reports in the Israeli press, Foreign Minister Golda Meir did not feel fit to bear the responsibility alone, and she referred the matter to the Cabinet. But the government remanded the decision to her, and so did the parliamentary Foreign Affairs Committee.[4]

When Foreign Minister Dr. Gerhard Schroeder announced in the *Bundestag,* on June 29, that his government had applied for the agreement, it seemed fairly certain that the Israelis had consented to Pauls (having no real reason to reject him.) The fact that he had been one of Hitler's officers was insufficient grounds, though it can be taken for granted that investigations as to the activities of the unit in which Pauls served in Russia were undertaken in Israel.

When at last the Isreali government agreed to accept Dr. Pauls, the German press, in unison, welcomed it. The *Sueddeutsche Zeitung* stated that it took a long time; yet, it spoke well for Prime Minister Levi Eshkol and Foreign Minister Golda Meir that they ignored the opposition to Pauls in the country, in the government and in their own party. *Die Welt,* July 10, praising Pauls' qualifications, wrote that those Israelis who had dealt with Pauls had spoken well

---

[4] *Maariv,* August 4, 1965.

of him. The paper expressed the hope that the number of Israelis thinking in the same manner would increase soon. On August 11, the day of Pauls' arrival in Israel, the country's biggest newspaper, *Maariv*, commented: "This can hardly be called a day of satisfaction . . . We would have preferred, if we are to have relations with Germany, that the first Ambassador would have been a personality whose past would have afforded no special investigation . . . ."

Security measures for the German diplomat had to be very strict in the first few months. Whenever he went for a swim in the pool of his Tel Aviv hotel (one floor of which, at first, served as the German Embassy) his bodyguards even had to dive with him.

The task ahead of Pauls was no easy one. Although he could expect politeness from the authorities intent on the establishment of diplomatic relations, the antagonistic feelings of the Israeli public were bound to persist. To gain the confidence of the Israeli people for himself and for the nation he represented appeared to be almost unattainable in August, 1965.

Perhaps, the dispute over Pauls would have lost its sting earlier, had it not been for Bonn's second appointment to the German Embassy in Tel Aviv; Dr. Alexander Toeroek was to act as Embassy Councilor and *Charge d'Affaires.*

Once this appointment had been announced, it became clear that it was another, perhaps, even more controversial one. Dr. Toeroek had served in the Hungarian Foreign Service under Nikolaus Horthy, a Facist, ruling with dictatorial and totalitarian methods long before Hitler came to power in Germany. In 1940, Dr. Toeroek represented the Horthy government as attaché at the Hungarian Embassy in Bucharest. In the crucial year of 1944, when the German Nazis marched into Hungary, and more or less dictated the affairs there, Toeroek was sent to Berlin as Legation Secretary.

The Hungarian Mission there may well have been a place for receiving or forwarding Nazi orders, including those concerning the annihilation of Hungarian Jewry. From March till July, 1944, over 400,000 Hungarian Jews had been shipped off to Auschwitz where the majority had been gassed, on arrival. It seemed very likely that only men loyal to the system in Hungary were delegated to Berlin, then. Toeroek remained in Berlin when the war ended, presumably, because he disliked the Communists' take over. He became Secretary of the Hungarian Red Cross and, in 1948, lectured at the Berlin Institute for Political Science. In 1950, he joined Bonn's Foreign Service, becoming a German citizen at the same time. First, Toeroek was sent to Tunisia. From 1959 till 1963, he served as ambassador to Togo. Then he worked in the Foreign Office in Bonn until his appointment to the German Embassy in Tel Aviv in 1965.

The Israeli public was stunned, as were the Germans, if one can credit most of the press reaction. The arguments against Dr. Toeroek were much more plausible for the Germans than the ones against Pauls. Toeroek had been an official of a Fascist administration which had become guilty of murder, a fact which seemed to have slipped the attention of Bonn's Foreign Office, according to statements to Israeli journalists. Their attention was drawn to the fact that Horthy was no longer in power in the last stages of war in Hungary, yet no mention was made that Toeroek also served under Hitler's puppet, Ferencz Szalasi. A German radio commentator asked how, after such an appointment, the Germans could still make the Israelis believe that they wanted to make friends with them. The *Neue Rheinzeitung* (near-SPD) asked, "Does the German Foreign Office always have to resort to diplomats who had served during the Nazi period?" The independent *Stuttgarter Zeitung* alluded to the possibility that the Foreign Office chose diplomats with a doubtful past for the Tel Aviv Embassy to express the Foreign Office's indignation that diplomatic relations with Israel came about without its doing: ". . . Any post from the south of the Sahara to North America would have been suitable for Toeroek, but not the one in Tel Aviv." *Die Welt* said, "It is not surprising that many Israelis, particularly those who emigrated from Hungary, bore unconcealed distrust of diplomats who carried out state business during the time when they feared for their lives . . ." [5]

Bonn's Foreign Office, however, insisted that Toeroek take his post in Israel and stated that Toeroek had been carefully screened before he had been allowed to join the Foreign Service and it was found that he had belonged neither to the Nazi movement nor to its Hungarian version. It was convinced that Toeroek had nothing whatever to do with the deportation of Jews from Hungary. A later attack on Toeroek by a Hungarian organization claiming to have documents proving that he had, after all, been a member of the Fascist movement, the *Pfeilkreuzler* (Arrow-Cross), added to the embarrassment of the German government.

The Israeli authorities once more were put to a hard test. The decision had been reached on diplomatic relations to Germany. It had

[5] All press comments, August 4, 1965.

been a difficult decision and they had made it for none other than political reasons. The Germans did not make it any easier for them, although there is reason to believe that the two appointments had been made in good faith. The trouble was that many Germans had never really bothered to do more than consider casually what had been done to the Jews under the Nazi regime. Guilty conscience, postwar political events and the need of integration in the free world had made them gloss over this past quickly. The Nazi criminals, alone—and they, a small minority—were considered responsible for the twelve years and all that had happened then; the ordinary Germans, somewhat their victims; all they had done was to obey orders and to do so out of fear for their lives. No wonder that they failed to understand the Israelis, who believed that without the active support of millions Hitler could not have built up the criminal state.

The two appointments, again, roused emotions in Israel against Germany. The Israeli government was, however, intent on carrying out the establishment of diplomatic relations. It really had no alternative. To reverse its decision would have meant that the chance to arrive at some rapport with Germany would have vanished for years. And this was of importance, considering Germany's role in Europe with which Israel urgently required association. Also, it would have meant leaving Germany entirely under Arab influence. Consequently, Israel was forced to accept the appointments, especially as there was no visible proof of crimes connected with either of the two diplomats. The feeling alone that the German government had not been exactly tactful when they nominated the two men who had been at least close to the crimes was not enough for rejecting them. It was clear that the newly established diplomatic relations were burdened before they actually started.

At a press conference in Bonn on July 5, Karl-Guenther von Hase, State Secretary and government spokesman, asked when the German government would grant agreement to the first Israeli ambassador to Germany, replied, "After we have thought it over a little." Von Hase apparently wanted to make it clear that the Federal Republic of Germany also would take its time over the application for Asher Ben-Nathan, as the Israelis had done in the case of Pauls. It is no secret that members of the German government wanted to demonstrate that they had some reservations concerning Israel's choice of its first ambassador.

Ben-Nathan had been connected with the secret German-Israel

arms deal and his nomination gave some Germans the idea that, perhaps, this deal (which had caused so much upheaval in German foreign politics) was to be continued. The *Sueddeutsche Zeitung* revealed the "mixed feelings" which the German government harbored against the Israeli appointment. They would have preferred, the paper said, someone who had not been connected with the arms deliveries to Israel. There was also a hint, here and there, that Ben-Nathan had hunted Nazis in Austria right after 1945, which caused more uneasy feelings. But when Asher Ben-Nathan arrived in Germany at last, the *Rheinische Post* (near CDU) called it a "historic moment." In his first statement on August 16, Ben-Nathan said that he was "fully conscious of the historic significance of stepping, as first Israeli Ambassador, on German soil."

The whole country looked at the man with surprise. He did not fit their picture of a Jew. Tall and handsome, blond and blue-eyed, upright and self-assured, this man was in no way what they had learned to believe about the Jews during the Hitler era. Moreover, he was by no means what people expected of a diplomat and an ambassador, considering his previous career as much as his unconventional nature. In both, he represented the Israeli, the people who had converted the homeland of the Jews into a haven for survivors.

For Ben-Nathan, born in Vienna in 1921 into a family which was scrupulously Jewish, there had been no problem of assimilation or any conflict. He was, first and foremost, Jewish. He had attended a Jewish school, and at the age of nine he had joined the Zionist Youth Movement. When Hitler came to power in Germany and there was imminent danger of Austria's invasion, his father bought an orange grove in Palestine.

In those years—until Hitler actually entered Austria in 1938—Ben-Nathan campaigned among the Jews of Vienna to accept the idea of Zionism. In the summer of 1938, Ben-Nathan left Austria for Palestine. He had to choose the peril of illegal immigration as the English did all to stop the influx of European Jews into Palestine beyond the quotas set for normal times. Ben-Nathan became a member of the *Kibbutz Meduroth Zeraim.* In 1944, he was entrusted by this Jewish agency [6] with his first political task. He collected information about the fate of Jewry in Europe and about Nazi crimes and criminals from what immigrants were able to tell him. After the

[6] Jewish agency for Palestine, 1929 to 1948, recognized as the official representative of the Jews in cooperation with the Palestine government in all questions concerning the Jews.

war, he was sent to his birthplace, Vienna, to help Jewish survivors in their efforts to reach Palestine (illegally, as the British restrictions on immigration still existed.) For two years he worked there, masquerading as a journalist, and when he left he had helped more than 100,000 survivors reach the shores of Palestine from the European camps via Vienna. Due to his activities there, the only photograph of Adolf Eichmann was found. In 1947, he was recalled and returned at first to his kibbutz until he was asked to help in the building up of the Jerusalem Foreign Office. In 1951, he started a two-year period of study in Geneva to catch up with his education which had been neglected during those years of helping the state to come into being. He studied political science, international law and economics.

In 1956, after three years in industry, Ben-Nathan was called to take up a post in the Defense Ministry which delegated him to Paris. There his responsibilities included the acquisition of arms to strengthen Israel's defense forces. It was then that he made his first contacts with Germany and Germans and was instrumental in effecting the arms deal between Israel and Germany. He reached the rank of Director General of the Defense Ministry. This led to the appointment of Ambassador to Germany—a record somewhat typical of many others who have helped to create the state of Israel.

For Asher Ben-Nathan, there were prospects for an easy start in Germany. No doubt the Germans were relieved that, at long last, the unnatural state of relations between the two nations had been overcome. The cordiality with which the Germans were finally ready to receive him was, to a great extent, the expression of honest sentiments. It was mixed, no doubt, with a good deal of wonder. And there was also curiosity to meet a man who represented a nation that had shown so much ingenuity in reconquering their homeland, especially among many young Germans for whom it was their first encounter with a Jew. It seemed as if there would be few obstacles, if any, for the work of an Israeli ambassador in Germany, though for him, personally, it may not have been as easy as that. But once the Israeli government had decided on the establishment of diplomatic relations with Germany, every Israeli official must have been aware of the implications—of the problems of contact with a nation that, twenty years before, had been connected with the most horrible of crimes.

On August 24, 10:30 a.m. sharp, Asher Ben-Nathan wrote his

name in the guest book of the Federal President in Bonn's Villa Hammerschmidt and presented his credentials.

The Bonn public took no interest in the arrival or departure of the new Ambassador, being so used to this sort of spectacle in Germany's small capital. Had it not been for television, it might have escaped the notice of the German public that the Israeli Ambassador now was officially instated and all the quibbling over diplomatic relations with Israel was over.

At 10:40 a.m., it was recorded that Ben-Nathan presented his credentials to the Hesse Chief Minister and Upper House president, Dr. Georg-August Zinn, deputizing for Federal President Heinrich Luebke, who was on vacation. The presentation, much less ceremonious than in Israel, took place without witnesses except for Walter Scheel, Minister of Economic Cooperation (standing in for the Foreign Minister), some officials of the German state and the Israeli Embassy councilors. Only the black top hats in the hall of the President's palace were a sign that a ceremony of significance was going on inside.

The Israeli Ambassador to Germany ended that day on which German-Israel relations had begun, *de facto,* by laying a wreath at the plaque of the Cologne synagogue commemorating the six million dead and taking part in a memorial service for them.

BIBLIOGRAPHY

Adenauer, Konrad, *Erinnerungen 1953–55* (*Memoirs*) Deutsche Verlag-sanstalt, Stuttgart, 1965.

Alexander, Edgar, *Adenauer und das neue Deutschland* (Adenauer and the New Germany), Paulus Verlag, Recklinghausen, 1956.

Baade, Fritz, *Neugestaltung unserer Politik in Nah–und Mittelost* ("Re-shaping of Our Policy in the Near and Middle East"), *Aussenpolitik*, No. 4, 1965.

Balabkins, Nicholas, "The Birth of Restitution," *The Wiener Library Bulletin*, London, 1967.

Baumann, Jürgen, *Wozu noch Auschwitz Prozess?* ("Why Still an Auschwitz Trial?") *Die politische Meinung*, September, 1964.

Ben–Gavriel, M.Y., *Israel und der Status Quo* ("Israel and the Status Quo") *Aussenpolitik*, No. 12, 1958.

Ben-Vered, Amos, "Israel und Deutschland," *Europa–Archiv*, 1965.

Berra, Xaver, *Mörder oder Opfer der Gesselschaft–eine Zwischenbilanz in den NS–Mordprozessen* ("Murderers or Victims of Society-Interim Results of Nazi Murder Trials"), *Werkhefte*, 1964.

Beutler, Werner, *Die deutsch–israelischen Beziehungen* ("The German-Israel Relations"), *Werkhefte*, 1964.

Blessin-Wilden, *Bundesentschädigungsgesetz* (*Restitution Legislation*), Verlag C.H. Beck, Munich, 1954–1955.

Boehm, Franz, *Deutsch–israelische Beziehungen* ("German–Israel Relations"), *Frankfurter Hefte*, 1965.

Boehm, Franz und Dirks, Walther, *Judentum, Schicksal, Wesen und Gegenwart* (*Jewry, Fate, Character and Presence*), Franz Steiner Verlag, Wiesbaden, 1965.

Brandt, Willy, *Deutschland, Israel und die Juden* ("Germany, Israel and the Jews") (Speech), Herzl Institute, New York, March 19, 1961. *Landeszentrale für politische Bildung* (Regional Office for Political Education), Berlin, 1961.

Bundesministerium für gesamtdeutsche Fragen:SBZ von A–Z, Taschen- und Nachschlagebuch über die sowjetische Besatzungszone ("Federal Ministry for all German Affairs, Soviet Occupied Zone from A to Z"), Bonn, 1966.

Dollinger, Hans, *Die Bundesrepublik und die Ära Adenauer, 1949–1963* (*The Federal Republic and the Adenauer Era*), Verlag Kurt Desch, Munich, 1966.

el Dessouki, Mohammad–Kamal, *Hitler und der Nahe Osten* ("Hitler and the Near East") (Thesis), Free University of West Berlin, 1963.

Eckert, Felix von, *Ein unordentliches Leben* (*A Disorderly Life*), Econ Verlag, Düsseldorf, 1967.

Elon, Amos, *In einem heimgesuchten Land* (*In a Tortured Country*), Kindler Verlag, Munich, 1966.

Evangelische Kirche Deutschlands ("Protestant Church of Germany"), *Evangelisches Jährbuch* (*Protestant Annual*), 1949.

Fischer, Alfred Joachim, *Israel und die Bundesrepublik Deutschland* ("Israel and the Federal Republic of Germany,") *Deutsche Rundschau*, Baden–Baden, 1957.

Fricke, Karl-Wilhelm, *Die SED und die Juden* ("The Socialist Unity Party and the Jews") *SBZ–Archiv*, December, 1964.

Ganther, Heinz, *Die Juden in Deutschland* (*The Jews in Germany*), Gala Verlag, Hamburg, 1959.

Giordano, Ralph, *Narben, Spuren, Zeugen* (*Scars, Traces, Witnesses*), Verlag Allgemeine Wochenzeitung der Juden in Deutschland, Düsseldorf, 1961.

Goldman, Botho, *Die Bedeutung des Abkommens zwischen der Bundesrepublik und dem Staat Israel vom 10.9.1952 für die wirtschaftliche Entwicklung der Bundesrepublik und Israel dargestellt am Beispiel der Erfüllungsperiode 52–53 bis 55–56.* ("The significance of the treaty between the Federal Republic of Germany and the state of Israel from September 10, 1952, for the economic development of the Federal Republic and Israel described on the basis of the period of fullfilment, 1952–53 to 1955–56.") (Thesis), Johannes Gutenberg University, Mainz, 1956.

Goldschmidt, Dietrich und Krau, Hans–Joachim, *Der ungekündigte Bund* (*The Unbroken Link*), Kreuz Verlag, Stuttgart, 1962.

Gollwitzer, Helmut, *Israel und Wir* (*Israel and We*), Lettner Verlag, Berlin, 1958.

Gross, Erwin, *Die Schuld der Kirche* ("The Guilt of the Church"), *Die Wandlung*, No. 2, 1947.

Grossman, Kurt R., "Germany's Moral Debt, The German–Israel Agreement," *Public Affairs Press*, Washington, D.C., 1954.

Henkys, Reinhard, *Die nationalsozialistischen Gewaltverbrechen (The National Socialist Crimes of Violence)*, Kreuz–Verlag, Stuttgart, 1964.

Heuss, Theodor, *Bergen-Belson, Heft 1 der Schriftenreihe Zwischen Gestern und Morgen* ("Between Yesterday and Tomorrow,") International Committee, Sonnenberg, 1952.

Heuss, Theodor, *An ünd uber Juden (Addressed to Jews and About Them)*, compiled and published by Hans Lamm, Econ Verlag, Düsseldorf, 1964.

Heuss, Theodor, *Statt und Volk im Werden (State and People in the Making)*, Ner Tamid Verlag, Munich, 1960.

Hottinger, Arnold, *Die Hintergründe der Einladung Ulbrichts nach Kairo* ("The Background to the Invitation of Ulbricht to Cairo"), *Europa–Archiv*, No. 4, 1965.

Jenhani, Habib, *Aspekte der Palästina Frage* ("Aspects of the Palestine Question"), *Deutsche Aussenpolitik* (DDR), No. 9, 1964.

Josephtal, Senta, *The Responsible Attitude, the Life and Opinion of Giora Josephtal*, Schocken Books, Inc., New York, 1966.

Kaul, F.K. *Der Fall Eichmann (The Eichmann Case)*, Verlag Das Neue Berlin, Berlin, 1963.

Kempner, Robert W., *Eichmann und Komplizen (Eichmann and Accomplices)*, Europa Verlag, Stuttgart, Zürich, Wien, 1961.

Kopp, Otto, *Adenauer, Biographische und politische Dokumentation (Adenauer, Biographical and Political Documentation)*, Seewald Verlag, Stuttgart, 1963.

Kreysler, Joachim und Jungfer, Klaus, *Deutsche–Israel Politik—Entwicklung oder politische Masche (German–Israel Policy—Development or Political Trick)*, Wolf Frhr. von Tucher Verlag G.m.b.H., Diessen–Ammersee, 1965.

Kusche, Ulrich, *Die deutsch–israelischen Studentenbeziehungen* ("The Relations of German–Israel Students"), *Diskussion*, February, 1967.

Küster, Otto, *Wiedergutmachung als elementare Rechtsaufgabe (Restitution As Elementary Legal Task)*, Verlag G. Schulte–Buhnke, Frankfurt, 1953.

Küster, Otto, *Die dramatische Struktur der Wahrheit (The Dramatic Structure of Truth)*, Ernst Klett Verlag, Stuttgart, 1967.

Lamm, Hans, *Der Eichmann–Prozess in der deutschen öffentlichen Meinung (The Eichmann Trial in German Public Opinion)*, collection of documents, Ner Tamid Verlag, Frankfurt, 1961.

Löbe, Paul, *Der Weg war lang, Lebenserinnerungen, (The Road Was Long, Memoirs)*, Arani–Verlag, Berlin, 1954.

Luchsinger, Fred, *Bericht über Bonn (Report About Bonn)*, *Deutsche*

Politik 1955–1965 (German Politics from 1955 to 1965), Verlag Fretz und Wasmuth, Stuttgart, Zurich, 1966.

Lüth, Eric, *Viel Steine lagen am Weg (Many Stones Lay On the Road)*, Marion von Schroeder Verlag, Hamburg, 1966.

Mansfeld, Michael, *Bonn, Koblenzer Strasse, Der Bericht des Robert von Lenwitz (The Report of Robert von Lenwitz)*, Verlag Kurt Desch, Munich, 1967.

Maor, Harry, *Über den Wiederaufbau der jüdischen Gemeinden in Deutschland nach 1945* ("About the Reestablishment of the Jewish Communities in Germany after 1945") (Thesis), Mainz University, 1961.

Marx, Karl, *Brucken schlagen. (To Build Bridges), Aufsätze und Reden aus den Jahren 1946–1962 (Essays and Lectures from the years 1946 to 1962)*, Verlag Allgemeine Wochenzeitung der Juden in Deutschland, Düsseldorf, 1962.

Meyer, Enno, *Juden und Judenfeinde in der christlichen Welt* (Jews and the *Enemies of Jews in the Christian World*,) Joseph Melzer Verlag, Cologne, 1962.

Müller, Peter, *Die Beziehungen der deutschen Studentenschaft den Studenten Israels* ("The Relations of the German Students to the Students of Israel"), *Diskussion*, April, 1965.

Noelle-Neumann, Elisabeth und Peter, *Jahrbuch der öffentlichen Meinung, 1947–1955 (Yearbook of Public Opinion)*, Verlag für Demoskopie, Allensbach, 1958.

Noelle-Neumann, Elisabeth und Peter, *Jahrbuch der öffentlichen Meinung, 1957 (Yearbook of Public Opinion)*, Verlag für Demoskopie, Allensbach, 1958.

Noelle-Neumann, Elisabeth und Peter, *Jahrbuch der öffentlichen Meinung, 1958–1964 (Yearbook of Public Opinion)*, Verlag für Demoskopie, Allensbach, 1965.

Noelle-Neumann, Elisabeth und Peter, *The Germans, Public Opinion Polls, 1947–1966*, Verlag für Demoskopie, Allensbach, 1967.

Pearlman, Moshe, *Die Festnahme Adolf Eichmanns (The Arrest of Adolf Eichmann)*, S. Fischer Verlag, Frankfurt, 1961.

Praeger, Frederick, *The Politics of Post-war Germany*, New York, 1963.

Presse- und Informationsamt der Bundesregierung (Press and Information Office of the Federal Republic), *Regierung Adenauer, 1949–1963* (Adenauer's Government 1949–1963), Bonn, 1963.

Schaichtel, Walter, *Was kommt nach der wirtschaftlichen Wiedergutmachung?* "What Comes After Economic Restitution?" *Der Volkswirt*, No. 46, November, 1962.

Schmidt, Heinz, *Die Judenfrage und die christliche Kirche in Deutschland (The Jewish Question and the Christian Church in Germany)*, Kohlhammer Verlag, Stuttgart, 1947.

Scholz, Arno und Oschilewski, Walter G., *Kurt Schumacher, Reden und*

Schriften (*Kurt Schumacher, Lectures and Writings*), Arani Verlag, Berlin, 1953.

Scholz, Arno und Oschilewski, Walter G., *Sein Weg durch die Zeit, Kurt Schumachers Leben und Leistung* (*His Progress Through Time—Kurt Schumacher's Life and Achievement*), Arani Verlag, Berlin, 1954

Schwelien, Joachim, *Jargon der Gewalt,* (Power Jargon) Ner Tamid Verlag, Frankfurt, 1961.

Shinnar, Felix E., *Bericht eines Beauftragten* (*Report of a Special Comsioner*), Wunderlich Verlag, Tubingen, 1967.

Staatsrat der Deutschen Demokratischen Republik (Council of State of the German Democratic Republic), *Die Deutsche Demokratische Republik und die UAR—gute Freund* ("The German Democratic Republic and the United Arab Republic—good friends"), Berlin, 1965.

Vogel, Rolf, *Deutschlands Weg nach Israel* (*Germany's Road to Israel*), Seewald Verlag, Stuttgart, 1967.

Wagner, Wolfgang, *Die Hallstein-Doktrin nach Ulbrichts Besuch in Agypten* ("The Hallstein Doctrine After Ulbricht's Visit In Egypt"), *Europa-Archiv,* No. 5, 1965.

Wagner, Wolfgang, *Der Rückschlag der Bonner Politik in den arabischen Staaten* "The Setback of Bonn's Policy in Arab States," *Europa-Archiv,* No. 10, 1965.

Wewer, Heinz, *Die deutsch-israelischen Beziehungen—Ende oder Neubeginn?* ("The German-Israel Relations—End or New Beginning?") Frankfurter Hefte, 1963.

Weymar, Paul, *Konrad Adenauer,* André Deutsch, London, 1957.

Wiesenthal, Simon, *Doch die Mörder leben* (*Yet, the Murderers Are Alive*), Opéra Mundi, Paris, 1967.

Zentralrat der Juden in Deutschland (Central Council of German Jewry), *10 Jahre Zentralrat der Juden in Deutschland* ("10 Years Central Council of German Jewry"), *Tribune,* No. 5, Düsseldorf, 1963.

Journals

Aussenpolitik, journal for foreign policy, No. 4, 1965; No. 12, 1958.

Der Spiegel, Hamburg, 1960–1965.

Der Volkswirt, journal for economists, No. 46, November, 1962.

Der Weg, journal for questions concerning Jewry, Berlin, 1947–1949.

Deutsche Aussenpolitik (DDR), journal for foreign politics of the German Democratic Republic, No.9, 1964.

Deutsche Rundschau, 1957.

Die politische Meinung, September, 1964.

Die Wandlung, No. 2, 1947.

Diskussion, journal for problems of society and German-Israel relations, Berlin, 1965–1967.

Europa-Archiv, No. 4, No. 5, No. 10, 1965.

Frankfurter Hefte, 1963–1965.

Freiburger Rundbrief, contributions to promote friendship between the old and the new people of God in the spirit of both Testaments, published by Dr. Gertrud Luckner, 1959–1966.

Israel Forum, published by Dr. Hans Landsberger, Rothenberg, 1964.

Israel–Informationsdienst (Israel Information Service) published by the Israel Mission, Cologne, 1953–1957.

Tribune, No. 5, Dusseldorf, 1963.

Werkhefte, 1964.

INDEX

INGE DEUTSCHKRON

INGE DEUTSCHKRON grew up happily in Berlin until Hitler came to power.

Her Jewish father a teacher and an active member of the Social Democratic Party, the child soon found that the Nazis made education, and life in general, impossible for Jewish children. Nevertheless, Inge Deutschkron and her mother were forced to remain in Nazi Germany (although the father managed to reach England shortly before war broke out) where she found herself financially unable to complete a kindergarten nursing course and worked in the only areas opened to Jews—as a servant and in a factory.

In 1943, with the help of Germans opposed to Hitler, Miss Deutschkron and her mother "disappeared," moving from place to place in fear of being deported to the annihilation camps. Having no ration cards, the girl worked as charwoman, sales clerk, laundry assistant—almost anything that would put food in their mouths. In the last months of the war, false names were assumed and forged documents procured.

Circumstances improved after the war and, in 1946, the Deutschkrons were fortunate enough to join the father in England. But, again, lack of money interrupted Miss Deutschkron's pursuit of education at London University and she accepted a post with the Socialist International (the alliance of the Social Democrat and Labor parties).

But, the world was beckoning so, in 1954, Miss Deutschkron

headed for Asia. She spent a year roaming about India, Burma, Nepal and Israel.

In spite of all the suffering, Germany was still "home" to this resilient woman and she headed for Bonn where she found a ready market for writing about her travel experiences. In 1958, *Maariv*, Tel Aviv's evening newspaper, was lucky enough to acquire Inge Deutschkron as its correspondent in Germany.

Although deeply attached to the Germans and their kind who, at the risk of their lives, helped the Deutschkrons to survive, she realized before long that her real home was Israel. She became an Israeli citizen with a view to settling there shortly.

"I wrote my first book on the persecution of children under the Nazis, in the hope that I could do something to make the Germans more aware of the crimes committed in their name, and make them and the rest of the world understand the consequences of state-ordered anti-Semitism or any other racial hatred. I shall go on doing so."